MEMOIRS
—IN EXILE——————

Confessional Hope and
Institutional Conflict

JOHN H. TIETJEN

Fortress Press   Minneapolis

MEMOIRS IN EXILE
Confessional Hope and Institutional Conflict

Scripture quotations unless otherwise noted are from the Today's English Version of the Bible, © 1976 by the American Bible Society. Used by permission.

Cover design: Patricia Boman

Interior design: Karen Buck

Library of Congress Cataloging-in-Publication Data

Tietjen, John H.
    Memoirs in exile : confessional hope and institutional conflict /
John H. Tietjen.
        p.   cm.
    Includes bibliographical references and index.
    ISBN 0-8006-2462-9 : $19.95
    1. Christ Seminary–Seminex. 2. Lutheran Church—Missouri Synod.
3. Tietjen, John H.   I. Title.
BV4070.C555T54   1991
207'.73—dc20
                                                                    90-3978
                                                                      CIP

The paper used in this publication meets the minimum requirements of American National Standard for Information Sciences—Permanence of Paper for Printed Library Materials, ANSI Z329.48-1984. ∞™

Manufactured in the U.S.A.   AF 1-2462

94   93   92   91   90   1   2   3   4   5   6   7   8   9   10

◆

CONTENTS

———————◆

PREFACE

I have a story to tell. As the events of the story were happening, people would say to me, "I hope you are keeping a journal so that you can write about this someday." I did not keep a journal. I did write notes to myself so that I would remember exactly how it was. I also kept the documents that record what happened, until five four-drawer filing cabinets were filled.

From time to time, while the events of the story were taking place, people would ask me, "When are you going to write your book? You're a historian, you know. You have an obligation to tell us what happened." But I was too embroiled in what was happening, too emotionally involved. I needed the distance of time before I could write. While the story was still going on, I did not know for sure how it was going to turn out.

Now I know. The calendar year 1988 was sabbatical time for me after eighteen years of responsibility for a seminary. The sabbatical gave me opportunity to review the tumultuous course of events in the last quarter century of my life. I was able to read again the documents and the notes I had written and to reflect on what happened and what it means. I now have a story to tell.

There are two reasons for telling the story and two intentions connected to the reasons. I owe a debt to posterity and need to pay that debt. True, the events of my story took place in a small corner of the church, and those events may prove to be, as some may already be convinced they are, nothing more than a tempest in a teapot. But I was a central figure in this tempest. I have had unique experiences and possess documents others do not have. I know some things few others know. I feel a responsibility to tell others what I saw taking place.

My first intention, then, is to tell what happened as I experienced it. I make no pretense at writing a definitive history of the events and the period I am describing. I was after all a partisan in the struggle about which I write and confess that I am partisan still. I tell the story from my perspective, as I saw it happen. What I write belongs, therefore, to the category of memoirs.

I also aim to be objective and fair as I write. Time has provided distance to reflect more dispassionately on the past, especially the emotional and controversial experiences of the more distant past. I do not write in order to engage in recrimination or to justify myself, although I confess, sinner that I am, that I may not always recognize when I am doing so. In any case, my purpose is not recrimination or self-justification but to tell events from my perspective so that my account can be available, should others undertake to write the broader history of what happened.

A second reason for writing is that the events about which I write have a dramatic shape. There are protagonists and movement in the story. There are conflict and resolution. There is meaning in the events I describe. Because I believe in the immanent presence of the transcendent God, I am convinced that there are meaning and purpose in history. Some of us, while we were experiencing the events, saw the dim outlines of the story taking shape. We experienced institutional death and transfiguration. We saw God at work in the midst of it all.

The story I have to tell is good news. My purpose is to share a contemporary version of the Bible's gospel of God. The story is this: Because of the death and resurrection of Jesus, the Christ, God is at work in the midst of death to create new life. The reality of the story and the gift of life belong to those who believe. Because the story is God's good news, there is a second purpose in telling it. I have no choice but to tell the story so that it may be the power of God for those who believe.

In paying tribute to his colleague Richard R. Caemmerer on the occasion of the publication of Caemmerer's autobiography, Andrew Weyermann coined the term "autozoegraphy." According to Weyermann, *bios* is the Greek word for biological life, *zoe* is the word the Fourth Gospel uses for the eternal life God gives to those who believe. "*Bios* is biological breathing, but *Zoe* is the quality of the eternal in the present," Weyermann wrote as he urged that all preaching be autozoegraphy.[1] As one who continually receives God's gift of life, the story I tell is frankly autozoegraphical.

The story is not mine alone. The institution that I served, Christ Seminary–Seminex, was paradigm for many others involved in the events I describe; I served as representative and symbol for them. I am deeply aware that my story is "our" story, the story of the people of Evangelical Lutherans in Mission, Christ Seminary–Seminex, and the

Association of Evangelical Lutheran Churches. I am confident that in reading my story those people will see their own. For their sake I need to tell our story so that we may continue to witness together to the enlivening work of God among us. It may be that others who read our story will find it to be theirs.

I am grateful to the Board of Directors of Christ Seminary–Seminex for the sabbatical that has made it possible for me to tell my story. I thank Lutheran Brotherhood for the grant from its faculty fellowship program that has assisted me in the project.

I am especially grateful to former colleagues Jeannette Bauermeister and John Damm for providing me with information about aspects of the story that I did not know. I am similarly grateful to former students David Abrahamson, Amandus Derr, Gerald Miller, Leon Rosenthal, and James Wind, who helped me understand the role of students at a critical point in the story. I thank my wife, Ernestine, for reliving the events with me and helping to prod my memory about the more personal events recounted.

I owe a special debt of gratitude to Walter Wangerin, Jr., who repeatedly took time out of his own writing schedule to give me counsel and guidance about how to tell the story. What a joy it is to acknowledge a former student as mentor!

With appreciation I acknowledge the help of former colleagues Paul Bauermeister and Andrew Weyermann, who carefully read the material as I produced it and offered invaluable criticism to improve it, and of Larry Neeb, who read and helped improve the completed manuscript.

In addition to the above, several former co-workers encouraged me to proceed when the project was in its early stages: Robert Bertram, Frederick Danker, Richard Koenig, and William Lesher. To them I am indebted for the impetus that carried the project through to its completion.

I also thank the Berkeley contingent of Christ Seminary–Seminex: Carl and Doris Graesser, Dorothy and George Hoyer, Clara and Everett Kalin, and Meta and Robert Smith. They gave me the gift of a computer that was the instrument for telling the story and that has forever changed my writing methods.

Finally, I thank the people of Evangelical Lutherans in Mission, Seminex, and the Association of Evangelical Lutheran Churches, fellow pilgrims on the road to the city that is to come and that comes down out of heaven from God. Without them there would be no story, and to them I dedicate their story with love.

John H. Tietjen

---◆

ABBREVIATIONS

To tell my story I have adopted throughout this book a style of abbreviations, many of them common among Lutheran church historians. In each chapter, I spell out the first usage of the synod or denomination or board. After that the common acronym is used. Publication data in the footnotes are cited by abbreviation throughout.

ACDC
: Advisory Committee on Doctrine and Conciliation. Formed in 1974 by J. A. O. Preus to delineate the controverted issues and composed of seven representatives from each side in the controversy that threatened to split the Lutheran Church-Missouri Synod.

AELC
: Association of Evangelical Lutheran Churches, the church body formed in December 1976 by those who found it impossible to continue to do ministry within the Lutheran Church–Missouri Synod.

ALC
: The American Lutheran Church, formed in 1960 by four Lutheran church bodies which had practiced church fellowship for three decades within a confederation known as the American Lutheran Conference. They were American Lutheran Church, Evangelical Lutheran Church, Lutheran Free Church, and United Evangelical Lutheran Church.

BB
: "Blue Book," as J. A. O. Preus's large report on the faculty of Concordia Seminary became known in the Lutheran Church–Missouri Synod. It contained summaries of alleged false doctrine by the faculty.

BC   *The Book of Concord.* Trans. and ed. Theodore G. Tappert. Philadelphia: Fortress Press; St. Louis: Concordia Publishing, 1959. The compendium of Lutheran confessional writings.

BHE   Board for Higher Education. The Lutheran Church–Missouri Synod board with overall responsibility for their colleges and seminaries.

BoC   Board of Control. The governing board of Concordia Seminary.

BoD   Board of Directors. The Lutheran Church–Missouri Synod governing board.

CLU   Committee on Lutheran Unity. The name of the group composed of representatives of the ALC, AELC, and Lutheran Church in America that recommended the formation of a new Lutheran church.

CNLC   Commission for a New Lutheran Church. The 70-member group created by the ALC, AELC, and Lutheran Church in America that submitted proposals eventuating in the formation of the Evangelical Lutheran Church in America.

CS   Concordia Seminary. The Lutheran Church–Missouri Synod seminary in St. Louis, also called the Seminary, not to be confused with Concordia Theological Seminary, Springfield, Illinois.

CTM   *Concordia Theological Monthly.* The journal of the faculty of CS. A journal with the same initials, *Currents in Theology and Mission,* was later published by Seminex. This title will be spelled out.

CTS   Concordia Theological Seminary, Springfield, Illinois.

ELC   Evangelical Lutheran Church. The church body formed in 1917 to bring together most of the Norwegian Lutherans in America. It helped form the ALC in 1960.

ELCA   Evangelical Lutheran Church in America, formed January 1, 1988, with the merger of ALC, AELC, and Lutheran Church in America.

ELIM   Evangelical Lutherans in Mission. The organization created in 1973 by those who were protesting Lutheran Church–Missouri Synod convention actions for the purpose of defending those who were under attack by the Lutheran Church–Missouri Synod administration.

ELS — Evangelical Lutheran Synod. The small church body composed of Norwegian Lutherans who chose not to join the ELC in 1917. It established fellowship with the Lutheran Church–Missouri Synod and later severed fellowship, declaring the Lutheran Church–Missouri Synod to be heterodox.

English District — A nongeographic district of the Lutheran Church–Missouri Synod originally charged with the responsibility of doing work in the English language in the predominantly German-speaking Lutheran Church–Missouri Synod. It led the way in espousing new causes and movements within the Lutheran Church–Missouri Synod.

FAC — Faculty Advisory Committee. Established in 1970 to help the CS administration understand the position of the faculty and to help the faculty reach decisions in dealing with J. A. O. Preus's investigation of CS.

FFC — Fact Finding Committee. The five-member group created by J. A. O. Preus to conduct the investigation of the teaching of the faculty of CS.

FLUTE — Fund for Lutheran Theological Education. The not-for-profit corporation established in 1973 to receive and disperse unsolicited funds given for the defense and support of the CS faculty.

LCA — Lutheran Church in America. Formed in 1962 by four church bodies: United Lutheran Church in America, Augustana Lutheran Church, American Evangelical Lutheran Church, and Suomi Synod.

LCMS — Lutheran Church–Missouri Synod. Established in 1847 as the German Evangelical Lutheran Synod of Missouri, Ohio, and Other States, the church body changed its name for its centennial anniversary. From longstanding tradition members often refer to the Synod and Missouri Synod interchangeably with LCMS.

LCUSA — Lutheran Council in the U.S.A. The cooperative agency for the Lutherans of America formed in 1966 as the successor agency to the National Lutheran Council, with the LCMS as a participating member.

LNTS — Luther Northwestern Theological Seminary, St. Paul, Minnesota. A combined seminary of the ALC and LCA, now a seminary of the ELCA.

LSTC   Lutheran School of Theology at Chicago. A regionally supported seminary of the LCA, now a seminary of the ELCA.

NCC   National Council of the Churches of Christ in the United States of America. The agency of cooperation for most of the Protestant and Orthodox churches in the U.S.A.

PLTS   Pacific Lutheran Theological Seminary, Berkeley, California. A regional seminary of the LCA, supported also by the ALC and the AELC, now a seminary of the ELCA.

SAC   Student Administrative Council. The central organization of the student body of CS.

Seminarians   Seminarians Concerned for Reconciliation Under the
Concerned   Gospel. Established in 1973 by CS students, it was the political arm of CS students in the LCMS controversy.

UC   University Club, St. Louis. The club facilities in the University Club building were leased by Seminex to house its operations from August 1975 to January 1982.

WTS   Wartburg Theological Seminary, Dubuque, Iowa. A seminary of the ALC, now a seminary of the ELCA.

CHRONOLOGY
OF EVENTS

5/19/69	John H. Tietjen elected president of Concordia Seminary (CS), St. Louis
7/12/69	Jacob A. O. Preus elected president of the Lutheran Church–Missouri Synod (LCMS)
5/17/70	Preus publicly announces intention to take action on alleged departures from the Synod's doctrinal position
9/9/70	Preus announces appointment of a Fact Finding Committee (FFC) to investigate the CS faculty
12/11/70	Interviews of faculty by FFC begin
1/5/71	Faculty announces decision to continue participation in FFC interviews under protest
3/27/71	Interviews of faculty by FFC end
7/15/71	LCMS Milwaukee convention defeats Preus's effort to require submission to convention-adopted doctrinal statements
7/15/71	LCMS Milwaukee convention turns FFC report over to CS's Board of Control (BoC)
9/20/71	CS BoC begins review of FFC report
12/13/71	BoC declines reappointment of CS faculty member Arlis J. Ehlen
1/4/72	CS faculty asks to meet with Preus over his ethics in the BoC's decision concerning Ehlen
1/11/72	Preus advises of impending disciplinary action against Tietjen
1/18/72	Tietjen and Preus meet to work out compromise

2/18/72	Preus withdraws from compromise agreement and gives the BoC "A Statement of Scriptural and Confessional Principles" to serve as standard for doctrinal review
3/5/72	Tietjen refuses to implement Preus demand that Ehlen be barred from teaching exegetical courses
6/17/72	BoC issues progress report to Preus, stating that it had not yet found false doctrine in the faculty
9/1/72	Preus issues his "Blue Book" (BB), a report condemning numerous unnamed CS faculty for teaching false doctrine
9/8/72	Tietjen issues *Fact Finding or Fault Finding?* to counter the BB
9/20/72	LCMS Council of Presidents announces controversy compromise
10/26/72	Preus acts against Council of Presidents compromise
1/15/73	CS BoC completes interviews with faculty, clears all of the charge of false doctrine
7/10/73	LCMS New Orleans convention affirms that convention-adopted doctrinal statements are binding
7/11/73	New Orleans convention adopts "A Statement of Scriptural and Confessional Principles" as binding doctrinal statement
7/12/73	New Orleans convention condemns CS faculty for teaching false doctrine
7/13/73	New Orleans convention requires newly elected CS BoC to deal with future of Tietjen as president
7/23/73	CS faculty issues "A Declaration of Protest and Confession"
8/13/73	CS BoC suspends Tietjen as president and faculty member, then delays implementation of its action
8/28/73	Conference of Evangelical Lutheranism organizes Evangelical Lutherans in Mission (ELIM)
9/29/73	CS BoC "vacates" Tietjen suspension
12/13/73	CS faculty member Arthur Carl Piepkorn dies
1/20/74	CS BoC suspends Tietjen as president
1/21/74	CS student body announces moratorium on classes
1/21/74	CS faculty announces that it considers the faculty to be suspended
2/17/74	CS BoC requires faculty decision to return to class or to be held in breach of contract
2/18/74	Faculty takes no action on board demand

2/19/74	Students decide to join faculty in resuming seminary education "in exile"
2/20/74	Classes of Concordia Seminary in Exile (Seminex) begin at St. Louis University and Eden Seminary
4/10/74	William Kohn resigns as executive secretary of LCMS Board for Missions
5/11/74	Partners in Mission begins functioning as the mission arm of ELIM
5/24/74	First class graduates from Seminex
6/21/74	Concordia Seminary in Exile is legally incorporated
8/26/74	Second ELIM Assembly is held in Chicago
10/12/74	CS BoC removes Tietjen from office as president and faculty member
2/1/75	Seminex governing board elects Tietjen president
4/14/75	Theological convocation is held to try to effect reconciliation
6/29/75	Missouri District official Oscar Gerken clears Tietjen of charges of false doctrine
7/4–11/75	LCMS Anaheim convention condemns ELIM, censures eight district presidents for ordaining Seminex graduates, authorizes their removal from office by Preus
8/13/75	Third ELIM Assembly authorizes formation of "a new association"
8/15/75	Seminex moves into its own facilities at 607 N. Grand in St. Louis
2/28/76	Coordinating Council for a new church organization is created
4/2/76	Preus removes four district presidents from office
6/19/76	English Synod is established out of the LCMS English District
12/3–4/76	Association of Evangelical Lutheran Churches (AELC) is organized with five constituent synods
5/12/77	Seminex board decision on staff reduction precipitates crisis
9/28/77	LCMS vice-president Theodore Nickel declares Tietjen removed from ministerial roster
10/28/77	Concordia Seminary in Exile changes its name to Christ Seminary–Seminex
4/14–16/78	AELC issues "A Call for Lutheran Union"
1/22–23/79	AELC joins American Lutheran Church—Lutheran Church in America Committee on Lutheran Unity

12/14/79	AELC is invited to join ALC-LCA Consultation on Theological Education
6/20/80	William Lesher of Lutheran School of Theology at Chicago (LSTC) meets with Tietjen in Denver to propose move of Seminex to the LSTC campus
10/3/81	Seminex board proposes merger of LSTC and Seminex
11/30/81	Representatives of Seminex and LSTC boards consider proposals for closer relations between the two schools
1/14/82	Seminex moves to new facilities at 539 N. Grand in St. Louis
1/29/82	Plan for three-way deployment of Seminex resources is proposed
5/82	LSTC, Pacific Lutheran Theological Seminary, Wartburg Theological Seminary, and Seminex boards agree to three-way deployment of Seminex resources
9/8/82	ALC, AELC, LCA conventions agree to unite and authorize a union process
9/82	Commission for a New Lutheran Church (CNLC) begins its work
5/83	Last Seminex commencement is held in St. Louis
8/83	Seminex moves to Chicago, Berkeley, and Austin
8/29/86	ALC, AELC, LCA conventions agree to form the Evangelical Lutheran Church in America (ELCA)
4/30/87	Constituting convention of ELCA begins
12/31/87	Seminex ceases to exist as an educational institution

PART 1 ────────────────────◆

"If Your Brother Sins Against You"

1 ———◆

CONTEXT FOR CONFLICT

We panted for breath in the mile-high air as we hurried as fast as our legs could carry us along the ten-block distance from Denver's downtown Hilton to the new Convention Center. We didn't talk. The gradually upward slope of the path made breathing even more difficult. In the distance the snow-capped Rocky Mountains framed our view as we rushed ahead.

Jacob A. O. Preus and I were late for the evening session of the Forty-eighth Convention of the Lutheran Church–Missouri Synod, which had begun earlier that day. It was Saturday, July 12, 1969, the weekend before the historic U.S. space launch that landed men on the moon. Preus and I were in a hurry because we wanted to hear the results of the second ballot for the office of president of the church body. According to synodical practice, numerical vote totals were never announced, but rumor had it that at the end of the first ballot Preus was ahead of incumbent Oliver R. Harms.

I did not expect Harms to be defeated, although I was very much aware of the campaign to oust him in favor of Preus. At the morning session executive director Walter Wolbrecht had departed from his prepared report to bemoan the open politicking that was going on in behalf of the Preus candidacy. Political campaigns for church office were contrary to the tradition of the Synod. Yet all the trappings of a political campaign were present at the Denver convention, including a campaign headquarters in a downtown hotel, lapel fishhooks to identify the party members, slates of approved candidates for office, and convention floor organization to assure votes according to the will of the party leadership.

3

Yet I thought that in spite of the campaign—perhaps even because of it—a majority of the delegates would return Oliver Harms to office.

Preus and I were hurrying to the Convention Center together because we had both been guests of honor at an intimate dinner in the Denver Hilton sponsored by Walter Rugland, president of Aid Association for Lutherans.[1] Rugland thought that a dinner would be a good way to help two seminary presidents get better acquainted while AAL leaders fostered relations with their two schools. Preus was president of the Missouri Synod's seminary in Springfield, Illinois, and some six weeks earlier I had been elected president of the Synod's seminary in St. Louis.

Not that Preus and I were strangers. He was an LCMS representative to the annual meetings of the Lutheran Council in the U.S.A., whose Division of Public Relations I served as executive secretary. Our paths had crossed at the council's annual meetings. Three summers earlier Preus and I had met in Concordia Seminary's dining room while I was teaching at a summer session there and Preus was present on official business. But Rugland was right in assuming that it would be helpful for us to get better acquainted.

As Preus and I entered the outer lobby of the Convention Center, the voice of Arlen Bruns, president of the Missouri Synod's Kansas District and chair of the Elections Committee, was resounding over the loudspeakers: "I report to you that in this election for the president of the Synod the Reverend Dr. Jacob Preus of Springfield, Illinois, received a majority and is elected to the president of the synod."[2] I was stunned. I looked at Preus. His jaw was set, thrust forward and upward, his lips pursed. He furrowed his brow and without a smile hurried into the Convention Center proper and made his way amidst applause to the platform to which Oliver Harms as chair was inviting him. I hurried to my seat on the convention floor, then listened as Preus told the convention that he was overwhelmed by the decision and needed to consult the governing board of his seminary before deciding whether to accept the election.

I was troubled by what had happened. I had expected to work closely with Harms. Now I was to work with a president whose candidacy had been proposed by people within the Missouri Synod whose understanding of the church's theology and mission was different from mine. Some of those people were hurling heresy charges against faculty members of the seminary to which I had just been called as president. They were opposed to the reelection of Harms because of his efforts to bring about fellowship with the American Lutheran Church.

The adoption of fellowship would mean that the Missouri Synod and the ALC would recognize each other as orthodox Lutheran churches and that their members could commune at the altars of each other's congregations. Fellowship with the ALC had become the chief issue at the Denver convention. As a member of the convention's Committee 3 on Church Relations I had voted with the majority in recommending that the convention vote for fellowship. Preus had become the presidential candidate of those who opposed fellowship with the ALC.

As Preus left the podium and made his way across the platform, I intercepted him as he reached the convention floor. I wanted to be the first to congratulate him and to wish him well. Even though there was foreboding in my heart, I wanted my handshake to convey my hope that Preus and I would be able to work together.

I was Oliver Harms's choice for president of CS. Harms himself told me that several years later, when in the midst of controversy he wanted me to know that he stood behind me. Alfred O. Fuerbringer had been serving as president of the LCMS's St. Louis seminary since 1954 and had reached the mandatory retirement age of 65. Early in the 1968–69 academic year, CS's governing board, its Board of Control, had begun the process of choosing a successor. LCMS regulations at that time specified that four Electors chose the president of CS on the basis of nominees submitted by a committee of the faculty. The Electors were the president of LCMS (Harms), the president of the Missouri District (Herman C. Scherer), the chair of the Board for Higher Education (Albert G. Huegli), and the seminary BoC voting as a unit.

The seminary Faculty Committee submitted five names to the Electors from among 65 nominated candidates. The confidentiality of the recommendation was so well preserved that to this day I do not know who the other four candidates were. Harms told me that in reviewing the five candidates he had decided to vote for me and that after some discussion his decision had convinced the others to do the same.

Harms had been elected president of the Missouri Synod at a convention in Cleveland in 1962, when John W. Behnken, who had presided over the Synod for twenty-seven years, decided to retire. Like Behnken before him, Harms was a father-figure. He stood more than six feet tall and was always impeccably dressed. Snow-white hair crowned a full face that was impassive most of the time except for gentle eyes. By the time of the Denver convention, cataracts made it difficult for him to read. He attributed the condition to his practice of reading the small print of the Lutheran confessional writings in *The Book of Concord* on the daily bus trip to his downtown office from his home in a St. Louis suburb, a practice he followed in order to get better acquainted with the doctrinal standards of Lutheranism.

Observers described the Cleveland convention as a turning point in the life of the Missouri Synod, signaling a move away from rigidity in theology and isolation in church life toward more openness in both theology and mission. Within a few years under Harms's leadership the LCMS had helped form the LCUSA, was proposing to enter into fellowship with the ALC, had begun discussions looking toward fellowship with the Lutheran Church in America, and had adopted a series of profoundly significant mission affirmations to help shape its work of outreach around the world.

Although I was an ardent supporter of the LCMS's new direction, I was still an unlikely choice for president of its St. Louis seminary. Established in 1839, eight years before the Missouri Synod, CS for more than a century had been a bastion of orthodoxy for the church body. The Synod's seminary in Springfield, Illinois, concentrated on the practice of ministry, had less rigorous admission standards, and prepared older men for ministry. In contrast the St. Louis seminary prided itself on its preoccupation with issues of theology, its faculty serving as arbiters of theological issues and as doctrinal reviewers of all material published by the Synod's publishing house. At the time of my election CTS was the largest Lutheran seminary in the United States with more than seven hundred students, six hundred of whom were preparing for ordination in the LCMS.

Under Fuerbringer's leadership CS had been undergoing a quiet revolution. Biblical studies were receiving major attention, replacing *dogmatic theology,* the task of organizing and systematizing the church's doctrine. Several members of the faculty were helping CS and the church body come to terms with contemporary issues of biblical criticism. One faculty member, Martin P. Scharlemann, created a storm of controversy when in 1959 in an essay to a pastoral conference he presented a frontal attack against the notion of biblical inerrancy, and many in the LCMS called for Scharlemann's removal from the CS faculty. Following Scharlemann's lead, younger CS professors, such as Norman Habel and Edgar Krentz, began to help their students and the Synod's clergy come to terms with some of the issues in biblical criticism.

I was surprised when Harms informed me by telephone of my election on the evening of May 19, 1969. I had responded to a form sent by the Faculty Committee to all those who were nominated, but I was not aware that I was one of the five being recommended by the committee. I had spent that day speaking at a conference of pastors in New Jersey and had gone to New York City for a dinner meeting, so I was not at home when Harms called to relay the news of the election. I called him back around 9:00 P.M. I was speechless when I heard the news.

I had little reason to assume that I would be a serious candidate, let alone the Electors' choice. I was an Easterner, born and raised in New

York City and serving in ministry in the greater New York metropolitan area since my seminary graduation in 1953. The East coast was a fringe area for the Missouri Synod and had a mind-set often out of touch with the Midwest, where LCMS members predominated. Since my ordination I had served in the Synod's English District.

During my years as a parish pastor I served also as editor of the *American Lutheran*, an influential independent journal within the LCMS, which advocated such causes as fellowship with other Lutherans, participation in the ecumenical movement, a common hymnal for all Lutherans, and responsible advocacy of social issues before state and federal governments. In other words, I was too liberal to be chosen. In addition, I had written a blunt letter to Harms a few years earlier when, after a year's delay in the publication of my book, I learned that Harms had personally intruded into the publication process because of his concerns about the book's content.[3]

The odds against my election were overwhelming. Yet what should and could not happen did. I felt I had no choice but to see the decision as the will of God.

◆ ◆ ◆

I had been diligently seeking to do the will of God for more than two decades. During my senior year in high school I had a spiritual experience in which I was convinced that God had called me into the ministry. My family was not especially religious. My parents had emigrated from poverty conditions of post–World War I Germany in the 1920s for a better life in America. My mother saw to it that my younger sister and I were baptized, attended Sunday school, and were confirmed in Lutheran congregations. Although during my youth they rarely attended church, my parents sought out congregations that conducted services in the German language. In such a congregation, I was confirmed on Palm Sunday 1942.

Emanuel Lutheran Church in the Corona section of Queens, New York City, was a congregation of the LCMS. Its pastor, Henry Pottberg, was a potbellied man with thinning gray hair and a white mustache, who preached thirty-minute sermons, dry as dust to my teenage ears, which nevertheless heard loud and clear his message of justification by faith. On one occasion, alone in our Queens apartment, I became terrified at the prospect of my death and of being catapulted before the judgment seat of God. I remembered the doctrine I had been taught and heard the Gospel: "Works don't justify; faith does. God has already justified you. You believe God's promise. Don't be afraid." Terror gave way to peace.

My young and tender faith was nurtured and strengthened within the context of an active youth group in Emanuel Church. I was attending

Stuyvesant High School in Manhattan, a premier New York City public school that specialized in mathematics and science, in preparation for embarking on an engineering career. Gradually my faith in God and my commitment to discipleship deepened. Among irreverent and agnostic fellow students I witnessed to my faith, sharing my views in student publications. One day, keenly aware of the presence of God, I felt myself called to make ministry rather than engineering my vocation.

I learned from Pastor Pottberg that the route to pastoral ministry in the LCMS lay through Concordia College in Bronxville, New York, and CS in St. Louis. I never thought to do otherwise. It was God I wanted to serve, and the Missouri Synod simply happened to be the church body to which my home congregation belonged.

During my schooling I gradually came to realize that serving God probably meant being the pastor of a congregation. My year of internship or vicarage under the tutelage of Alfred W. Trinklein, pastor of St. Matthew Lutheran Church at the upper end of Manhattan, fired within me a passion for parish ministry. Nevertheless, in my final year at CS I gave serious thought to the possibility of graduate study. I had been an excellent student, and some of my professors were urging me to consider teaching as a way to do ministry. The seminary was ready to offer me a fellowship to spend an additional year in St. Louis in pursuit of a master's degree in New Testament. George V. Schick, professor of Old Testament, urged me to go to his alma mater, Johns Hopkins University, to pursue a doctorate in Old Testament.

As I prayed for God's guidance, I went for counsel to Jaraslav J. Pelikan, then a budding historian of theology serving on the seminary faculty, who had profoundly influenced my theological development. I came away convinced that I should leave to God the question of whether I should serve in parish ministry or in teaching but that there was no better time than the present to pursue graduate studies that would make possible a ministry of teaching. I was also convinced that I had probably learned most of what I could learn at CS and that I would find it more challenging to do graduate study at another school.

In our conversation Pelikan stated his conviction that biblical studies were going to be an issue within the LCMS in the near future and predicted serious conflict as people came to terms with the results of biblical research. Under the protective shell of my Missouri Synod environment I was already experiencing the tension between traditional LCMS views on the inspiration and inerrancy of the Bible and historical criticism, whose results I had to confront in my exegetical studies. I decided that I wanted no part of any impending battle over the Bible. Instead of biblical studies I would follow Pelikan in devoting myself to historical theology. I would do so at Union Theological Seminary in New

York, to which Pelikan's teacher at the University of Chicago, Wilhelm Pauck, had recently moved.

My experience at Union Seminary challenged my Missouri Lutheranism. To pass the qualifying doctoral examinations I had no choice but to come to terms with biblical criticism. I discovered in Luther's writings on the Word of God a solution for the problems of biblical inerrancy raised for me by my Missouri Synod heritage. The ecumenical environment made me, if anything, more of a confessional Lutheran, although it also gave me a profound appreciation for the convictions of other Christians and generated within me a commitment to be an active participant in the ecumenical movement.

Once the decision to do graduate study in New York had been made, I received a call to become a part-time assistant pastor at Grace Lutheran Church in Teaneck, New Jersey, where my former seminary roommate, John S. Damm, had gone to serve as an assistant pastor two years earlier. After receiving a Master of Sacred Theology degree from Union Seminary in 1954 and completing my course work for the degree of Doctor of Theology, I was called to be pastor of a Lutheran church in neighboring Leonia, New Jersey, in 1956.

In Leonia I had the opportunity of combining my scholarly pursuits with practical ministry. For a doctoral dissertation I focused on nineteenth-century Lutheranism in America and wrote on "The Principles of Church Union Espoused in the Nineteenth Century Attempts to Unite the Lutheran Church in America." The dissertation served as the basis for a history of Lutheran union efforts in America. The published book described three ways in which Lutherans had tried to unite in the past and proposed that Lutherans could come together in one church if they could recognize as sufficient the unity they already had in their subscription to the Scriptures and to the Lutheran Confessions.

My interest in Lutheran unity was more than scholarly. In Leonia, a community of 7,500 people, were two Lutheran churches. The congregation I served was Calvary Lutheran Church, a member of the LCMS. Five blocks down the street was Holy Trinity Lutheran Church, a congregation of the United Lutheran Church in America, which in 1962 became a part of the LCA. The two congregations, established in the late 1920s, had been competing against one another for three decades.

Both congregations counted between two hundred and two hundred fifty communicant members and were quite small in comparison to the Roman Catholic, Presbyterian, Methodist, and Episcopal churches in the community. Alvin Rudisill, the pastor of Holy Trinity Church, was also a recent seminary graduate. He and I decided to do what we could to overcome the hostility of the past for the sake of a united Lutheran witness in the community. The cooperation we initiated culminated, after both of us had gone, into a union of the two congregations as Holy Spirit Lutheran Church, which joined the ALC to avoid the problem of having to choose between either former parent organization.

Parish ministry taught me a great deal about life and matured my spirituality. I came to understand my Christian commitment in terms of discipleship, and in my ministry I tried to exemplify it. I sought to conform my life to Christ's and to live the life of Jesus in my own. My years in Leonia provided me much experience in seeking to know the will of God concerning my ministry. I received a variety of invitations to do ministry elsewhere: to be pastor in other congregations; to begin a Lutheran high school in Queens, New York City; to write curricular materials for the Missouri Synod's Board for Parish Education; to teach theology and later to head the theology department at Valparaiso University; to teach historical theology at CS. Those invitations necessitated a good bit of soul-searching.

While I was trying to decide what to do about the first invitation to serve at Valparaiso University, Prem Gary, a member of my Leonia congregation, came to see me. A new convert to the Christian faith, Gary was head of an international business corporation and delighted in meeting with me to trade his worldly wisdom for my spiritual insights. Gary was a large man with thinning gray hair, whose full face was quick to show emotion. On this occasion his advice was direct: "Pastor, don't go to Valpo. Stay here a while longer. You're young. There isn't a better place for you to learn about life."

I turned down the invitation to Valparaiso, as I did the others, because I became convinced that it was God's will that I continue in parish ministry where I was. Through it all I discovered that if you genuinely want to know God's will and open your heart to hear God speak, God's will becomes clear to you. The invitation to teach historical theology at CS caused me special pain. My wrestling with the will of God was particularly intense. I really did want to accept, and several times I was ready to announce my decision to go to St. Louis.

On a Sunday evening during that time, Prem Gary appeared at the door of our home and asked to come in for a few moments. He sat down in our living room and leaned forward, a smile of compassion lighting up his face. "Pastor," he said, "I know you've made your decision. I felt the emotion in the way you prayed the liturgy this morning. But I don't know what you've decided."

I marveled at his insight. "Yes," I responded, "I've made my decision. I'm staying." And then I explained that in wrestling with the decision, I had discovered a truth about myself: I dearly wanted the prestige and honor of being a seminary professor. That was the real reason I had engaged in graduate study. For the sake of my own soul it was necessary for me to exorcise the demon of unholy ambition and therefore to say no to the seminary. When Gary's eyes overflowed with tears, mine did, too.

To my surprise, several years later, when I was invited to head up the Division of Public Relations of the newly forming LCUSA, I found it easy to say yes. Although as a magazine editor I had some experience in communication, I did not know much about public relations and was untried in administration. What made the difference was not the work I was being asked to do but the cause of the LCUSA itself. The LCUSA was the agency of cooperation for 95 percent of the Lutherans in America. Members at its founding were the ALC, the LCA, the LCMS, and the Synod of Evangelical Lutheran Churches.[4] For the first time in its history the LCMS was to be a member of a major cooperative agency, and I was being asked to help implement that by being a LCMS member of the LCUSA's staff. As the organization that was to bring together the three major Lutheran churches of America, LCUSA held promise of being the means to bring about Lutheran union. I was convinced that as I had worked for Lutheran union on the local level, it was now God's will that I should do so at the national level.

My time with LCUSA was a blessing to me. I learned not only about public relations but about news writing, film production, ministry to those in the armed forces, and representing the church before the federal government and the United Nations—all areas of LCUSA's work that were the responsibility of the division I served. I developed good professional and personal relations with people in the news media, which was not without significance later when news media gave so much attention to the controversy within the LCMS.

C. Thomas Spitz, Jr., general manager of LCUSA, himself a LCMS member of the staff, saw my potential as an administrator and invested in my development in the field of management. I returned the investment by leading the way in getting the council and its divisions and departments committed to a planning process. After three years as a staff member of LCUSA, I again received an invitation from CS, this time to serve as its president. As one who had worked to know and do the will of God, I had to believe that CS was where God now wanted me to serve. I accepted the invitation, ready to carry out new responsibilities as leader of a major institution of a changing church body.

Indeed, a major process of change was under way in the LCMS. The barriers of language had come down during the generation following World War I. As a result, the people of the Missouri Synod experienced acculturation in the American environment, and the church body itself became an American denomination.

The German Evangelical Lutheran Synod of Missouri, Ohio, and Other States had been founded in 1847 by a coalition of immigrants committed to genuine and orthodox Lutheranism. Under the leadership of C. F. W. Walther, professor and president of CS in St. Louis and for many years president of the church body, "Missouri" and "Missourian" became adjectives for a theological stance and a way of life within American Lutheranism. They connoted a fascinating blend of strong congregational autonomy with strict conformity to doctrinal standards.

The Missouri Synod constitution specified that the synodical organization was purely advisory and without legislative authority as far as its congregations were concerned. At the same time it required the president of the Synod to supervise the doctrine taught by its members and to assure conformity with the Synod's doctrinal standards. According to the Synod's constitution (Article VIII.C), all doctrinal matters were to be decided by the Word of God, that is, the Bible, and all other matters by majority vote. The Synod's founders did not say how one was to discern the position of the Bible in the course of a doctrinal dispute, simply assuming that the teaching of the Scripture would be clear. The system worked as long as Synod members were willing to accept theologians like Walther and Francis Pieper, Walther's successor as president of CS, as sole arbiters of scriptural truth.

Missouri Lutheranism insisted that unity in doctrine and in practice was required for any form of ecclesiastical relationship, all the way from organic union to simple cooperation. Convinced that it was not one in doctrine and in practice with other churches, the Missouri Synod did not participate in the gradual amalgamation of Lutheran synods, in the formation of ecumenical agencies, or even in American Lutheranism's first agency of cooperation, the National Lutheran Council. In support of its policy of isolation the Synod cited Rom. 16:17 with its injunction to avoid those who cause division contrary to accepted doctrine. It joined with several other churches in forming the Evangelical Lutheran Synodical Conference in 1872 only when theological discussions with those churches had demonstrated that they were doctrinally orthodox. But that organization was divided within a decade of its founding when its members could not agree on how to articulate the Bible's teaching on election, or predestination.

For more than a half century the Missouri Synod grew by leaps and bounds through a vigorous policy of meeting German immigrants as they arrived in their new homeland and shepherding them into Synod congregations. The Synod's system of parochial schools taught Lutheran orthodoxy and the German language to the children of the immigrants.

Doctrine, language, and educational system combined to keep Missouri Synod Lutherans aloof from the mainstream of American life but also produced a theologically informed, homogeneous, dynamic community.

But acculturation long delayed could not be denied and began in earnest as a result of World War I. The war cut off the flow of German immigrants into the United States, and postwar government policy restricted future immigration. The Synod could no longer look to immigration as a major source of growth and had to recognize its mission to the people of the United States. The war made the German language and German parochial schools unpopular, reinforcing the use of English and encouraging involvement in the public school system. Through the 1920s and the 1930s most Missouri Synod congregations made the transition from German to English in worship and instruction.

Acculturation and Americanization had a profound impact on the Missouri Synod. People with ethnic backgrounds other than German joined its congregations. Missouri Synod young people, like other American young people, went to college in increasing numbers. Missouri Synod seminary graduates went on to universities for graduate study, first in safe areas, such as history, literature, or language, then in the more dangerous areas of religion and theology. In their jobs and communities Missouri Synod people rubbed shoulders with members of other Christian churches. Missouri Synod people traded with other Americans in the marketplace of American ideas and attitudes.

Acculturation produced change in the Synod. The process of change, begun in the 1940s, accelerated in the 1950s and 1960s. Curricular materials for church and Sunday school imported new educational methods from the secular culture. New hymns and liturgical forms changed patterns of worship. Pastors joined local ministerial associations. Missouri Synod missionaries began to cooperate with other Christians in evangelistic outreach. New faculty members at Missouri Synod colleges and seminaries had graduate degrees from institutions outside of the Synod. Professors at Synod institutions and some clergy began to come to terms with more than a century of historical criticism of the Bible.

The Missouri Synod found a way to participate in forming the successor agency to the National Lutheran Council, LCUSA, and considered whether to join the Lutheran World Federation. Under the patient leadership of Oliver R. Harms it was asked to declare fellowship with the ALC and to continue a process that looked toward fellowship with the LCA.

Change is usually difficult to endure. In a sociological organization it can be traumatic. Controversy erupted within the LCMS over the changes it was experiencing. The Missouri Synod always had its share of those who saw it as their calling to guard the Synod's orthodoxy. During the 1920s there were those who opposed the efforts of a Synod commission to reach doctrinal agreement with the three synods that were in the process of forming the (old) ALC of 1930. The opponents secured the rejection of the commission's recommendation of fellowship in 1929. During the 1940s and 1950s the opponents of efforts to bring the Missouri Synod and the (old) ALC into fellowship coordinated their work through the publication of a journal, *The Confessional Lutheran.*

In the late 1950s several students at CS, notably Herman Otten, made accusations of heresy against professors there, particularly Horace Hummel and Martin P. Scharlemann, professors of exegetical theology. *The Confessional Lutheran* complained bitterly about the growing liberalism of the Missouri Synod and demanded that CS and synodical officials take action against the teachers of false doctrine. In an effort to stem the outcry, the CS governing board did not renew Hummel's teaching contract. At the 1962 Missouri Synod convention Scharlemann was induced to withdraw his essay from circulation and to make a public apology for the furor he had caused, although not for what he taught—the compromise that CS president Alfred Fuerbringer had worked out with Synod president John Behnken to keep Scharlemann on the faculty.

Opposition to the change within the Missouri Synod was reorganized following the 1962 Synod convention. Herman Otten, who had been denied approval for ordination by the CS faculty, had begun publishing a weekly journal, first called *Lutheran News* and then *Christian News*, which stridently called for the ouster of CS and synodical officials. By the time of the 1965 Missouri Synod convention a new leadership group had organized and had begun to use the political process to stop the changes within the Synod.

Present in the leadership group were two real politicians: Milton Carpenter, Democrat and erstwhile treasurer of the state of Missouri; and Robert Hirsch, Republican and state senator from South Dakota. Others included E. J. Otto, parish pastor from Quincy, Illinois; Edwin C. Weber, president of the Synod's Michigan District; Waldo Werning, staff member of the South Wisconsin District; Karl Barth, pastor of a congregation in the South Wisconsin District and later its president; and Jacob A. O. Preus, president of Concordia Theological Seminary, Springfield, Illinois. Preus was soon to become the group's candidate to unseat Harms as president of the Synod.

Jacob Preus, or "Jack" as he was known to everyone, had grown up as the son of a politician. His father had served as governor of Minnesota. Though Jack Preus may have long been a Missourian at heart, he did not begin his ministry in the Missouri Synod. He prepared for ministry at Luther Theological Seminary in St. Paul, Minnesota, at that time a seminary of the Evangelical Lutheran Church, one of the churches that helped form the ALC in 1960. Preus was ordained in 1945 after receiving a call from a congregation of the ELC in St. Paul.

Preus had been unhappy with the theological climate at Luther Seminary during his student days. In 1947 he left the ELC for the Evangelical Lutheran Synod, a splinter group that emerged when the ELC was formed to bring Norwegian Lutherans together in 1917. In 1949 Preus published a revision of a 1948 convention essay, "What Stands Between," in which he cataloged the alleged false doctrines that made it necessary for him to leave the ELC.

Preus's brother Robert had preceded him into the ELS by transferring from Luther Seminary to Bethany, the ELS seminary in Mankato, Minnesota, early in 1947. Together the Preus brothers led a movement to get the ELS to sever fellowship relations with the LCMS. Their efforts succeeded in 1955. Within three years both brothers were serving in positions of considerable responsibility within the Missouri Synod. Robert Preus became a professor of systematic theology at CS in St. Louis in 1957. A year later Jacob Preus was teaching Greek and handling public relations at Concordia Theological Seminary in Springfield, Illinois.

The Springfield seminary was in the process of coming out from under the shadow of the St. Louis seminary and the position of second-class citizenship in the Missouri Synod. The process of building and improving the Springfield seminary had begun under Walter Baepler, president during the 1950s, and had developed rapidly under his successor, George Beto. With first-rate younger professors and improved facilities, the Springfield seminary was on its way to challenging the St. Louis seminary for preeminence in the Synod.

Abruptly Beto resigned in 1962 to return to Texas to head its prison system, and Jacob Preus was named acting president. The selection of Beto's successor was not made until after Oliver Harms was elected president of the Missouri Synod later in 1962. Harms had a part in naming Jacob Preus president of the Springfield seminary, a position that gave Preus considerable influence within the LCMS. Preus courted the more conservative constituency within the Synod, and within a few years several of the younger "stars" among the Springfield seminary faculty—John Heusmann, Curtis Huber, Richard Jungkuntz, and Bernard Kurzweg—had left for other positions.

From his position as president of the Springfield seminary, Preus joined the group that had decided to stop the tide of change within the Synod by utilizing the political process. The group worked hard to elect delegates to synodical conventions who shared their objectives and through whom they could elect their own candidates to positions of power within the Synod. They had modest success at the 1967 convention in New York. By the time of the 1969 convention in Denver they were well organized and ready to try to capture the presidency. They decided that Jacob Preus was their best candidate, and he agreed to be their man. The group campaigned on a platform of being against fellowship with the ALC, the cause with which Harms had identified himself. Preus, who was a member of the top-level Missouri–ALC commission that was recommending fellowship to the two churches, dissociated himself from that recommendation, calling for more time for consideration of all the issues involved.

The opposition group launched a campaign journal, *Balance*, and later organized as Balance, Incorporated, in Jacob Preus's home. The journal, together with the effective propagandizing of *Christian News*, convinced a majority of the delegates to the 1969 convention that Harms was leading the Synod down the primrose path of liberalism. Those delegates decided to replace Harms with Jacob Preus—by about thirty votes if the rumors of the election returns are correct. And then, after seeing Harms in action for a few days, they approved by a vote of 522 to 438 Harms's proposal of fellowship with the ALC.

Several nights after Preus's election I was enjoying an after-session drink with a number of religion editors who were attending the Synod convention. With us was Lester Heins, former religion editor of the Toledo *Blade*, who was serving as director of communications for the ALC. Puffing on his pipe, his bushy eyebrows lowered, Heins said to me, "John, you don't have to accept that seminary presidency now." "But, Les," I said, "I've already accepted it." "Sure," he responded, "but they've changed the rules on you. You thought you were going to work with Oliver Harms. Now they've given you Jack Preus. You can back out of it if you want to."

I thought about what Heins said but felt I couldn't do what he was suggesting. It was true that the ground rules had been changed on me. Instead of a Synod president who wanted to lead LCMS into the future, I now would have to work with one elected by people who wanted to turn back the clock. But I had accepted the appointment as president of CS with the conviction that it was what God wanted me to do. *What did God have in store for me?* I wondered. Deep within I felt a premonition: The way of the disciple leads to a cross.

2 ——◆

AGENDA OVERHEARD

The sun had set on a family celebration of Easter. It was about 8:30 P.M. on March 29, 1970, when the phone rang in our home on the campus of Concordia Seminary. On the line was Frederick Danker, CS professor of exegetical theology. He said he had some important information to share, sensitive information that made it unwise for him to come to my house. I drove to Danker's house in Clayton. Waiting for me outside, Danker quickly got into the front seat of my car and suggested that I drive around.

The students called Danker "Red Fred" because of his frizzled red hair, to distinguish him from his brother, "Black Bill," also a member of the CS faculty. Lean and wiry, Danker moved like a man always in a hurry. He talked just as rapidly with colorful language and unexpected but appropriate turns of phrases accompanied by vigorous gestures. I knew him chiefly from his reputation as a first-rate scholar and a demanding teacher. His expectations of thorough exegesis by students had become legendary. Although I was completing my seventh month at CS, the visit with Danker in my car was the first time he and I had talked alone.

Danker spoke while I drove. He said that he had gone to his office in Sieck Hall on the campus Easter Sunday afternoon after preaching that morning. As he worked at his desk with the window open, he overheard a conversation taking place in an office just down the hall. The conversation was between Jacob A. O. Preus, president of the Lutheran Church–Missouri Synod, and his brother Robert Preus, professor of systematic theology at CS. The conversation began at 3:15 P.M. and continued for a little more than half an hour. Danker wanted me to understand that it was not his nature to bear tales. He could not help but hear the talk through his window, even though it was sometimes muted, enabling him to catch only bits and pieces. What he heard was serious and troubling enough that he felt he had to share it in confidence with me in my capacity as CS president.

According to Danker, the Preus brothers had in mind a CS investigation. When Danker began overhearing the conversation, Robert Preus was reporting to Jack on theological discussions taking place among faculty members. As Danker reported it, Robert Preus said that the exegetes had disavowed statements attributed to them by a member of their department, Martin Scharlemann, and were now clamming up. As overheard by Danker, Robert Preus singled out Everett Kalin, a younger member of the faculty and an expert on the formation of the scriptural canon, as one who simply must be made to answer.

Danker continued: Jack informed his brother that Jack was planning to carry through on his intention of conducting an investigation into the faculty's teaching. One option would be that he ask the CS Board of Control to conduct the investigation. A second option was to get Scharlemann to ask the BoC for an investigation. Robert Preus proposed that in any investigation by the BoC, Edwin Weber, first vice-president of the Synod and Jack Preus's representative on the BoC, should put the questions to faculty members and be instructed to insist on yes-or-no answers.

According to Danker, Jack Preus worried that a BoC-conducted investigation would likely wind up as a hung jury. Robert agreed, asserting that there were too many liberals on the BoC, including its chairman, for the BoC as a whole to do a good job of investigating the faculty. Jack then said that the third option was to handle things through an investigative committee. Robert agreed, pointing out that a committee would have a dual advantage: it would enable Jack to claim that he was fulfilling his presidential responsibility as supervisor of doctrine, and at the same time it would make it unnecessary for him actually to do it himself.

There was discussion of personnel for the committee. Danker heard two names. One was that of Paul Zimmermann, who had served with Jack Preus at Bethany College during his years in the Evangelical Lutheran Synod and who had become president of Concordia College in Ann Arbor, Michigan. Another was that of Elmer Foelber, a member of the editorial staff of Concordia Publishing House and, according to Robert Preus, thoroughly familiar with the writings of the faculty members.

When Danker finished, he handed me a single page of typewritten notes, summarizing the conversation he had overheard.[1] I thanked him for the information and told him that for some time I had been wondering how the move against CS would begin. Perhaps he had just told me.

I came to CS with great expectations but also with twinges of foreboding. The election of Jacob A. O. Preus as president of the LCMS just two months after my election as CS president portended problems for the chief theological institution of the Synod because Preus had been elected on a platform that promised a theological housecleaning within the Synod. I had no sooner set foot on campus than my problems began.

I arrived in St. Louis on a hot and humid Sunday afternoon on September 1, 1969. With my wife, Ernestine, and our four children, I had driven from our house in Leonia, New Jersey, in our station wagon crammed with clothes and linen for our new home. We had to return to New Jersey later in the month to close the sale of our house and to move our furniture and other belongings. But we needed to be in St. Louis before then for the beginning events of the CS 1969–70 academic year and for school opening for our children.

CS had scheduled a faculty retreat for September 2–3 at Monticello College in Monticello, Illinois. The theme for the retreat was "The Gospel and the Theological Task," the title of an article I had contributed for a *Festschrift* edition of the *Concordia Theological Monthly* published the previous June in honor of Alfred O. Fuerbringer.[2] I had written the article a year before its publication and had no idea that its appearance would coincide with my election as president of the seminary whose faculty published it. In the article I made distinctions between such terms as *gospel, doctrine, dogma,* and *theology,* terms that Synod pastors tended to equate in their theological discussions. I argued that not every doctrine was a dogma. *Dogma* embraced the doctrines of the creeds and confessions that we in the church had designated as essential for the integrity of the gospel and by which we agreed to norm all our teaching. I argued further that there could be differences in theology that were not disagreements over the nature of the gospel and pointed to the theological variety in the New Testament as illustration. In addition I argued that theology could not be done in a vacuum but needed to be shaped by the situation to which it was to be addressed. My article and six others written by CS faculty members were to serve as the basis for theological discussion at the retreat.

The plans were for my family to stay temporarily in the home occupied by faculty member Carl Graesser and his family, who were away on a sabbatical leave, until our permanent house was ready. My instructions were to pick up the key to the Graesser house at the home of my sister,

Wilma Weyermann, whose husband, Andrew, was professor of homilet-ics and ethics. We had no sooner received welcoming hugs and sat down in the Weyermann living room than my brother-in-law handed me a document. His round face reflecting his normal concern with the serious side of life, he tried to smile as he said, "I'm sorry to have to do this, but you had better read this before the faculty retreat tomorrow. It has been distributed to all the members of the faculty."

In my hands were three single-spaced typewritten pages with the heading, "*SOME ANIMADVERSIONS* on The Theme of the Retreat: 'The Gospel and the Theological Task.'" Sandwiched in between a preface and a conclusion were eight numbered paragraphs, each of which was headed with the title "Animadversion." At the end of the document the author identified himself: "MARTIN H. SCHARLEMANN, Graduate Professor of Exegetical Theology." I thanked Weyermann for alerting me early to the problem and said that I would deal with the document later that day.

An *animadversion,* according to *Webster's New Collegiate Dictionary,* is "a critical and usually censorious remark" or "adverse and typically ill-natured or unfair criticism." Scharlemann no doubt intended the first meaning of the word, but the second applied as well. In his preface Scharlemann claimed that he had in mind all the articles that were to be under discussion at the retreat, but his eight animadversions dealt only with the article I had written. Scharlemann criticized my article for what it said, for what it did not say, for lack of clarity, and for inner inconsist-ency. He especially objected to my assertions about the relativity of all human formulations of the gospel and about the need to have specific situations in mind in the task of formulating theology. Although he had not written a word about any of the other articles to be discussed, he summed up his conviction this way: "I have come to the reluctant conclu-sion that the articles referred to in the *Festschrift* do not flow from the central principle of Lutheran theology." Animadversions were a fasci-nating way to welcome a new seminary president!

I regarded Martin Scharlemann as a personal friend. He had arrived on the faculty of CS in my final year there as a student, and I had taken a course from him in philosophy and another in New Testament. When he was under attack during the early years of my parish ministry, I had personally written to CS and synodical officials in his behalf. As editor of the *American Lutheran* I had supported CS editorially in its carefully nuanced understanding of the Scriptures as the Word of God.[3] As a pastoral delegate to the 1962 LCMS convention in Cleveland I grieved as I listened to Scharlemann apologize in order to keep his job. Several years later, when I taught in CS's summer school, I was Scharlemann's guest for dinner and a welcome visitor in his home.

Because of our friendship I was puzzled by Scharlemann's attack. I never did have use for the acerbic nature of so much of the theological debate that took place in the Missouri Synod. Perhaps the Scharlemann animadversions were only an example of the kind of theological debate I would have to expect from members of a seminary faculty. I had heard that Scharlemann was upset that he had not been elected CS president. I did not understand how he could have imagined the he would be chosen in view of the controversy he had precipitated a decade earlier. Perhaps his animadversions were his way of letting me and everyone else know that he considered me less qualified than he for the presidency. In any event, at the retreat, both during the sessions and privately, I engaged Scharlemann in discussion of my article in an effort to come to an understanding with him. I thought I had been successful. But the welcome I received from Scharlemann in St. Louis was only a token of the opposition that was to come.

In spite of the cloud Scharlemann cast over it, the faculty retreat went well, enabling the faculty and me to get to know one another and launching the procedures for a new academic year. The year began officially one week later at the opening communion service in the CS chapel on the evening of September 10, 1969. I had arranged to be installed into office at that service along with several other new administrators. Although an academic inauguration would be held in November, I wanted it to be clear that I was in fact president as the school year began. To install me into office, I had invited Bertwin L. Frey, president of the English District, the Missouri Synod district to which I had belonged since my ordination in 1953. Though my predecessors had belonged to the geographical district in which CS was located, first called the Western District and then the Missouri District, I intended to continue to belong to the English District. Not only did I identify with the progressive direction of the English District but I also assumed, based on experience during my parish ministry when a neighboring pastor tried to remove me from office, that I could count on the leaders of the English District to assure me fair treatment in the event of any trouble.

When I picked Frey up at the St. Louis airport to bring him to the opening service, he told me that along with F. Dean Lueking, pastor of a prominent congregation in River Forest, Illinois, he had taken the initiative to organize a movement within the Missouri Synod to resist the anticipated onslaughts of Jacob Preus's administration. Short and wiry with curly, graying hair, Frey's body showed the results of disciplined daily exercise. His face flushed as he spoke, Frey said that if one side in the Synod had organized politically to espouse its causes, then a counterorganization was necessary. He wanted me to know that he stood ready to help if CS should come under fire. "Stay strong!" he told me as we arrived for the service.

Following the rite of installation I presided and preached at the communion service. I had given careful thought to what I wanted to say and had concluded that I needed to preach as much to myself about personal ministry as to the assembled CS community about its mission. Although it was normally my practice to preach on the assigned texts of the church year, I chose a specific text for the opening service sermon: Luke 14:25–33 contains the injunction of Jesus to count the cost of discipleship just as a builder must count the cost before erecting a tower and a general does before sending troops out against an enemy army.

To all in the assembled community—faculty, students, and families beginning a new academic year; entering students starting preparation for ordination; new administrators ready to use their talents in a new location; and myself, a new president just installed into office—I spoke about the need to count the cost before embarking on our ventures. I pointed out that for those who want to follow in Jesus' steps to do ministry, the cost of discipleship is nothing less than to walk the way of the cross. I made it clear that I personally had counted the cost and was ready to pay the price.

To celebrate my inauguration as sixth president of CS in its 130th year, a specially created committee had planned a week-long series of events under the theme "Seminary—In God for the World." The inauguration itself took place on the morning of November 10, 1969, in the auditorium that served as the CS chapel, amid the pomp and pageantry of academia with the CS faculty and representatives of over 100 educational and ecclesiastical organizations participating in the robed procession. Among those who brought official greetings were Jacob A. O. Preus, president of the LCMS, and Frederik A. Schiotz, president of the American Lutheran Church, the church body with which Missouri had entered fellowship relations just four months earlier.

In preparing the inaugural address I had solicited the counsel of the CS academic and administrative leaders and of the student body officers in order to reflect their ideas in what I said, thus indicating the collaborative style of leadership I hoped to give. In the address I described what I felt was CS's overarching purpose: "to help the church achieve its mission of bringing God's life to the world."[4] I pointed out the implications of such a purpose for CS's understanding of itself as an educational institution, for the notion of ministry underlying its curriculum, and for its relation to the church. I wanted to make it clear that the direction in which I would seek to lead CS would be determined not by personal or political agendas but by commitment to the church's mission to the world.

As an alumnus I had reflected on what was happening at CS from time to time during the course of my prior ministry. I appreciated the younger faculty who were being assembled under the leadership of then academic dean Arthur C. Repp to replace older faculty who had been my professors, some of whom were, frankly, no longer capable teachers. I rejoiced at the new emphasis on the Scriptures and on teaching future pastors to be interpreters of the Scriptures themselves instead of relying totally on the interpretation of others. I was grateful for the transition from dogmatics to confessional theology that was taking place in the area of systematics.

But I did not appreciate what I thought was less than candor in the seminary's repeated claims that nothing had really changed in CS teaching. I resented the efforts to demonstrate that what was happening at CS was really the "old" Missouri Synod after all. I thought that it would have been not only more honest but also more helpful for CS to capitalize on the changes that were going on by showing how those changes were enabling CS and the LCMS to be more faithful to the Synod's confessional position.

I was deeply grateful that CS was providing its graduates with a solid theological foundation, but I worried about the growing gap I saw opening between theology and ministry, with theology being understood by more and more graduates as an intellectual occupation. As I saw it, theology had no reason for being except to serve the church's mission, and the purpose of seminary education was to provide the church not with theological eggheads but with pastors. Therefore I was pleased that, even before I arrived at CS, my friend and former roommate John Damm had been assigned (under the auspices of the Theological Education Research Committee appointed by the Missouri Synod's Board for Higher Education) to do the homework necessary for revising the seminary curriculum. As sometimes happens among friends, Damm and I not only thought alike but could often read each other's minds. Damm had a year to produce a report, and then he and I could work together in revising the curriculum.

To give CS new leadership, information was needed about its alleged problems with its constituency. In my work with the Lutheran Council in the USA I had initiated a research project to ascertain what image the American public had of the Lutheran church. The project, completed after I left LCUSA, was designed to be a benchmark against which to measure the results of major public relations efforts by Lutherans in the United States. I proposed to the CS's administrative council that we initiate a similar research project to ascertain CS's image within the LCMS.

Robert Grunow, director of CS relations, and his associate Larry Neeb, director of communications, were enthusiastic. Both were relatively new, their positions only recently created. The attacks on CS had made clear the need for CS to do a better job of communicating with the Synod. A developing financial shortage in the Synod nudged CS into its own development and fund-raising program. Grunow, his black hair combed back, outgoing and at times unctuous in his relations with others, had come from the parish to CS to raise funds. Neeb, a compactly built young man, muscular and athletic, his hair cropped short but already showing signs of receding, was a recent CS graduate who had taken on the communications task. In my opinion he was a genuine diamond in the rough.

With the assistance of Grunow and Neeb we engaged the services of Frank Block and Associates, professional advertising and marketing consultants in St. Louis, to conduct the research. So that public attention would not skew the results, we kept the effort confidential among CS's chief administrators. Because it would be difficult to get an accurate sample of the laity of Missouri without more public attention, we agreed to sample only the Synod's clergy and to limit our contact to parish pastors in the U.S. That approach would enable us to assess the clergy's continuing-education needs as well.

The survey, conducted by telephone during February 1970, revealed that CS had an image problem with only a small percentage of the pastors throughout the Missouri Synod, primarily older clergy and graduates of the seminary in Springfield, Illinois. Less than fifteen percent took some exception to the statement: "Concordia Seminary, St. Louis is true to sound Lutheran principles." Pastors identified the area of pastoral counseling as the one in which they most needed continuing-education help. Sixty-eight percent of the respondents expressed themselves in favor of relations with the ALC.[5]

The survey results were encouraging. CS was not in serious trouble with the clergy of the LCMS and therefore presumably not with the majority of the laity. Nevertheless, work needed to be done in order to reassure the small number of clergy who had reservations about our Lutheran commitment. The survey had given us the means by which to determine the effectiveness of future CS relations efforts.

I shared the survey results with CS's governing board and with the faculty. I arranged for the faculty to review the results in workshops in order to produce a plan of communication between CS and the Synod. We wanted to confirm the views of those who thought well of us and to change the minds of those who had doubts about us.

I led the way in the communications task, speaking to a large number of the Synod's district conventions during winter and spring 1970, using the same format everywhere. I began with a simple confession of my personal faith, following the formula of the Apostles' Creed, so that the convention delegates would have a basis on which to relate to a new CS president. I could tell that the directness and the simplicity of the confession had a profound effect. Acting on my convictions about the need for honesty, I dealt at some length with my perception of the problem between CS and the Synod: CS's use of historical criticism, which some pastors in the Synod equated with what they had been taught as "higher criticism" during their seminary days. I pointed out that our faculty made use of historical criticism with solid Lutheran presuppositions about the Scripture as the Word of God and without the faith-destroying presuppositions of higher criticism. I concluded with information about CS that would be of interest to pastors and their congregations.

A month after I arrived in St. Louis, Jacob Preus invited me to dinner. He extended the invitation at the October 1969 meeting of the Commission on Theology and Church Relations, its first meeting since Preus's election as president, which I attended as one of the faculty's representatives on the commission. Preus told me that as a former seminary president, he wanted to share some thoughts with me about how to run a seminary.

Our dinner meeting took place on November 3, 1969, at the Missouri Athletic Club in downtown St. Louis, where Preus as president of the Synod was a member. We sat at a table for two out of the mainstream of activity in the cavernous dining room. Preus was affable, conversing most of the time with an amiable grin that seemed to temper the seriousness of what he said. He made good on his promise to tell me how to run CS. He said my biggest problem was going to be how to be my "own man." According to Preus, it was not Alfred O. Fuerbringer, my predecessor as president, but Arthur C. Repp, CS's vice-president for academic affairs, who really directed CS. Preus insisted that I would have to get rid of Repp if I wanted to be in charge.

Toward the end of the meal the real reason for the dinner invitation became clear. Preus told me that he considered his election as president of the Missouri Synod to be a mandate to straighten out the Synod theologically. He said that he intended to carry out the mandate and in the process to bring CS back into the mainstream of the Synod. I stated that I assumed that he would be following the constitutionally prescribed procedures, which stipulated that access to the faculty would be through my office and that any decisions concerning faculty would be made by the CS governing board.

I assured Preus that he could count on my cooperation in any approaches to the faculty and that I would be glad to help him deal with his concerns. I pointed out that I, too, was concerned that our faculty be faithful to their commitment to the Missouri Synod's doctrinal position. That position, I pointed out, was stated in Article II of the Synod's constitution: acceptance without reservation of the Scriptures as the written Word of God and the only rule and norm of faith and practice and of the confessional writings in *The Book of Concord* (1580) as a true and unadulterated statement and exposition of the Word of God. I wanted it clearly understood what I expected the standard to be for any review of faculty teaching. I added that, until it could be proven otherwise, we had to presume that the faculty members were faithful to their confessional vows.[6]

As I drove home that night, I reflected that a shift was probably under way in the ideology of the Preus party. Preus had been elected Synod president on a platform that was opposed to fellowship with the ALC. Yet after electing Preus, the Synod had approved fellowship. From my perspective, Preus needed a new issue to consolidate his power. He needed another platform on which to stand in order to unite his followers against something. It looked to me as though false doctrine was going to be the issue and CS was going to be its focus.

On December 15, 1969, at a meeting of the CS Electors held in conjunction with a meeting of the BoC, Preus again made his intentions clear concerning the CS faculty. At the November meeting of the BoC, held on the day of my academic inauguration, I had proposed that Richard P. Jungkuntz be called to the faculty to fill a vacancy in the area of New Testament and church history. Jungkuntz had been serving as executive secretary of the Commission on Theology and Church Relations until he was removed a month earlier and was seriously considering appealing the action as the basis for a civil suit. Jungkuntz was already serving as a CS guest professor, and his academic and scholarly abilities were beyond question. I assumed that Preus might be happy to have Jungkuntz out of his hair and that the honeymoon condition of my early months as president might enable me to secure Jungkuntz's services.

My recommendation required that the Electors meet to consider whether to authorize Jungkuntz as a candidate for a faculty position. LCMS regulations for choosing a professor were similar to those for electing a president. Four CS Electors made the decision: the president of the Synod, a representative of the Synod's BHE, the president of the Missouri District, and the BoC functioning as a group. A majority of these four entities had to give prior approval for the BoC to issue a call to a prospective faculty member. The Electors postponed action on the Jungkuntz candidacy pending the outcome of the decision by Jungkuntz on whether to appeal his removal from office. Several months later, after Jungkuntz decided not to appeal, the Electors did not approve his candidacy.

In the course of the discussion at the December meeting about Jungkuntz's candidacy, Preus announced that he was considering undertaking an investigation of CS to get at the false doctrine being taught there. I was deeply distressed by his statement and challenged it at the meeting. I pointed out to Preus that he had precluded the purpose of any investigation if he was already convinced of the presence of false doctrine without first ascertaining the facts. Contrary to the provisions in Matthew 18, he had not even talked to anyone he suspected of teaching false doctrine. (In Matt. 18:15–17 Jesus gives procedures to follow "if your brother sins against you," requiring personal, private conversations for the purpose of reaching understanding and reconciliation.) As I spoke, I watched Preus glower at me, his jaw jutting out pugnaciously, but he made no response. The meeting participants quickly returned to the agenda.[7]

The provisions of Matthew 18 were again the subject of a conversation I had, this time with Martin Scharlemann in early February 1970. In my continuing efforts to reach out to him, I had asked him to come to my office. There, wisps of gray hair combed back on his head, his pale face set in a passionless pose, his lips slightly parted, Scharlemann told me that he considered the situation at CS to be so intolerable that he was seriously thinking about asking the president of the Synod to conduct an investigation. In my response I pointed out that there were many other things he needed to do before he was entitled to take so drastic a step. In the spirit of Matthew 18 he needed to talk to the faculty members about whose teaching or actions he was concerned. In addition, he had the responsibility of sharing his concerns with me so that I might use my office to try to resolve any problems.

I asked Scharlemann about whom he was concerned and what the issues were. He named two fellow members of the exegetical department, Everett Kalin and Ralph Klein, and said that his basic concern was about their views on the inspiration of the Scriptures. So I arranged for a meeting with Scharlemann, Kalin, and Klein in my office in order to deal with Scharlemann's concerns. The discussion was frank and cordial and led to further meetings to discuss another of Scharlemann's concerns, the orders of creation, which referred to structures such as government and family that were presumably built into the very fabric of human life.

The issue of orders of creation made it clear to me that Scharlemann's objections to Kalin and Klein were not primarily doctrinal but social. Those two faculty members were the most outspoken on social issues and were in close touch with campus student activists. As a chaplain and brigadier general in the Air Force Reserves, Scharlemann did not take kindly to the protests of CS students against the Vietnam War and to the support that Kalin and Klein gave to such activities. In any event, the discussions demonstrated to me that there were no real basic doctrinal disagreements among the three faculty members.[8]

While the discussions of Scharlemann's concerns were taking place, conversations between the members of the exegetical and systematics departments were renewed. Those conversations had begun the year before my arrival with a not-so-hidden agenda of dealing with the cleavage reported by students in the approach to the Scriptures by faculty members in the two departments. The renewed conversations demonstrated that another agenda was now in operation. These are the conversations on which Robert Preus reported to his brother Jack below Frederick Danker's open window. With Scharlemann often serving as inquisitor, Robert Preus, Richard Klann, and Ralph Bohlmann joined with him in trying to get members of the exegetical department to commit themselves on controversial issues. But early on, most of the faculty sensed that something besides scholarly dialogue was sought. It was no longer safe to explore the truth.

Danker's report of the Easter Sunday agenda heard through his window clarified a number of things in my mind. First, there was a connection between the internal discussions going on within the faculty and Jacob Preus's determination to get at the "false doctrine" supposedly at CS. Scharlemann, Robert Preus, and others were doing their best to get some of their colleagues to state for the record their position on controversial issues, so that those positions could then be revealed in Preus's investigation of the faculty. Second, Martin Scharlemann, the courageous and honest exegete who had led the way in helping the Missouri Synod confront the basic issues in biblical studies, had already allied himself with Robert and Jacob Preus to undo the very principles and procedures he had helped introduce at CS. He was ready to request an investigation of the faculty, if Jacob Preus asked him to do so. Third, and most important to me, Jacob Preus had decided to approach the faculty through an investigative committee. He did not intend to follow the established procedures of dealing with particular individuals about whom there were specific concerns. He intended to ignore Matthew 18.

◆ ◆ ◆

Subsequent events proved how well Danker heard the conversation outside his window. On April 9, just eleven days later, I received from

Martin Scharlemann a copy of a three-page letter sent that day to Jacob Preus in which Scharlemann detailed his concern about the "theological climate" prevailing at CS and requested that "a competent committee of inquiry be created to look into the matters that threaten to deface the Lutheran character of the life and instruction going on at Concordia Seminary.[9] It did not matter that we were in the process of dealing with his concerns in fraternal discussion. It did not matter that the discussions, as Scharlemann himself acknowledged in his letter to Preus, had "proved to be constructive." He had been encouraged to ask for the appointment of an investigative committee, and he had done so.

What was I to do? I asked Arthur Repp to come to my office. Contrary to the counsel Jacob Preus had given me about Repp, I learned that I did not have to remove him from office in order to be in charge at CS. Far from it! Ever since I arrived in St. Louis, Repp had demonstrated that he was a most competent and loyal administrator. He was interested in the results of a job well done, not the glory. When he presented the facts to back up a recommendation he was making, the decision to be made was evident, but he always made it clear that the decision was mine.

Repp sat down in his accustomed place in a chair across from me at my desk. With bushy black hair atop his head, a perpetual five o'clock shadow on his chin and jowly cheeks, he looked at me with a trace of a smile on his lips, his dark eyes shining brightly through rimless glasses. I handed him the correspondence from Scharlemann and said, "Doc, I received this today. What do you think I should do about it?"

Repp shook his head in dismay several times as he read Scharlemann's letter. Then, in his characteristically blunt fashion he said, "You can't ignore that, John. You've got to do something about it. First, he's challenging your leadership as president. In fact, he's saying you don't count as president. You can't let him get away with that and survive for long. But there's a much more important reason. He's refusing to follow Matthew 18, and he's asking for a procedure that has no connection to Matthew 18."

Repp explained how the many attacks against members of the faculty over the past decades had produced specific procedures to assure both the accountability and the protection of the faculty. At the heart of the procedures was Matthew 18 with its requirement that accuser meet accused in an effort to resolve the problem. Only if that discussion should prove unsatisfactory could there be a next step, which required the CS administration to deal with the problem. Then, only if that should prove unsatisfactory, could the issue come before Synod officials.

"We aren't perfect here, John," Repp said. "I think you knew that even before you came here. But we have tried to figure out how to make sure that our faculty are dealt with as Christians as we hold them to their confessional commitment." He stopped, unsure if he should say what was on his mind, and then decided to continue. "People use Matthew 18 if their goal is to gain the brother. They look for another way if they are out to get him."

After reflecting on Repp's counsel, I decided to make an issue both for the faculty and for the BoC of my ability to deal with problems at CS without any outside help and of the sufficiency of the Matthew 18 due process procedures without an investigation of CS. The day after I received Scharlemann's letter I announced a special faculty meeting for April 16 to secure a faculty action on the basis of which to ask for a vote of confidence from the BoC.

Scharlemann chose not to attend the meeting, stating afterward that he had a previous appointment. Most faculty members were stunned and appalled when I read Scharlemann's letter to them. In the course of the discussion Arthur Carl Piepkorn, a close friend of Scharlemann, who was serving as chair of the systematics department and had distinguished himself as an army chaplain, broke down in tears when he tried to speak. After the meeting he explained to me that his distress was because he realized what the demon of ambition was doing to his good friend. Other members of the faculty commented to me about the change in Scharlemann ever since I was offered the CS presidency and he was not.

The faculty gave me its vote of confidence. In its action the faculty disputed the need for a special committee of inquiry and affirmed its readiness to continue mutual theological discussion to ensure continuing faithfulness to the Lutheran confessional commitment. It declared the bylaw procedures to be adequate and preferable for achieving faculty unity and solidarity and pledged its support to me in my efforts to ensure that the faculty remain faithful to its avowed confessional position.[10]

Armed with the faculty action, I made an issue of Scharlemann's request for an investigative committee at the meeting of the BoC on April 20, 1970. The BoC gave me its vote of confidence. In its action it declared that the Scharlemann letter had bypassed the proper procedures for achieving faculty unity and solidarity. The BoC placed itself squarely behind my efforts to carry out the responsibilities of my office to ensure that the faculty would remain faithful to its confessional commitment.[11]

My efforts were to no avail. During the board meeting Jacob Preus came to the CS campus for the purpose of hand-delivering a document to me in my capacity as executive officer of the BoC. (So began a regular pattern of operation in which Preus would hand me major controversial documents either during or just before a board meeting.) The document announced the creation of a Fact-Finding Committee for the purpose of dealing with disturbances created by "alleged departures from our

Synod's doctrinal position on the part of individuals serving in various capacities within our church." In an accompanying letter Preus stated that he was directing the committee to "begin its work with Concordia Seminary, Saint Louis, Missouri, because of its strategic importance for the life and work of the synod" and asked the BoC "to cooperate with the Committee in every possible way."[12]

In response to the Preus materials, the BoC declared its readiness to cooperate with the FFC "under the appropriate section of the *Handbook*," by which the BoC meant the Synod bylaws dealing with supervision of educational institutions.[13] The BoC was not about to give away its synodically mandated supervisory responsibility. Unofficially, board members encouraged me to follow through on my announced intention of meeting with Preus as soon as possible to try to dissuade him from the use of an FFC.

I met with Preus the next day in his office in the Lutheran Building in downtown St. Louis. I reported the BoC's action and explained why I thought the decision to create a FFC was unwise. I explained how the Scharlemann letter undermined my office as president and that his decision was now going to compound the problem. I asserted that I was convinced that the bylaw procedures in the synodical *Handbook* were adequate and preferable for him to carry out his constitutional responsibilities to supervise doctrine and would enable him to achieve the objectives he had announced for the FFC. Staring at me impassively, he agreed to think it over.[14]

Several weeks later, under date of May 15, 1970, Preus wrote to inform me that as a result of our conversation he had decided for the time being at least to try to carry on the contemplated interviews himself with the help of the vice-presidents and other resource people. He went on to say that he might have to resort to a special committee if "this procedure does not prove to be feasible" and that he would be in touch with me shortly "for setting up a schedule of interviews on these matters." At the same time, Preus released an issue of *Brother to Brother*, an occasional newsletter from his office to the clergy of the Synod, under the date of Pentecost 1970 (Pentecost was on May 17 that year). In the newsletter Preus stated that he had become convinced of the need to take decisive action concerning alleged departures from the Synod's doctrinal position. He reported that he had considered appointing a special committee "to consult with the individuals involved and to present its findings and recommendations to my office" but that he had decided to undertake personally with the assistance of the vice-presidents and other resource persons "the task of interviewing certain individuals against whom complaints have been lodged repeatedly." He went on to reserve the right to create a special committee if he should find that necessary. "I might add," he concluded, "that my initial approach will be to several faculty members of our St. Louis seminary. President John Tietjen and the Board of Control have assured me of their sincere cooperation."

A delay occurred before Preus and I arranged a meeting to consider procedures for his contacts with faculty members. We met on July 6 from 2:00 to 4:00 P.M. in the Board Room in Pieper Hall on the CTS campus. President Preus brought with him Herman Scherer, president of the Synod's Missouri District and therefore a member of the CTS's governing board, and Herbert Mueller, secretary of the Synod and Preus's arbiter on constitutional issues. I asked those who shared administrative responsibility for the faculty with me to be at the meeting: vice-president for academic affairs, Arthur C. Repp; academic dean, Walter Wegner; and chairpersons Arthur Carl Piepkorn of the systematics department, Edgar Krentz and Alfred Sauer of the exegetical department, John Constable of the historical department, and Andrew Weyermann of the practical department.

Preus took charge at the beginning of the meeting, and Walter Wegner took extensive, almost verbatim notes.[15] Although Preus had announced to the Synod that his initial approach was going to be to "several" CS faculty members, at the outset of our meeting he requested that all faculty members supply him with copies of all their writings, including doctoral theses, conference essays, *CTM* articles, copies of classroom tests together with what the professors considered to be the correct answers to test questions, classroom syllabi, and unpublished essays. He explained that he did not want to get involved in a "hassle" based on oral reports of what faculty members taught, including reports of what they said in their classrooms or tape recordings made by students. He said that he would ask certain people to read the material to be supplied by the faculty but that any evaluation made would be his.

I objected to what looked to me to be a fishing expedition that put a cloud of suspicion over every member of the faculty in a process that seemed to assume that they were guilty until they proved themselves innocent. While affirming his right and responsibility as synodical president to supervise doctrine, I pointed out that the Synod's constitution specified that his supervisory authority was to be carried out in the case of CS through the BoC and therefore insisted that any findings or recommendations of the investigation would have to be turned over to the BoC. I urged that it would be much better to follow the bylaw procedures for dealing with specific people concerning whom there were suspicions or complaints. Other faculty members supported my position, and Piepkorn's arguments seemed particularly effective in getting Preus to change his mind.

Preus agreed that it would be simpler if he did not have to deal with all the faculty members. He expressed the hope that out of the process could come an adequate judicial system according to which a plaintiff could get some action and a harassed professor could get some relief. At one point he agreed that he would limit his inquiry to those in the exegetical department. Finally he agreed that he would limit his inquiry to specific individuals about whom he had received criticism and to specific writings that had been called into question. His procedure would be to conduct interviews with these individuals and then, if not satisfied, to bring his concerns to the BoC through me.

I was pleased with the results of the meeting. I felt that we had secured the use of the due process procedures of the Synod's bylaws, reaffirmed the role and responsibility of the BoC, and prevented unnecessary trauma for most of the faculty members. But Preus had the last word and unilaterally altered the agreement. He did so, he said, partly because of the public attention to his proposed investigation in the press that summer.

Investigative reporter Robert Teuscher broke the news of Preus's plans for an investigation in the July 13, 1970, edition of the St. Louis *Globe-Democrat*. Carried later in the day by the St. Louis *Post-Dispatch*, the story was distributed by AP and UPI wire services to newspapers all over the country. Public attention increased as a result of the report of a private interview Preus gave to staff writer Betty Medsger of *The Washington Post*, published in its July 27, 1970, edition. The story quoted Preus as wanting the Missouri Synod to establish new procedures that would make it easier "to oust pastors and seminary professors not 'in line' with official church doctrine." *Newsweek* reported on the investigation in its August 3, 1970, issue under the caption, "Hunting Lutheran Heretics."

From my experience as public relations executive of LCUSA, I had learned how important it was to accentuate the positive in dealings with the press. I therefore prepared a statement for public release in which I denied that the members of our faculty taught false doctrine and presented what they did teach on such issues as the virgin birth and the resurrection of Jesus Christ. Disputing the need for any extraordinary procedures in dealing with teaching at CS, I stated that I nevertheless welcomed Preus's investigation. "First, it will demonstrate how truly Lutheran we are," I said. "Second, it will help our church clarify what it really means to be Lutheran." I had no doubt about the commitment of the faculty to the Lutheran confessional position. I expected the investigation to produce sharp controversy that would involve the Missouri

Synod in a learning experience about the meaning of Lutheranism, with our faculty serving as teachers.

I incorporated the substance of the news release in a column I wrote for the summer issue of the CS newsletter. Preus cited those remarks as his second reason for changing his mind about how he was going to investigate CS. In a letter to the BoC dated September 9, 1970, Preus accused me of questioning his right to conduct an inquiry, denying the need for interviews, and seeking to discourage him from "asking the professors at the seminary what they believe." Therefore "in the interest of maximum objectivity and fairness and in the hope of promoting good will and trust," Preus decided "to revert to the mode of procedure" he had originally proposed, namely a FFC.[16]

3 ──◆

FISHING
EXPEDITION

The faculty interviews by Lutheran Church–Missouri Synod president
J. A. O. Preus's Fact Finding Committee were coming to an end. It was
Friday, March 5, 1971. The interviews had been going on twice a month,
two days at a time, since the middle of December. Four faculty members
had been interviewed separately during a day, each interview extending
for an hour and a half to two hours. After the interviews scheduled for
March 26 and 27, forty-six members of the faculty would have been
interviewed.

The interviews were held in the board room in the Lutheran Building at 210 North Broadway in St. Louis, headquarters of the LCMS. A
glass-topped mahogany table filled the long room from one end to the
other. High-back, thickly cushioned leather chairs that rocked and
swiveled were arranged around the table. To the back of each chair was
affixed a label bearing the name of one of the nineteen members of the
Synod's Board of Directors. On the wall behind the chair at the foot of
the table was a large painting of the ornate official seal of the LCMS,
with crosses and stars and grapevines, proclaiming the center of the
Christian faith—*Jesus Christus Dominus Est* (Jesus Christ is Lord)—and
heralding the watchwords of the Lutheran Reformation—*Sola Fide, Sola
Scriptura, Sola Gratia* (Faith Alone, Scripture Alone, Grace Alone).

The FFC members seated themselves around the foot and right
side of the table. Occupying the leather chair at the foot was Paul W.
Streufert, pastor of a congregation in Rocky River, Ohio, who as fourth
vice-president of the Missouri Synod attended the meetings of the BoD
in this same room. Affable and ingratiating, his oval face and pointy

nose flushed a deep red, he had made it clear that he did not want to be on the FFC and was present only because the responsibility of his office required him to do whatever the president of the Synod asked him to do.

Next to Streufert at the end of the table sat the chair of the FFC, Paul A. Zimmermann, president of the Synod's junior college in Ann Arbor, Michigan, who had a reputation in the Synod for his attempts to demonstrate the inerrancy of the Bible in scientific and historical matters. Serving as chief interrogator, his hands busily managing the mounds of documents in front of him, his eyes darting behind his glasses from paper to committee members to person being interviewed, he gave the impression that he was doing work too important and serious to smile.

To the right of Zimmermann sat Karl L. Barth, newly elected president of the Synod's South Wisconsin District. When he was not managing the tape-recording equipment for the committee, he was leaning back in his chair with arms folded, his shock of combed-back, graying curly hair resting against the cushion, his eyes looking out from a pock-marked face with questioning suspicion, his lips occasionally parting to show pleasure or displeasure.

Farther up the table sat H. Armin Moellering, pastor of a congregation in Palisades Park, New Jersey, who had a doctorate in the Greek classics. He and I were anything but strangers. As neighboring pastor during my time as parish pastor in Leonia, he had brought official charges against me to the president of the English District because of the activity of my congregation in working for unity with the other Lutheran congregation in town. He had been unsuccessful in getting me removed from office. "Red" was his nickname, although his hair had thinned and turned white. He liked to lace his sonorous speech with clipped, properly accented German quotations. Next to Moellering sat Elmer Foelber, member of the editorial staff of Concordia Publishing House, who had once been a professor of English at the Synod's junior college in Fort Wayne, Indiana, and was now near retirement. Peering out from under bushy gray eyebrows through thick rimless glasses, a lighted cigar in hand, he seemed to have difficulty staying awake.

The faculty member to be interviewed on this early evening of March 5 was Robert W. Bertram, professor of systematic and historical theology. He sat in the seat reserved for interviewees, next to Streufert and across from Zimmermann. Bertram was well known to the committee members. He had been teaching at Concordia Seminary since 1963 following distinguished service as head of the department of religion at Valparaiso University and was popular as essayist and lecturer in the pastoral conferences of the Missouri Synod. Round-faced with laugh lines emanating from eyes that were always ready to sparkle with good humor, he wore a dark beard that compensated for thinning hair on top of his head. I sat to Bertram's left, managing two tape recorders so that both Bertram and I could have a tape of the interview.

The interview had begun with Bertram explaining his work as a teacher of systematic theology and his hopes for the future of his craft. Paul Zimmermann's questions had led Bertram to describe his confessional commitment and the relevance of Lutheran confessional theology in the contemporary world. Karl Barth shifted the direction of the conversation.[1]

Barth: What about *sola scriptura* as formal principle? Do you think these terms that we have used—formal principle and material principle[2]—are still worthwhile? Is the primary question as we approach systematics, "What do the Scriptures say?" or "How does this relate to the Gospel of Christ?" Are these two things mutually exclusive? I am thinking of very practical things now confronting our own church as far as the ordination of women is concerned. I have heard, and this is not from anybody on your faculty, but a fellow pastor of mine said to me, "The question is not whether the Scriptures plainly teach for or against the ordination of women but whether this impinges on salvation." Now, I am asking, I guess, to go back to the original thing. How do you see *sola scriptura?* Is this still a valid thing, this formal principle? How does this get practical in approaching dogmatics?

Bertram: It certainly is practical. I would take the two questions with which you started and link them together. "What does the Scripture say?" and "What does the Gospel say?" are inseparable questions. They are not really two questions. But you could make one question out of them and say, "What does the Scripture informed by the Gospel say?" Then we are off and away. And if in the face of that kind of question you would say, "Is the *sola scriptura* question essential, is it primary, is it practical?" I would say, yes, to all of those. As to the other question, where you used the example of the ordination of women and asked, "Does that impinge on salvation?" I think I would be inclined to turn that around and say—because at least offhand I see no immediate way in which that does impinge on salvation—I would turn it around and say, "Does salvation impinge on *it?* Does the Gospel of Christ, as that Gospel is rehearsed in the Scriptures of Old and New Testament, have implications for such things as the ordination of women?" I would say that it does.

Barth: So many of these things, though, have a quite indirect relationship to the . . . Whether I maintain faith in . . . Whether you are talking about capital punishment or civil obedience or a host of other things, if you qualify your statement on *sola scriptura* . . . I don't recall just exactly what you said, the Scriptures in the light of the Gospel, or whatever, aren't you in danger of changing the formal or the material principle, changing them around?

Bertram: I don't know where the distinction between formal and material principles originated . . .

Barth: That was my original question. Do you still think this is valid?

Bertram: I am not so sure I do. First of all, I don't think the terms mean much to people today, this old Aristotelian distinction between form and matter. If we could be sure that the people with whom we are using such terms did understand the—let's say—Aristotelian roots of those terms, then I would feel a lot more at ease using them, because one of the first things that any good Aristotelian would have said is that you can never have form without matter or matter without form. Now as long as we could be sure that all of the parties to the discussion would understand that—that in other words you can't have Scripture (if that is the *forma*)—for Christian theological purposes you can't use Scripture without letting it be informed by the *materia,* which in this case is, say, the doctrine of justification by faith alone—okay, then I would grant the validity of that kind of language. . . .

That raises the question: Is it still important to distinguish between the Scriptures and the Gospel which gives them life? I don't know. In the history of theology distinctions are always made for some purpose. And I would have to answer that question—Is the distinction still a worthwhile distinction?—by cross-examining and counter-asking, What is the *purpose* you have in mind for making the distinction? Then I could say maybe, maybe, the distinction is valid. My own reading of the situation is that right now what we need like we need a hole in the head is to *distinguish* the Scripture from the Gospel. Rather what we need right now is to see a kind of symbiosis between them. You can't talk sensibly about Scripture without talking about the Gospel. And you can't talk sensibly about the Gospel without talking about *that* Gospel which is the Gospel of the Holy Scriptures.

Barth: The reason for the question that you hinted at, said I want to know what the reason would be—the reason would be whether it would be possible then to enjoy within the church a diversity on a host of different things that perhaps Scriptures talk plainly but which would not by any means destroy faith in the Gospel. I mentioned several examples. That would be the reason for . . . Would this mean, if we don't want to distinguish Scripture from the Gospel, that we could permit a diversity doctrinally limited only by the Gospel in the sense of the way of salvation?

Bertram: Okay. I think I catch the drift of your question. If I don't, you will ask it again. A diversity "doctrinally" already loads the terms in a way in which I wouldn't feel at ease with them. The only "doctrine" that I find the Lutheran Confessions operating with is the *doctrina evangelii,* the doctrine of the Gospel. And about *that* doctrine there is no diversity. That is one reason I said before that I don't see *The Book of Concord* as being a denominational document. It is meant to confess, starting with the Catholic Creeds all the way through to the Solid Declaration, it is intended to confess the doctrine of the Gospel, not a Lutheran doctrine of the Gospel. We would all say, "Obviously not that." Not even a Lutheran perspective on the doctrine of the Gospel. It means to be confessing one faith, the only faith there ever was—the same one faith, one Lord, one baptism, one God and Father of all. That is what the apostolic churches confess. So I don't feel at home with the language of "doctrinal diversity," I suppose. But on the other hand . . .

Zimmermann: Excuse me, just for clarification, you are talking about the Formula of Concord and use the term Gospel. Are you using it in the sense of the Formula, the broad sense, the Gospel as including the Law concept plus all of the supporting doctrine all the way from creation through eschatology?

Bertram: Yes, the broad sense, that is right, for which the typical terminology of the confessors is to refer to these as "articles." These are articulations of one dimension or one sector rather than another of that single Gospel. Maybe it would help if I dug into a particular example.

Bertram discoursed on LCMS Resolution 2–31, which dealt with the historicity of the Genesis account of the creation, Adam and Eve, and the fall. The resolution says, Bertram pointed out, that the teachings that God created humanity in God's image and that God subjected a fallen humanity to corruption and mortality are essential to the pure and clear teaching of the gospel. Bertram went on to point out that the resolution does not make the same claim for the six-day creation, the historicity of Adam and Eve, and the historicity of the fall. Bertram cited the illustration as evidence of the dilemma in which the Missouri Synod found itself: "It wants to say the Biblical thing. It also—and for this I would say *Gott sei dank!*—it also feels under evangelical obligation to say what it is the Scripture does say only if you can show how what the Scripture says is relatable to the clear and pure teaching of the Gospel."

Zimmermann and Bertram discussed whether, for the clear and pure teaching of the gospel, it was necessary to affirm the historicity of Adam and Eve and of the fall. Zimmermann conceded that it was not necessary for the sake of the gospel to affirm a six-day creation. Bertram said he would not find it objectionable if someone declined to accept the historicity of Adam and Eve for exegetical reasons. Zimmermann then took Bertram up on his proposal to discuss the virgin birth of Jesus as another illustration of his point about the inseparability of Bible and gospel.

Zimmermann: Now let me tie it in with this. Could I say, I think that the virgin birth in Matthew is a *midrash*, a sort of pious spiritualization which somehow found its way into the New Testament, and I still believe that

Christ is Redeemer but I cannot believe the doctrine of the virgin birth? Could I go to the Confessions and say that I think that there is then an exegetical question, too? After all, it is only based on a couple of passages. I understand that as a midrash whereas the confessors took it literally. Therefore it is obviously an exegetical question.

Bertram: Now let me get this straight: What is an exegetical question?

Zimmermann: The virgin birth.

Bertram: The virgin birth of our Lord . . . I would first of all feel an obligation to hear out from a man who had difficulties with this just what his difficulties are with it. If he would say, "Well, I hesitate to affirm the virgin birth of our Lord because there is such scant reference to it in the New Testament," I would say, "Well, ordinarily that is a difficulty that is worth taking seriously. Do you have any more objections to it? Would you prefer to limit your sources to the somewhat more circumstantial descriptions of our Lord's virgin birth in Luke?" . . . Well, maybe he says, "I think the reason Luke elaborates the story of our Lord's virgin birth as fully as he does is due to a mistranslation of Isaiah 7 and that a legend came out of this septuagintal translation to which Luke then wanted to respond, and he wanted to describe our Lord in terms of that legend and that the Christian gospel is not necessarily bound by that." I would say, "Well, if that is so, that would also be worth taking seriously."

But suppose he would say, "Well, I have another objection, and that is that I don't believe that if Jesus was fully human that it is human enough for him to have been born only of one parent." Now then, there we are beginning to get into what I would call a somewhat more theological, substantive theological question. Now I think I would want to counter by saying, the big question is, what is the function which the doctrine of our Lord's virgin birth—and I would regard this as an "articulation" of the "doctrine of the Gospel"—what is the function which the doctrine of our Lord's virgin birth performs? That is a little harder to bring off. Is our Lord said to have been "conceived by the Holy Ghost, born of the Virgin Mary" so that thereby he would be excused from any shadow of coming in the chain of original sin? That has been one solution, one explanation, that has been proposed, although there is little biblical evidence for that. I know of one theologian whom I respect who is supposed to have said to one of his seminars in Germany when tackled on this point, *"Es is einfach biblisch."* It is simply biblical. I think, going back to our question of before, to relate it to the clear and pure essential teaching of the Gospel is still obligatory on us. How can we relate the Luke reference to our Lord's virgin birth to the Gospel? And until we do, we haven't really done the full theological task.

Zimmermann: Now having done the full theological task . . . but is that different . . . or if we can't see how that could be done . . . going back to this man who says it is simply biblical and therefore we accept it, is there anything wrong with his answer? Isn't that fundamentally where you start, as it is written?

Bertram: No.

Zimmermann: That is not what you are saying?

Bertram: Yes, surely that is where you start. But I was saying no to "Is there something wrong with that?" I would say that, because it is biblical, this is where you start, that is true. And a man had better have pretty good reasons for dismissing something when it is *einfach biblisch.*

Zimmermann: If it is *einfach biblisch,* are there any reasons for dismissing it that can stand?

Bertram: No, no. There are no reasons for dismissing it. But I don't think those are the only two alternatives. The question is whether he believes, teaches, and confesses it. And why does he believe, teach, and confess it? Finally why he ought to believe, teach, and confess it is integral, it is ingredient to the Gospel. And that is the alternative to dismissing it. The alternative is not simply to say, I believe it because it is in the Scriptures, but to say, I believe it because it says what it does about Jesus Christ who is my Lord.

Zimmermann: Now if a man operating on . . .

Bertram: Let me just add this, that the kinds of events which are recorded by the thousands in Scriptures are not to be dismissed. They are asserted, claims are made for them, for their facticity, their happened-ness, their historicity. But if that is all that we can say in our preaching and our teaching and our confessing, then I would say these accounts are still in limbo. They haven't been assimilated to the kind of proclamation of the Gospel that it is our job as doctors of the church to work out for them.

Armin Moellering entered the discussion about the significance of the virgin birth, arguing on the basis of a statement from Swiss theologian Karl Barth that the loss of the teaching concerning the virgin birth would seriously impair the teaching concerning the incarnation. Bertram responded that, according to his reading of Matthew's account of the virgin birth, what would be impaired is not the incarnation but the teaching about the glory of the cross, the humiliation of God in the Suffering Servant.

Moellering: Would there be in the repudiation of the, I think, rather clear-cut witness in Matthew, in the repudiation of that witness to the virgin birth, would there be an impairment to the inviolability of Scripture, even before I know exactly how to handle this difficult thing in relating it to the gospel?

Bertram: I am more interested in the inviolability of *that* Scripture which is the Scripture of the gospel. I catch, still, a kind of two-story operation here: the Scripture is one thing, and the gospel, whether you ever get around to impairing that or not, that you can take in stride later.

Moellering: No, no. I see you as making some kind of distinction between the inviolability of Scripture and the inviolability of the Gospel.

Bertram: No, I don't want to—that is exactly what I *don't* want to do.

Moellering: Yeah, so that I would say a priori I will accept this saying because it is witness to one of the Scriptures and it is highly desirable that I see how this relates to the Gospel, but I can't call it in question or even put it on ice in the interim because that would subvert the inviolability of Scripture. That is a very dangerous precedent to set, isn't it?

Bertram: It certainly is. But now, so you have accepted it. What have you done? Is that faith?

Moellering: Well, let's say, is it bowing before the authority of Scripture?

Bertram: Is that faith?

Zimmermann: (*sharply*) Would you please answer the question?

Bertram: (*loudly*) It is not faith! Suppose a man does accept the virgin birth, does this make him a Christian? Has he believed the Gospel? I am asking rhetorical questions.

Moellering: Let me turn things around. If he rejects the virgin birth, which is clearly witnessed to in the Scriptures, because he can't still relate it to the specific Gospel, what then happens?

Bertram: You make it sound, Armin—well, excuse me for saying so—you make it sound as though the two alternatives, the mutual disjunction, is between accepting the virgin birth because it is Scriptural—which I am all in favor of doing as phase one, shall I say, the beginning phase of something bigger that has to be done—or on the other hand rejecting it and therefore being an unbeliever. Now what I am saying is that even if a person accepts the virgin birth and accepts it for no other reason than that it is in the Bible, that still is not what the Bible itself calls *pistis* [faith].

Moellering shifted the discussion to Bertram's views concerning whether the apostle Paul was the author of the Letter to the Ephesians, a topic that occupied the rest of the interview.

The interview with Bertram gave no hint of the storm of controversy that had surrounded the beginning of the fact-finding investigation and that almost aborted it after it had begun. Missouri Synod President Jacob A. O. Preus announced his decision to investigate CS by means of a FFC in a letter to the BoC, which the board dealt with at its meeting on September 21, 1970. In the letter Preus named the five members of the committee and assured the BoC that the committee's findings would be shared with them. Preus explained that he had decided to conduct his inquiry by means of a committee to ensure maximum objectivity and fairness because of all the public attention given to the announcement of his decision to conduct the inquiry himself.

At the board meeting I presented a case against the need for a special investigative committee, arguing on the basis of the Missouri Synod bylaws that the BoC was the committee established by the Synod for the purpose of governing CS, and it should now serve the president of the Synod in carrying out his stated responsibility to supervise doctrine in the Synod in relation to CS. The BoC understood the implications in the appointment of the committee and was eager to get to Preus before news of the committee's appointment became public knowledge. It resolved to ask Preus to come to its October 19 meeting so that the BoC could discuss with him its proposal that the BoC conduct the investigation for him.

Preus did not meet with me so that I could explain the BoC's action in person. I did my best over the phone, and by telephone five days later Preus told me that he had reviewed the matter and had decided to abide by his decision to appoint a committee. He asked me to be present for a meeting of the committee on October 2 so that I could be informed about the procedures to be followed and what would be expected of me and the faculty.

On October 1 Herbert Kuenne, chair of the Missouri Synod's Commission on Constitutional Matters, telephoned to ask me to attend a portion of the commission's meeting later that day. When I arrived, Kuenne informed me that the commission had previously affirmed that the president of the Synod was within his constitutional rights in appointing a FFC and was now reconsidering its decision. Kuenne told me that the commission welcomed my thoughts on the issue.

I responded that I had been unaware of the commission's previous action and regretted that I had not been informed about the reason for my presence so that I could have prepared appropriately. I told the commission what I had said to the BoC and asked for the opportunity to make a formal presentation on the basis of a carefully prepared brief. The next day Preus gave me a copy of the commission's original opinion, dated April 29, 1970, issued a few days after I had first urged Preus not to appoint a special committee. Preus also gave me a copy of the commission's October statement, reaffirming its original opinion.

On the evening of October 2 I met with Preus and the FFC. They handed me a list of objectives for their investigation, which included lofty aims: " . . . the strengthening of our synodical bond . . . to protect the seminary against unfounded criticism . . . to ascertain facts underlying the criticism . . . to make certain that our future pastors are taught the Word of God in its truth and purity, that they are firm in their confessional subscription, and that our Synod, reassured of these facts, may continue to move forward in its proclamation of the Gospel. . . . "

Preus and the FFC announced that the FFC would do its work without presuppositions and would make no judgments. It would interview all members of the faculty in biweekly meetings on Fridays and Saturdays and would present a report to the president of the Synod, who in turn would report to the BoC and to the Synod. In advance of the interviews the committee asked to review a long list of materials, including catalogs and student publications, minutes of faculty and board meetings, course outlines and syllabi, a complete bibliography of all faculty publications, copies of all essays delivered since 1965, and copies of graduate examination questions and answers for the previous two years. Contrary to Preus's earlier statement that I as CS president should be present for all interviews, the committee proposed that individual faculty members should have the privilege of choosing a faculty member in place of me.

I reported the results of my meeting with Preus and the FFC to the CS faculty on October 6. In view of the considerable stake the faculty had in the whole fact-finding procedure, I recommended the creation of a special faculty committee to serve as a channel for faculty opinion and to provide me with counsel on issues of concern to the faculty. The faculty elected a Faculty Advisory Committee composed of five members: Robert W. Bertram, articulate systematic theologian, who was gradually being recognized as a leader among the faculty; Richard R. Caemmerer, Sr., the senior member of the faculty, revered by several generations of students who had studied preaching with him; Alfred O. Fuerbringer, my predecessor as president, who was wise in the ways of the Missouri Synod and had extensive contacts with Synod leaders;

Edgar M. Krentz, New Testament scholar recognized for his sharp mind and his ability to communicate; and Leonhard C. Wuerffel, former dean of students now on modified service, who was respected for his wisdom and his understanding of people.

I met with the FAC to review the faculty's options in responding to Preus's plans for a FFC investigation. They worked quickly to produce recommendations for consideration by the faculty at meetings on October 13 and 16. On October 13 the faculty asked that "just cause be given for such an investigation and for the extraordinary procedure" and requested that Preus "discuss personally with the faculty the reasons for this investigation and its proposed procedures before its actual inception."[3] On October 16 the faculty adopted a statement of twelve concerns, which it commended to me as counsel. At the center of its concern over procedure was the issue of the criteria to be used in evaluation of the faculty's teaching. Concern number six read: "We state our conviction that Article II of the [Missouri Synod] Constitution states those criteria in an unalterable fashion."[4]

I shared the faculty's requests and concerns along with the agenda material distributed for the October 19 meeting of the BoC. I also reported to the BoC the deep concern among the students as expressed to me at meetings of the student body Administrative Council and the student Commission on Seminary Concerns. Students were particularly upset about not being able to get firsthand information because of the confidentiality that had surrounded the investigation. I had assured the students that I would brief them fully following the BoC meeting.

Shortly before the meeting, Andrew Weyermann, member of the faculty and my brother-in-law, came to my office. He had been chosen by a number of the younger faculty to share their concerns with me and to report to them what I was thinking. Their selection of Weyermann for the task was an expression of their confidence in him and of their perception of the good relations between us. We liked and respected each other.

Weyermann, tall and athletic, a college basketball star who loved classical music and serious cinema, sat somewhat stiffly on the green leather chair in my office, his face flushed. He began, "John, some of the troops are very worried about this Fact Finding Committee. They don't agree with your PR stance about welcoming the investigation. They think we should refuse to participate and let Preus figure out what he wants to do about it. Not all of them think that way, mind you. In fact, it's a small minority. But they want you to know that they're not gung-ho to get involved with this so-called Fact Finding Committee."

I reviewed with Weyermann the factors that the officially elected FAC had considered before making their recommendations. "What grounds do we have to say no?" I asked. "The constitution gives Preus the responsibility of supervising doctrine. We can argue until we're blue in the face that he is supposed to exercise that responsibility through the Board of Control. The fact is, he has in hand a statement from the Commission on Constitutional Matters that says he is within his rights to appoint such a Fact Finding Committee, that the bylaw provisions dealing with the Board of Control don't take away the responsibility given him in the constitution. What if we refuse to participate and our board tells us we must? Then we've got our own board against us, and that would put me in a hopeless position."

"There's an even more important factor," I continued. "The people out in the church simply won't understand our refusal to participate. They'll want to know what we're afraid of, what we've got to hide. After all, Preus says that the committee is only going to do fact finding; it isn't going to make any judgments; it's all for the purpose of protecting the seminary! We may think that's hogwash, but try to convince the people of the Synod that it is. If we say no, Preus will just go to the next Synod convention and get the convention to tell us to knuckle under. I think the only course open to us is the one the faculty has chosen. We have stated our conditions for participating in the investigation, and now I've got to do everything I can to get the board to make the faculty's conditions its own."

"As I said," Weyermann responded, "most faculty agree with the course we're on. They think we've got to make the best of a bad situation. We've got to make sure that we say to that Fact Finding Committee what we want the Synod to hear. We've got to see the investigation as an opportunity to do what we have been called to do—to teach. But I don't mind telling you, John, I am personally uneasy, very uneasy. Down inside of me something tells me that we're making a terrible mistake."

Preus and FFC chair Paul Zimmermann were present at the October 19 board meeting, distributed the opinions of the Commission on Constitutional Matters, and explained the proposed procedures of the investigation. After long discussion, board chairperson George Loose turned the chair over to vice-chairperson Kurt Biel in order to challenge Preus's decision to conduct the investigation by means of a special committee instead of through the BoC. Leaning over the table toward Preus, the usual smile gone from his Florida-tanned face, Loose told Preus that in his twenty-five years of experience with synodical conventions, the conventions had never authorized special investigations instead of following the Synod's bylaws; always they had insisted that such investigation be the responsibility of the Synod's duly elected boards and committees.

Preus countered that the BoC would be expected to carry out its bylaw responsibilities after the FFC had made its report. Loose asked that the record show it was his opinion that the BoC was in a better position than anyone else to assess what was going on at CS, that the procedure was irregular and contrary to the expressed will of the Synod, and that the proposed investigation was a blow to the Synod's democratic polity and a threat of spiritual tyranny.[5]

After Preus and Zimmermann had gone, the BoC debated what to do about Preus's proposed investigation. It finally recognized that it had no real choice but to declare its readiness to cooperate with the FFC and to ask the faculty to do the same. Then the BoC adopted a series of major proposals concerning the investigation for presentation to Preus. It asked that, in addition to interviews and examination of written documents, the FFC should be present for worship at CS, visit classrooms, and meet with students in order to experience the community within which the teaching was taking place. It urged that Preus report to the Synod immediately about the procedures for the investigation to obviate confusion, misinformation, and misunderstanding. It urged that the FFC "base its findings solely on Synod's doctrinal position according to Article II of the Synod's constitution." It asked Preus to meet with the faculty to discuss the investigation personally before its inception. In addition to a number of other recommendations, it declared that "the president of the seminary or his representative is entitled to be present for every activity of the committee which includes personnel of the seminary community."[6]

A week later I received Preus's response to the BoC proposals. Preus declined to meet with the faculty. He agreed that the FFC should attend CS classes and worship but rejected the proposal concerning criteria. Synodically adopted doctrinal statements were to be among the criteria for assessing the faculty's position. He insisted that there be no public report of the investigation beyond the announcement that was to appear in the Synod's journal the next week.

I considered the issue of criteria to be so critical that I insisted that the BoC would have to decide what to do about Preus's response before interviews with faculty members, the first of which were scheduled for November 12–13, could begin. As I told the CS BoC at the November 16 meeting: "Such a linking of synodically adopted statements with the Scriptures and the Lutheran Confessions as criteria for determining faith and life strikes at the heart of the Lutheran confessional principle. It is one thing to honor and uphold synodically adopted statements and resolutions. It is quite another to make those statements a criterion by which to assess faithfulness to confessional commitment. . . . Therefore, before the actual inquiry begins, it is absolutely essential that there be unambiguous agreement on the criterion by which 'facts' concerning doctrinal positions are to be determined. There should be no inquiry apart from such agreement."[7]

The BoC chose not to reach such an agreement. Instead, after pondering what to do, it adopted a resolution proposed by Missouri District president Herman Scherer. A kind and gentle man who never raised his voice, speaking at board meetings only to propose compromise, Scherer read from a prepared statement: "we reiterate our readiness to cooperate with the special committee and . . . we pray that as a result of the inquiry God may be glorified, His church edified, and His will done."[8]

Along with Martin Scharlemann and Robert Preus, three other CS faculty members supported Missouri Synod President Jacob Preus in his approach to CS. Some of them, in their efforts to sniff out heresy among their colleagues, had fostered an environment that made free and open theological discussion nearly impossible in meetings of the faculty. Individually they had voted against faculty resolutions dealing with the proposed investigation. Their opposition to their colleagues and their rejection of my leadership became public when the faculty as a whole tried to reassure the people of the LCMS of the orthodoxy of their confessional commitment.

At a meeting of the faculty on November 3, 1970, the newly created FAC proposed that the faculty issue a declaration concerning their confessional commitment as a way to counter the questions about faculty loyalty that had been raised by the proposal to investigate. The declaration was a simple reaffirmation of the commitment required in Article II of the Missouri Synod constitution together with quotations from the Augsburg Confession and the Formula of Concord through which the faculty made it clear that they would submit to no other doctrinal standard than the one specified in the LCMS constitution. The faculty resolved to ask members "to affix their signatures to the proposed declaration as a reaffirmation to one another and to the church of their confessional commitment . . . and that should there be any member of the faculty who is not able to sign the declaration he be invited to submit a written explanation of the reason to President Tietjen."[9]

Five faculty members declined to sign the declaration. Except for Martin Scharlemann they were members of the systematics department:

Ralph A. Bohlmann, reputed to have received more nominations for CS presidency than anyone else and to have been upset at being denied the election; Richard Klann, immigrant from Germany after World War II, whose ever-present smile belied a rapier tongue; Robert Preus, brother of the president of the Synod; and Lorenz Wunderlich, kind and friendly member of the faculty's old guard. The five joined together in giving two reasons for not signing the declaration. First, they described the declaration "as a device to neutralize or impede the investigation of our seminary." Second, they stated: "We are convinced that there are basic theological differences within the faculty, including matters pertaining both to the interpretation of Holy Scripture and to the meaning of confessional subscription in the Lutheran Church."[10]

I was concerned about how their response would be received because I believed that to the average member of the Missouri Synod, a "basic theological difference" meant a doctrinal difference, a disagreement over the doctrine of the gospel as that doctrine is drawn from the Holy Scriptures and affirmed in the Lutheran confessional writings. Is that what the minority members were alleging existed within the faculty? That seemed to be the implication in their refusal to join in a reaffirmation of confessional commitment.

I wrote to each of the five, asking them to explain. I requested them to provide me with evidence in support of their allegation about the existence of basic theological differences. I asked each to name the faculty members with whom he had these differences. I explained that I was acting on the basis of the Missouri Synod bylaws, which required that I mediate "controversies and disagreements among members of the faculty."[11] I was determined to follow the procedures of Matthew 18 that required face-to-face encounters between accuser and accused for the purpose preserving relations of fellowship.

What followed was an incredibly long and complicated internal struggle, which was never officially resolved. The minority members declined to answer my questions and appealed instead for a hearing with the BoC. After repeated efforts to get them to cooperate with me failed, the BoC granted them a hearing at its February 15, 1971, meeting and received from them a document entitled "Data on Theological Differences," which was in effect an attack on my leadership. The BoC supported me in my understanding of my bylaw responsibility and in my efforts to get at the issue of alleged theological differences. When after more than a year my efforts proved fruitless, I turned the problem over to the BoC so that, under the terms of the bylaws, it could serve as arbitrator. The BoC met with the five faculty members several times for extended periods. The issue was still in process when the 1973 convention of the Missouri Synod precipitated events that made the process irrelevant.

◆ ◆ ◆

The first set of FFC interviews took place on Friday and Saturday, December 11 and 12, 1970. As president I was the first of the faculty members to be interviewed. The interview on December 11 dealt with my personal theological position, although I was repeatedly asked how I would act as president over against hypothetical situations within the faculty. At the last of the scheduled interviews, on March 27, 1971, I would present a report in my capacity as president on "Doctrine and Life at Concordia Seminary, St. Louis." Arthur Repp, vice-president for academic affairs at CS, reported on December 11 in his official capacity, presenting an "Evaluation of the Doctrinal Position of the Faculty."

Martin Scharlemann was one of three faculty members interviewed on December 12. At the outset of the interview Scharlemann submitted to the FFC an eight-page document he had drafted, entitled "A Report on Concerns," which he described as his theological evaluation of the problem at CS.

I asked the committee not to receive the document. I stated that, although I had no objections to their knowing how Scharlemann saw things at CS, by receiving the document they were intruding into an internal CS problem. I pointed out that the interviews were for the purpose of asking individual faculty members about their faith and teaching, not for the purpose of commenting on the teaching of their colleagues. I reminded Scharlemann that I had repeatedly asked him to submit such material to me; only recently, I had asked him and four other faculty members to submit to me documentation of their allegation concerning theological differences at CS. I reminded the committee that officers of CS had been asked to provide overall evaluations of CS and the faculty, and that they had already received one such evaluation from the seminary's vice-president for academic affairs (Repp).

Paul Zimmermann as chair of the FFC announced a brief recess for the purpose of consulting with the other members. When the meeting resumed, Zimmermann read from a letter dated November 30, 1970, from Jacob Preus, written in response to questions Zimmermann had posed in a letter dated November 17. Preus's letter authorized the FFC to receive not only documents such as the one Scharlemann had submitted but statements by individual faculty members about the theological position of other faculty members. It further authorized the FFC to investigate any papers that faculty members had written as exploratory essays for the purpose of engaging the faculty in discussion. Preus's letter stated, "I am sending a carbon copy of this reply to President John Tietjen so that he will be fully informed."[12]

On the basis of the letter from Preus and in response to my request that the FFC not receive the Scharlemann document, Zimmermann ruled: "It is the committee's opinion that the instructions from President Preus enable us to receive information of this kind." I informed Zimmermann that I had not received a copy of the Preus letter and that if I had received it I would have immediately protested it. I stated: "I have to inform you that I protest your ruling and will so inform my board of control."[13]

Later that day as I drove from downtown St. Louis to my home, my stomach tied up in knots, I tried to cope with the host of emotions assaulting me. I felt betrayed by a friend and colleague whom I had supported when he was under attack. I was apopleptic about what seemed to be the duplicity of Preus. I wondered whether Preus and Zimmermann had made sure I never received the copy of the letter that would have enabled me to intervene in time. Even worse, I was overcome with despair over my own ability to carry out the responsibilities of my office in the face of the Preus onslaught against CS and over the possibility of ensuring due process for the members of the faculty.

When I got home and shared what happened with my wife, I told her that I now had a little better understanding of what it was like to be in hell. As I wrestled with God over what was happening, I found comfort in my call. I reminded myself that through the instrument of the church, God had called me to my present position and that I could count on God to provide the wisdom and strength needed for the tasks to which God had called.

The regular monthly meeting of the BoC took place two days after the first round of the FFC's interviews, on December 14 and 15, 1970. The BoC shared my concern over what had happened in the Scharlemann interview and resolved to ask Preus to instruct the FFC to restrict its questions to the personal doctrinal position of individual faculty members and that "faculty members not be asked or permitted to comment on the doctrinal position of their colleagues."[14] The faculty, meeting on December 15, endorsed the BoC's action and again extended its invitation to Preus to meet with them. Preus again declined.

Writing under date of December 24, 1970, Preus responded to the BoC action. He cited the opinion of the Commission on Constitutional Matters as giving him authority beyond the bylaw prescriptions. Quoting from his November 30 letter, he reiterated his instructions to the FFC. Then, addressing the BoC, he added, "I am willing, in deference to your concerns and to your request, to further instruct the Fact-Finding Committee when the theological climate of the seminary faculty is being explored that a professor, if he feels called upon to state the conflicting views of other men on the faculty, refrain from identifying them beyond a vague general identification such as 'professor x' or 'one of my colleagues.' In other words, I do not wish such persons to name names or to make charges against others who are not present."[15]

Preus had turned down the BoC's request and had compounded the problem by authorizing a procedure that I believed made a mockery of the Matthew 18 provisions concerning face-to-face meetings. What could be done? Preus no doubt expected the BoC to back down as it had done after his response to its requests concerning the investigation a month earlier. I had no reason to think it would do otherwise. The next round of FFC interviews was scheduled for January 8 and 9. The BoC would not meet again until January 18.

The FAC and I spent Christmas week in long meetings, reviewing alternative courses of action. We simply could not continue to participate in the FFC's interviews without some action; in our opinion, Preus had authorized procedures that were unethical. We gave serious consideration to refusing to participate in any further interviews, thus changing the whole course of Preus's investigation. But our concern was that such an action would be misunderstood by the people of the LCMS, who would conclude that we had backed out because we had something to hide. We reasoned that the people of the LCMS were the ones who would ultimately decide the future of CS and the Synod and that is was essential that the people be fully informed about what was happening in the Preus investigation.

The FAC decided to recommend to the faculty that it continue to participate in the FFC interviews but in a state of protest and that, in announcing its protest, the faculty send an open letter to Preus explaining the reasons for the protest and the objections to the investigation itself. The protest resolution was hard-hitting. It described the Preus decision as intolerable, unscriptural, unethical, divisive, and disruptive. The accompanying open letter faulted Preus for placing the entire faculty under a cloud of suspicion, for refusing to meet with the faculty to discuss the investigation, for declining to affirm Article II of the Synod's constitution as the only doctrinal standard of the investigation, for failing to provide a written statement of mutually accepted procedures for the investigation, and for his insistence on the extraordinary procedure of a FFC. The faculty adopted the FAC's recommendations at its meeting on January 5, 1971. The faculty action was front-page news with banner headlines in the January 17 issue of the LCMS publication, the *Lutheran Witness Reporter*.

Preus was present at the January 18 meeting of the seminary BoC. He brought with him Paul Zimmermann and Paul Streufert of the FFC and Herbert Mueller, secretary of the Synod and member of the Commission on Constitutional Matters. After extended discussion the BoC decided to postpone action to a special meeting to be held on January 27. At that meeting, after considering several alternatives, the BoC resolved to try to make peace by urging all parties—Preus, the FFC, the FAC, and me—to meet and to "exert every effort to reach a clear understanding and an amicable solution so that the peace of the Church may be preserved. . . . "[16]

The FAC and I met with Preus and the FFC in extended meetings on February 6 and 20 and hammered out agreements on most of the issues. On the key issue that had precipitated the faculty protest and open letter it was agreed: "The Fact Finding Committee will not request or receive statements by a faculty member about the doctrinal position of a colleague, either by name or anonymously, or about the faculty in general or a portion of it. Such testimony, if necessary, is to be made in accordance with the provisions of the Synodical *Handbook,* beginning within the Seminary community. The Fact Finding Committee may ask faculty members about theological issues, including issues on which their colleagues may also hold positions of their own. However, the faculty member being interviewed is to be asked only about his own position."[17] It was also agreed that Preus would turn over the Scharlemann statement to the BoC.

On the issue of the doctrinal standard for the investigation it was agreed that "Article II of the synodical constitution will serve as the sole criterion by which the Fact Finding Committee will assemble facts for report to the president of the Synod and as the sole criterion by which the president of the Synod will make a judgment about the facts reported to him." Preus agreed to meet with the faculty "in the near future." It was further agreed that it was no longer necessary to agree on a written set of guidelines for the interviews since most of the interviews had already been held.[18]

At a meeting on February 25 the faculty resolved: "Since its purpose has been achieved, our protest is no longer necessary. Just as we cooperated fully with the president's inquiry following our protest, so we declare that we will continue to cooperate and now no longer under protest."[19] The faculty's strategy of going public seemed to have worked because they had prevailed on two key issues. But the FFC investigation was still intact.

The FFC's interview with Robert Bertram, reported earlier in this chapter, was in many ways typical of all the interviews. Paul Zimmermann was in charge of the examination, assisted by Karl Barth and Armin

Moellering. Paul Streufert and Elmer Foelber spoke sparingly and then only in ways that seemed less than helpful to Zimmermann's purpose. The content of the Bertram interview was also typical of the other interviews, although no faculty member was more eloquent than Bertram in describing the inseparable connection between Scripture and gospel. As in the Bertram interview, in their questions addressed to other faculty members the FFC members operated with an assumption that affirmed an authority of the Scripture apart from the gospel, which faculty members refused to allow.

A case in point was the interview with Andrew Weyermann, professor of homiletics and ethics who worked with a passion to teach students that a sermon is for the purpose of preaching the gospel. When Barth asked him about the implication of the Reformation slogan, *sola scriptura*, for the Bible's authority, Weyermann explained that for him the Scriptures were authoritative because they are "the cradle that holds Christ." The Scriptures themselves say, he pointed out, that they were "written for our hope. They have an intention and a function. Their intention is to point to Christ, and their function is to give hope."[20] He went on to say that every passage of Scripture must be understood in the light of the intention to point to Christ and the function of giving us hope. To Barth's explicit proposal that the Bible is authoritative apart from its gospel content, Weyermann insisted that the Bible is authoritative only when the two are held together.

As the interviews came to an end, I enlisted the help of several faculty members in analyzing the questions asked by the FFC in order to establish what they were after and what assumptions lay behind their interrogation. We deduced from the questions that there were seven basic areas of concern.[21] Among them were authority as it relates to the Bible and the Lutheran Confession, ethics and social action, communion and church fellowship. But the primary, almost obsessive, concern was with the Bible and how to interpret it.

One large area was the Bible's historicity or facticity and, in that connection, the use of the historical-critical method. For example, did Jesus actually speak the words attributed to him in the Gospels? Did the miracles happen? Did John the Baptist preach in the wilderness, wear clothes of camel's hair, and eat locusts and wild honey? Another area was predictive prophecy and its fulfillment. For example, is Isaiah's description of the son that is to be born (9:7) a prediction of the birth of Jesus? A third area dealt with the meaning of inspiration and inerrancy. For example, did the Holy Spirit so guide the writers of the Scripture that they were preserved from error when they wrote?

In my final session with the FFC, during the discussion that followed my official report on the doctrinal situation at CS, I spoke of my observation that, in every one of the interviews with the faculty, FFC members had demonstrated their preoccupation with facticity in the Scriptures. I said that in response all faculty members had made it clear that while they presupposed the factuality of events described in the Scripture, they stressed the gospel message present in the events. Referring to the account of the wedding at Cana (John 2:1–11), I said, "You can have water changed into wine as fact and not have the truth present in that passage." I went on, "To talk about the historical events as if they themselves were important is to miss the whole point of the New Testament. Even the disciples did not understand until they believed."[22]

Early in April 1971, after the last of the FFC interviews, Andrew Weyermann visited me at home. His visits as an informal liaison with the faculty were becoming a regular habit. As we sat in my study, Weyermann asked how I felt about the interviews. I told him that I felt fairly good about them but was glad that they were over. I asked him if he still felt it was a mistake to agree to them. He answered: "Yes, I do. I know all the arguments about why we had no choice but to go along with them. I think we should have said no and made them come after us one by one. There's no telling what Preus is going to do with all that material we gave him."

"True, Andy," I responded. "But what our faculty said in those interviews is on the record for us, too, and we can make use of it. In many ways our faculty gave a magnificent witness. They did what I said the investigation would do—show how Lutheran we really are. They made it unmistakably clear that the Scriptures are for them the only rule and norm of faith and of practice."

"But," I went on, "they were eloquent in making it clear that it was the Scripture proclaiming the gospel that was the only rule and norm. Zimmermann and his committee were working with a notion of scriptural authority that separated the Scripture from the gospel. Our faculty insisted that it was not enough to locate the authority of Scripture in a theory of inspiration of the Scriptures. They affirmed the inspiration of the Scriptures, but they insisted that the inspired Scriptures were authoritative because of their gospel content."

"Yes, we did what we had to do," Weyermann said. "When people want to throttle you with facticity and inerrancy, you have to insist on the gospel meaning in the facts as more important than the facts themselves. Only the gospel saves, not the historical facts."

"But, John," he added, "the other side does have a point. How much gospel do you have left if you don't have a historical event in which to ground it? Can we proclaim Jesus as the divine physician if the miracles of healing didn't happen? The tragedy of the situation in our Synod is that we can't engage honestly and openly in the pursuit of truth without being hounded out of the church for doing so. When the fact finders hear us stressing the gospel meaning of an event rather than the event itself, they're afraid we don't think the event happened. When some of our peers out in the theological world hear us affirming that the event happened, they're afraid we mean it. We have to be able to decide whether the account of the virgin birth is a midrash and whether John the Baptist did wear a coat of camel's hair, or whether those were devices the early Christians used to tell us who Jesus is and what God did through him.

"And then we have to come to terms with what God actually did through Jesus. There has to be an event in which the gospel is grounded or our gospel is our own illusion. For me that issue has to be decided in each instance on the basis of the Scripture text itself and not on the basis of a preconceived notion that ours is a world in which miracles don't happen. After all, with God all things are possible. For me there is one bedrock event on which everything else depends and which gives us a gospel to proclaim, and that is, Jesus raised from the dead. But even Jesus' death and resurrection is not good news in and of itself. There is good news—we have a gospel to proclaim—because, as Paul has pointed out [Rom. 4:25], Jesus was put to death for our trespasses and raised for our justification."

"Andy," I replied, "I think our faculty was grappling with that issue right in the presence of the fact finders. It's just that they had to take into account who they were talking to and what use those people were going to make of what they said. I'm proud of them."[23]

As I reflected on the interviews, I thought it was appropriate for them to have taken place under the watchful eye of the official seal of the Missouri Synod. Through the witness they gave, our faculty integrated the Reformation slogans of Faith Alone, Scripture Alone, and Grace Alone in proclaiming the center of the Christian faith: Jesus Christ is Lord.

4 ———◆

CONVENTION
STALEMATE

"May your president leave the podium and make a statement of personal privilege?"[1]

The question was posed by Jacob A. O. Preus from the rostrum to the delegates of the Forty-ninth Regular Convention of the Lutheran Church–Missouri Synod assembled in the Milwaukee Arena in Milwaukee, Wisconsin. It was midafternoon on Thursday, July 15, 1971. The convention had begun the previous Friday evening. It was now the fourteenth session of what had proven to be a tumultuous convention characterized by long lines of delegates waiting at microphones for their turn to speak, by challenges on parliamentary procedure, and by shouts of points of order and pleas for personal privilege. The president of the Synod, who was chairing this session, decided to avail himself of a plea of personal privilege and was leaving the rostrum to come down to a microphone on the floor.

The arena floor was jammed with convention delegates. A thousand voting delegates, half of them pastors, half laity, almost all of them men, sat at long tables in rows facing the platform where the chair presided and committee reports were presented. Another five hundred advisory delegates, most of them clergy, sat at tables in an area behind the voting delegates. In back of the rostrum on the platform, behind a huge altar used for convention worship, was the convention logo, a black cross superimposed over an open Bible and a flying dove and emblazoned with the convention theme, "Sent to Reconcile."

From opening day the convention proceedings had been charged with emotion. The unofficial political party that had secured the election of Jacob Preus as Missouri Synod president two years earlier was hard at work behind the scenes. Circulating among the delegates were lists of candidates preferred by the Preus party for election to boards and commissions. An opposition party for Synod moderates, as the news media labeled them, aware that there were no real liberals in the Missouri Synod, had been organized since the last convention under the leadership of two Synod pastors, Bertwin L. Frey of Fairview Park, Ohio, and F. Dean Lueking of River Forest, Illinois. The convention was polarized between the two groups, and crucial resolutions were adopted by close votes.

The delegates had just completed action on a resolution that had been introduced two days earlier and had been discussed and amended several times in afternoon sessions three days in a row. Resolution 2-21 was entitled "To Uphold Synodical Doctrinal Resolutions." It came from floor Committee Number 2 on Theological Matters and was presented by its chair, George F. Wollenburg, dour-faced, clerically garbed president of the Synod's Montana District. Most of the Preus-appointed members of the committee shared Preus's basic theological stance and could be expected to act in keeping with that view.

At the first business session of the convention on Saturday morning, July 10, Preus had devoted more than half of a lengthy "President's Report" to the issue of doctrinal statements adopted by conventions of the Synod. In a carefully reasoned presentation of the issue, Preus argued that statements of doctrine adopted at synodical conventions should be binding on members of the Synod unless it could be shown that they are contrary to the Scriptures. He wanted the convention to act so that the issue would be resolved once and for all. Preus summarized the question for which he wanted a clear and simple answer: "Does an evangelical and confessional church body such as ours have the right and duty to adopt doctrinal statements which are in complete conformity with Scripture and the Lutheran Confessions—and then expect her pastors, teachers, and professors, out of faithfulness to Scripture and the Confessions, to believe, teach, and confess according to such statement?"[2]

The resolution presented by Committee Number 2 on Theological Matters gave Preus the clear and simple answer he wanted. After a long preamble and a series of five "Whereas" paragraphs that gave the rationale for the proposed action, Resolution 2-21 began: "*Resolved,* That the Synod once again declare its doctrinal resolutions to be of binding force until it can be demonstrated to the Synod that they are not in accord with the Word of God." Additional resolveds required those who had trouble with synodically adopted doctrinal statements to bring their concerns "to the attention of the Synod through the appropriate channels" and to "refrain from expressing their dissent except through procedures established by the Synod." A concluding resolution required the members of the Synod to support the Synod's president in carrying out his responsibility to assure conformity with the doctrinal resolutions of the Synod.[3]

Even before debate on the resolution began, while it was still being introduced, long lines of delegates formed at the microphones to speak. The allotted time ran out before the vote could be taken, and discussion was resumed in the session the next afternoon. At that time it was moved and seconded to substitute for the resolveds of Resolution 2-21 the resolveds of Resolution 5-24, a resolution whose text had been distributed to the delegates but which had not yet been presented to the convention.

Resolution 5-24 was the product of Committee Number 5 on Constitutional Matters, which had also been assigned the issue of the status of the Synod's doctrinal statements because of its relation to the issue of the Synod's confessional basis as described in Article II of the LCMS constitution. The resolution, although clearly affirming the "desirability of the formulation of doctrinal statements," nevertheless declared that "such doctrinal formulations are subordinate to the Lutheran Confessions." The resolution also distinguished between doctrinal resolutions formulated and adopted at synodical conventions and those adopted after presentation by "officially authorized groups" and after careful study by congregations and clergy. Reaffirming the action of the 1969 convention about honoring and upholding doctrinal statements "as valid interpretations of Christian doctrine," the resolution urged that "in the case of the aforementioned more formal and comprehensive statements of belief . . . the ministry of the church regard these formulations with special seriousness" and that those who disagreed with the formulations share their objections with those who were responsible for the supervision of their teaching and participate in a joint study whose envisioned outcome would be unanimity.[4]

Resolution 5-24 was a more moderate response than Resolution 2-21 to the issue of the status of doctrinal statements in the Synod. But the moderate camp of Frey and Lueking had no floor organization, and the Preus party did. After debate had been cut off, the motion to substitute Resolution 5-24 for 2-21 failed by a vote of 450 to 469.[5]

The first challenge to the action Preus wanted from the convention in Milwaukee had failed, but the struggle was not over. Lloyd Goetz, president of the Synod's North Wisconsin District and chair of its Council of Presidents, received permission to read a statement on the status of the Synod's doctrinal statements that had been adopted at a meeting of the council on February 27, 1970. It was immediately moved and seconded to substitute the resolveds of the statement Goetz had read[6] for the resolveds of Resolution 2-21. The allotted time ran out before the vote could be taken.

The resolution of the Council of Presidents was even more moderating than the wording of Resolution 5-24. Its content was a series of quotations from the resolutions of the Denver convention of 1969 and the Cleveland convention of 1962. It urged the members of the Synod "to honor and uphold the synodically adopted statements as valid interpretations of Christian doctrine and not to give them more or less status than they deserve." It asked "all who believe these synodically adopted doctrinal statements to be faulty in their formulation of Scriptural doctrine" to present their concerns to the Commission on Theology and Church Relations. It prayed that "unity may be restored and strengthened in our Synod on the basis of the Scriptures and the Lutheran Confessions."

When the issue came back on the floor of the convention on the afternoon of July 15, Preus no doubt assumed, in view of the rejection of Resolution 5-24, that the statement from the Council of Presidents would have a similar fate and that the motion as originally presented would then be adopted. When debate was halted and the votes counted, the substitute motion had been approved, 485 to 425. Preus had been defeated on what for him must have been the key issue of the convention, as his presidential address made clear.

Speaking from the chair, an exasperated Preus asked for a point of personal privilege. Knowing that he would be challenged if he tried to make it from the rostrum, he descended to the convention floor, to the first microphone on the right-hand side, facing the platform. A hush came over the delegates. Turning just a bit so that he could see at least some of the delegates, the normal smile gone from his face, Preus thrust his jaw out and spoke:

"Brethren, it's rather regrettable that this action took place yesterday afternoon of injecting into the discussion the statement of the Council of Presidents. There's nothing wrong with it. It was, as I said in the discussion, done in answer to a request that I made. But it has caused us an enormous amount of parliamentary procedure. I was up half the night talking to people who questioned whether it could be introduced and things of this kind, and it shows the difficulty of doing something that is not processed through a floor committee. However, it is parliamentarily perfectly satisfactory, as we indicated to this brother over here"— Preus pointed to a delegate whom he had addressed from the chair on the issue of the legitimacy of the substitute motion—"to have a substitute motion."

Stabbing the air repeatedly with his right hand, Preus made his point: "However, this needs to be said—and here is the substance of what I wish to say. We have had a great deal of difficulty down through the years with the whole matter of the status of doctrinal resolutions of

Synod and whether or not people are to be expected to abide by them, particularly those in the pastoral, teacheral [sic], and professorial office. I said nothing to this convention, in my president's address, that meant more to me personally and administratively and theologically than that first section dealing with this subject. I labored on that for many weeks, and it represents my entire—it represents my heart and my soul as well as my mind. What has been done by this substitution is to bring us back to where we were at Denver. It is my opinion that Resolution 2-21 in its resolveds advanced us some and gave us some way of having—some way of dealing with theological vagaries and aberrations and charges and counter charges, whereby people who have doubts or who wish to launch something on the church would not constantly keep the church in a turmoil over these matters but would use the proper channels and work through their district presidents, etc."

With a voice sometimes scolding, sometimes pleading, his face flushed, Preus continued: "Now by this, what you've done is, you've simply moved the entire discussion of all such matters back to the Denver Convention, with all the attendant confusion that has gone on in the church on doctrinal matters. Now I don't say this with any disrespect to the Council of Presidents. They are men I dearly love and they are men who are attempting to maintain doctrinal discipline in their various districts. But quite frankly, we have not had very adequate machinery for this. And it was the—I'm sure that the work of Committee Number 2 in developing 2-21 was an attempt to help this situation. Not to impose a law upon the church or to put people in academic or intellectual chains, but rather to create a procedure for dealing with matters of this kind which would be workable and would be evangelical and also would give the church an opportunity—the majority of us just want to preach the Gospel and do the kind of job that we know God wants us to do—to get the theological arguments out of the center stage and over into an area where they can be dealt with. Therefore I must say that I express a great deal of regret, as the one who is given the task of supervisor of doctrinal life, at this particular turn of this matter. It will cause us a great deal of difficulty."[7]

Confusion hung in the air as Preus moved away from the microphone and toward the platform. Several people in the Preus party tried to amend or recommit the resolution that had already been adopted and were ruled out of order. No one had the understanding or the presence of mind to get someone who had voted for the motion to move that it be reconsidered.[8] The convention turned its attention to other matters. Preus had made his plea too late and without advance consultation with the people of his party about how to respond to what he said. He did not get what I concluded from his report and speech from the floor that he wanted out of the

Milwaukee convention: authorization to use synodically adopted doctrinal statements to discipline those who taught what he called "theological vagaries and aberrations."

◆ ◆ ◆

The status of doctrinal statements adopted by the Missouri Synod had been a controversial issue for more than a decade. The stakes were high. At issue was the meaning of confessional commitment. How the issue was resolved decided what answer would be given to what it means to be Lutheran. Would Lutheran mean the teaching of the Scripture affirmed in the Lutheran Confessions, or would it mean what church conventions by majority vote decide that it means?

The issue of the status of doctrinal statements first came to a head at the LCMS convention in San Francisco June 17–27, 1959. Those within the Synod who identified with the causes championed by the archconservative publication, the *Confessional Lutheran*, were insisting that the Synod clearly reaffirm its traditional doctrinal position. By that they meant something other than the Lutheran Confessions. A conference of pastors in the Synod's Texas District had proposed that the convention require all pastors, teachers, and professors in the Synod to subscribe not only to the confessional writings in *The Book of Concord* but to the "Brief Statement," a formulation of doctrine adopted by LCMS in 1932 to serve as the basis for doctrinal discussions with the American Lutheran Church and which had been reaffirmed by several previous conventions as an expression of the doctrinal position of the Synod. Floor Committee Number 3 on Intersynodical and Doctrinal Matters, chaired by Texas District president Roland Wiederaenders, was given the responsibility of dealing with the proposal.

The ninth resolution proposed by the Committee on Intersynodical and Doctrinal Matters dealt with the issue and received notoriety during and after the convention as Resolution Number 9. The resolution declared that " . . . every doctrinal statement of a confessional nature adopted by Synod as a true exposition of the Holy Scriptures [the "Brief Statement" was one such doctrinal statement] is to be regarded as public doctrine (*publica doctrina*) in Synod" and stipulated that " . . . Synod's pastors, teachers, and professors are held to teach and act in harmony with such statements."[9] After three sessions and a plea in behalf of the resolution by President John W. Behnken, the resolution was adopted.

A storm of protest against Resolution Number 9 erupted in various parts of the Missouri Synod. The English District in 1960 and the Atlantic District in 1961 declared the controversial resolution to be unconstitutional and asked the LCMS to do the same at its convention in 1962. The Southeastern District asked the 1962 convention to rescind the resolution because it altered the Synod's confessional standard. The basic constitutional argument was that Resolution Number 9 had the effect of amending Article II of the Synod's constitution by adding doctrinal statements to the Synod's doctrinal basis without following the procedures for amendment specified in Article XIV.

I personally was deeply concerned about the issue and actively involved in the effort to undo Resolution Number 9. As a pastoral member of the English District I was a major participant in its convention decision. I was invited to make a presentation to the Southeastern District on "The Lutheran Confessional Principle," especially geared for the laity, prior to the action taken by that convention on the controversial resolution. I published the essay in the *American Lutheran*[10] as a contribution to the discussion prior to the 1962 convention and editorialized on the issue several times. As a pastoral delegate to the 1962 convention I participated in the effort to declare the resolution unconstitutional.

Another delegate to the 1962 convention played perhaps the key role in the convention's ultimate decision. Edward Lind, an attorney and a member of an English District congregation in Princeton, New Jersey, succeeded in getting the English District's Board of Directors to request the Synod's Committee on Constitutional Matters to render an opinion on the constitutionality of Resolution Number 9. Lind personally met with the attorney member of that committee, Herbert F. Kuenne, and convinced Kuenne that the controversial resolution was indeed unconstitutional. Kuenne convinced the committee, and the committee's opinion decided the issue. Meeting in Cleveland, Ohio, June 20–29, 1962, the LCMS's forty-fifth convention declared "Resolution 9 of Committee 3 of the 1959 synodical convention unconstitutional on the ground that said resolution has the effect of amending the confessional basis of the Constitution of the Synod without following the procedure required by Article XIV of the Constitution."[11]

Then in Resolution 3-17 the convention addressed the issue of the status of synodically adopted doctrinal statements. Reaffirming the confessional basis of Article II of the Synod's constitution, the convention resolved "to beseech all its members by the mercies of God to honor and uphold the doctrinal content of these synodically adopted statements." It asked those who had problems with the statements to share their concerns with a newly established Commission on Theology and Church Relations, and that commission was asked to study the status and use of doctrinal statements in the Synod.[12]

The Commission on Theology and Church Relations had been established to provide guidance and leadership in dealing with a host of theological issues that were disturbing the life of the LCMS. Under Oliver R. Harms as newly elected president of the Synod and with the capable guidance of Richard P. Jungkuntz as executive secretary, the commission produced a variety of documents and opinions on issues of biblical interpretation and on issues relating to cooperation and fellowship with other Lutherans. To the convention of the Missouri Synod meeting in New York City, July 7–14, 1967, the Commission on Theology and Church Relations reported the results of its deliberation on the status and use of doctrinal statements.[13] In effect the commission reasserted the position adopted at the 1962 convention. Its report included a quotation from *BC* on the distinction between the Lutheran confessional writings and "other good, useful, and pure books," making it clear that doctrinal statements were not to be used the way the confessional writings are to be used, namely, as standards according to which "all other writings are to be approved and accepted, judged and regulated."[14] The convention made the commission's position its own.

Several overtures to the convention of the Missouri Synod in Denver, Colorado, July 11–18, 1969, called for the use of the "Brief Statement" as a means of discipline and required action once again on the status and use of doctrinal statements. The convention resolved to "urge its members to honor and uphold the synodically adopted statements as valid interpretations of Christian doctrine and not to give them more or less status than they deserve."[15]

The issue of the status and use of synodically adopted doctrinal statements came to a head in the investigation of the faculty of Concordia Seminary. When we insisted that only the Scriptures and the Lutheran Confessions, not the Synod's doctrinal statements, could be used in assessing the doctrinal position of the faculty, the faculty and I were articulating the position that the Missouri Synod in its conventions had been promulgating for a decade.

We had reluctantly agreed to submit to Preus's investigation with the belief that the investigation would demonstrate not only how Lutheran we were but what it means to be Lutheran. For us Lutheran identity consisted of commitment to the Lutheran confessional writings and their central teaching of justification by faith as summary and statement of the teaching of the Holy Scriptures. No other written documents, no matter how true, could decide for us how to understand the Scriptures, especially if the documents did not have the voluntary and unreserved commitment of those required to teach in accord with them. When Preus at first refused to agree with us that only the Scriptures and the Confessions and not synodically adopted doctrinal statements were to be the standard for evaluating us, we had to object. At stake in using synodically adopted doctrinal statements to determine what the Scriptures teach was the loss of what it means to be Lutheran.

While the criterion issue was still unresolved, the CS Faculty Advisory Committee arranged for a presentation to the faculty on "The Binding Nature of Synodical Resolutions for a Pastor or Professor of the Lutheran Church–Missouri Synod."[16] The essay was presented by Arthur C. Repp, CS vice-president for academic affairs. The essay and a faculty resolution based on it were presented to CS's Board of Control to help board members understand that what was at stake in the argument was nothing less than the Lutheran confessional principle.

Among Repp's arguments against the binding nature of synodical resolutions, his first and most important point was: "The principle is un-Lutheran." Repp cited the Formula of Concord[17] in asserting that for Lutherans the Scriptures are "the only rule and norm according to which all doctrines and teachers alike must be appraised and judged." Then he pointed out that Lutherans stand together on the platform of the Lutheran Confessions as their confessional witness to what the Scriptures teach. They can be held to teach in accord with these documents because they have voluntarily committed themselves to them as secondary norms (*norma normata*) that give witness to the primary norm that is the Sacred Scripture (*norma normans*). Once again citing the Formula of Concord, Repp asserted that other writings, such as synodically adopted doctrinal statements, can be "accepted and used as helpful expositions and explanations," but the Lutheran confessional writings alone are the "single, universally accepted, certain, and common form of doctrine which all our Evangelical churches subscribe and from which and according to which, because it is drawn from the Word of God, all other writings are to be approved and accepted, judged and regulated."[18]

Repp allowed for the possibility that the time might come "when it would be necessary for the Lutheran Church to formulate a new confession. A part of the Lutheran Church, such as the Missouri Synod could, indeed, draw up such a new confession for new needs in a new day provided, as Sasse[19] pointed out, 'This new Confession would presuppose and safeguard the doctrinal content of *The Book of Concord.*' To pursue that course, however, the Missouri Synod would need to go a much more complicated route than the simple adoption of doctrinal statements at a delegate Synod." All the members of the Synod would have to be involved so that the new Confession would indeed receive the voluntary commitment of those to be normed by it.

In asking the Milwaukee convention to make the Synod's doctrinal statements binding on pastors, teachers, and professors, Jacob Preus set himself against the position the LCMS had espoused in its conventions for the past decade. Perhaps he assumed that such a course was part of the mandate given him in his election two years earlier. The disappointment he expressed in his convention floor statement after his request had in effect been turned down was because Preus apparently envisioned the binding nature of doctrinal statements to be the foundation stone in a new system of discipline within the Missouri Synod.

Preus had talked about a new system of discipline from time to time since his election at the convention in Denver. He hinted at the subject in his dinner conversation with me on November 3, 1969, when he announced his intention to move against CS. In the meeting that department chairs and I had with him on July 6, 1970,[20] Preus said: " . . . we have a situation in the church—with incessant complaining and belly-aching—which calls for some action since people feel that protests are being made but nothing ever happens. I hope that out of this will come an adequate judicial system according to which a plaintiff can get some action and a harassed professor can get some relief."[21]

What Preus had in mind concerning "an adequate judicial system" became more clear in a candid interview he gave to Betty Medsger of the *Washington Post* as reported in its July 27, 1970, edition. According to Medsger, Preus said "that he wants to establish procedures that would make it possible to oust pastors and seminary professors 'not in line' with official church doctrines." Medsger reported Preus saying that "he hopes appropriate judicial channels will be proposed and approved at the church's next national meeting in July 1971 in Milwaukee." Preus was quoted as saying: "We need to set boundaries beyond which a man cannot go and still remain a pastor or teacher in our church. Those boundaries need to be worked out very carefully." What Preus meant by "judicial channels" and "boundaries" was explained in another quotation in the Medsger article: "I think the church has a right to pass resolutions on a doctrinal matter and expect its pastors and teachers to adhere."

Preus was convinced that the Missouri Synod did not have adequate procedures for discipline. He was also convinced that the doctrinal standard set in Article II of the Synod's constitution was not sufficient for assuring doctrinal orthodoxy. When in January 1971 the faculty of CS publicly took him to task for refusing to make Article II the standard of evaluation in the investigation,[22] Preus told students in an interview in the CS student newspaper, "Article II is O.K. for 1839" [the date when CS was founded], but it does not deal with such present problems as the inerrancy of the Scripture and the use of higher critical methods." Those problems, he explained, "cannot be settled by sixteenth-century Confessions."[23]

So Preus looked to the Milwaukee Convention to change the direction of the past decade and declare synodically adopted doctrinal statements binding on its pastors, teachers, and professors. In his President's Report Preus argued that the requirement of Article II to teach what the Scriptures teach, "far from prohibiting us from adopting doctrinal statements as a Synod and asking our people to adhere to them, actually compels us to adopt such statements as the course of events and the needs of the church develop." Preus argued that since the Synod convention is a representative delegate assembly, therefore the resolutions it adopts "must . . . be considered as the expression of the church body and must be regarded as valid and binding unless they are in conflict with the Word of God."[24]

Preus made it clear in his report that a decision in favor of the binding nature of doctrinal statements would have practical results. It would enable him to ensure that the Synod's pastors, teachers, and professors "preach and teach according to the official position of our church."[25] It would enable him to put an end to a much too permissive variety of biblical interpretation and diversity in doctrine present in the Synod. Preus gave seven examples of what he meant by too much variety and diversity, examples that came straight out of the Fact Finding Committee's interviews with the faculty, although Preus did not say so and did not accurately reflect the position taken by the faculty. Preus called attention to differences in understanding of what constitutes "doctrine" in the Lutheran Confessions. He cited differences of opinion on the inspiration and inerrancy of Scripture and on the nature of the Bible's authority. He found fault with a confusion of the formal and material principles in theology and with views concerning miracles in the Bible that were not totally literalistic.

Then Preus drew the conclusion: "The question that has to be answered by this convention is whether we are willing to allow such matters (and many more) to be regarded as open questions on which we may take any position we wish. . . . If we do not want this kind of latitude because we feel that it threatens the faith we confess and the message of reconciliation with which we have been entrusted, let us state clearly to all concerned that deviations from the official position of our church must be dealt with and cannot be permitted."[26] He cited his investigation of CS as an illustration of a course of action designed to assure doctrinal purity in the Synod. Preus counted on the Milwaukee convention to establish the principle that synodically adopted doctrinal statements were binding. Then he would make use of statements already adopted and of statements yet to be approved to require the Synod's teachers to conform to a strict "Missouri" Lutheranism or to get out.

As the CS faculty prepared for the Milwaukee convention, we tried to determine how convention proceedings would affect us. It was not until shortly before the convention began that we received a copy of the President's Report and thus became aware of Preus's agenda for the convention. Up until then we assumed that our first concern had to be what the convention might do about Preus's investigation of CS and the FFC's report.

FFC chair Paul Zimmermann had told me on March 27, 1971, when the faculty interviews were completed, that the FFC hoped to produce a report to Preus as soon as possible. Preus would then turn the report over to the BoC. April and May passed without any report. When the BoC met on June 21, 1971, a little more than two weeks before the Milwaukee convention, still without any report, some of us began to wonder whether Preus might not be planning to make use of the report in Milwaukee.

Preus turned over the FFC report to me on June 30, 1971, in a meeting I had arranged with him for the purpose of presenting a progress report from the BoC on its dealings with five faculty members who now constituted a minority group within the faculty.[27] Our meeting was fascinating from a number of viewpoints. Preus told me that he might want to talk to individual faculty members to clarify features of the FFC report because the answers they would give might be different under less emotional circumstances. I took that to mean that he planned a tactic of seeking to divide in order to conquer. In our meeting Preus told me that he hoped our relations would be much better in the next year and that he expected to be working closely with me and with the BoC, which could expect anywhere from one to five new members as a result of the Milwaukee convention.

As I returned to CS, I felt encouraged by the hope that perhaps we could expect a thaw in the cold war we were experiencing. A cursory reading of the FFC report, however, put the chill back in my spine. I concluded that Preus's announced expectation of working closely with the BoC and me meant that he expected that the elections at the Milwaukee convention would measurably improve his support among BoC members.[28]

Not until the evening before the day of adjournment did the issue of the CS investigation come to the floor of the Milwaukee convention.

Committee Number 2 on Theological Matters presented a resolution (2-28) that directed the BoC "to take appropriate action on the basis of the [FFC] report, commending or correcting where necessary." The resolution asked the board to report progress to the president of the Synod and to the Board for Higher Education and asked the president of the Synod to report on the progress of the BoC within one year.[29]

A delegate moved that the report be released to the convention delegates. George Loose, chairman of the BoC, explained to the convention in his mellifluous bass voice that there had been an agreement between the BoC and the president of the Synod that the report of the FFC would come first to the BoC, that the BoC itself had not yet met to receive the report, and that he had only seen the summary portions of the report.

I stated to the convention that I did not object to release of the report but questioned the fairness of doing so since the faculty had neither seen it nor been informed that it had been completed. I pointed out that fairness would require that distribution of the report be accompanied by the faculty's response to what the report had to say about the faculty's confessional position. I told the delegates that I would arrange for them to receive the faculty's response in due time if they should decide to receive the report. I wanted it clearly understood that we did not intend to sit idly by should the report be released.

When vice-president Roland Wiederaenders and vice-president and FFC member Paul Streufert spoke against the release of the report, the motion asking for the report was withdrawn, and the committee's resolution was adopted. Thus the premature release of the FFC report was averted. But the issue of the Preus investigation was very much alive.

Election of board members was for us at CS a key issue of the Milwaukee convention. Who would comprise the BoC that would have the responsibility of taking action on the FFC report? According to a procedure in which half the members of the BoC were elected at each biennial convention, the terms of five of the eleven members came due at the Milwaukee convention; all five were eligible for reelection. Two of the five were laity, Melvin C. Bahle of St. Louis, and Erwin M. Roschke of Des Plaines, Illinois; one was a member in the teacher category, Paul G. Nickel of St. Louis; and two were pastors, Kurt W. Biel of Orlando, Florida, and John W. Ott of St. Louis.

At the 1969 convention the Preus party had succeeded in getting control of the committee responsible for submitting nominations to the 1971 convention. The Convention Nominations Committee renominated the incumbent board members except for Ott, who had had a heart attack in the previous year and decided for reasons of health not to be nominated for reelection. The committee nominated three other pastors, two other laymen, and one other teacher, all of whom were closely identified with Preus, some of them leaders in the Preus party.

I was eager for the reelection of all four incumbent board members. However, we needed another pastoral nominee to replace Ott. It chilled me to think of the consequences if one of those proposed by the Convention Nominations Committee were to be elected. I took a few friends into my confidence to reflect on potential candidates whom we could nominate from the floor and whose name recognition would make them electable.

As we sifted through candidates, it occurred to us that a prominent St. Louis pastor who was completing his term as a member of the Synod's Board of Directors had been designated to give the devotions at the close of each convention day. William A. Buege was well known throughout the Synod for his published sermons and as the pastor of Christ Lutheran Church in Minneapolis, made famous because it had been designed by the renowned architect Eero Saarinen. Buege had served as the dean of the chapel at Valparaiso University before coming to a parish in St. Louis. Six foot, three inches tall, garbed in clerical clothes with a huge cross suspended on an ample chest, a balding head topping a cherubic face, Buege combined in his person theological competence and a pastoral heart. In addition to being well known, Buege would be receiving major convention exposure through his presentation of the evening devotions.

We decided that Buege was our candidate. We arranged for him to be nominated from the floor without letting him know that CS was behind his nomination. We let it be known through the Frey-Lueking organization that we were hoping all our friends would vote for Buege and the BoC incumbents. A hitch developed at the time of the nominations from the floor. In addition to Buege, the name of Peter Mealwitz was placed in nomination. Mealwitz was a pastor from Ohio, a member of the English District, and a good friend of mine. I immediately told him my concern. I informed him that Buege was our candidate, that Mealwitz's nomination would mean that the votes of those supporting CS would be divided, and that I hoped he would withdraw his name from the ballot. He did.

The first election returns did not bode well for us. Walter Dissen, a layman from North Olmsted, Ohio, one of the candidates of the Convention Nominations Committee, was the first board member to be elected, thereby replacing one of the two lay incumbents. Then Erwin Roshcke and Paul Nickel were reelected. Finally, William Buege was elected and Kurt Biel was reelected over the three Preus pastoral candidates. Those of us from CS breathed a sigh of relief.

In retrospect, we received Walter Dissen in place of Melvin Bahle, from our standpoint a serious loss; but we received William Buege in place of John Ott, from our standpoint a major gain. The complexion of the BoC would not change all that much. Preus's party had not succeeded in taking over the BoC. In view of the Preus defeat on the issue of the binding nature of doctrinal resolutions, the standoff on the FFC report, and the election of members to the BoC, what had been featured as a gathering "Sent to Reconcile" turned out to be a convention stalemate.

◆ ◆ ◆

Four of us from CS shared a suite at the Schroeder Hotel during the convention. Ernestine and I were in one bedroom separated by a living room from a bedroom shared by Richard R. Caemmerer, Sr., and Arthur C. Repp, two faculty members with the longest tenure at CS. After the evening session on Thursday, July 15, 1971, the four of us gathered in the living room of our suite for a nightcap. For us the major issues had now been decided, and we looked forward to going home the next day. Jackets and ties and shoes came off as we sat down to relax and review the events of what had been a tumultuous day. Nursing his scotch and water, a mischievous twinkle in his eye, Repp, who knew this was Ernestine's first time at a Missouri Synod convention, said, "Well, Ernestine, what do you think? Isn't a Missouri Synod convention an uplifting spiritual experience?"

"Doc," Ernestine responded, "if this convention is any indication of what conventions are like, they're awful. All the words about God are a cover-up for the use of power. What I can't get over is how angry so many of these supposedly Christian people are—not just the delegates, the visitors, too. They don't know who I am as I sit among them, and I hear what they say. They seem so afraid to face the truth."

As Repp and Caemmerer smiled, I said, "I think we dodged a bullet today. I don't mean keeping the Fact Finding Committee report under wraps. I mean the convention's action on doctrinal statements."

"Right, John," Caemmerer said. Setting down his glass of wine and leaning back in his chair, closing his eyes, Caemmerer said, "*Sola Scriptura* is what these Preus partisans talk about, but Scripture alone isn't really enough for them. They insist on convention resolutions to tell everybody what the Scripture says."

"The Lutheran Confessions aren't enough either," Repp said. "How many pages are there in the Tappert edition of *The Book of Concord*? Six hundred? It doesn't matter. It's not enough. The Confessions don't say what these people want them to say about innerancy and inspiration and facticity. They've got to have doctrinal resolutions to spell out their position on those issues."

"Will they give up now that they didn't get their way?" Ernestine asked.

"I'm afraid not," I responded. "These people never give up. They need doctrinal statements. They've got to make doctrinal statements binding so that they can legislate what everybody has to believe. If they do succeed, church conventions will tell us what the Bible teaches about Adam and Eve and a six-day creation and Jonah and the whale, and a lot more. You'll either have to agree, keep quiet, or get out."

"Well, John," Repp said, "you were right about this controversy showing what it means to be Lutheran. The Preus people have a very different understanding of what Lutheran is. They think the Lutheran Confessions are not enough to witness to what the Scriptures teach. They think we have to have a system of doctrine that spells out everything in detail to nail down what the Bible teaches. They think they know exactly what the Bible teaches and that they have a right to tell us what we have to believe and teach."

"Right!" Caemmerer said. "The two views about Lutheranism that are in contention right now are as different as a box is different from a platform. The Preus people think of Lutheranism as a box. You have to be in the box to be a Lutheran. The box tells you what you can believe and what you can't believe. If you don't agree on the truth in the box, you have to get out. But Lutheranism is really a platform on which to stand. The Scriptures and the Lutheran Confessions that witness to what they teach are the ground of our life together. They are the platform on which we stand to witness to what we believe. As rule and norm the Scriptures help us make sure that we speak the Word of God when we witness. The Confessions free us up to witness to what is the heart of our faith—Jesus Christ—and the good news that we are justified by faith in him."

We finished our drinks and bid each other good night, secure in the knowledge that the Milwaukee convention had not succeeded in making us move off the platform into the box.[30]

PART 2 ────────────────◆

"If He Will Not Listen to You"

5 ——◆

NO RETURN

Missouri Synod president Jacob A. O. Preus and I were eating club sand-wiches at the Crest House on Broadway and Chestnut Street in down-town St. Louis. We were at a small table in the center of the crowded restaurant. The time was approximately 1:00 P.M. on Tuesday, January 18, 1972. We had been in conversation several hours already, having begun earlier in the day in Preus's office in the Lutheran Building. His puckish face seemed ready to break into a grin:[1]

Preus: You're a president, John, as I am. Every president has got to be practical. He has got to be realistic. The trouble is, I never know when you are speaking as John Tietjen and when you are playing the role of seminary president. I want to talk to you as John Tietjen.

Tietjen: Okay.

Preus: You could be a big influence on your faculty to keep them in check. As I've observed them in recent years, they've decided that they're going to be the theological leaders in the Synod to change the Synod's theological thinking. Look at the articles they write and the papers they deliver at pas-toral conferences, to say nothing about what they do in the classroom. I've noticed that you have a lot of influence with the faculty. They have full confidence in you. That's not strange, considering what they're going through. They've got a common problem, so they naturally look for a leader. You've given them leadership, and they respect you for it. But in your leadership you have been intransigent in defending the faculty and in supporting what they have been doing. You and I might be able to avoid a collision course if you would give up your intransigence and exert a moderating influence on the faculty to hold them in line.

Tietjen: You're right, Jack. I do have considerable influence with the faculty. They respect my leadership. I have particular goals and aims for Concordia Seminary. My frustration is that for more than a year I have been unable to do the job I was called to do. On any number of occasions I have made clear my understanding of theological education and of the role of Concordia Seminary in the life of the church. You've heard me. You know that my emphasis has been and still is that theology must be in the service of ministry.[2] But we can't get at the TERC Report[3] or the task of revising the curriculum because of the investigation you've imposed on us. I'm confident that the faculty would let me lead them and the whole seminary institution in making sure that theology serves ministry. And that, Jack, could be a major way of meeting your concern about the direction the faculty has taken in recent years. In fact, because of my influence and my leadership the faculty is already stating its position much more moderately and responsibly.

Preus: Well, they certainly need to do that.

Tietjen: You say I am intransigent in my defense of the faculty. I suppose so, though the word is yours, Jack, not mine. It's the responsibility of my office to defend the institution and its faculty. I have no choice but to protect their good name. Look, Jack, I made a basic assessment of what you were up to from the time you made your first move against the seminary, and my actions are based on the assessment I made. It's my assessment that from the beginning control has been the name of your game. You want control of the seminary. That includes the faculty and means that you want some faculty members replaced. Control also includes my office and means that I have to be replaced. I'm not particularly concerned about my job or my future, but I'm not about to let you have your way.[4] Since we're an institution under attack, it's essential that we defend ourselves properly, and that accounts for what you call my intransigence.

Preus: John, you know the parable[5] about the king with ten thousand men and what he does when he discovers that his enemy is moving against him with twenty thousand men. I'm the king with twenty thousand men. The letter I sent you[6] was my way to mobilize my twenty thousand. But for the sake of the Synod I've decided against the collision course. I don't want to see heads roll. I get no pleasure out of seeing a man lose his position. I feel for Ehlen's[7] wife and his children. But something has got to be done to restore the Synod's confidence in the seminary. It would be very helpful if we could talk about theological issues. There are some things that just can't be allowed at the seminary.

Tietjen: It sure would be helpful if the discussion could move to a consideration of issues instead of persons. Our fear of what you are after was confirmed at the December board meeting when you asked the board not to reappoint three faculty members. I welcome a discussion of the issues, but not in a context of whether or not someone is to be dismissed from the faculty. I don't want a collision course, either. If you're interested in working out some compromise solution to the problem between us, I am ready to explore the possibilities. But we have to have mutual agreement on objectives and on procedures by which to reach them. Otherwise, in a short time one of us might feel that he had been double-crossed.

The Crest House dialogue reported above is only an excerpt from a much longer conversation, to which I will return. The conversation took place because of an agreement made the day before at a meeting of Concordia Seminary's Board of Control. The problem for which the conversation was supposed to begin to find a solution had been building ever since the convention of the Lutheran Church–Missouri Synod in Milwaukee the preceding summer. The convention had directed the CS BoC to act on the report of Preus's Fact Finding Committee.

Preus and FFC chair Paul Zimmermann were present at the September 20, 1971, meeting of the BoC to transmit the report officially. Technically and for the record that is all they did. Actually, Preus did much more. He read to the BoC a ten- or twelve-page single-spaced typewritten letter in which he told the BoC what it had to do about the report. He accused specific faculty members of false doctrine, told the BoC to investigate me because of my defense of the faculty's use of historical criticism, insisted that faculty contracts that were coming due should not be renewed, and said that the BoC had to find a way to remove certain tenured faculty members. Preus gave the BoC one year to carry out his instructions. He made it clear that if they failed to do so, he would take matters into his own hands.

When Preus finished, BoC members sat in stunned silence. One by one they let Preus know how he had demeaned them by telling them what they had to do about a report on which a Synod convention had given them responsibility to act and which they had not yet even received. William Buege, attending his first BoC meeting since his election at the Milwaukee convention, stated that in the light of Preus's letter he doubted that he could serve on the BoC and keep his integrity. I insisted that Preus would have to read his letter to the faculty the next day or I would report in detail what he had said. Preus and Zimmermann stepped out of the room to confer. When they returned, Preus announced that he was withdrawing the letter and that he wanted the BoC to act as if he had not read it.

Preus liked to tell his friends that the Missouri Synod was made up of Germans and that Germans liked nothing better than to be told what to do. But I think he badly overplayed his hand in telling the BoC what to do. Although technically Preus's letter had been stricken from the record, BoC members and I knew what he had said. As I wrote immediately following the meeting, "Though the board officially received nothing but the Fact Finding Committee's report and the resolutions of the Milwaukee convention, the board members know what Preus wants out of them. It will be mighty difficult for them not to be pressured by the gun to their head."[8]

The FFC report consisted of typewritten transcripts of the taped interviews with each member of the faculty, a committee summary of each interview, a Summary of Report prepared by the committee consisting of forty pages purporting to present observations without judgment, and a collection of other items, including reports on classroom visits, selected syllabi, catalogs, public relations materials, and student periodicals.[9]

The BoC took seriously the responsibility the Synod convention in Milwaukee had placed upon it. To ensure the accuracy of the transcripts of the faculty interviews, the BoC asked each interviewed faculty member to compare the typescript with the tape in his possession and make any corrections deemed necessary. The BoC also invited each faculty member to respond to the FFC's summary of the interview. The BoC decided to extend its October meeting by almost a full day in order to participate in a faculty-led discussion on the historical-critical method and to begin a process of interviews of its own in relation to the FFC report. At my request the BoC decided to begin the interview process with me and with two chief administrators, vice-president for academic affairs Arthur Repp and dean of students Kenneth Breimeier. It also granted my request to present an analysis of the FFC's Summary of Report, as the only person from CS who had been present for all faculty interviews.[10]

The BoC conducted one interview with me at its October 1971 meeting. Not until its February 1972 meeting was it able to give serious attention once again to its synodically imposed responsibility to review the FFC report. First, a series of letters from Preus,[11] and then Preus's personal involvement in the issue of renewal of several faculty contracts, absorbed the board's time and attention.

One issue in Preus's letters had to do with news stories reporting the results of the BoC's September meeting, for which Preus held me accountable—as if the media, already tuned in to the investigation for a year, would ignore the BoC's decisions regarding the investigation. Another issue, on which Preus was insistent—in fact, demanding—was that all interviews with faculty personnel should be tape recorded. But the BoC understood its task at this point to engage faculty in fraternal discussion of the interviews conducted by the FFC. The time for tape recorders would come if there should be a need for judicial proceedings.

The major issue raised in Preus's letters was whether to reappoint seven members of the faculty whose four-year contracts expired at the end of June 1972. According to synodical requirements, faculty members had to be given six months notice if it was the BoC's intention not to renew their contracts, and so it was necessary to decide on reappointment before December 31, 1971. For Preus the problem was compounded by the bylaw regulation that any faculty member with seven years of service within the Synod's system of higher education would automatically receive tenure. Thus any of the seven who were reappointed would in due course receive tenure.

The faculty members in question were Mark Bangert, David Deppe, Arlis Ehlen, Wi Jo Kang, Ralph Klein, Duane Mehl, and Robert Smith. Preus requested that these faculty members be interviewed so that the BoC could be "completely satisfied with their doctrinal position," and Preus asked to be present for those interviews.[12] Then Preus insisted that the BoC "go through the material dealing with these men which was prepared by the Fact Finding Committee." Preus wrote: "I do not wish to imply that all of these men are guilty of false doctrine or that they should not be reemployed but I am saying that I believe you owe it to all concerned to examine these men prior to renewing their contracts."[13]

The BoC invited its members to submit written questions to faculty members whose contracts were up for renewal. Three BoC members, Charles Burmeister, Walter Dissen, and Herman Scherer, availed themselves of the opportunity, addressing questions to Deppe, Ehlen, Kang, Klein, and Smith. The responses of the faculty members were distributed along with the agenda material for the December meeting.

Preus was present for the BoC meeting on December 13, 1971, and brought Paul Zimmermann of the FFC along with him. The meeting was held in the board room on the second floor of Pieper Hall on the CS campus. A rectangular mahogany table filled the room; with eighteen chairs around the table, it was difficult to fit in additional chairs to accommodate more people. George Loose as chair presided at the end of the table farthest from the door. I was at the other end. Members tended to take the same seats meeting after meeting, and when additional people were present, as on this occasion, it took some shuffling before everyone found a place. Preus had taken a seat close to the head of the table to Loose's left, and Zimmermann sat next to him.

Loose invited Preus to share his thoughts with the BoC. As Preus started to speak, he turned on a small tape recorder in front of him. Loose interrupted, begging Preus's pardon, and asked him what his purpose was in using a tape recorder. Preus's face reddened, his eyes squinted, and his jaw moved up and down as if he were chewing gum. Looking straight ahead and not at Loose, he said that the tape recorder was only to record his presentation so that he could give BoC members copies of it. At the end of his presentation he picked up the recorder, and with an elaborate hand movement, turned it off.

In his presentation Preus said that he did not object to the reappointment of some of the faculty whose contracts were coming due, but did have concerns about some. He named Deppe, Ehlen, Klein, and Smith, adding that he was sure he could take care of his concerns with Deppe just by talking to the man. Preus had a proposal for the BoC: decline to renew the contracts of Ehlen, Klein, and Smith, and then give me and Repp the opportunity at a later time, after the BoC had thoroughly reviewed their doctrinal position, to propose new appointments for them. He described this as a fair and evangelical procedure that would relieve the time pressure concerning these professors. Preus stressed his concern that at this time he could not tell the church that these men were doctrinally sound.

To me it seemed that Preus's goal was to remove the three men from the faculty. He hoped that the BoC members would think that in the course of the next six months, after they had done their work on the FFC report, it would still be possible to keep these three on the faculty through new appointments. Preus, however, could block new appointments either by action of the Board for Higher Education, a group firmly in his control, or through the Electors, whose decisions were also in his control. I announced that if the BoC declined to renew the contracts of any of the seven, I would not propose that person for a new appointment.

After Loose asked about Preus's problems with the three faculty members, the BoC decided that Preus should interview the three that same day in the presence of the BoC, and that the BoC would reserve the right to conduct its own interview on the basis of the FFC materials at a later time. Smith, Klein, and Ehlen were interviewed. Preus asked Smith about his views on the inspiration and inerrancy of Scripture. He asked Klein his position on predictive prophecy. He asked Ehlen about the existence of angels and a personal devil and the historicity of the Genesis account of Adam and Eve.

After supper and a plenary session, the BoC returned to its consideration of contract renewal. Repp, speaking for me, argued strongly for the reappointment of all seven professors. Preus restated his proposal to decline the reappointment of Smith, Klein, and Ehlen with the understanding that I would be given opportunity to submit new appointments for them. Board member Walter Dissen made the motion for Preus. Voting separately on each of the men, the BoC voted no on declining the reappointment of Smith and Klein and yes on declining the reappointment of Ehlen. They then voted to reappoint Smith, Klein, and the other four faculty members whose contracts were up for renewal.

Repp and I then pressed the BoC to give a formal statement as to why it did not reappoint Ehlen. In the discussion that followed it was clear that a number of BoC members were dissatisfied with Ehlen's position on the existence of angels and a personal devil. A motion was made and passed to reconsider the decision not to reappoint Ehlen. A motion was then made to reappoint him, and that motion was tabled. The BoC resolved to convene a special meeting the following week to consider the tabled motion.

Arlis J. Ehlen was a most unlikely candidate to be at the center of a controversy. Quiet and reserved, mild-mannered, he was almost shy. Forty years of age, he was married and the father of three. He had done graduate work at the University of Bonn in Germany and at Brandeis University and received his doctorate from Harvard University in 1965. He had served for three years at CS before entering Harvard and had subsequently served congregations in Rochester, New York; and Yuba City, California. He taught for a year at LCMS's Concordia College in Oakland, California, before rejoining the CS faculty in 1968. His specialty was Hebrew poetry. Tall and thin, speaking softly and without emotion, he wore glasses that made him look the scholar he was.

Ehlen asked to be present at the special BoC meeting on December 20, 1971, a procedure that Repp and I had proposed to give him an opportunity to meet the BoC's concerns. The meeting began at 6:00 P.M. At 6:30 Ehlen was invited in. He sat next to me, presented his own personal statement of faith, and then responded to questions.

After almost two hours, the interview seemed to be at an end. Then Preus, who had been ominously silent for most of the evening, asked a series of questions based on what he said were student notes from Ehlen's classes that had appeared unsolicited on Preus's desk. The questions had to do with the account in Exodus 14 of the crossing of the Red Sea by the Israelites and the facticity of the events described there. Ehlen responded that some of what Preus reported was clearly what he taught, some of it was obviously a misunderstanding of what he taught, and some of it he did not and would not teach. Ehlen tried to lead Preus and the BoC members through the complex exegetical issues involved in the Exodus account.

At 8:50 P.M. Ehlen was excused. Reading from a typewritten statement he must have prepared before the meeting, Preus claimed that at the December 13 meeting the BoC had not given sufficient time to the interviews of Smith and Klein; that he and other BoC members still had unanswered questions about the position of these two; that the FFC report had not been seriously considered in interviewing them; and that the BoC had voted to reconsider its decision to reappoint Ehlen even though Ehlen's responses on the existence of angels or a personal devil were so unsatisfactory that "even the chairman of the Board stated that he would be reluctant to permit Professor Ehlen to teach his confirmation class."[14]

Preus continued full force. He cited his constitutional responsibility to supervise doctrine and said that he was acting after consultation with the Synod vice-presidents. He "respectfully and earnestly" called upon the BoC to reconsider their reappointment of Smith and Klein, to decline to renew the contracts of Smith, Klein, and Ehlen "pending full-scale further interviews involving specifically the President of the Synod and those Board of Control members who still have unanswered questions," and to instruct me to have copies of my letters informing the three men of the BoC's decision on his desk by Wednesday morning, December 22. He ended with a threat: "I consider this matter of such great importance that I hope and pray that this particular solution to the immediate problems will find favor with you and prompt you to accede to this appeal, thus making it unnecessary for me to consider what other action to take under the circumstances."

An extensive discussion followed on whether Ehlen should be reappointed. I challenged the use of student notes in the interview process, insisting that Ehlen had every right to confront whoever was the source of the notes. Finally, the BoC acted on the tabled motion to reappoint Ehlen. The votes were 4 affirmative, 5 negative, and 1 abstention. If the person who abstained had voted in the affirmative to create a tie, the chairperson could have cast a vote, which might have reversed the decision. In any event, the BoC's original decision of December 13 stood. Arlis Ehlen was not reappointed to another four-year term as a member of the faculty. The BoC chose not to give a reason for its action.

CS was in recess for the Christmas holidays. Students and many faculty were scattered across the country for family holiday reunions.

The campus was a different place when students were gone. Its natural beauty was still there, the Tudor Gothic architecture still held visitors in awe, but the life had gone out of the place. Walking through the empty campus was like wandering through a cemetery.

I knew that students and faculty would be deeply disturbed when they heard what had happened at the December 20 meeting and would want to do something about it on their return. During the holiday break I worked on the response to the FFC report that the BoC had authorized me to make. Classes resumed on January 4, 1972. The faculty met later that day for its regular monthly meeting. The Faculty Advisory Committee, which the faculty had elected to serve as liaison between the faculty and me for issues relating to Preus's investigation, presented two recommendations for action. The proposals were made by the committee's chairperson, Alfred Fuerbringer, my predecessor as CS president.

One action was a letter addressed to the BoC on behalf of Arlis Ehlen. Identifying with Ehlen's exegetical approach and confessional position, the letter was intended to request ever so gently that the BoC reconsider its action and to reappoint Ehlen. Individual faculty members and executive staff signed the letter, and all agreed to keep the matter in confidence.

The second action was a letter addressed to Preus dealing with his use of student notes from Ehlen's classroom presentations in the course of Ehlen's BoC interview. The letter faulted Preus for not following the "evangelical practice that has been traditional among us." It reminded him that the student whose notes he had used had not brought his concerns to Ehlen, that the student had not taken his concerns to me as president of CS to provide me with an opportunity to deal with the matter, and that Preus himself had not first discussed his concerns personally with Ehlen before making them an issue at the BoC meeting. Calling attention to the "moral implications" of Preus's action, the faculty stated, "Such a practice could lead also to a breakdown of healthy student-teacher relationships in the classroom and become an unevangelical model for our future pastors in their relationships with one another and with their parishioners."[15]

The faculty asked Preus to meet with a small delegation of faculty members "no later than Wednesday, January 12," because of the "critical importance of this issue." As its delegation to meet with Preus, the faculty named five of its active senior members: Herbert J. A. Bouman, Richard R. Caemmerer, Sr., George W. Hoyer, Herbert T. Mayer, and Arthur Carl Piepkorn. All of these professors had been at CS a decade earlier when the use of classroom notes without following "evangelical practice" had been an issue in the charges of false doctrine made against

Martin Scharlemann and Horace Hummel, a professor no longer on the faculty.

Student body president Kenneth Ruppar arranged for a student convocation following the chapel service on January 5. He asked me to report on what happened at the December BoC meetings. Arlis Ehlen was asked to make a statement. Both of us were to respond to questions.

I was concerned about what the students might do. For more than a year they had been standing by, watching Preus's investigation and its effects on CS. Eager to be of help, many were frustrated because there seemed to be nothing they could do. Many were determined to do something about the decision not to reappoint Ehlen.

Earlier in the day a cartoon appeared in the *Spectrum*, a student news publication, depicting a dove, a symbol for the Holy Spirit, bearing a huge head of Jacob Preus, dictating to CS on the reappointment of Arlis Ehlen. Before the convocation, I told dean of students Kenneth Breimeier that we would have to send Preus an apology from those who were responsible for the cartoon. The apology was published in the January 7 issue of *Spectrum* and dispatched to Preus the same day along with a personal apology from me. Preus was not available to talk to me by phone when I tried to reach him.

The student convocation took place in the large auditorium where chapel services were held (plans to build a separate chapel had never been completed). The auditorium was a large room with a balcony, seating more than five hundred people. It was filled with students. A single microphone had been set up at the front of the floor of the auditorium. Ehlen and I spoke from the microphone.

In my report[16] to the students on what had taken place at the two December BoC meetings I stressed that the BoC had acted legally on the basis of the authority given to it in the Synod's bylaws and that students needed to act on their calling as students and not try to arrogate to themselves the responsibilities of the seminary's governing board. Ehlen's statement was low key, simply reporting factually the topics he had been asked to address and what he had said. Although he did not make much of an issue of it, he reported that Preus had made use of what Preus had called "unsolicited" reports of statements made in class by Ehlen, which unnamed students had presumably furnished Preus.

In the course of the question period one student asked me if any student had the right, in light of Matthew 18, to circulate classroom notes of faculty members to others in the Synod without first talking over concerns privately with the faculty member. I responded by reading a CS policy statement adopted on April 5, 1960, during a time when students at CS and others in the Synod had to be reminded of Matthew 18 and its implications for processing criticisms against certain faculty members. I pointed out that on the previous day the faculty had requested a meeting with President Preus to discuss the issue and that I would have more to say after that meeting.

In response to another student's question I pointed out that no one should think we were playing ecclesiastical games. The stakes were high, and anyone who felt compelled to act had better first count the cost. I believe the students understood clearly what their calling was and acted responsibly. They deluged the BoC with signatures from present students, past students who had been in Ehlen's courses, and absent student interns, asking the BoC to reverse its decision. Faculty members also sought to rouse their friends among the Synod clergy to communicate to the BoC. A flood of correspondence engulfed the BoC at its January and February meetings.

Concern about Preus's credibility arose in another way. Under date of December 20, 1971, the day of the second BoC meeting that month, Preus wrote similar letters to Ralph Klein and Robert Smith in which he asked them to restate in writing their answers to the questions he had addressed to them at the December 13 meeting. In both letters Preus said that he was making the request "for your own protection as well as mine."[17] Preus wrote to Klein: "I am interested, not only in the fact that you are a thoroughly orthodox theologian, but also that you be protected from false charges." Preus needed the material, he said, in order to deal with people who would be saying that the BoC meeting was a whitewash. He added, "I cannot operate with people on the basis of a fuzzy memory of a forty-minute interview." In Smith's letter the interview was described as a "pleasant chit chat."

In separate responses both Klein and Smith expressed incredulity that Preus could want the information he had requested for their "protection" when later on the same day the letters were written Preus pressed the BoC not to renew their contracts. "How can I believe you?" Smith asked. "You have tried to have me removed from my teaching position and livelihood. I cannot in any way interpret that as an action to protect me or my family."[18] Nevertheless, both professors responded in detail to Preus's questions, correcting his misinterpretations of what they had said. Klein wrote that he was mystified by Preus's reaction to the interview: "I heard Chairman Loose ask several times at the end of the interview whether there were any more questions. None were forthcoming, and in fact there seemed to be expressions of satisfaction on all sides—including from you."[19] Smith pointed out that Preus did not even use all of the forty minutes allotted for the interview.

"Contrary to what you now say," he wrote, "you were allowed ample time for airing your concerns."

◆ ◆ ◆

On Tuesday, January 11, 1972, a bombshell exploded, threatening Armageddon at the January 17 BoC meeting. On that day I received a letter from President Preus, dated January 7 although delivery service between the Synod offices and CS regularly provided for same-day delivery of mail. In the letter Preus said that on the basis of provisions in the Synod's constitution he was officially "advising, admonishing and reproving" me as CS president and holding me responsible for actions which, he wrote, "constitute an obstruction and a frustration of the Synodical President in the performance of the duties laid upon him by his oath of office."[20] Such official advice, admonition, and reproof could only mean that disciplinary action was to be imposed on me.

What were the reasons for such a severe and unprecedented course of action? Preus gave two reasons in his letter. The first was the "judgmental and unethical letter" the faculty had adopted on January 4, the letter that asked for a meeting with Preus to talk about his use of classroom notes in the Ehlen interview. According to Preus, the faculty acted without full possession of the facts. The second reason was the January 5 issue of the *Spectrum,* in which, according to Preus, "there appears material which verges on the blasphemous, shows a lack of understanding of Christian ethics, and again is based on misinformation." Although Preus acknowledged the apology and retraction in the January 7 *Spectrum,* "this cannot undo the damage which has been done to all concerned."

Preus announced in his letter that because of the "serious and far reaching significance of these two actions," he was sending copies of the letter to the members of the BoC, the Synod's BHE, and the LCMS Board of Directors. Instead of meeting with a faculty delegation he would "deal with these matters only in the presence of yourself and the Board of Control." He would be at the board's January 17 meeting and would have the synodical vice-presidents along for aid and counsel.

I convened the FAC to consider what really lay behind Preus's letter and to prepare for whatever might come at the January BoC meeting. One theory proposed was that Preus was using the two reasons cited in his letter to do what he had intended to do all along—namely, force me out of office as president. The stream of letters to me from his office since the previous September had the purpose of making a case that I was willfully functioning as an "obstruction and a frustration" in the performance of his duties as president of the Synod. The faculty letter and the *Spectrum* cartoon simply provided him with the occasion to make his move.

Another theory was that the faculty letter questioning his ethics had caused him to panic. Perhaps he realized he had crossed the line of what was acceptable behavior in going after professors. He had done what at the outset of the investigation process he had told the faculty he would not do.[21] He assumed that the faculty and I were engaged in a process that would result in public accusations against him on ethical grounds. He decided to move against me by accusing the faculty of being "judgmental and unethical" and seized upon the *Spectrum* cartoon to reinforce his attack.

Truth is probably expressed in both theories. My assessment at the time was more complex.[22] As I saw it, the BoC's decisions on reappointment were a major defeat for Preus, and he did not intend to let the matter rest. So he wrote to Klein and Smith to get in writing documentation he could use against them. On January 5 he wrote me a blunt letter reiterating his "order" to make transcripts of all faculty interviews with the BoC. If the BoC had reappointed Ehlen, he probably would have moved against the BoC, but its decision confused the situation for him.

In the meantime events took place over which Preus had no control. As I saw it then, he interpreted the events as a full-scale CS attack on him. He may have held me responsible for a story in the December 29 St. Louis *Globe Democrat* reporting on the BoC's action. The faculty's request to meet with him probably seemed to him to be preparation for a public attack on his ethics. He was infuriated by the *Spectrum* cartoon and probably assumed that I had called the student convocation to foment student action. The deluge of letters to the BoC from around the church suggested that some organized effort was under way.

So Preus apparently decided to move against me, putting into operation a plan he had probably prepared earlier for use if I should step out of line. It would call for my ouster, or at least suspension, on the grounds that I was willfully obstructing his efforts to supervise doctrine in the Synod. The groundwork was prepared through the battery of letters from his office ordering me to carry out his directives. In any event, we at CS had to take Preus's letter with utmost gravity. He had sent copies of it not only to the BoC but to the two boards on which he could count for support, the Synod's BHE and BoD. We prepared for Armageddon.

On January 13 I responded to Preus's letter with a blunt letter of my own. I asserted that I found it incomprehensible that he should send such a letter "before you have even spoken to me about your concerns." I wrote: "I might have been able to clarify some things for you if you had . . . given me the opportunity to speak to you when I called you on January 7 to share information with you about the two matters to which you refer in your letter."[23] I told him I saw no connection between the constitutional provisions he cited in his letter and the reasons he gave for "advising, admonishing and reproving" me. I told him I had no choice but to send my letter to all those to whom he had sent his and would be ready to talk to him about his concerns at the meeting of the BoC.

In the meantime the FAC and I organized on the assumption that by the end of the January BoC meeting I would no longer be functioning as president. We established a series of task forces under the jurisdiction of a central committee to handle media communications, contacts with the church, the writing of materials, student relations, finances, and legal matters. We named personnel for the task forces and the central committee, drew up a tentative schedule for the time immediately following the BoC meeting, including a moratorium on classes, and devised telephone and letter-writing campaigns.[24] The students organized a prayer vigil that was held during the whole time the BoC was in session, which the students invited BoC members to attend.

The fateful meeting of the BoC began at 2:00 P.M. on January 17, 1972. Preus was in attendance with the five Synod vice-presidents: Roland Wiederaenders, first vice-president and full-time officer of the Synod, short and roly-poly in stature, speaking with a gentle voice in his new role as moderating influence and mediator in the Preus administration; Theodore Nickel, parish pastor from Chicago and chair of the Synod's Commission on Theology and Church Relations, short and balding, wearing a clerical collar, shrill of speech, seemingly relishing his role as theological policy maker; Edwin Weber, pastor from Fraser, Michigan, and Preus's representative on the BoC, with a strong physique, the face of a Bavarian and a German-English accent to match; Paul Streufert, parish pastor from Cleveland and member of Preus's FFC, red-faced and sleepy-eyed; Guido Merkens, parish pastor from San Antonio, tall and athletic. It was an imposing group. All seats in the board room were filled.

As the meeting began, Chairperson George Loose asked Preus what he wanted included on the agenda. Preus responded that he was asking the BoC to give consideration primarily to the theological issues raised in the interview of Arlis Ehlen and, in the process, to deal with the question of whether Ehlen should be given cause for the decision not to reappoint him. For more than an hour the vice-presidents dominated the discussion, arguing the pros and cons of giving cause.

I tried to figure out what was going on. What was Preus up to? Did he not intend to follow through on his letter of admonition and reproof? When the discussion on giving cause petered out, I asked Preus what else he and the vice-presidents wanted to discuss. Preus said something about the BoC standing at a crossroads and that he preferred not to discuss the actions about which he had written in his January 7 letter to me; he wanted instead to discuss the theological matters that were the real problem behind the December BoC meetings.

Conversations on theological matters proceeded until the meeting was recessed for supper and continued after supper for almost three hours. Members of the BoC were minimally involved in the discussions while the vice-presidents, especially Nickel, dominated. I found it necessary again and again to point out how the CS faculty was being prejudged and how views were being attributed to the faculty that they did not acknowledge as their own. As the hours wore on, I realized that Preus did not intend to follow through on the threat in his letter of January 7.

Finally, Preus stated that at a meeting of the BHE, when his letter of January 7 was being considered, it was proposed that the BHE arrange for a meeting between Preus and me. Preus stated that he felt he should meet with me apart from the auspices of the BHE. Roland Wiederaenders underscored the need for the two of us to meet so that we could work together "in mutual confidence and trust." Preus promised to get together with me as soon as possible, and I stated my readiness to meet with him to try to resolve whatever issues needed our attention. At 9:45 P.M., amidst a feeling of euphoria, Preus and the vice-presidents left the meeting. Preus asked me to meet him the next morning in his office.

Why had Preus backed off from what he himself in my subsequent meetings with him described as the "collision course" he was pursuing? As we at CS pieced things together, several factors probably contributed to the change. Preus cooled off when he realized things were not as bad as they first seemed. CS made no public accusation against him on ethical grounds. He received letters of apology for the *Spectrum* cartoon. He began to realize the consequences of his projected course of action. He had attended meetings of the Council of Presidents and of the Commission on Theology and Church Relations the week after he sent his letter, and cooler heads may have counseled against carrying out his plans.

By the time Preus participated in the BHE meeting on January 15, he probably no longer wanted to press the issue. He secured from that group the proposal for a meeting with me that he could use as a way out at the BoC meeting. At his meeting with the Synod's vice-presidents prior to the BoC meeting, Roland Wiederaenders probably proposed the course of action that he requested at the BoC meeting—namely, that the discussion focus on theology instead of procedure. In the course of the meeting Preus discovered that I was not geared up for a major assault on him on ethical grounds. By the end of the meeting he was ready to propose that the two of us should meet to resolve the issues without the need for the presence of the BHE or anyone else.

As I drove downtown for my 11:00 A.M. meeting with Preus, I felt like someone who had been hauled before a firing squad and then, when rifles were raised for execution, had been given a reprieve. Although I was wary of what Preus might have in mind for our meeting, I was determined that personally I should be frank and open and ready to grasp opportunities to resolve the problems between Preus and CS. We met in Preus's office, just a short distance from the board room where a year before I had spent many Fridays and Saturdays with faculty members in FFC interviews. Preus sat at his desk. I sat in the chair opposite him.

After agreeing on items we wanted to discuss, Preus and I started talking about the faculty's letter to him concerning his use of student notes in the Ehlen interview.[25] Preus said he was upset with the faculty action because it singled him out as the only person to make use of classroom notes when board member Charles Burmeister had also made use of such material and perhaps others had, too. I pointed out that the faculty's action was based on Ehlen's report and that Ehlen either did not know or did not remember that Burmeister had made use of student notes. In any event, I said, the faculty would have automatically made a distinction between use of such notes by a lay member of the BoC and by the president of the Synod. I reminded him of how sensitive the issue was for the CS community in view of the problems the faculty had experienced a decade earlier.

I tried to make Preus understand the problem in his action: He had prejudged Ehlen and asked that he not be reappointed on the basis of material he had never discussed with Ehlen, some of which the professor denied teaching. We came to no agreement, and Preus asked me to inform the faculty that we were engaged in conversations and that any decision about a meeting would await the outcome of our discussions. I did not agree to do that but made it clear that I would keep the faculty from pushing him on this issue for the time being.

We talked next about Preus's correspondence with Professors Klein and Smith. Preus simply could not understand why we had a problem with his letters to them. After all, he had not simply argued against reappointing them; he had proposed a procedure by which their views could be more fully ascertained and by which they might then be reappointed. In response I said that I was going to speak bluntly and frankly: I told Preus that I considered his proposal to be a deliberate deception.

When he rejected my accusation, I told him that I was speaking as a Christian and brother in Christ and that I had a serious fault to lay before him: It was un-Christian to assume that professors were guilty and to require them to prove their innocence, as he was doing. I pointed out that he had asked that Klein and Smith not be reappointed because of their doctrinal views when he had not discussed those views with them. Preus objected to my requiring him to follow the procedures of Matthew 18. I told him that he was not listening to me. I was talking not about procedures he should follow, but about what was in his mind and heart. I was finding fault with an attitude that refused to give the benefit of the doubt and to put the best construction on things, words that paraphrased Martin Luther's catechism explanation of the Eighth Commandment and its prohibition against bearing false witness.

Preus erupted in anger, insisting that he had only wanted to find out the facts about the two professors and that I had tried to rush their appointments through without a thorough review of their teaching. After I reviewed the course of events since September, he calmed down. He said that he had been led to believe that Klein denied there was any messianic prophecy in the Old Testament and that Klein's answers had satisfied him. He said he had problems with Smith's view of an inspired community. When I pointed out that the term was his and not Smith's, he said he would look it up in the article Smith had written to which he was objecting.

Preus and I then talked about my problems with his intrusion into meetings of the BoC and its consequences for our relations with each other. I said that in my opinion he simply refused to accept the fact that I was president of CS. He shot back that in his opinion I refused to accept the fact that he was president of the Synod. I laughed, and we agreed that we both understood each other on that point. He responded to my basic complaint by saying that he had to intrude into the BoC's affairs because, unlike other executives in the Synod, I did not keep him properly informed about what was going on at CS.

Preus introduced our next agenda item, and it became clear to me that we were now dealing with the real reason he wanted to meet with me. Preus presented a lengthy assessment of the political climate of the Synod. Then he said something like, "I'm the president of this church body, and you're a president, too. Every president has a sense of history. I don't want to go down in history as the person during whose presidency the Missouri Synod was split." Therefore, he said, he had decided to change the collision course on which we had been heading. He looked at his watch and suggested that we continue the conversation over lunch.

I have already reported the heart of our conversation at the Crest House. Our lunchtime conversation continued with Preus proposing that one course of action could be to review the FFC report to determine what issues needed to be discussed. I said that I welcomed any procedure that would focus on issues but that it was essential that we come to an understanding as to what would be done with the FFC report. When Preus agreed, I said that it was crucial that we come to that understanding before the next meeting of the BoC since I was expected to give my assessment of the FFC report at that meeting. On the one hand, I told Preus that I would not want to give my assessment if we could find a compromise way of dealing with the problem. On the other hand, if the report was to be given any standing, it would be necessary for me to demolish it; I had done the homework and had the wherewithal to do so. I pointed out that I understood how important the report was to Preus and how much he was bound up with it. That is why it was necessary for us to find a way around the report that would be acceptable to him. The report had to be removed in order to make it possible for us to focus on theological issues. Preus said that he had no intention of publishing the report.

As the time drew near 2:00 P.M. Preus said that he wanted to consult with a few people. He mentioned Paul Streufert, Paul Zimmermann, Herbert Mueller, and Roland Wiederaenders. He suggested that I consult with others, too. We agreed to an all-day meeting on January 31. Preus said that neither his office nor mine would be advisable because of interruptions and suggested that we meet in his home. I left the Crest House convinced that the doors to conciliation were wide open, and I was determined to make the most of it.

I was therefore totally unprepared for my phone conversation with Preus two days later. He called me, returning the call I had tried to make to him the day before. I had agreed to report to him the outcome of the faculty meeting on January 18, and that was the purpose of my call. I told him that I had arranged for the faculty to do no more than to approve the action of a faculty committee in its efforts to arrange a meeting with Preus and had reported that Preus and I were in discussion on that and other issues.

Preus told me that he was deeply disturbed by the faculty action and that what I should have done was to have them withdraw their letter. Under the circumstances he could have no further meetings with me because I had not acted in good faith. No matter what I said, Preus remained adamant, insisting that he could not meet with me unless the faculty withdrew its letter or met also with others who had used classroom materials. I told him I thought he was making too much of the faculty action. He asked to see a copy of it and said he would arrange a conference call with his vice-presidents to discuss the matter.[26]

After the phone conversation, I tried to figure out what had happened. I concluded that what Preus was after in the meeting with the

BoC and in the meeting with me was to eliminate the issue of the appropriateness of using classroom materials in the interview with Arlis Ehlen. Apparently, he expected me to call the faculty off on that issue on the assumption that he and I would then be able to talk about other issues. I began to wonder whether Preus ever really had compromise in mind. Perhaps I was walking into a trap.

Nevertheless, I persisted in my efforts to find a conciliatory way through the problem. That same day I talked with Roland Wiederaenders and shared with him what had happened. Wiederaenders and I had developed good relations since my arrival in St. Louis two years earlier. Together with Richard Schultz, president of Concordia Theological Seminary in Springfield, Illinois, we served as the Missouri Synod's Colloquy Committee, which had the responsibility of approving for pastoral ministry those who did not follow the normal route to ordination through either of the Synod's seminaries. We alternated the location of our monthly meetings between the St. Louis and Springfield seminaries. Wiederaenders and I spent time together driving to and from Springfield every other month, and we became good friends. Wiederaenders told me he was sure Preus would meet with me. When I called Preus's office on January 24 to ask about our meeting, Preus's secretary said he had asked her to arrange for the meeting on February 10 instead of January 31.

I prepared as hard as I knew how for that meeting with Preus. I assumed that he would be ready with a full-blown proposal with a discussion of theological issues based on the FFC report as its centerpiece. I therefore felt it necessary to have a proposal of my own to present. At our January 18 meeting I had talked about the need to have mutual agreement on objectives and on procedures by which to achieve them. I drew up a list of both objectives and procedures, presented them to the FAC for reaction, and revised them on the basis of the responses I received.[27] My approach was to try to find a way to resolve all the issues that were bound up in the controversy rather than to deal with them piecemeal.

On February 10 I met again with Preus in his office. To my surprise he did not present a proposal for us to discuss. I presented my list of objectives and procedures, and they became the agenda for our meeting. I explained my list of twelve objectives one by one, and Preus was in agreement with every one of them:

1. Role of the president of the Synod as supervisor of doctrine upheld.
2. Concerns of the president of the Synod dealt with.
3. Commitment of professors to Scripture and Confessions assured.
4. Cloud of suspicion removed from CS.
5. Responsibility of the BoC to carry out the Milwaukee resolution concerning the FFC report affirmed.

6. Rights of CS faculty to fair treatment assured.
7. Action on the FFC report concluded without controversy and report filed.
8. Reputation and good name of the president of the Synod, the members of the FFC, and faculty members preserved.
9. Reputation and good name of Professor Arlis Ehlen preserved.
10. Rights and responsibility of the CS president recognized.
11. CS freed to return to concentration on theological education.
12. Concerns of most people in the field satisfied.[28]

Preus and I had much more to talk about when it came to my list of procedures by which to achieve these objectives. I proposed a twofold process. One part of the process called for the BoC to complete its review of the FFC report, isolating issues for discussion and taking whatever action it deemed appropriate. I envisioned a situation in which the BoC would find no false doctrine among faculty members. Preus insisted on the need to allow for the possibility that the BoC might find false doctrine.

The second part of the process called for theological discussion of issues that had been mutually accepted by the BoC, faculty, and Preus. The penultimate procedure stated: "Board of Control through the seminary president structures meetings with faculty to which the president of the Synod is invited as a participant and arranges to work through the issues with all deliberate speed."[29] Another procedure called for the BoC and Preus to produce and release a statement to the Synod reporting the BoC's assessment of the FFC Report, the plans for meetings, the isolation of issues, and the agreement on theological principles. One final procedure called for the BoC to reengage Arlis Ehlen for a one-year contract "to provide opportunity for his participation in the discussions and for later review of his position with the faculty."[30] We agreed that I would produce a revised version of my list of objectives and procedures on the basis of our discussion and that we would meet again the morning of February 18, the day the next BoC meeting would begin.

Present with Preus for the February 18 meeting were Roland Wiederaenders and Arthur Ahlschwede, executive secretary of the BHE. We discussed my revisions of the list of objectives and procedures. Preus questioned bits of wording but took no issue with the substance of what I had presented. Preus was not sure about the procedure calling for Ehlen to receive a one-year contract, but he let it stand. He told me that he had asked Ahlschwede and the vice-presidents of the Synod to attend the meeting of the BoC with him and planned on being present from the beginning of the meeting. I felt a twinge of anxiety but dismissed it, assuring myself that Preus was only providing for full participation in a historic meeting that promised to put an end to the CS controversy. I left feeling good about our accomplishments and eager to present the results to the BoC later that evening.

At 4:30 that afternoon I received a call from Roland Wiederaenders, who reported that he was "in Jack's office" and that Preus had decided that he could not agree to the last of the nine procedures after all, the one calling for a one-year contract for Ehlen. I swallowed hard and told Wiederaenders that I had already prepared the materials for distribution to the BoC but would make it clear in my presentation that the procedure relating to Ehlen was not a part of our agreement. I assured myself that eight-ninths of a loaf was better than none.

The board room in Pieper Hall was once again crowded. It was 7:00 P.M. when the BoC meeting began on February 18, 1972, the first of a four-day meeting to deal with the massive accumulation of work that had backed up over the past months and to fulfill the BoC's responsibilities with respect to the FFC report. Instead of my usual seat at the foot of the table, I was sitting about one-third of the way up the table on the right side looking toward the head. Preus had positioned himself, as he usually did, to the left of Loose as chair of the meeting. It was therefore difficult for Preus and me to look at each other when we spoke.

At Loose's request I reported on my meetings with Preus. With a great sense of expectation, I presented the statement of objectives and procedures on which we had agreed. It did not take long for me to realize that something was very wrong. As I distributed the document on procedures, Preus stated that he was not totally agreed with the proposed order or wording of the procedures. I did not respond but explained the procedures and the reasoning behind them at some length. When I had finished, Preus repeated that he did not agree with the order in which the procedures were listed. He said the BoC needed a chronology and a bill of particulars for doing its work on the FFC report. I remained silent. In the course of discussion it became clear that Preus was disavowing the statement of procedures.

BoC member Kurt Biel wanted to know if the BoC should assume that what Preus called a bill of particulars would be forthcoming from him. Preus responded that he would want to talk to the vice-presidents about that but that he had prepared a paper for the BoC's consideration dealing with the basic issues and would like to discuss that document. "There it is," I said to myself, "the reason for the entourage." Apparently Preus had been going through the motions with me when all along he had a different purpose in mind for the BoC meeting. I had been double-crossed.

Finally I spoke. With a sick feeling in my stomach I said that I did not understand what was happening because I had participated in meetings in which Preus and I had come to an agreement on both objectives and procedures. Preus interjected that I had written every word of the objectives and procedures. Although he agreed with me on the objectives, the procedures were unacceptable to him both in wording and in the order of presentation. Again I said I did not understand because that very morning we had agreed on these documents for presentation to the BoC. Late in the afternoon I had agreed to remove the procedure relating to Arlis Ehlen from the list. Looking straight at Roland Wiederaenders, I said, "You were there this morning, Roland. Did we or did we not have an agreement?" Loose declared a recess so that Preus and I and others could consult.

Preus, Wiederaenders, Ahlschwede, and I went to my office down the hall. I was deeply disturbed. Once the door to the office closed, I said, "Jack, you lied." Preus erupted in anger and headed for the door. Wiederaenders calmed him down, but Preus clearly had no intention of pursuing the method of conciliation I had proposed. He had his own plan, and he was working it.

When the meeting resumed, Wiederaenders explained that there had been an agreement between Preus and me. Ahlschwede ventured the opinion that there was much more agreement than disagreement between us. After further futile discussion, the BoC resolved to urge Preus and me to continue to meet with Wiederaenders and Ahlschwede "in an effort to come to an understanding regarding objectives and procedures as soon as possible." Given what had happened, I knew there was no hope for any such meetings.

Then the BoC dealt with what I concluded was the real reason for Preus's presence at the meeting. Preus's supporters among the BoC members were all set for it; they even knew the name of the paper Preus wanted to present. Walter Dissen made the motion, and Vice-President Weber seconded it: "that the Board take up for discussion the paper of President Preus titled A STATEMENT OF SCRIPTURAL AND CONFESSIONAL PRINCIPLES."[31] Preus said the purpose of the document was to give the BoC guidelines for its work of dealing with the FFC report. He claimed that the guidelines were derived directly from the Scriptures and the Lutheran Confessions and summarized the public doctrine of the LCMS as expressed in statements adopted by the Synod.

While presumably agreeing with me on one of the nine conciliation procedures—namely, that the president of the Synod, the BoC, and the CS faculty would mutually agree on the theological principles to be used in discussing doctrinal issues—Preus had now presented unilaterally the principles that were to guide the discussion of issues. In fact, he had submitted a "doctrinal statement" by which to norm the teaching of the faculty even before the Synod in convention had adopted it and even though the Milwaukee convention had refused to declare doctrinal statements binding. Our proposed effort at conciliation was a shambles.

During the rest of its four-day meeting the BoC tried valiantly to get caught up on its responsibilities. It heard a report from CS professor John Damm, author of the proposals of the Theological Education Research Committee, which had major implications for the curriculum and for CS's understanding of its mission. It participated in a presentation by faculty members led by Edgar Krentz on the historical-critical method, one of the issues it had to consider in its review of the FFC report. It dealt with a number of internal problems. It asked me to draw up a list of the issues in the FFC report that needed to be discussed with the faculty.

The BoC also dealt with the consequences of its decision not to renew the contract of Arlis Ehlen. On the issue of whether to give a reason for its decision, the BoC decided to announce publicly that "a majority of the members of the Board of Control with varying individual reasons found the contract renewal of Dr. Arlis Ehlen as a professor not desirable at the time they were obliged to cast their votes."[32] Toward the end of the meeting, the BoC decided to engage Ehlen to teach for one year so that it could include him in its proposed discussion of issues and in its review of the FFC report, an action that infuriated Preus.

The day after the meeting Preus wrote me a letter in my capacity as executive officer of the BoC in which he issued a directive that I "see to it that Doctor Ehlen teaches no course in which he will have opportunity to advocate his higher critical views concerning biblical interpretation, effective at the beginning of the spring quarter of the 1971–72 school year."[33] I sent the letter to the members of the BoC on the assumption that it was intended for them since it was addressed to me as executive officer. In an accompanying letter I stated that the BoC's policies did not make it possible for me to accede to the directive without specific instruction from the BoC. If they wanted to give such instruction, they would have to meet before March 6, the day the spring quarter was to begin.

On March 2 Preus sent me another letter, this time addressed to me in my capacity as CS president. He made it clear that he was reissuing his directive about Ehlen's teaching responsibilities in his constitutional capacity as the one who supervises all employees of the Synod. He insisted on an answer before the beginning of the spring quarter. In a letter sent to Preus on March 5 I informed him that it was not possible for me to do what he asked without further direction from the BoC. In my letter I pointed out contractual problems, practical difficulties, and consequences for accreditation that would flow from obeying his directive.

I stated that Preus's directive would be in order only if Ehlen were teaching or advocating false doctrine in the classroom, and that acting on his directive would raise suspicion concerning Ehlen's doctrinal orthodoxy. I pointed out that Ehlen was eligible for a call anywhere in the Synod and that the BoC would not have decided to reengage him if it had reason to conclude that he taught false doctrine.

Another reason, which I gave in my letter to Preus, subsequently received major attention both in the press and throughout the LCMS. I stated that Ehlen did not teach his courses, as Preus claimed in his letter to me, in order "to advocate his higher critical views concerning biblical interpretation," but in order to "use every exegetical tool at his disposal to assist his students in discovering what God is saying to us in the sacred text." I stated that if by "higher critical views" Preus meant historical-critical method, "then it is not possible for Dr. Ehlen to teach any of his assigned courses at a seminary level of instruction, thus taking the text of the Holy Scriptures with utter seriousness, without using historical-critical methodology." I added, "Nor is that possible for any other faculty member who teaches a course in biblical interpretation, regardless of the department to which he may belong."[34]

Preus was present at the March 20, 1972, meeting of the BoC and read a thirteen-page letter to which six appendices totaling another seventeen pages were attached, in which he made a major issue of my response to his directive. Preus insisted that the BoC should reprove me for my action and require me to fulfill his directive. He had already arranged to have the BHE veto the BoC's decision to offer Ehlen a one-year contract. In the course of the meeting he tried to bargain with the BoC by suggesting that the BHE might be willing to approve the one-year appointment if the BoC would give assurance concerning what Ehlen would and would not teach. Three separate times during the meeting Preus asked the BoC to act in such a way as to comply with his directive to me. The BoC's only response was to decide to meet with Ehlen, "no later than the next Board meeting,"[35] before taking any action.

Actions at the February and March meetings of the BoC set the basic course for the foreseeable future. The CS controversy had reached the point of no return. There would be a collision after all.

Sometime in between the expectation of Armageddon at the January board meeting and the end to the prospects of conciliation at the February board meeting—I do not remember the date—Leonhard Wuerffel invited me to his home for a personal conversation. Wuerffel was dean of students when I was a CS student and had served in that capacity until shortly before I returned as president. He was now CS placement director and was teaching courses in the field of pastoral care and counseling. Stockily built with a squarish head, black hair in a closely cropped crew cut, Wuerffel treated me like a younger brother. At meetings of the FAC, of which he was a member, I sensed him watching me and could feel his concern.

I was no stranger to the Wuerffel home. I had visited there frequently during my student days, enjoying the hospitality of the family. Wuerffel's wife, Margaret, typed my Bachelor of Divinity thesis, which led me to make even more visits to their home. For our personal conversation Wuerffel invited me into his study. Looking at me intently without a trace of a smile, he explained that he was concerned about me and the stress I was experiencing. I laughed and told him that I ran a mile every morning to stay in shape and get rid of frustration. But there was no way to laugh off his concern.

He wanted to know how I felt about getting more than I bargained for in becoming CS president. I told him that I believed God had called me to the position and that I was ready to do whatever God expected of me. But, I added, I was disillusioned about the institutional church and distressed to discover that so many people in high office acted as if the church were just another organization, a corporation whose business was religion. I myself was finding it necessary to work hard to keep functioning as a Christian.

We talked about the distinctions that have to be made between the church as a spiritual communion and the church as an empirical institution, with Wuerffel underscoring the institutional aspect of the church's nature. He was glad to see that I was realistic about the church being a human organization that functions according to the rules and laws that pertain to any human organization. Compromise is a fact of life in any human organization, he wanted me to understand. You may have to compromise in this controversy, he told me. Don't be afraid of compromise, he counseled, and don't feel guilty about it. I told him I didn't have any problem with compromise unless I was expected to compromise people— if the compromise meant that I had to offer people up as scapegoats. I couldn't do that, I said. To me people meant more than institutions.

Wuerffel smiled for the first time and said that offering up scapegoats would do no good in the present circumstances. He said that he had been observing Jacob Preus for some time and was convinced that the man was driven by the need to use power and to exercise control. It would not be enough to offer him the scalps of a few faculty. He wanted control of CS as evidence of his power in the Synod.

Wuerffel's words reminded me of the time during one BoC meeting when I had left the meeting to get something from my office and found

Preus sitting in the chair behind my desk. His face flushing a deep red, Preus stood up and explained that he had just sat down to make a phone call. I told Wuerffel that I knew all about the temptation of power. Like my namesake John, the Son of Thunder among Jesus' disciples, I had to cope with the desire for power myself. If power was the name of the game, I said, I was at a distinct disadvantage. I lacked the instincts and experience to know how to impose it on others. I was convinced that disciples of Jesus were expected to use their lives in serving others, not in ruling over them.

Wuerffel pointed out that it was easy enough to follow Jesus' words about serving instead of ruling if you did not sit in a seat of power. What was really difficult was to give your life in service to others when you occupied a seat of power, as a seminary president did. Your obligation as a disciple was to use the power of the institution in behalf of others and not for yourself or even for the institution.

As our conversation continued, I told Wuerffel that I did not think being a Christian meant that you had to be naive. While we did our best to be as harmless as doves, we had every right to be as wise as serpents. I intended to continue to stand up to Preus's use of power, but I did not intend to fight fire with fire. Mindful of the humanly institutional character of the church, I would try to live by and to foster the church's nature as a spiritual communion of the people of God. Let Preus and his associates grasp for power to advance their cause. I would do my best to do what was right and hope that the people of the church, who would make the ultimate decision, would do the same.

6 ———◆

PREJUDGED

On September 18, 1972, Helen Dietrich, my secretary at Concordia Seminary, knocked on my office door and said that a President Haak wanted to see me. I held out my hand in greeting to Rudolph A. Haak of Springfield, Illinois, president of the Central Illinois District of the Lutheran Church–Missouri Synod. I ushered him over to chairs arranged for conversation in front of an unused fireplace in my oak-paneled office. Set into the mantel were five tiles, each bearing the name and years of service of one of my predecessors in the office of CS president, and on the wall above the mantel hung their portraits, constant reminders of the weighty tradition of responsibility I had inherited.

Haak and I had not had much opportunity to become personally acquainted. Just two years earlier he had been elected president of one of the most conservative districts within the Missouri Synod. Haak was about fifty years of age, not quite six feet tall, of moderate build, and his face showed gentle lines creased by compassion in years of pastoral experience. Haak was in St. Louis to attend a meeting of the Council of Presidents scheduled to begin later that day on the CS campus. Getting quickly to the point, Haak said that at the meeting of the Council of Presidents he wanted to try to find a way through the crisis that was confronting the Missouri Synod in order to prevent impending disaster.

The crisis to which he referred had been precipitated by the publication of two documents within the past several weeks that had exploded like bombshells on the Synod. One document, published under the date of September 1, was a 160-page report from Missouri Synod president Jacob A. O. Preus, based on the report of the Fact Finding Committee, which condemned the faculty of CS for teaching and condoning false doctrine.[1] The second document was a 34-page analysis of Preus's investigation of CS, issued a week later to counter Preus's report, in which I described the FFC report as unfair, unreliable, untrue, less than scriptural, and un-Lutheran.[2]

The Council of Presidents was composed of the presidents of the Missouri Synod's forty districts,[3] the five synodical vice-presidents, and the president of the Synod. The group had its own organization with a chair, Wilbert E. Griesse of Fort Smith, Arkansas, president of the Mid-South District, and with a secretary, Richard L. Schlecht of Ann Arbor, Michigan, president of the Michigan District. The group met several times a year for mutual consultation. Although it had only advisory authority, the Council of Presidents consisted of the chief elected pastors of the Synod, and its recommendations carried considerable weight.

Haak asked me whether CS faculty members would be willing to participate in local forums held in districts throughout the Synod in which the focus of discussion would be their own written confessions of faith formulated in relation to the issues in controversy. I asked Haak why he thought such a course of action would ameliorate the present crisis. He said that we needed to find a method different from the present process of investigation, accusation, and recrimination. We needed to put our trust in the Holy Spirit, he said, and also in the power of the means of grace that are in operation when brethren engage in mutual conversation. He felt it was necessary that the faculty have the opportunity to be heard in their own words and to present and defend what they taught among their peers in the church. The faculty members would learn much from the people of the church, and the people in turn would learn much from the faculty in such free and open discussion.

Although I couldn't imagine that Preus would be in favor of Haak's proposal, I was not going to be the one to discourage it. I told Haak that I felt sure the CS faculty would respond positively. After all, they were claiming that Preus and the FFC had misrepresented them, and they had announced their readiness to speak openly to anyone on the issues in controversy. I told Haak that if the Council of Presidents would see his proposal as a helpful way through the crisis, I felt sure that our faculty would produce the confessions of faith and participate in the forums.

Two days later, I was invited to attend the meeting of the Council of Presidents to participate in the discussion of potential solutions to the crisis. To my amazement, the Council was giving serious consideration to Haak's proposal as a centerpiece of a solution. Several sessions and much discussion later, the Council agreed on an action. The Council had extracted from Preus and me a joint statement, signed by both of us, in which we urged "full and frank discussion of the theological issues that are before the Synod" and declared that in issuing our documents "each of us had the purpose of illuminating the issues that are troubling our Synod and not of engaging in personal recrimination."[4]

The Council resolved that because "the doctrinal position of many of the professors at the Seminary has been called into question," each of the faculty members should be asked to "assure the church of his Biblical and confessional stance by setting forth (in writing), for use in discussion forums, what is believed, taught and confessed, giving special attention to the theological issues in controversy among us today. . . . " In addition the Council urged the seminary Board of Control to continue to follow the procedures of Matthew 18, giving every accused professor a fair hearing in which the accused would have the opportunity to face his accuser and to know specifically what the accusation was. The Council suggested that a "fiduciary committee" consisting of the accused and the accuser, a theologian chosen by each, and a pastoral moderator be the forum for dealing with accusations, and the members of the Council offered to fulfill the pastoral role.

The Council of Presidents thus called for a return to the procedures of Matthew 18, a plea that I had been making ever since Preus announced his investigation. The action envisioned face-to-face discussions between faculty members and the people of the church, which could result in a situation in which some in the church would make accusations of false doctrine against faculty members. The Council's action prescribed a pastoral process for use by the CS BoC in dealing with the accusations.

Under the date of September 21, 1972, Wilbert Griesse sent a letter to all the pastors of the Synod reporting the Council's action. Giving thanks to God for the preservation of unity, the Council's members believed that they had found a way through the crisis in the Synod. Jacob A. O. Preus was a party to the decision, as was I.

The Preus document, partially responsible for the crisis, had a long title: *Report of the Synodical President to the Lutheran Church–Missouri Synod, in Compliance with Resolution 2-28 of the 49th Regular Convention of the Synod, Held at Milwaukee, Wisconsin, July 9–16, 1971.* In view of the title, it is not surprising that the document received a nickname: the "Blue Book," because of the color of its cover. The Preus report was not unanticipated, but few could have predicted what its contents would be. As the full title stated, Preus issued it in compliance with a resolution of the Missouri Synod's 1971 convention. Resolution 2-28 of that convention had required the BoC of CS to report to Preus the results of its review of the FFC report and had required Preus to report the BoC's progress to the membership of the Synod in one year.

The BoC's good intentions of dealing with the FFC report had been thwarted for a time over the issue of contract renewals and the status of faculty member Arlis Ehlen. The BoC was finally able to turn in earnest to the FFC report at its February 1972 meeting. It had determined to isolate issues in the FFC report and to deal in depth with those issues before dealing with faculty members.

At the BoC meeting February 18–21, 1972, Professor Edgar M. Krentz discussed the issue of the historical-critical method. At the March 20, 1972, BoC meeting Professor Robert W. Bertram aided the BoC in considering the nature of confessional commitment. On April 17, 1972, Professor Norman Habel dealt with the relationship of fact and faith in Christian theology. The meeting on May 15, 1972, included a formal debate on the thesis, "A Lutheran theologian may legitimately use historical-critical methodology in interpreting the Scriptures," with Edgar Krentz speaking in the affirmative and Robert Preus in the negative.

Jacob Preus had something more in mind when he talked about getting at the issues. At the February meeting of the BoC Preus had presented "A Statement of Scriptural and Confessional Principles," a document that he said was "not to serve as a new standard of orthodoxy, but rather to assist you in identifying areas which need further attention in terms of the Synod's doctrinal position."[5] Despite his disclaimer, what Preus seemed to have in mind was that the BoC should use the document as a yardstick for assessing whether the positions of individual faculty members as reflected in the transcripts of their FFC interviews were in accord with "the Synod's doctrinal position." Preus said as much in a letter dated March 3, 1972, when he sent "A Statement of Scriptural and Confessional Principles," which he had said was for use by the BoC, to all congregations, pastors, and teachers of the Synod. In his letter Preus raised the question of how the BoC would be able to know whether the position of faculty members "is in complete accord with the Bible and the confessional position of our church as we have been taught it." He explained that he had drawn up "A Statement" so that the BoC would know what the Synod's position was and could use it in carrying out its mandated responsibilities. "The board of control may well request the faculty members of the St. Louis seminary to indicate their stance toward these guidelines," he wrote.

Preus made the point in person at the meeting of the BoC on March 20, 1972. He asked the BoC to use his statement as "guidelines" for assessing the position of the faculty, and he urged the BoC to invite the faculty to state their position in relation to his statement. In a carefully worded motion, the BoC resolved to receive Preus's statement "as guidelines to his assessment of the issues confronting our Synod and as to his understanding of how the issues should be resolved."[6] It asked the faculty to respond to Preus's statement by the April BoC meeting if possible.

"A Statement of Scriptural and Confessional Principles" was a five-page printed document consisting of six sections: Christ as Savior and Lord, Law and Gospel, Mission of the Church, Holy Scripture, Original Sin, and Confessional Subscription. The section on Holy Scripture comprised two-thirds of the material. Each section and subsection began with words to the effect, "We believe, teach, and confess . . . ," implying that what Preus had in mind was a new confessional statement for the LCMS. Each affirmative paragraph was followed by an antithetical paragraph that began with something like, "We therefore reject the following views . . . ." Sixty-two of the sixty-seven antithetical statements were by Preus's own assertion[7] alleged to be descriptions of the teaching of members of the CS faculty.

With the assistance of the Faculty Advisory Committee I organized the faculty for a speedy response to the Preus document. On April 4, 1972, the faculty adopted and published its response.[8] The response was in two sections dealing with the relation of "A Statement" first to CS and then to the Synod.

The faculty denied that the positions rejected in "A Statement" were descriptive of their teaching: "The positions . . . are in most cases not the position of any member of this faculty. In a few cases they are at most caricatures of positions of one or more of our colleagues. But in almost every case the distortion is so severe that it does not represent the actual position of any of us." The faculty response went on to indict "A Statement" as "invalid both as an assessment and as a solution of presumed problems at our Seminary." In the second half of its response the faculty warned the Synod against the "endorsement" that Preus had invited in the final paragraph of "A Statement." The faculty described the document as theologically inadequate with "a spirit alien to Lutheran confessional theology," and it condemned the effort to make binding dogma out of mere theological opinion.

Preus did not take no for an answer. In a letter to the BoC dated April 14, 1972, he expressed disappointment over the faculty response. He wrote that the BoC would need some kind of principle by which to evaluate the faculty, once again urging the use of his "A Statement." "Otherwise," he wrote, "I am frank to say that I do not really know how you are going to proceed. I think it is imperative for you to be able to tell the church in your report exactly what kind of principles you did use in evaluating the position of the faculty." Preus urged the board to ask each member of the faculty to respond individually to "A Statement" and reported that it was his intention to meet with the faculty in the near future.

Preus kept his long-delayed promise of meeting with the faculty, bringing the five synodical vice-presidents and Missouri District president Herman Scherer with him. The meeting took place in the lounge of Pritzlaff Hall on the CS campus on May 17, 1972. In a large room that had once served as the reading room of the CS library, the faculty and the synodical officials sat on sofas and chairs. It was a warm day in St. Louis, and the casement windows were open. By previous agreement between Preus and me there were to be two presentations, the first by Preus to the faculty, the second by Robert Bertram in behalf of the faculty to Preus. Preus and Bertram spoke from a lectern that had been set in front of one of the open windows.

After a lengthy recounting of the history of recent theological problems in the Synod, Preus presented a list of thirteen items that he said "represent a sample of theological issues and doctrinal positions which disturb the church and which are, nevertheless, held by some of the professors of this seminary."[9] Then he presented a series of requests to which he wanted answers in writing. The first request was directed to me and asked that I state whether I was in agreement with any of the thirteen positions in his list and what I had done about ministering to faculty who were in agreement with any of the statements. His major request of the faculty was that by June 1 each faculty member present a response to the positions presented in "A Statement."

Bertram's presentation was in two sections. In the first Bertram detailed the faculty's concern "that you, President Preus, have become simultaneously public judge and public prosecutor, employing the double power both to press the accusations and to determine the verdict."[10] In the second section Bertram summarized the faculty's conviction about the priority of the gospel in the context of Scripture, the Confessions, the Christian community, and CS, and expressed the faculty's desire to discuss that priority with him.

I was simultaneously frightened and amused at the game of hard ball I saw being played. Did Preus think we were going to fall into the trap he laid for us and actually let him use "A Statement" as a yardstick for our teaching? Did he really expect the BoC to find fault with the faculty for refusing to acknowledge positions articulated in "A Statement" as their own, when the BoC was hearing faculty members describe their positions in their own words? Did Preus expect the people of the Synod to think that we held positions we had publicly disowned?

The faculty responded to Preus's requests through action taken at a special meeting on May 30, 1972. In a letter to Preus the faculty stated that to comply with his request that it "show point by point and individually where we agree or disagree" with "A Statement" would be to give the statement "precisely that confessional status as a test of orthodoxy which you say you do not wish it to have."[11] The faculty therefore reiterated the response it had made on April 4. I responded by letter on June 12, 1972, to the request Preus made of me. I said simply that I had "ascertained the positions of individual faculty members and [had] assured myself through personal discussion that members of the faculty [were] not teaching contrary to their confessional commitment."

In the meantime the BoC had asked a committee consisting of William Buege, Charles Burmeister, and Paul Nickel to assist it in drawing up a progress report to fulfill the responsibility laid upon it in Resolution 2-28 of the 1971 convention. At its meeting June 16–17, 1972, the BoC put the finishing touches to the report and sent it on to Preus and to the Board for Higher Education. The report described in detail what the BoC had done to fulfill its responsibilities of dealing with the FFC report and pointed out a number of extenuating circumstances that prevented it from making more progress. After describing the issues that were under consideration, the BoC reported: "A basic issue lies at the root of the issues . . . and comes to the surface again and again no matter what the topic for discussion may be. From one perspective the issue is not doctrine but method. How does a Lutheran theologian carry out the task of interpreting the Scriptures? . . . Looked at from another perspective the issue is very much doctrinal. It is the question of the proper relation between the Scriptures and the Gospel in the task of Scripture interpretation."[12]

The BoC described its plans for dealing with the issues under consideration and for interviewing faculty members. Then came the blockbuster: "In its careful review of the Fact Finding Committee report and in the interviews and discussions held with faculty members the board to this date has found no false doctrine among the members of the seminary faculty. Though unsubstantiated accusations against the faculty as a whole and individual members continue to be made, the board has not been required to deal with any formal charge of false doctrine."

Preus did much more than report to the Synod on the progress of the BoC in its review of the FFC report. In his 160-page BB he made it clear that he had weighed both the CS faculty and the BoC in the balance and found them wanting. The content and format of the book indicated that its publication must have been in the works for a long time. The material was color-coded. Green sections included material of which Preus was explicitly the author. Blue sections consisted of report material, including a long historical introduction and many summaries of the "findings" of the FFC. White sections included many pages of excerpts from the transcripts of the faculty FFC interviews and from the published works of faculty members, which were presented as alleged evidence in support of the FFC's "findings." A six-page table purported to contrast the position of the Synod in one column and the divergent positions held by various members of the faculty in another column. Among the material colored blue, after all the "findings" and the "evidence," way in the back of the book, appeared the report of the BoC.

The names of faculty members were not attached to quotations from their transcripts. Instead faculty members were designated by letters of the alphabet. Because twenty-nine faculty members were quoted, the designations ran from Professor A through all the letters of the alphabet to Professor CC. For example, quotations from my transcript were designated as those of Professor I; Robert Bertram was Professor R; Arthur Carl Piepkorn was Professor J; Robert Smith was Professor H. It did not take faculty members long to figure out what face to attach to each letter.

One paragraph in the long historical introduction is particularly revealing about what was going on in the process of the CS investigation:

> The six topics treated in the *Statement* reflect the major issues discussed in the committee's interviews with the professors. In each of these areas the *Statement* presents a brief summary paragraph which attempts to state what the Synod affirms, as well as a number of short statements expressing views which contradict that position. These antithetical statements include many of the specific concerns about faculty members expressed within the Synod in recent years. They were included in the *Statement* to give the faculty every opportunity to reject any views for which they may have been unjustly criticized. The *Statement* was intended to facilitate the task of the Board of Control as it dealt with the professors on the basis of several hundred pages of interview transcripts. It was shared with the church not only to provide information on which issues were under discussion but to offer guidance in applying Holy Scripture and the Lutheran Confessions to those issues.

In my assessment, the report said that, contrary to the assertion that the investigation was only interested in finding the facts of the faculty's doctrinal position and was making no judgment, the FFC from the outset worked with a construct of the six topics that were later published in "A Statement" and asked its questions of faculty members on the basis of that construct. In fact, the FFC had before it something like the two-column table that appeared in its original report to Preus and then was published in the BB, and faculty members were given opportunities in the interviews to align themselves with positions in one column or the other. The "faculty" column as opposed to the "Synod" column had been drawn up "in several instances" on the basis of "questions and concerns about faculty members expressed within the Synod in recent years." Then the yardstick that was used in gathering the evidence was turned over to the BoC in the form of "A Statement" for it to use in finding the faculty guilty.

To put it bluntly: Before the interviews began, faculty members had been prejudged as guilty. The interviews were designed to give the faculty the opportunity to put their heads in a noose, and through the use of "A Statement" the BoC was supposed to hang them.

The Preus report bluntly contradicted the BoC's progress report: there *was* false doctrine at CS. The BB summarized the charge:

a. A false doctrine of the nature of the Holy Scriptures coupled with methods of interpretation which effectually erode the authority of the Scriptures.
b. A substantial undermining of the confessional doctrine of original sin by *de facto* denial of the historical events on which it is based.
c. A permissiveness toward certain false doctrines.
d. A tendency to deny that the Law is a normative guide for Christian behavior.
e. A conditional acceptance of the Lutheran Confessions.
f. A strong claim that the Seminary faculty need not teach in accord with the Synod's doctrinal stance as expressed in the Synod's official doctrinal statements and resolutions.[13]

Five of the six accusations are really about alleged attitudes or tendencies, which Preus and his supporters might find distressing but which surely do not qualify as false doctrine in the traditional understanding of the phrase. Only the first of the six accusations specifies a charge of false doctrine, namely, concerning the nature of the Holy Scripture. That charge is developed at great length, and most of the material in the BB is devoted to it.

What was the faculty's false doctrine concerning "the nature of the Holy Scriptures"? The BB puts it this way:

Within the faculty the doctrine of the Holy Scriptures is subverted to the point where, in effect, a false doctrine is proclaimed regarding them. The faculty does indeed proclaim its allegiance to the Scriptures as the primary norm of Christian doctrine. However, in fact, the majority hold a view of the Scriptures which in practice erodes the authority of Holy Writ. Verbal inspiration, as it is commonly understood in the Synod, is not taught by all. The inerrancy of the Scriptures is severely limited. The Gospel (the primary teaching of the Scripture) is regarded as virtually exclusively normative in such a way as to detract from the normative authority of the whole Scripture. This is sometimes called "Gospel Reductionism."[14]

On the basis of such words, many careful readers of the BB had a difficult time understanding what was the faculty's false doctrine concerning the nature of the Scripture. From Preus's point of view it was false doctrine not to repeat the formulas about verbal inspiration and inerrancy as they were "commonly understood in the Synod." It was false doctrine to refuse to accept an understanding of the Scripture's authority separated from its gospel content. The basic accusation is broken out in detail in twenty-six sections filling a hundred pages in the BB, covering topics such as inerrancy, authority, miracles, prophecy, and authorship of biblical books. In each case the "findings" are summarized to show the disagreement between the position of the faculty and the Synod, and then quotations from faculty transcripts and publications are presented as evidence. No effort is made to link the evidence material to what the "findings" say about it. It is simply assumed that the material is self-evident proof of what the "findings" section states.

In a concluding section of the BB[15] Preus took on CS and revealed his expectations for the future. First he devoted almost a page to explaining why he as president of the Synod was exempt from following the procedure prescribed in Matthew 18. Then he criticized the CS BoC, the faculty, and me for not using "A Statement" for the purpose for which he had issued it. Then he faulted the BoC for submitting a progress report instead of completing its work on the FFC report. Charging that "some professors at the Seminary hold views contrary to the established doctrinal position of the Synod," Preus insisted that the BoC should remove those professors from their teaching positions. He asked the BoC to complete its work on the investigation by February 1 so that he could include it in his report to the Synod. Preus's next words were ominous: "The convention will then decide whether the action of the Seminary Board of Control is satisfactory or, if not, prescribe whatever action the convention determines proper and appropriate."

Turning his attention to me, Preus charged that I had failed to carry out my office because I had been present at all the faculty interviews and had not done anything about the false doctrine revealed in those interviews. He demanded that the BoC deal with me "personally and first of all" as to my confessional stance and my "failure to exercise the supervision of the doctrine of the faculty as prescribed in the synodical *Handbook.*"

None of us at CS could have imagined the contents of the BB. By its publication Preus demonstrated publicly that, as Bertram had told him in his meeting with the faculty on May 17, 1972, Preus had taken on the role of both prosecutor and judge. We realized full well that for us the BB was a disaster. Its size, its color-coded pages, its many quotations from transcripts and publications gave the appearance that there was weight and validity in the contents. We knew that only a few people in the Synod would bother to read it and that fewer still would take the trouble to see if the supposed evidence presented in quotations and publications did in fact support the assertions made in the "findings." We knew that few people would actually read the "findings." The *conclusion* was what everyone would understand. Through his investigation Preus had found the whole faculty guilty of false doctrine.

As we read the BB, stunned by its contents, at a loss to know what to do, Herbert J. A. Bouman stopped by my office. Tall, somewhat stoop-shouldered, with graying hair and a trim gray mustache, the soft-spoken Bouman had been professor of systematic theology at CS since 1954. He was always ready to tell people how the responsibility given him by CS to teach the Lutheran Confessions had moved him away from the legalisms of his past to a full appreciation of the centrality and sufficiency of the gospel. Bouman had come to share with me a quotation from the Lutheran Confessions for my encouragement. The quotation was from the Apology of the Augsburg Confession: "The saying is certainly true that there is no defense against the attacks of slanderers. Nothing can be said so carefully that it can avoid misrepresentation."[16]

We of the CS faculty considered the BB to be outrageous slander. How could we defend ourselves? We needed to counter the Preus attack immediately. We could not afford to spend weeks analyzing Preus's report and securing full faculty agreement for a response.

In my desk drawer lay a document I had prepared several months earlier. It was a full response to the FFC report. I had secured from the BoC permission to share the FFC report with five or six members of the faculty for the purpose of receiving their assistance in drawing up a response. I had intended to present the response to the BoC and to make the response public if the FFC report was released to the Synod.

During my Crest House conversation with Preus,[17] which I had assumed was for the purpose of working out a compromise, I told him that I had produced the response but was reluctant to use it if there could be another way through the controversy. Although there was to be no compromise, the BoC's preoccupation with the problem relating to the contract of Arlis Ehlen and the BoC's determination to deal with faculty members in discussion of major issues raised by the investigation led me to keep my response in my desk drawer.

Preus remembered what I had told him and twice asked me to share my response with him,[18] but I did not want to interfere with the BoC's efforts in dealing with the FFC report and in making a progress report to the synod. I told Preus so in declining to share my response. Frankly, I also did not want Preus to know what I had in reserve should he decide to publish the FFC report.

The response I had produced dealt with the FFC report, not with the BB. Yet the BB was based on the FFC report, included major portions of it, and repeated its basic "findings" in a rearranged form. After intense discussion the FAC and I decided that we should publish my report as an analysis of the investigation that had led to the publication of the BB and immediately undertake writing a response to the BB itself.

Within a week's time, through the hard work of our communications director, Larry Neeb, we published my thirty-five-page response under the title: *Fact Finding or Fault Finding? An Analysis of President J. A. O. Preus' Investigation of Concordia Seminary.* The publication was mailed to all the clergy of the Synod together with an accompanying letter from me and a declaration of the faculty, adopted September 12, 1972, repudiating the BB. *Fact Finding or Fault Finding?* delivered its blows without kid gloves. I presented the conclusions up front:

1. The fact finding process was conceived in a prejudgment that has shaped the inquiry, predetermined its results, and subjected the seminary to treatment that is *unfair.*
2. The procedures employed by the Fact Finding Committee have produced results that are *unreliable.*
3. The Report is a strange blend of half-truths, misunderstandings, and distortions which make the profile it presents *untrue.*
4. The views of Scripture interpretation which lie behind the investigation and shape its results are *less than Scriptural.*
5. The theology which lies behind the inquiry and the Report, by whose standard the theology of the faculty was measured, is *un-Lutheran.*[19]

Major sections of the response were devoted to providing evidence in support of these five assertions. Edgar Krentz wrote the section dealing with the concept of the Scripture that lay behind the investigation. Robert Bertram produced the section taking issue with the theology behind the report. I wrote the rest of the material. The second half of the document was a detailed analysis of the FFC report section by section and concluded with responses from those who had assisted me in dealing with the report, in which they criticized how the FFC report had dealt with their positions as stated in the interviews.

In my letter accompanying *Fact Finding or Fault Finding?* I pleaded for a "return to the fraternal relations for assuring doctrinal fidelity that have characterized our Synod throughout its history." I pointed out that the Preus investigation had circumvented long-established means to ensure soundness of doctrine. "In his report on the seminary," I wrote, "President Preus has presented allegations about faculty members without saying who they are, without first having brought his concerns to those faculty members individually, and without even inquiring whether he has understood them correctly." I stated that Preus had in effect taken away from the BoC the jurisdiction over the FFC report that the 1971 Synod convention had given it. I pointed out that Preus had "accused us of false doctrine in a way that completely ignores the due process procedures designed to protect us all from malicious slander." I asked, "Do we really want to exchange our evangelical way of dealing with one another under the supervision of elected boards and officials for a new procedure that avoids brotherly confrontation and discussion and counts on votes for a resolution?"

"No," the Council of Presidents seemed to say as a result of the efforts of Central Illinois District president Rudolph Haak during its meeting on the CS campus September 18–21, 1972. As reported, the Council of Presidents urged face-to-face meetings between the faculty and the members of the Synod on the basis of confessions of faith prepared by members of the faculty; urged the BoC to continue to insist on the procedures of Matthew 18; and offered the services of members of the Council of Presidents in the process of dealing with formal charges of false doctrine against individual faculty members.

Less than a week later, on September 26, 1972, Haak met with the CS faculty to urge a positive response to the action of the Council of Presidents. The faculty asked the FAC to propose a response to the request of the Council of Presidents. At a meeting on October 5 the faculty approved the committee's recommendation, thanking the Council of Presidents "for the pastoral and evangelical course of action recommended in its resolution." They accepted the invitation that the faculty should, "both corporately and as individuals," set down its faith in writing for use in discussion forums "in order to edify and unify the church," and agreed that their material should be ready for consideration by the Council of Presidents at its next meeting in November.[20]

Haak worked hard to enact the Council of Presidents' proposal. In a letter to Council chair Wilbert Griesse he reported the faculty's favorable response and urged that faculty members be invited "into our districts to meet with circuit pastors or with other small groupings." In a letter to Griesse and Council program committee chair Carl Heckmann, president of the Texas District, Haak proposed that the Council follow through on its desire to discuss the issues by inviting the CS faculty to make presentations at the Council's November meeting on historical criticism and on the relation of the gospel and Scripture.[21]

Were we really going to embark on a new solution to the controversy? In the meetings the Council had called for between Preus and me, with Roland Wiederaenders serving as moderator and mediator, I raised the issue of the significance of the Council of Presidents' action. Preus made it clear that he had no intention of changing his course.

The first of these meetings was held in Preus's office on October 12, 1972. Preus stated that he was pleased with the adoption of the Haak proposal because it was a compromise. He said that the specific wording of the proposal was not important; what was important was not *what* happened but *that* it happened, namely that the Council of Presidents felt that it had taken a significant step to cool things down. Preus emphasized that no action of the Council of Presidents could interfere with his exercise of his responsibilities and that he intended to fulfill those responsibilities. Pointing out that no one believed Adolf Hitler when he wrote of his intentions in *Mein Kampf*, Preus said that people could trust him to do exactly what he said he would do. It was his intention, he said, to get everything settled before or during the 1973 Missouri Synod convention.

The subject of Haak's proposal came up again at our next meeting, held in my office on October 20, 1972. Preus mentioned Haak's suggestion concerning a program for the next meeting of the Council of Presidents involving presentations by CS faculty members. Preus said that such a proposal was simply turning back to the way things were before 1969 and was therefore completely unworkable.

Haak and Preus held a long telephone conversation on the evening of October 26, 1972 (I do not know who initiated the call). The next day Preus summarized in a letter what he had said to Haak.[22] He said that Haak's commission from the Council of Presidents to meet with the faculty had already been discharged: "Any continuing meeting by you with faculty groups was not in the original commission by the Council of Presidents." Preus pointed out that the Council could not interfere with the constitutional responsibilities of those already involved in dealing with the CS matter. "Hence I indicated to you," Preus wrote Haak, "that publication of the individual statements by faculty members, distribution to the circuits, and discussion there by faculty members would short-circuit the proper synodical procedure. Therefore the statements should be given to the Board of Control and thence to the synodical President before any further use is made of them."

Haak also wrote to Preus the day after their telephone conversation, an anguished three-page letter.[23] Haak wrote:

I am not really surprised, but I am disappointed, that you chose to discourage my personal discussion of their faith confessions with members of the faculty. Validity for this and responsibility to perform this are not derived from a resolution of the Council of Presidents nor from the Synod's president, but from the Lord of both. There is no "appropriate" or "out of season" time to do this but it is always in order and *urgent* (2 Tim. 4:1–2). . . . To curtail or stop this activity again reduces our work to human strategy in carrying out a kind of "game" over which we must have control. Do we no longer believe that the Spirit of God is active in Christian witness, in confession, absolution, and correcting activities? What about the Word as a power of God? . . . I favor (heavily) the Lord's strategy.

After expressing his disappointment that his program proposal for the next meeting of the Council of Presidents had been rejected, Haak wrote that he could not remember what Preus had told him to do with the faculty's written confessions of faith:

Please count on me to do nothing. The chief reason is that I have no authority to say what should be done. Secondly, I feel that there need be no "watch-dog" restrictions placed upon them. If they choose to tell anyone in the church what they believe, praise the Lord! If what they say is right, praise the Lord! If what they say is wrong, then we correct them, praise the Lord! So I beg of you to have me excused from whatever it was that I should do. . . .

Other than this one thing, our phone conversation as I remember it last evening stands. I shall not be seen among the Seminary faculty except for authorized reasons. Having said what I did in the earlier paragraphs, I don't see how I can do you a greater honor. In fact, sound logic (in case you have missed it) tells me that I have placed you above God. I confess that I will have to think about this some more.

The proposal of the Council of Presidents initiated by Haak was doomed. Yet the action stood, and the CS faculty had to follow through on their agreement to produce confessions of faith. Indeed the faculty wanted to do so. The Council had given us another opportunity to show "how Lutheran we are" and "what it really means to be Lutheran."

Under the date of November 22, 1972, just prior to the November meeting of the Council of Presidents, I informed the Council by letter that the faculty had finished its work and had completed the individually written statements of faith that the Council had asked them to produce. I stated that in addition the faculty had approved for presentation to the church a document entitled "Affirmations of Faith and Discussion of Issues," in which the faculty's affirmations of faith were explicated in sections that dealt with nine issues intended for discussion in the Synod.

The faculty document was a group effort, produced by the FAC and reflecting the position of the faculty as a whole. Yet there was a primary author, Norman Habel, professor of exegetical theology, whose essays on the Genesis accounts of the creation and the fall had produced controversy within the Council of Presidents and in pastoral conferences some years earlier. An Australian by birth, physically lithe and wiry with a thin face and piercing eyes, Habel had creative genius as poet, storyteller, and communicator and was therefore chosen by the FAC to help produce the faculty's common witness.

The "Affirmations of Faith" section consisted of ten statements of faith that were developed into paragraphs and grouped in three sections similar to the three articles in the Nicene Creed. The purpose of the affirmations was to provide a proper grounding for the subsequent discussion of controversial issues. The faculty did not want to plunge into a consideration of the issues without expressing the context of faith within which the issues needed to be discussed.

The "Discussions of Issues" section included material for dealing with nine issues confronting the LCMS. The issues were framed in the ways the faculty wanted to discuss them, but they came to grips with the areas of controversy raised by the FFC. They included such topics as the account of creation, humanity's fall into sin, miracles, prophecies, gospel and Scripture, the Holy Spirit in relation to the Scripture and the church, and more.

At its November meeting the Council of Presidents asked for copies of the faculty statements. Larry Neeb, CS communications director, arranged to have them published in two volumes under a single title (which he supplied), *Faithful to Our Calling, Faithful to Our Lord.* Volume 1 presented the faculty's united confession of faith and the nine issues for discussion. Volume 2 consisted of the individual confessions of faith of forty-six members of the faculty. We sent the two volumes to the Council of Presidents and to all the pastors of the Synod.

The Council of Presidents never arranged discussion forums throughout the Synod for faculty members to talk about the theological issues in controversy. Although in September 1972 Preus was happy for the "compromise," by November it appeared that there would be no program of discussion forums. Less than two years later, Rudolph Haak was defeated for reelection as president of the Synod's Central Illinois District.

The meetings between Preus and me under the pastoral care of Roland Wiederaenders got nowhere. After the meetings on October 12 and 20 we met one more time, on November 13. My goal in the meetings was to work out a compromise, and so I kept pressing Preus for "terms of a settlement." In response to his *Mein Kampf* reference, I told him that I believed him about his intentions for the impending convention in New Orleans and wanted to know if we could not find another way through the problem.

In our meeting on October 20 Preus said there were several things I could do to help bring about a settlement: I could show the church that I was really dealing with the problems about which the people in the church were concerned. He said that he knew of a small church body in which a problem between the seminary and the synod had been solved by the seminary president's firing a couple of professors and replacing them with people more to the synod's liking. Preus told me that I could do the same. He said that it was essential that I understood one thing clearly: There were two irreconcilable theologies in the Synod, and the New Orleans convention was going to have to choose one and reject the other.

Preus's goal for our meetings was to produce a clear formulation of the issues. He insisted that the two of us needed to bring in others from our respective groups in order to define the issues. I refused to do so. I concluded that he was counting on our meetings to be the means by which to define the "two theologies" that were present in the Synod. In other words, I was supposed to help him in his program of showing the Synod that it had to choose between two irreconcilable approaches.[24]

For the 1972–73 academic year there was a changing of the administrative guard at CS. Arthur C. Repp, who had served first as academic dean and then as vice-president for academic affairs for two decades, reached sixty-five, the mandatory retirement age for school administrators. I decided to keep the position of vice-president for academic affairs vacant for the time being. I rearranged the administrative responsibilities in academic affairs and appointed John S. Damm as academic dean. Damm was the logical choice because of his work with the Theological Education Research Committee. Our close friendship proved to be a bonus during a time of intense conflict. Like the other three chief administrators—Kenneth Breimeier in student affairs, Robert Grunow in seminary relations, and William Krato in business management—Damm tried to manage all but major issues so that I could deal with the larger problems resulting from the Preus investigation. CS was blessed with competent and dedicated administrators who saw to it that we functioned effectively as a seminary while we tried to defend ourselves from attack.

The paper war between Preus and CS had its ugly consequences. We began to receive hate phone calls at home, and Ernestine had to invoke a rule that only she would answer the phone in order to spare our children the abuse at the other end of the line. My family accompanied me when I agreed to speak to a Bible class in a church in north St. Louis. After listening for a while, my eleven-year-old daughter, Mary, wanted to know why some of the people were so angry with me.

In our weekly meetings in my office Damm and I stuck closely to the business of academic affairs, only rarely digressing to talk about the controversy. On one occasion, when the heat of the conflict was particularly intense, I needed to talk about what was happening. I told Damm that I thought it was ironic that I should be involved as a major protagonist in a church conflict. As a student studying the Reformation period of church history, I had been convinced that Martin Luther was too polemic and preferred the more irenic Philip Melanchthon. As a parish pastor I had tried to be a reconciler, pouring oil on troubled waters in families and in the congregation. Now I was carrying the flag and leading the CS troops into battle.

Damm knew that there was more on my mind and helped me express it. I told him that I now understood from experience the truth of Lord Acton's famous saying, "Power tends to corrupt; absolute power corrupts absolutely." There is no way to use power without being corrupted by it. There is no way for the church to be a human institution without being involved in sin, and that makes it difficult for the empirical church to express what it means to be a spiritual communion. In spite of my best intentions not to do so, I was fighting fire with fire. We had no choice but to counter Preus's BB with a publication of our own. Look at the disastrous consequences for the life of the church, I said. Yet what else could we do? Should we refuse to defend ourselves from unjust attacks?

Damm reminded me of my statement that the controversy would be a learning experience for the people of the LCMS, helping them to grow in their understanding of what it means to be Lutheran. He said that if the conflict did have such a result, it would, like the Reformation itself, be worthwhile. He told me that the faculty was deeply grateful for my leadership.

I told Damm that I had been haunted by the words of T. S. Eliot in *Murder in the Cathedral* ever since I first heard them:

> The last temptation is the greatest treason:
> To do the right deed for the wrong reason.

It's not enough to do the right deed, I said. The motive has to be right, too. How can you stay a Christian in the midst of conflict, I asked rhetorically. In the midst of conflict, even if you think the deed is right, how can you keep your heart pure from anger or pride, from self-righteousness or the desire for revenge? I struggle with God every day to know what the right deed is and to do it for the right reason, I told Damm, but I have no way of knowing whether I am doing the will of God.

Damm reflected on what I said and then reminded me of Martin Luther's counsel when action is necessary and you cannot be sure whether your intended action is in accord with the will of God. *Pecca fortiter*, Luther said: "Sin boldly." Trust that the grace of God is all-embracing enough to cover your action even if it is contrary to God's will. You don't have to justify yourself, Damm told me; God has already done that in Christ.

7 ———◆

VERDICT

The day of decision had arrived. January 15, 1973, was a gray and overcast day in St. Louis. A biting wind and the damp winter air put a chill in your bones. This was the day the Board of Control of Concordia Seminary in St. Louis had decided to complete the action that had been mandated by the 1971 convention of the Lutheran Church–Missouri Synod. Resolution 2-28 of that convention had instructed the BoC "to take appropriate action" concerning the CS faculty on the basis of a report of a Fact Finding Committee appointed by Synod president Jacob A. O. Preus, "commending or correcting" the individual members of the faculty.

The temperature inside the board room of Pieper Hall on the CS campus was warm enough to elicit beads of perspiration on my upper lip. Perhaps it was not the temperature. The atmosphere in the room was so tense that all speech sounded shrill and stretched. Ever since the investigation had begun, I had insisted that the only properly constituted authority to render a judgment about the faculty was the BoC. Now the time for judgment had come. The BoC would have to decide whether to "commend" or "correct" the faculty—and me among them.

It was 1:30 P.M. The meeting had begun at 8:25 A.M. in executive session. One after another, six faculty members had appeared to answer questions put to them by BoC members concerning their doctrinal position on one or more issues that had surfaced in the course of the investigation. The six were the last of the twenty-nine faculty members that the BoC had felt it necessary to interview. At noon the BoC recessed for lunch, dividing into four standing committees to meet with CS administrators concerning the

121

seminary's regular work. At 1:00 P.M. the BoC members were back in executive session and quickly concluded the last of the six faculty interviews.

Seated at the head of the table, farthest from the room's entrance and framed by a lancet window, was the chair of the BoC, George Loose, pastor of a congregation in Pompano Beach, Florida. His suntanned face wore an almost perpetual smile under wavy golden hair carefully set in place. The remaining BoC members sat five on one side of the table, five on the other, and I sat at the foot of the table closest to the door.

To Loose's right sat August Beckemeier, St. Louis attorney, dressed in a pinstriped suit, wearing rimless glasses, squinting whenever he had something to say. He rested his left arm on the table as he looked down the length of the table toward the door. Next to him sat Kurt Biel, pastor of a congregation in Orlando, Florida, former district president, his thick shock of red hair turning gray, his freckles showing through his Florida tan. Next came Eugene Fincke, vice-president of a major St. Louis bank, leaning back in his chair, wearing a dark blue suit that highlighted the whiteness of his wavy, combed-back hair. To Fincke's right sat Erwin Roschke, a corporate executive from Chicago, nearly bald, wearing a gray suit, a slight smile formed on his lips. Closest to me sat Edwin Weber, third vice-president of the Synod and Preus's representative on the BoC, leaning forward with both arms resting on the table, his hair cropped short on a head that seemed to merge, neckless, into huge shoulders.

To Loose's left sat William Buege, pastor of a congregation in a St. Louis suburb and vice-chair of the board, his bald head and cherubic face topping a large frame clothed in clerical black. Next to Buege was Paul Nickel, teacher and principal in a Lutheran parochial school in a St. Louis suburb, toying with pencil and paper, wearing a brown suit, his wavy brown hair neatly combed. To Nickel's left sat the board's secretary, Walter Dissen, an attorney from North Olmsted, Ohio, wearing a navy-blue suit, his thin face dominated by a pointy nose, all his materials for the meeting laid out in stacks in front of him. Next came Herman Scherer, member of the BoC by virtue of his office as president of the Missouri District, short in stature, his thinning gray hair combed back, his hands folded in his lap. To my right was the board's treasurer, Charles Burmeister, St. Louis investment counselor, leaning back in his chair to take in the whole scene, his thick graying hair arranged in pompadour fashion.

The meeting was already in progress when Fincke and then Beckemeier arrived. Both had missed the morning session. Walter Dissen had made a motion to bar me from any portion of the meeting in which the BoC would deliberate on whether to commend or correct the faculty, on the grounds that I had an interest in the outcome of their decision. Loose ruled the motion out of order, stating that as the BoC's executive officer

I was entitled to be present and needed to be present so that I could be properly informed in order to implement the BoC's actions. Dissen appealed the chair's ruling. By a voice vote the ruling was sustained.

Charles Burmeister then moved "That each Board member submit in writing this personal commendation or correction on each member of the faculty." But the BoC as a whole was not satisfied with his proposal nor with an amendment to it. Paul Nickel's motion established the procedure to be followed: "That the Board consider each professor individually and vote on commending or correcting by ballot."[1]

The BoC then turned its attention to what it meant when it took action to "commend" or to "correct." "By consensus it was established that to commend was equivalent to stating that a professor was not guilty of false doctrine but was teaching in accord with the Scriptures and the Confessions. To correct was the equivalent of saying that a professor was not teaching in accord with the Scriptures and the Confessions and was therefore open to the charge of false doctrine." The BoC decided that, in instances in which it voted to "correct" an individual faculty member, it would then specify the false doctrine with which the faculty member was charged.

What was the BoC's understanding of doctrine that could be judged true or false? A year before, Preus had urged the BoC to use his "A Statement of Scriptural and Confessional Principles" as guidelines for assessing the faculty and had told the BoC that it had better be ready to tell the Synod what principle it had used to distinguish truth from error. August Beckemeier moved "That the Board's understanding of 'Doctrine' is that as reflected in the document titled, *Report of the Commission on Theology and Church Relations, A Review of the Question, 'What Is a Doctrine?'*" That document had been produced by the Commission on Theology and Church Relations before Preus was elected president of the Synod and had been approved and commended to members at the Synod's 1969 convention. Beckemeier's motion carried.

The BoC was moving closer to its time of decision, but it was still not ready. Kurt Biel proposed that they not vote on whether to commend or correct Arlis Ehlen, Walter Bartling, and Carl Meyer; the BoC agreed. Ehlen was technically no longer a member of the faculty, although he was still on the campus and receiving salary. Bartling had left the campus to accept a position as an institutional chaplain in Atlanta. Carl Meyer had died of a heart attack a month earlier. Dissen proposed that the BoC not vote on H. Lucille Hager, director of the CS library, because she had not been interviewed by the FFC. The BoC agreed.

There was one more motion. The BoC agreed with Herman Scherer's proposal "That the results of the balloting on whether to commend or correct appear in the protocol copy of the minutes and be made available to Synodical President J. A. O. Preus." Not even the faculty was to learn the individual vote totals. Around 3:00 P.M. the BoC began to discuss faculty members one by one, proceeding in alphabetical order, in each case concluding its discussion with a written ballot to commend or to correct.

◆ ◆ ◆

The BoC's action to commend or correct faculty members was the culmination of a process that began in September 1971, when the BoC received the report of Preus's FFC. The BoC spent many hours in several meetings coming to grips with the issues raised in that report. In September 1972 it began the process of interviewing individual faculty members.

A month earlier, at a rare August meeting, the BoC resolved to begin its interviews with Arthur Carl Piepkorn and to request him "to make a presentation on the subject of inerrancy."[2] The proposal to do so was initiated by Charles Burmeister and Eugene Fincke, both supporters of Preus's goals in the investigation. I was perplexed by what seemed to me an unwise decision on their part. Piepkorn had argued in writing against the use of the term *inerrancy*. Perhaps they wanted to establish at the outset of the interviews that CS faculty members were opposed to the "traditional" position of the Missouri Synod.

Piepkorn was graduate professor of systematic theology, a senior member of the faculty who had been teaching at CS since 1952. At the time of his election, rumor had it that then-CS president Louis J. Sieck outmaneuvered Missouri Synod president John W. Behnken when Sieck arranged to call Piepkorn to CS while Behnken was in Europe. Ramrod erect with close-cropped hair, Piepkorn exhibited his military training. He had been on active duty as an army chaplain from 1940 to 1951: senior chaplain of the U.S. occupational forces in Germany in 1945; commandant of the Chaplain School in Pennsylvania from 1948 to 1950; and president of the Chaplain Board when he retired from active duty as a colonel in 1951.

Always dressed publicly in clerical garb, his kindly thin face with the demeanor of an ascetic, bespectacled, Piepkorn expected the best from himself and his students. Like a Renaissance man, he knew a great deal about almost everything. His scholarship was legendary. Everything he wrote was documented with extensive footnotes. When Oliver Harms succeeded Behnken as Missouri Synod president, Piepkorn was appointed as one of the participants to help launch the Lutheran-Catholic dialogue and had a profound influence on them.

Through his classroom teaching Piepkorn helped shape the confessional understanding of a generation of students. He was always available to students, who admired him and called him "Father Arthur Carl" or "the Pieps." He taught me in my last (his second) year at CS, and I count him as one of the three or four teachers who were of major influence in the development of my theology. From him I gained an appreciation for a Lutheran evangelical-confessional identity within a catholic and ecumenical context. As a seminary president I could not have wanted a better theologian for the BoC to interview in initiating its theological discussions with individual faculty members.

The interview with Piepkorn took up two-and-one-half hours on the afternoon of September 18, 1972. All BoC members except Erwin Roschke were present. I moved over from my customary place so that Piepkorn could have ample room for his materials at the foot of the table. BoC members had before them a number of documents. One was the thirty-one-page corrected typescript of Piepkorn's interview before the FFC. Another was the eleven-page summary of the interview prepared by the FFC. A third was a fifteen-page response to the summary that Piepkorn had submitted to the BoC a year earlier along with eight attachments totaling another thirty-four pages. Still another document was Piepkorn's previously published sixteen-page article on inerrancy.[3] Also under consideration were the eight quotations from Piepkorn's transcript and published works in Preus's *Report of the Synodical President*, the so-called Blue Book. In the course of the meeting Piepkorn distributed a thirteen-page typescript of his statement on inerrancy and a five-page response to the use of his transcript and published works in the BB.[4]

In his presentation to the BoC Piepkorn stated that the words "inerrant" and "inerrancy" have been applied to Scripture relatively recently and do not occur in the Lutheran symbolical books or in the Scriptures themselves. He explained that some Lutherans in the nineteenth and twentieth centuries had insisted on the use of the terms to conserve Lutheran orthodoxy's doctrine of the truthfulness of the Scriptures. Piepkorn's basic thesis was that we should avoid applying these words to the Scriptures because the terms are not useful for communicating what Lutherans must say about the Scriptures. Piepkorn quoted from a work by Robert Preus, a strong proponent of the use of the word inerrancy, to show that the term has to be hedged about with so many qualifications as to render it meaningless and not useful in describing what must be said about the Scriptures. In his characteristically scholarly fashion, Piepkorn gave innumerable illustrations from the Scriptures to document the point that the qualities of the Scriptures do not include great precision in formulation, stenographic fidelity in reporting exact words, prosaic literalism in interpretation, bibliographically accurate citations of author and title, comprehensive documentation, carefully harmonized chronologies, a modern historiographic sense, consistent adjustment of sources to one another, and meticulously exact descriptions of attendant historical, physical, and other scientific details.

Piepkorn stressed three points. First, "The church correctly . . . affirms that the sacred scriptures are true. This much it must say; more it cannot say." Second, we must be clear on the purpose for which God gave the Scripture, not "to satisfy our curiosity . . . or to give us information about the subject matter of secular disciplines," but "to enlighten us in our native darkness about himself and about his saving purpose for human beings; to create and establish in us faith in Christ as God's son; to provide us with instruction . . . ; to give us the right mindset . . . ; to provide our hope with encouragement. . . ." Third, as we try to understand the purpose of an author or a passage, we should recognize our own limitations and "not expect or demand complete agreement in method or in results."[5]

In the discussion that followed, Piepkorn explained the reason he believed what he said in his interview and what he wrote in his published works as they were quoted in the BB. He faulted the FFC, in its summary of his transcript, for not understanding his words, for distorting his position, for putting words in his mouth, and for a selection of sentences that was tendentious. In response to a question about the assertion in the "Brief Statement"[6] in support of inerrancy, Piepkorn declared that the subscription he made at his ordination did not include that document but that he recognized himself as bound to the Scriptures and the Lutheran Confessions.

After the interview ended and Piepkorn was excused, the BoC spent about ten minutes discussing what it had heard. William Buege made the motion, and the BoC adopted it: "That in accord with Resolution 2-28 the Board of Control, having interviewed Dr. Piepkorn this day and having reviewed the Fact Finding Report materials concerning him, go on record as commending Dr. Piepkorn for his confession of faith made this day as being in accord with the Scriptures and the Lutheran Confessions and declare that it is satisfied with his explanation of his doctrinal position."[7] By common consent it was agreed that the BoC's action should be reported to Preus and to the Synod's Board for Higher Education.

I was happy with the BoC's decision. Was this a sign of things to come? What would happen when the BoC had to deal with less articulate and less experienced responders?

Encouraged by the results of its interview with Piepkorn, the BoC decided to meet for two days in October to interview me and six members of the faculty: Kenneth Breimeier, Frederick Danker, Everett Kalin, Herbert Mayer, Arthur Repp, and Alfred Sauer. The BoC had already interviewed me for a total of four hours a year earlier. The decision to interview me again was occasioned by Preus's insistence in the BB that the BoC "deal personally and first of all" with me as to my confessional stance and my alleged failure to exercise supervision of doctrine at CS.

The seven interviews took place at the BoC meeting October 15–16, 1972. A month before, following the interview with Piepkorn, the BoC had acted immediately to commend or correct him, but it did not continue that practice following the subsequent interviews. After each interview there was discussion about what procedure to follow, but no action was taken.

Two letters from Preus occupied the BoC's attention at the October meeting. A month before, Preus had asked the BoC what it intended to do about his instructions in the BB regarding unnamed professors whose positions Preus had declared contrary to the established doctrinal position of the Synod and regarding me for not disciplining such professors. The BoC had responded by stating simply that "the Board will proceed under Milwaukee Resolution 2-28."[8] In a letter of September 25, 1972, Preus repeated his question and said the BoC's answer was ambiguous. He wanted to know whether the BoC was going to require me to carry out the duties of my office. He asked, "Is the Board going to permit the kind of teachings indicated in my report to the church to continue to be taught at the Seminary?" In a letter of October 10, 1972, Preus responded to the BoC's action concerning Piepkorn. Piepkorn was "Professor J" in Preus's report to the Synod, he said, and he wanted to know if Piepkorn had retracted the statements quoted in the report.

The BoC decided to respond "by respectfully informing [President Preus] that it has taken account of his concerns and is seeking to meet them, that it is in the process of interviewing members of the faculty and President Tietjen in accord with its responsibilities under Milwaukee Resolution 2-28, that it will present a further report on its progress in taking action on the basis of the Fact Finding Report, and that it will at that time present more detailed information on its action concerning Dr. Piepkorn as requested by President Preus."[9]

In his letter of October 10 Preus had also renewed his request to make tape recordings of the interviews. Walter Dissen made the motion to do so at the October BoC meeting, but the BoC decided otherwise. Instead, so that there could be a record of each interview, the BoC decided that I should draft a summary of each interview in consultation with the interviewed person, for use by the BoC alone. The BoC thus would have summaries of interviews to refer to when ultimately making its decision to commend or correct and when submitting the final report of its action.

Six more professors were interviewed at the BoC meeting November 19–20, 1972: Robert Bertram, Richard Caemmerer, Carl Graesser, Norman Habel, George Hoyer, and Carl Volz. The BoC also continued its interview with me at several different times during the meeting. A new feature was added to the interview process. Walter Dissen had mailed questions to the faculty members in advance so that they could respond in writing. Each professor was asked from four to nine questions based on the quotations of that professor's transcript or published works as quoted in the BB. All professors presented their answers in writing at the time of the meeting, and this material was included in the summary of the interviews that I drafted.

The BoC decided to interview Holland Jones, Ralph Klein, Edgar Krentz, Edward Schroeder, and Robert Smith at its December meeting. In addition it asked that I arrange for four or five other faculty members to be standing by, in case time permitted additional interviews. I arranged for John Constable, David Deppe, Wi Jo Kang, Erwin Leuker, and Walter Wegner to "stand by." Walter Dissen knew the names of only the five professors named by the BoC, so he could submit questions only to those five. All of the ten except Wi Jo Kang were interviewed in December.

Now only six of the faculty members quoted in the BB had not been interviewed: Robert Conrad, John Damm, William Danker, Alfred Fuerbringer, Paul Goetting, and Wi Jo Kang. The BoC decided to interview these six at its January 1973 meeting and to take action at that time on whether to commend or correct the faculty members.

What kinds of things were discussed in the faculty interviews before the BoC that would serve as grist for the mill of decision concerning the faculty's doctrinal position? Most of the questioning began with citations of the faculty members' transcripts or published works in the BB and moved on from there to clarify what faculty members were saying. In prepared introductory statements, some faculty members showed how they had been misquoted or misunderstood by the FFC and the BB. Most faculty members prefaced their remarks with confessions of their faith, in some cases making use of the statements they had prepared at the request of the Council of Presidents.[10]

Herbert Mayer called attention to the use made by the BB of one of his conference essays to imply that he espoused an un-Christian "process theology." He pointed out that the FFC had asked him no questions about the essay. Rejecting "process theology" as a description of his theological position, he stated that the essay had been written before there was such a thing as "process theology." The allegation in the BB, he said, had done him a grave injustice.[11]

Frederick Danker was asked to explain a statement he made to the FFC in response to a question about Jesus' resurrection. Danker had been asked whether he could have taken a picture of Jesus rising from the dead if he had been at the tomb on Easter morning and had a camera with him. Danker responded, "Well, let's say this, that if you had a camera on the occasion I am sure you would have broken it." Explaining his statement, Danker said that God's activities are always much more than they appear to us; those who think they can film a miracle show that they do not understand what a miracle is. Citing John 6:14–15, Danker said that the crowds saw the "sign" of what Jesus did but failed to grasp the true miracle of it all, that Jesus was the bread of life for them, not a baker-magician to satisfy their interests in making him king.

Everett Kalin was asked whether it was his view that God continues to inspire his people today and that the Scriptures are therefore not unique. He agreed that God does continue to inspire but affirmed that the Scriptures are unique. He said the difference between the Scriptures and Christian proclamation today is that the Scriptures are the prophetic and apostolic testimony. He rejected the notion that what he was saying meant that the only difference between a pastor's inspiration today and the inspiration of the apostle Paul is that the pastor is centuries removed from the event. Other people saw those events as well, he said, and their writings are not Scripture. Faithful people were appointed by the Lord to give apostolic testimony to God's reconciling work in Jesus Christ. The key, he concluded, is apostolic testimony and the content of that testimony, Jesus Christ.

Arthur Repp was asked to clarify his statement to the FFC that the creation account in Genesis was not intended to be a literal description of a one-time event. Repp pointed to the figurative expressions and the anthropomorphic language in Genesis 1. He called attention to the variations in the two creation accounts of Genesis 1 and 2. Most important, he said, was the poetic, polemical, and liturgical structure of these chapters, which takes them out of the category of straight reporting, or history, and he described that structure in detail.

Asked about his views on the Book of Jonah, Alfred Sauer pointed out that the BB had dealt with his views under the rubric of an alleged permissive Christology. Describing various possible interpretations of Jesus' words in reference to Jonah, Sauer expressed his preference for the view that Jesus did not speak to the question of whether the account of Jonah is historical or parabolic. According to Sauer, it would have been possible for Jesus to affirm that his stay in the grave would be like Jonah staying in the fish for three days without thereby asserting that the

Jonah account is in fact historical. Sauer cited analogies between Abraham Lincoln and Paul Bunyan, and between the Allied defeat of Germany and St. George's slaying of the dragon.

One of the questions Walter Dissen put to Richard Caemmerer concerned a statement in Caemmerer's transcript that began, "Faith does not depend on the facts . . . ." Dissen wanted to know "can our faith in the forgiveness of sins through Jesus Christ thus stand apart from the facts, the documentation and the historical accuracy of Christ's crucifixion, death and resurrection?" Caemmerer responded:

> I do not say that Christ's crucifixion, death, and resurrection did not happen or that it makes no difference whether they happened. They are the cornerstone of my faith and the central message of the preaching of every Christian. What I tried to say in the transcript is that God's way of working faith is not in first place to document the veracity of those accounts, for faith is God's gift through the Holy Spirit. Jesus said to Thomas eight days after the first Easter, "Because thou hast seen, thou hast believed; blessed are they that have not seen and yet have believed" (John 20:29). Our faith accepts Christ's crucifixion, death, and resurrection for life and salvation. What leads it to accept is not human proof or reasoning, but God and the Gospel.

Edgar Krentz was asked whether it was an acceptable standard to measure an interpretation of Scripture by what it does to the proclamation of Jesus Christ as Lord, thus raising the issue of the "authority" of the gospel in relation to the "authority" of the Scripture. Krentz responded that it was not only an acceptable standard but a necessary one; that if he did not use it, he could be accused of being un-Lutheran and sub-Confessional. His language, he pointed out, was a rephrasing of the language of the Lutheran Confessions, which speaks of "making Christ necessary," of "honoring God," of "magnifying Christ." That, he said, is a touchstone by which to evaluate everything in Lutheran theology. Far from proposing it as a new criterion, he was using the criterion *The Book of Concord* makes it necessary to use. Thus, if an exegete denied Christ's power to raise the dead, it would be essential to show him that such a denial is a denial of the gospel. If he affirmed Christ's power to raise the dead but argued on the basis of the text that Christ did not do so, then the question has to be settled on the basis of the textual evidence. Krentz pointed out that if we say in advance that we know what a text of the Bible says, we are no longer allowing it to function in its role as rule and norm.

With Walter Dissen's questions, the issue of the historicity of Adam was raised again and again in the interviews. Robert Bertram dealt with the issue at length to try to help BoC members understand what was at stake in the faculty members' united position. He answered Dissen's question in writing:

> If all we mean by a "historical person" is an individual human being like you or me, then that will hardly do to describe Adam. "One man"? Yes, that he is. But not merely "one man" as you or I am "one man." No, Adam is "one man" the way Christ is "one man." . . . He is not just one man among "the many" the way you and I are. Somewhat like Christ—somewhat, yet not exactly—Adam is one man *for* the many. He is the one *through* whom the many are made what they are, sinful and mortal (Rom. 5:19). . . .
>
> That does not mean merely that Adam was chronologically the first individual in a long series of individuals. True, that is part of his story, too. After all, some sinner had to be the first one. But that hardly explains why you and I and his other descendants should have to die, much less why we should have had to become sinners in the first place. . . . Adam is . . . , shall we say, our fallen human nature.

Bertram said that he was not talking about an abstraction, a mere theological idea, but about something that is as real as any historical person but more by far than a historical person:

> Adam, as Paul says elsewhere, is the one "in [whom] all die," as Christ is the one in whom "all shall be made alive" (1 Cor. 15:22). But it would be meaningless to talk that way about Adam if he were just a "historical person" in the distant past, over and done with. He is also, as the Lutheran Confessions say over and over, "*der alte Adam*" [the old Adam]. What is that? "He is what is born in us from Adam" (LC, Baptism, 65). He is a being still very much present and mortally powerful. . . . That Adam, in which we all go on sinning and dying, can be defeated by nothing less than our dying and rising with Christ, beginning with our baptisms.

Then Bertram drove the point home:

> But *that* dimension of Adam, which the Gospel is all about, gets badly short-changed by much of the present preoccupation with Adam as a "historical person." That preoccupation is an effective way to distract sinners from their real problem and leave them terribly vulnerable.

Predictive prophecy was an issue raised in many of the interviews, especially for teachers of the Old Testament. Faculty members tried to help BoC members distinguish between the use of the term *Messiah* in the technical sense used by Old Testament scholars and in the broader sense used in the Lutheran tradition. They distinguished between the more immediate fulfillment of a promise in the history of the Israelite people and the ultimate fulfillment in the coming of Jesus, such as in Isa. 7:14.

They pointed out that for New Testament writers "fulfillment" meant ever so much more than "prediction-coming-true." So, for example, Norman Habel wrote:

> The Promise of God in the Old Testament assumed many forms. One of these forms was the specific assurances given to David and subsequent audiences in Israel about a future royal figure. These royal promises and expectations we term "messianic," in distinction from hopes and promises relating to a coming prophet, a new covenant and similar themes. All of these promises must be viewed, for us, from the vantage point of their fulfillment as a total. In Jesus Christ all the promises and plans of God are "yes" and "amen." For the Israelite who heard the message of God to David (in 2 Sam. 7), the promise was immediate, relevant and salutary. In Solomon the promise was first fulfilled and God was shown to be faithful. Of the many applications, reaffirmations and expressions of that promise to David throughout Israel's history, none could match the splendor, impact and surprising disclosure of God's grace in the final fulfillment which was Jesus Christ.

My interviews with the BoC in the course of its October and November meetings were of a different character from the faculty interviews. In the BB Preus had accused me of failing to fulfill the responsibilities of my office and insisted that the BoC should "deal with" me. Therefore, in addition to questions about my theological position on the issues in controversy, I was questioned about my conduct in office. I was asked if I would do anything differently as far as the CS investigation was concerned if I had it to do over. I said that I was often confronted by the question, that some had told me that my policy in handling the situation involving Arlis Ehlen had proved to be a failure and that I should have acted differently. I said that I had carefully reviewed the sequence of events in the Ehlen situation and was satisfied that in the light of the events as I knew them at the time I had made the right decisions.

Someone wanted to know if I felt equally confident about the rightness of my decision to reply to the BB with a document of my own. I answered that it was my opinion that the BB was such a disaster for the Synod and CS that it had to be countered. I had not wanted to release my response to Preus's investigation, not even to the BoC, I explained, but the publication of the BB made the response necessary. I added that if the BoC was of the opinion that things should be done differently from the way I was doing them, I would appreciate the counsel.

I was asked to explain what I meant by the terms *sub-biblical* and *un-Lutheran* in my response to characterize the FFC report. I said I had explained what I meant in my response and cited the sections. I summarized the criticism: separating the formal and material principles, making the gospel just one doctrine among many instead of the whole of

Christian teaching, and separating the authority of the Scripture from the authority of the gospel.

I was asked to comment on Preus's allegation in the BB that I had failed to exercise doctrinal supervision over the faculty. I pointed out that I had been present at all the faculty interviews with the FFC and knew from my close association with faculty members what they were teaching. I repeated what I had written in my response to the BB—namely, that the FFC's descriptions of the teaching of faculty members were distortions. Some of the views for which faculty members had been criticized were simply not their views, and others were in fact perfectly proper. Thus I had exercised doctrinal supervision but had come to a completely different conclusion than had President Preus.

Asked what I meant by the term "genuine doctrinal issues," which in the letter accompanying my response to the BB I had said must be dealt with, I cited the relation between Scripture and gospel as an example. I described how some in the Synod make of the gospel one doctrine among many to be found in the Scripture, whereas the Lutheran Confessions make the gospel the content of the Scripture and the key to understanding everything in the Scripture. I called attention to the danger of accepting an authority of Scripture which is divorced from the authority of the gospel and stressed the importance of keeping Scripture and gospel together, especially in a time of controversy. I described the formal and material principles as two sides of the same coin that cannot be separated: "The gospel we preach is the gospel of the Scriptures; we use the Scriptures as rule and norm for our teaching of the gospel. At the same time the gospel is the key to our understanding of the Scriptures; we use the gospel to assure that our understanding of the Scripture is correct."

Through the interview process the BoC members heard individual faculty members describe in their own words what they taught about the issues in controversy. The BoC had received the evidence to determine whether in fact the BB distorted what the faculty told the FFC and whether wrong conclusions had been drawn from the transcripts. Eleven men would have to make up their minds as to whether individual faculty members were teaching in accord with the Scriptures and the Lutheran Confessions.

Preus had made both the accusation and the judgment that "some professors at the Seminary hold views contrary to the established doctrinal position of the Synod." He claimed that the BoC could "readily" determine who they were by looking at the transcripts of the FFC report. When the BoC decided from its review of his transcript that Arthur Carl Piepkorn was not among them, Preus objected and called attention to the citations of Piepkorn's transcript in the BB as evidence of Piepkorn's need to retract his views. Did all the citations from the transcripts in the BB need to be retracted? Did Preus believe that all twenty-nine faculty members cited in the BB held views contrary to the established doctrinal position of the Synod? Would finding two faculty members among the twenty-nine be enough to bring peace?[12] In choosing whether to commend or correct, the eleven members of the BoC had a weighty decision to make, not only for the members of the faculty but for CS and the Synod as well.

◆ ◆ ◆

At approximately 3:00 P.M. on January 15, 1973, the BoC began deliberating and balloting on commending or correcting the faculty. On my yellow note pad I wrote the names of forty-seven members of the faculty in alphabetical order in a column on the left-hand side of two pieces of paper.[13] I did not include Walter Bartling, Arlis Ehlen, H. Lucille Hager, and Carl Meyer, whom the BoC had exempted earlier. I did include Arthur Carl Piepkorn, and wrote next to his name, "Already approved."

As the results of the ballots were reported, I recorded them in three columns, labeled "Commend," "Correct," and "Abstain." In two cases a fourth column was necessary, labeled "Interview," meaning that a BoC member voted to interview a faculty member who had not yet been interviewed. In three cases there were votes to "commend with reservation." The chair ruled that these votes should be counted as "to commend."

By 5:30 P.M. the balloting had proceeded alphabetically through M. The BoC moved to Koburg Hall to conduct its ordinary business with CS administrators over the dinner hour. Eugene Fincke excused himself for the remainder of the meeting. At 6:30 P.M. the BoC was back in executive session.

The BoC discovered that there were two faculty members on the remaining list who had not been interviewed by the FFC, so it decided not to vote on Eldon Pedersen, CS's director of athletics, and Kenneth Siess, who had joined the faculty after the investigation had begun and taught in the area of pastoral care and counseling. When they got to my name, I offered to excuse myself, but the BoC decided to postpone a decision on "whether to commend or correct President Tietjen."[14] When balloting on all faculty members was completed, the BoC decided to create a committee to draft a report of its action. George Loose and William Buege were named members of the committee, and I was asked to serve as a resource person.

Then the chair asked me if I would leave the room so that the BoC could consider what it should do about me in fulfilling its responsibilities.

About a half hour later Paul Nickel came to my office and asked me to return. I was told nothing. I discovered what had transpired only when, some time later, I read the bare facts in the minutes:

> The Board then proceeded to discuss the matter of meetings between Synodical President Preus and President Tietjen and the subject matter scheduled for the meetings. Also discussed was the *Report of the Synodical President* as it pertained to President Tietjen.
> The Board again discussed whether to commend or correct President Tietjen, Chairman Loose turning the chair over to Vice Chairman Buege during this time.
>
> *Motion:* That the Board remove from the table for consideration the doctrinal position of President Tietjen within the scope of Milwaukee Resolution 2-28 only. (Motion—Biel, Second—Beckemeier)
>
> *Action:* Motion Carried. (Dissen recorded against.)
>
> The Board then balloted on whether to commend or correct President Tietjen.

As I reflected on the meaning of the words, I concluded that three options must have been under consideration. One was to respond to Preus's request in the BB to "deal with" me in my alleged failure to exercise doctrinal supervision over the faculty. A second option was to postpone any action and to await the results of further meetings between Preus and me, the next one of which was scheduled for March. A third option was to treat me like any other member of the faculty interviewed by the FFC and to vote simply to commend or correct me within the context of the responsibilities of Milwaukee Resolution 2-28. The third option prevailed.

The meeting over, I sat at the desk in my office, benumbed, the two pages of the yellow pad in front of me. I studied the results of the BoC's action:

Faculty Member	Commend	Correct	Abstain	Interview
Bangert	9	—	2	—
Bergt*	8	—	3	—
Bertram	6	4	1	—
Bohlmann	9	—	2	—
Bouman	8	—	2	1
Breimeier	10	—	1	—
Caemmerer	8	2	1	—
Conrad	7	3	1	—
Constable	8	—	3	—
Damm	8	2	1	—
Danker, F.	8	2	1	—

* Bergt, Lessmann, Thiele, and Werberg were neither cited in BB nor interviewed.

Faculty Member	Commend	Correct	Abstain	Interview
Danker, W.	8	2	1	—
Deppe	7	2	2	—
Fuerbringer	7	2	2	—
Goetting	9	1	1	—
Graesser	6	5	—	—
Grunow	10	—	1	—
Habel	6	5	—	—
Hoyer	8	—	3	—
Jones	6	5	—	—
Kalin	7	4	—	—
Kang	8	2	1	—
Klann	7	2	2	—
Klein	6	5	—	—
Krentz	8	3	—	—
Lessmann*	8	3	—	—
Lueker	9	1	1	—
Mayer	6	5	—	—
Mehl	8	1	2	—
Piepkorn	Already approved			
Preus, R.	7	1	2	—
Repp	6	4	—	—
Sauer	6	4	—	—
Scharlemann	5	2	2	1
Schroeder	7	3	—	—
Smith	7	3	—	—
Thiele*	8	2	—	—
Tietjen				
Vincent	8	1	1	—
Volz	7	2	1	—
Wegner	7	3	—	—
Werberig*	9	1	—	—
Weyermann	9	1	—	—
Wuerffel	9	—	1	—
Wunderlich	10	—	—	—

* Bergt, Lessmann, Thiele, and Werberg were neither cited in BB nor interviewed.

I took pen in hand and wrote in the columns next to my name the results of the ballot concerning me, as George Loose had given them to me at the end of the meeting: Commend—7; Correct—3. Later, when I received Dissen's minutes, I discovered that there were notations next to the names of Caemmerer and Smith, indicating that Dissen had recorded his vote to correct them, and there were notations next to the names of Sauer and Tietjen, indicating that Burmeister, Dissen, and Weber had recorded their votes to correct Sauer and me.[15]

I sat in my office, drained of all emotion. Five faculty members had squeaked by with a one-vote majority, three more by a two-vote majority. All BoC members except those solidly in the Preus camp had voted to approve me. The BoC had made it clear to me that it was not through with its consideration of the issues and might want to conduct more interviews. But the decision had been made to commend everyone, to correct no one. I reached for the phone to call a few trusted members of the Faculty Advisory Committee so that they could discreetly let faculty members know that things had gone well but I was not yet at liberty to share the results.

◆ ◆ ◆

I assisted George Loose and William Buege in drawing up a draft of a report that was mailed to all members of the BoC on February 12, 1973, as part of the agenda material for the BoC meeting on February 19. The central issue at the meeting was not the wording of the report but who should receive it. Buege argued that he was not unwilling for the report to go to President Preus and to the BHE, but he insisted that it should go to the Synod in convention because a Synod convention had mandated that the BoC should take action on the FFC report. The BoC agreed that after sending copies to Preus and the BHE, the report should then be included as part of the CS general report to the 1973 Synod convention. It would therefore be among the materials distributed to convention delegates. The day after the BoC meeting I hand-delivered copies of the report to the office of President Preus (he was out of the country) and to BHE executive secretary Arthur Ahlschwede and arranged for a joint news release by CS and the Synod's Department of Public Relations.

It took two months to learn what Preus intended to do about the BoC's action. In an April 27, 1973, issue of *Brother to Brother,* his occasional newsletter, he included a two-page item on the BoC action. He described the problem: The BoC had reported that it found no false doctrine at CS when only six months prior Preus had reported to the Synod, "on the basis of the documentary evidence of the Fact Finding Committee," that false doctrine "was indeed being promulgated at the Saint Louis seminary, particularly with regard to the doctrine of the authority of Holy Scripture."

Preus blasted away at the BoC: Its action was only by majority vote. In a number of cases the difference was only one or two votes. It interviewed only twenty-nine of the forty-five on whom it voted. It did not use his "A Statement of Scriptural and Confessional Principles" and therefore had no guiding principle by which to distinguish truth from error. It had made no tape recordings of the interviews and therefore had nothing to refer to beyond summaries, which presumably were suspect because I had prepared them. It insisted that the issues were only theological, not doctrinal. The interviews held by the BoC plus the faculty's documents published as *Faithful to Our Calling, Faithful to Our Lord* plus the document I published as *Fact Finding or Fault Finding?* "all substantiate the findings of the Fact Finding Committee as well as the findings and charges of the *Report of the Synodical President*," Preus concluded.

The first sentence of his final paragraph almost made me laugh. "I am informed," he wrote, "that the report of the Board of Control to the convention will consist of four parts, one by the board and three supplemental reports by individual members." Who informed him of that? Certainly not the BoC, which had submitted a single report and did not even know that some of its members were submitting reports of their own. Preus was apparently making another intrusive, preemptive move into the internal affairs of the BoC in an attempt to negate its action. The reports of individual members would be given the same status as the report of the entire BoC itself. Apparently, Preus was gearing up for a convention showdown. As he put it in *Brother to Brother*, "There can be no doubt that this issue ought to be resolved by the highest authority in the Synod, namely, the synodical convention itself. This can be done in New Orleans."

As the bylaws of the Synod required me to do, I had stressed the authority of the BoC to render a judgment about the CS faculty. I had been confident that the elected members of the BoC, if they had all the facts and could meet personally with the faculty, would recognize how Lutheran the faculty's teaching was. Their decision justified my confidence. Now the BoC had joined the faculty and me in taking the CS's case to the people of the Synod. I was confident that the New Orleans convention would justify our confidence in the people.

8 ——◆

RIVERGATE

"The chair recognizes Dr. John Tietjen at microphone nine." The voice speaking from the rostrum belonged to Guido A. Merkens, parish pastor from San Antonio, Texas, who a few days earlier had been reelected as one of five vice-presidents of the Lutheran Church–Missouri Synod, in the process moving up from fourth to second vice-president. Tall, with the physique of a linebacker, Merkens was chairing Session 11 of the Fiftieth Regular Convention of the Missouri Synod assembled in the Rivergate convention center in New Orleans.

It was evening on Wednesday, July 11, 1973. The convention had begun the previous Friday and still had two days to go. The mood was tense. Herbert Mueller's words had come true. In the *Convention Workbook* the secretary of the Synod had reported, "There are those who say that some of the sons of Missouri will be coming back to New Orleans to reenact in their own way the Battle of New Orleans."[1]

The selection of New Orleans as a convention site coincided with the conclusion of a year's celebration of the Missouri Synod's 125th anniversary. People were remembering that the Synod's Saxon forebears had landed in New Orleans on their arrival in America. At a time when the bungled break-in at the Watergate Hotel in Washington, D.C., was dominating the news, people were amused to learn that the Missouri Synod's Battle of New Orleans was happening in a place called Rivergate.

When Merkens invited me to speak, I was at a microphone in the rear of the hall. I was in the section reserved for advisory delegates, those who could speak at the convention but not vote and who wore blue badges instead of the red badges of voting delegates. At this convention not only were advisory delegates relegated to a separate section, as was done at the previous convention, but the section for voting delegates was cordoned off and ushers were stationed to keep out anyone not wearing a red badge.

Shortly before, I had entered the section where more than a thousand voting delegates were seated at long tables. In fact, I found it necessary to enter this reserved section often during the convention. By now the ushers knew who I was and with a smile simply acknowledged me without asking me what my business was. This time I had gone through the section up to the rostrum and delivered a note to the secretary of the Synod. The note requested that I be recognized at microphone nine for the purpose of raising a question of privilege when Resolution 3-09 came to the floor that evening. I made the request in advance and in writing because the three microphones in the rear of the hall for use by advisory delegates were so far away from the rostrum that it was difficult for the chair to see them. I did not relish having to go through gymnastic gyrations or to make loud noises to get the chair's attention.

Resolution 3-09 was one of the actions that Synod president Jacob A. O. Preus wanted the New Orleans convention to adopt, one he considered indispensable for settling the problems in the Synod.[2] It proposed to settle the "seminary problem" by condemning the position of the faculty of Concordia Seminary, St. Louis. After a long historical introduction and a three-page "Preamble," the resolution described the teaching of the faculty that was to be condemned: "a. subversion of the authority of Scripture (formal principle); b. 'Gospelism' or 'Gospel reductionism' whereby the authority of Scripture is reduced to its 'Gospel' content; c. denial of the third use of the Law, i.e., the function of the Law as guide for the Christian in his life."

The resolution called on the Synod to "repudiate that attitude toward Holy Scripture . . . which reduces to theological opinion or exegetical questions matters which are in fact clearly taught in Scripture." What were such matters? The resolution listed examples: "facticity of miracle accounts and their details; historicity of Adam and Eve as real persons; the fall of Adam and Eve into sin as a real event . . . ; the historicity of every detail in the life of Jesus as recorded by the evangelists; predictive prophecies in the Old Testament which are in fact Messianic; the doctrine of angels; the Jonah account."

The resolution called on the Synod to recognize that the theological position defended by the faculty "is in fact false doctrine running counter to the Holy Scriptures, the Lutheran Confessions, and the synodical stance. . . . for that reason," the resolution continued, quoting words from one of the Lutheran confessional writings, the faculty's position "'cannot be tolerated in the church of God, much less be excused and defended' (FC, SD, Preface, 9)."[3]

Lewis C. Niemoeller, chair of Committee Number 3 on Seminary Issues, parish pastor from Springfield, Illinois, and a member of the leadership in the Preus party, presented Resolution 3-09, reading it in its entirety including the lengthy introduction and preamble. When he was finished, the chair called on me at microphone nine. Addressing the chair, I asked for the privilege of speaking to Resolution 3-09 in behalf of the faculty of CS. When several delegates asked that I go up front to speak from the platform, Merkens put the question to the delegates, and they agreed. Delegates turned around in their seats to watch me as I made the long walk from the rear of the hall to the speaker's podium.

On the wall behind the platform, raised high in the air, was the logo of the convention, a Latin cross emerging from converging lines and set within a circle whose circumference was a jagged edge. To many of us for whom that logo was the center of attention during the convention proceedings the circle looked for all the world like a rotary saw. Now from the speaker's podium I was going to make a supreme effort to keep the buzz saw of a convention resolution from ripping up our CS faculty.

Beginning with a short personal confession of faith, I told the delegates that Resolution 3-09 was asking them to condemn the faculty for teachings that the faculty refused to recognize as their own. We affirm the formal principle, I told them; we affirm the authority of the Scripture; we affirm the reality of creation and the fall; we affirm the third use of the law; we reject "gospel reductionism" while we affirm the gospel as the material principle of theology; we reject "fideism" while we affirm the centrality of faith.

I said that the accusations in Resolution 3-09 illustrated the problem: the faculty was not being heard. As a faculty we had said that the Fact Finding Committee report had misunderstood and misrepresented us and that the "Blue Book" had done the same. Now the resolution before the convention was doing it again. I pointed out that the faculty did get one fair hearing. Our Board of Control listened to us and after careful consideration, voting on the faculty one by one, had affirmed that we were not to be accused of false doctrine but were teaching in accord with the Scriptures and the Lutheran Confessions.

"Therefore tonight I urge you," I pleaded with the delegates, "please do not compound the problem any worse than it is. Do not condemn us wrongly on the basis of judgments which we refuse to acknowledge as our position. There are ways of dealing with accusations of false doctrine. They have not been followed. Do not violate your own bylaws. There has to be a better way to deal with this issue. Several have been proposed to the convention. . . . In the name of our Lord Jesus Christ, who shed his blood for us, I ask you, find a better way."[4]

As I made my way back to the rear of the hall, Niemoeller introduced Eugene Klug, professor of systematic theology at the Synod's seminary in Springfield, Illinois, and a member of Committee Number 3, to respond. Klug said that while he appreciated what I said, the committee had spent a great deal of time for months prior to the convention discussing the issues. Their study had involved documents prepared by the CS faculty, reports of the FFC and of the BoC, and many other items. The committee was convinced, Klug concluded, that the statements in the proposed resolution were correct.

In the discussion that followed, a delegate moved to remove Resolution 3-09 from consideration by the convention, but a majority voted no. Then Paul Bretscher, parish pastor from Valparaiso, Indiana, and son of a retired CS New Testament professor, made an impassioned plea that the faculty not be condemned without being heard. Bretscher pointed out that three representatives chosen by the faculty were among the convention's advisory delegates and that the convention had an obligation to listen to them at a time and in a setting that allowed for careful deliberation. With Bretscher making the motion, the convention agreed to suspend the standing rules to allow "not less than three hours" for discussion of Resolution 3-09 "at a more reasonable time," giving the three faculty representatives an opportunity to speak, and granting me "speaking privileges equal to that of the floor committee."[5] I was asked to meet with Bretscher and Niemoeller to work out the details. Perhaps it was still possible, I said to myself, to shut the buzz saw down.

Both sides in the controversy had been gearing up for months for the Missouri Synod's Battle of New Orleans. Because voting delegates made the convention's decisions, delegate selection was crucial. The Missouri Synod's districts were divided up into electoral circuits with one pastor and one lay person chosen from each circuit. Each pair of delegates represented from seven to twenty congregations involving an aggregate communicant membership ranging from fifteen hundred to ten thousand.

There was a time in the not too distant past when pastoral delegates were chosen and congregations were asked to name a lay delegate on the basis of whose turn it was to represent the circuit. The Preus political party had put an end to that benign process in preparation for the Denver convention in 1969. Now each side in the controversy worked for the election of delegates who were favorable to the causes it espoused. The Preus party had the benefit of experience in getting circuits to choose the delegates they wanted. But the counterorganization headed by Bertwin Frey and Dean Lueking was learning fast.

A meeting of district contact people of the Preus party (held in Chicago on April 2, 1973) reported that 60 percent of the delegates were in the Preus camp and could be counted on to vote accordingly.[6] Amandus J. Derr, a CS student, reported an assessment out of the Frey-Lueking camp, according to which 45 percent of the delegates were conservative, 45 percent were moderate (conservative and moderate were used as party labels), and the leaning of the remaining 10 percent was unknown.[7] Derr had been instrumental in establishing an ad hoc organization of CS students called "Seminarians Concerned for Reconciliation under the Gospel" and had secured a list of the names and addresses of all voting delegates to the convention. His organization wrote to the delegates to champion the cause of the CS faculty.

The Preus party told its story through the journal *Affirm*, published by Balance, Inc. There was at first no comparable opposition journal. In September 1972 a group of clergy and laity in St. Louis began issuing *INFO* to provide accurate information on the controversy and to espouse causes different from that of the Preus party. We at CS understood that, just as Preus had goals for the 1971 convention, so he would have specific goals and proposals in New Orleans. We had to have proposals of our own. It was not enough simply to report what the BoC had done in reviewing the faculty on the basis of the FFC report. We had to take seriously the controversy in which the Synod was embroiled and propose ways to deal with it. Because of the BoC's preoccupation with its review of the faculty and its report to the Synod, the faculty took the initiative through its Faculty Advisory Committee.

The FAC had been created by the faculty at the beginning of the CS investigation to serve as an interface between the faculty and me. Its purpose was to advise me concerning faculty thinking on issues under discussion pertaining to the investigation, as well as to advise the faculty on what action to take. It had become an efficient and invaluable instrument for CS action. The plain fact was that the faculty could not afford to do any squabbling or disagreeing in faculty meetings. There was a direct pipeline from faculty meetings to Jacob Preus's office through some of the five "minority" faculty members who identified with the Preus cause, especially Robert Preus, Jacob's brother.

The FAC served as forum and channel for discussion and expression of disagreement. The committee had the heavy responsibility of making sure that it had properly heard faculty members on issues that were under consideration and that its proposals were what the faculty wanted to do. Everyone understood that the faculty would vote for whatever the FAC proposed. The FAC and I worked together closely to assure responsible action by faculty and administration.

On March 6, 1973, on recommendation of the FAC, the faculty agreed to submit an overture to the New Orleans convention, proposing a program for resolving the synodical controversy through fraternal discussion. The proposal called for local and regional discussion in all the districts of the Synod convened by the district presidents for discussion of issues determined by a special commission consisting of the president of the Synod, six district presidents elected by the Council of Presidents, and the presidents of the Synod's six terminal schools. The faculty invited the BoC to join with it in submitting the proposal to the New Orleans convention.[8] The BoC amended the proposal slightly and adopted it under the title "To Seek Reconciliation through Fraternal Discussion" at its meeting March 19, 1973.[9]

At Missouri Synod conventions all overtures were channeled through floor committees composed of convention delegates with the responsibility of making recommendations in the form of resolutions presented to the convention for action. The prerogative of deciding the number and jurisdiction of floor committees and of appointing the committee members gave the president of the Synod enormous power over the convention. It had been the tradition to appoint committees that were representative not only of the various convention constituencies but of the differing points of view as well. Thus it was possible for committees to thrash through the various sides of issues and reach compromises that facilitated debate on the convention floor.

Jacob Preus changed the tradition, first at Milwaukee in 1971 and then at New Orleans in 1973. Committees crucial for achieving Preus's goals for the convention had a large majority of people who could be counted on to help him. People who were not his supporters were appointed to committees whose work was irrelevant to his goals. At the New Orleans convention, as at the preceding one in Milwaukee, I was assigned to the floor committee on evangelism—a topic that was not on most delegates' minds.

For Preus's goals at New Orleans, as events at the convention ultimately demonstrated, the two crucial floor committees were Committee Number 2 on Theology and Church Relations and Committee Number 3 on Seminary Issues, a committee created for this convention alone. The committee ranks were filled with hard-line Preus party members and followers.[10] Committee Number 3 met several times before the New Orleans convention. At a meeting on May 18, 1973, it requested the presence, separately, of the BoC, the FAC, and me. It became painfully clear at the meetings that we could expect nothing but trouble from the committee and that our only hope was on the floor of the convention itself.

Committee Number 3 turned down two CS requests to distribute materials to the delegates. The delegates had copies of Preus's BB with its damaging allegations against the faculty. In the interest of fairness we asked to distribute the faculty's own response[11] but were refused. When the BoC learned that the *Convention Workbook* contained not only the BoC's two-page report to the convention but two additional reports by its own members, one by Walter Dissen and Edwin Weber, the other by Charles Burmeister and Eugene Fincke, totaling six pages, the BoC drafted a reply[12] to the "supplemental reports" and asked that the reply be distributed to delegates. The committee said no.

Six weeks before the convention, a report circulated that Jacob Preus had said at a meeting with his supporters in Oklahoma, "Tietjen must go." Confronted with the report at a meeting of the Council of Presidents, Preus acknowledged the statement and repeated it with emphasis. The *Convention Workbook* had any number of overtures calling for my dismissal, for the firing of the faculty, and for the ouster of the BoC. Ominously, the June issue of *Affirm*, the publication of the Preus party, asked the New Orleans convention, should other efforts fail, to do "what hitherto had been—amongst us all—the unthinkable: close the Sem."

Yet it was impossible to know what the people of the Synod were thinking or what the convention delegates would do. In my characteristic fashion I took pencil and yellow pad in hand on the eve of the convention and wrote down my assumptions concerning what would happen.[13] Besides his reelection, Preus's two main goals at the convention seemed to be the adoption of a doctrinal position for purposes of discipline, and the control of CS. For the sake of those goals I figured that Preus would back off from other issues, such as severing fellowship with the American Lutheran Church. I expected Preus to work for the approval of "A Statement of Scriptural and Confessional Principles" as a binding doctrinal statement, for control of the CS BoC through the election process, and for my removal from office by convention action.

It was of course possible that Preus would not be reelected. In that event, I wrote on my pad, we could expect the convention to deal CS a blow for the sake of balance. "Even under the best of conditions," I wrote, "the turmoil has been so widespread that Concordia Seminary can expect some rebuke or punishment." But, I consoled myself, "In a polarized convention people in the middle will put forth major efforts to avoid a split and to bring about a compromise." No doubt my future would be part of that compromise. I figured that I would not have to go through the ordeal of being president of CS much longer. If that was what was required to accomplish God's will of peace and unity in the Synod, I was prepared to pay the price.

Two years earlier the Missouri Synod had changed the rules for the election of its president and first vice-president. The convention in 1971 had approved a process in which the Synod's congregations were invited to submit single nominations for the office of president and for first vice-president, which were both full-time positions. The five candidates receiving the highest number of nominations became the slate for each office.

The Preus party had its candidate. Around whom should the opposition rally? The leadership of the Frey-Lueking organization decided that the candidate should be Oswald C. J. Hoffmann, popular and dynamic speaker of "The Lutheran Hour," international radio program of the Synod's Lutheran Laymen's League. One-time professor at the Synod's Concordia College in Bronxville, New York, and former director of public relations for the Synod, Hoffmann was well known not only in the Synod but in Protestant and evangelical circles for his commitment to the work of Bible distribution, for dramatic preaching, and for clear witness to the Christian gospel. A big man with jowly cheeks, Hoffmann's piercing eyes and booming bass voice held audiences in rapt attention.

Would Hoffmann stand for election? A few good friends, I am among them, were delegated to meet with him to sound him out. Hoffmann had been one of my professors in college. When he became "Lutheran Hour" speaker, I assisted him for a number of years in recording his sermons in a New York City broadcasting studio. Hoffmann was too awesome a figure to me for the two of us to become close friends, yet I was someone he trusted and could speak to him frankly. Visiting him in his home, I told him in delicate terms about the intention of some of his friends to sponsor his candidacy for president of the Synod. I made it clear that his friends would not persist against his wishes. It was not necessary for him to say yes, I told him, but it was essential that he say no if he did not want his friends to proceed. When Hoffmann did not respond, I concluded that he was on board and so informed Dean Lueking. A few others who spoke to Hoffmann made the same report.

Thus we were all stunned a few months later when Hoffmann's name was removed from the list of presidential candidates. The change in the election procedures specified that nominees for the office of president or first vice-president had to give their prior consent not just to be a candidate but to serve if elected. Hoffmann stated that the procedure requiring prior consent was in violation of the traditional Missouri

Synod view of the call, that he could not decide whether to accept a call until he had received it, and that he would not violate his conscience by giving his prior consent.

Did Hoffmann's action mean that he had assessed the situation and decided he could not win? Was he trying to keep his relations with the Lutheran Laymen's League in good shape in the event that he should lose? Was he announcing that he would be a candidate only if there was a ground swell of popular support evidenced by a decision to change the offending procedure? The statement that accompanied his announcement sounded like he was still a candidate: "I earnestly request of the members of our church that instead of arguing with each other in bitterness and fear, we open our hearts to the Word of God and to one another, praying with confidence toward God for the well-being of Christ's church throughout the world, working with one another as servants of the Lord Christ rather than as masters of worldly power, and witnessing with lips and life to the saving power of Christ's Gospel."[14]

The Frey-Lueking organization decided to try to eliminate the prior consent procedure so that Hoffmann could be nominated from the floor in New Orleans. If the effort failed, their candidate would be William H. Kohn, executive director of the Synod's Board for Missions. But Hoffmann's decision had taken the wind out of the campaign sails. It was no longer possible to communicate a clear alternative to reelecting Jacob Preus.

In traditional Missouri Synod fashion the election of a president was among the first items of business at the New Orleans convention. The move to eliminate the bylaw requiring prior consent to serve failed. The voting for synodical president took place without Hoffmann's name on the ballot. On the first ballot Jacob Preus received 606 votes, 77 more than needed for a majority, to William Kohn's 340.

Of equal importance to us at CS were the elections for members of the BoC. The terms of four members came due at the New Orleans convention. Ineligible for reelection were George Loose, the BoC's chair, and August Beckemeier, both of whom had supported the BoC's action in finding in favor of the CS faculty. Renominated were Charles Burmeister and Eugene Fincke, both of whom were solidly in the Preus camp.

The two pastors proposed by the Nominations Committee gave the delegates a clear choice. One was Alfred Buls, pastor of the congregation closest to the seminary, where many of the faculty and their families were members. A former district president, Buls was a good friend of the CS community. The other candidate was Ewald J. Otto, parish pastor from Quincy, Illinois, editor of *Affirm* and author of its June editorial entitled "Close the Sem." The Preus party had learned a lesson from the Milwaukee convention BoC elections, when they divided their votes among several candidates while we had only one.[15] There was only one obvious "conservative" candidate for the pastoral position on the BoC.

In addition to Burmeister and Fincke, four other lay candidates were nominated for three board positions. We decided to endorse one of them, Robert W. Clup, a professor from Norman, Oklahoma, and to nominate two candidates of our own. One was Jay Pfotenhauer, a judge from San Francisco who had served as member of the Synod's Board of Directors before the Preus ascendancy and whose name was well known in the Synod. The other was Elmer Kraemer, well known to the Synod laity as editor of the *Lutheran Layman* and then of the *Reporter,* a newspaper published by the LCMS. I had personally spoken to Pfotenhauer and secured his consent to be a candidate. To our disappointment, after his nomination, even though he was not at the convention, he withdrew as a candidate.

The election returns were not known until midway through the convention. In view of other convention actions, the results were not surprising. Burmeister and Fincke were reelected. From among the other laity the choice was Alfred Briel, senior partner of an accounting firm in Evansville, Indiana, and a relative by marriage of Robert Preus. Chosen from the two pastoral candidates was Ewald J. Otto. Jacob Preus now had at least a six-to-five majority on the BoC.

CS was not the only institution to feel the results of the elections. The Preus party had published an election guide so that Preus's supporters would know for whom to vote. Out of a possible 147 candidates listed in the guide, 143 were elected. The Preus party took control of all the major boards and commissions of the Synod. Asked to comment on the elections in an interview for KFUO, the Missouri Synod radio station in St. Louis, "moderate" leader Dean Lueking laughed as he said, "We've lost everything but our scruples."[16]

Jacob Preus's program for the New Orleans convention became clear to me as the two chief convention committees, Committee 2 on Theology and Church Relations and Committee 3 on Seminary Issues, produced their resolutions for convention action. The first chief issue, like a major premise in a developing syllogism, had to do with the binding nature of doctrinal statements, the issue that Preus had hoped and failed to settle at the 1971 convention. Formulated by Committee 2 as Resolution 2-12, it was presented by Committee 3 at Session 4 on Monday morning, July 9, 1973, as a joint resolution of the two committees, a sign of its importance. The resolution[17] asked that Article II of the Synod's constitution be understood as requiring the formulation and adoption of doctrinal statements that are binding on the members of the

Synod. After presenting the resolution, Committee 3 chair Lewis Niemoeller called on the president of the Synod to make a statement.

Preus stated that he had received criticism because of his efforts to maintain the doctrinal position of the Synod. It was now up to the convention delegates to decide which doctrinal position the Synod should hold. While everyone in the Synod professed to accept Article II of the synodical constitution, under its umbrella many questions had not been resolved. These included such matters as the historicity of Adam and Eve, original sin, New Testament miracles, the third use of the law, and the origin, nature, and authority of Scripture. In his *Report to the Synod* he had said that the Synod was at a crossroads. Now it was time for the delegates to choose a direction.[18]

"Someone in this church," Preus said, "ought to have the authority to determine how we today interpret and confess our Lutheran faith and the authority to maintain it in our pulpits and classrooms." Preus asked, "Is the Synod helpless? Do we have no way to determine what is to be preached in our pulpits, taught in our classrooms and in our confirmation classes?" He concluded: "As we begin this discussion on the binding nature of doctrinal resolutions, please remember what is at stake. We must retain our synodical voice and keep the authority of the Synod to bind its spiritual leaders to the understanding we have of our faith and to empower our officials to act when departures from our biblical and confessional position take place."[19]

The weight of the presidential office was now behind the joint resolution, but action had to be postponed when time ran out. Resolution 2-12 was back on the floor for consideration the following morning. In a tumultuous session several efforts to amend the motion were defeated, as were several efforts to close debate. A delegate served notice that he would on the next day introduce a motion to change the standing rules to allow for the possibility of closing debate after a prescribed procedure by a simple majority vote. Finally, a two-thirds majority vote closed debate. By a standing vote of 653 to 381 the convention acted to interpret the doctrinal article of the Synod's constitution as requiring the adoption of binding doctrinal statements.

That same evening the second major Preus convention issue was before the delegates, the minor premise in the developing syllogism. It was Resolution 3-01, presented as another joint resolution of Committees 2 and 3. Resolution 3-01 called on the delegates to declare Preus's "A Statement of Scriptural and Confessional Principles" to be in all its parts scriptural and in accord with the Lutheran Confessions.[20] After thirty minutes of discussion a motion to close debate failed. Former president Oliver Harms was rebuffed when the delegates refused to extend time in order to allow him to make a statement to the convention.

The organization under the leadership of Bertwin Frey and Dean Lueking had arranged for nightly meetings in a local hotel to enable supporters to reflect on the day's events and to plan the next day's strategies. After the debate on Resolution 3-01 the meeting room was packed with deeply concerned delegates. I arrived late and had difficulty squeezing in.

In the front of the room stood F. Dean Lueking, tall, his tan suit accenting his fair features, a smile on his face, his tenor voice straining to be heard in the crowded room. Lueking, expressing the convictions of most of the people there, was saying that Resolution 3-01 was *the* convention issue of conscience. It was the practical case for the theory that had been approved that morning—namely, that the Synod was required to adopt binding doctrinal statements. "A Statement of Scriptural and Confessional Principles" was being offered as such a binding doctrinal statement required by the present situation in the Synod. Regardless of its content—and there was much in it to criticize—what was wrong with it was that it was to be used in addition to and in place of the Lutheran Confessions as the standard by which to determine scriptural teaching. Its adoption struck at the very heart of the Lutheran confessional principle. It had to be vigorously opposed and, if approved, its adoption had to be protested.

The assembled group agreed on a strategy. Although they knew from five days of convention experience that they did not have the votes to block the passage of Resolution 3-01, perhaps they could keep the convention from voting on it by making it impossible to get the two-thirds majority necessary to close debate. If and when the resolution was adopted, they would record their negative votes. They would expect pastoral delegate Samuel J. Roth to tell them how. Roth, a St. Louis parish pastor, was one of the key figures behind the publication of the journal *INFO*. Through his clear, reasoned, and forceful speeches on the floor of the convention, he had been recognized by both sides as the delegate who spoke for the convention minority.

When the business session began the following morning, lay delegate Gilbert LaHaine, Sr., of Lansing, Michigan, made his motion to change the rules of the convention to permit closing debate after specified intervals of time by a simple majority vote. After considerable discussion the delegates voted by a two-thirds majority, 668 to 333, to close debate on the motion. However, the vote on the motion to change the rules did not receive a two-thirds majority, the count being 548 for and 479 against. Nevertheless, Jacob Preus, who was in the chair at the time, declared the motion adopted and the rules changed.

In the afternoon session lay delegate Melvin Donaho of Plattsburgh, New York, holding a copy of the latest revised edition of *Robert's Rules of*

Order, challenged the legality of the morning session action of changing the rules by less than a two-thirds majority vote.[21] Vice-president Edwin Weber was in the chair at the time, and parliamentary chaos descended on the convention floor. After an hour of confusion the delegates voted 579 to 386 to sustain Weber's ruling that the convention had followed *Robert's Rules of Order.* In its determination to adopt the Preus program the convention had violated its own rules and had throttled the only tool the minority had to stop the Preus buzz saw.

After the rules were changed, there was no question but that the convention would adopt Preus's "A Statement of Scriptural and Confessional Principles" as a binding doctrinal statement. The issue came to the floor again that afternoon, Wednesday, July 11, 1973. A motion from the floor proposed that the resolution should be referred to the Council of Presidents. During the morning session former president Oliver Harms had been given the opportunity to address the convention that he had not been given the night before. He had proposed that the convention turn over to the Council of Presidents the issues on which it was finding it impossible to come to agreement, including the issue of adopting "A Statement." When debate was shut off by a simple majority vote, the motion to refer was declined.

Additional amendments were also rejected. Finally debate was terminated by majority vote, and Resolution 3-01 was adopted 562 to 455. Fifty-five percent of the convention delegates had made "A Statement of Scriptural and Confessional Principles" binding on the whole Synod.

Immediately raising a point of privilege, Herman Neunaber, president of the Synod's Southern Illinois District, stated how he intended to deal with the resolution for those in his district who had conscience problems with it. Samuel Roth then asked for the floor. Short of stature with a youthful face that belied his age and maturity, Roth was standing in front of a microphone on the right side in the front of the convention hall. Speaking softly and calmly, his tenor voice without emotion, his demeanor respectful, Roth said:

> I speak to a matter of conscience. It is important to me to record my dissent to this vote because I am deeply convinced that it is a mistake which the Synod will regret and I hope someday will correct. I have studied the president's "Statement" thoroughly. I accept it as a helpful tool for study but not as a measure of my orthodoxy according to the sacred Scriptures. I invite those who feel as I do to join me in recording their dissent. I ask the chair out of respect for our conscience to grant us this privilege. We will do so in an orderly way, the red badges coming in a single file to the secretary's desk, the blue badges to a point in their section. And we ask those who care to join us in one—repeat, one—stanza of "The Church's One Foundation."[22]

With Samuel Roth leading the way, hundreds of delegates rose from their seats to record their dissent to the action of the convention in adopting Resolution 3-01. As they did so, they sang one stanza of the hymn as Roth had requested, but they sang it over and over again, linking arms, many of them in tears. For at least ten minutes they sang, until all the dissenting votes had been submitted.

Shaking his head as he left the convention hall, veteran news reporter Erik Modean of the Lutheran Council News Bureau said to me, "Never in all my years of going to conventions have I seen anything like it."

The major and minor premises of the syllogism were in place. Now the convention had to draw the conclusion. Resolution 3-09 condemned the faculty for holding positions that "A Statement of Scriptural and Confessional Principles" described as contrary to the position of the Synod, and that document was now a binding doctrinal statement. I have already described the presentation of Resolution 3-09 to the convention, my address to the convention in behalf of the CS faculty, and the convention decision to hear from the three elected representatives of the faculty before taking action on the resolution.

Resolution 3-09 came back on the floor as the first order of business Thursday morning, July 12, 1973. Vice-president Roland Wiederaenders had been assigned to chair the session. I had helped make the arrangements to provide for presentations and discussion in an orderly way. Each of the three elected faculty representatives was to make a ten-minute presentation on one of the three charges of false doctrine in the resolution. Following each presentation there was to be a forty-five-minute period for discussion. At the end of the three presentations and the ensuing discussion the regular rules of the convention would apply.

Edgar Krentz of the CS faculty addressed the issue of the faculty's alleged rejection of the formal principle and the consequent "subversion of the authority of Scripture." Tall, thin, and wiry, his sandy hair cut short and wearing a full beard, Krentz chose his words with care. He explained that he and all the members of the faculty accepted the Bible as the inspired Word of God and the only rule of faith and practice and to underscore the importance of careful exegetical study in order to hear what the Bible actually teaches.

Robert Bertram was the next faculty representative to speak when the discussion period had elapsed. Of medium build with thinning black hair and a clipped beard, stressing first one side of an issue, then the other, Bertram spoke to the charge of "gospel reductionism." Rejecting the label, he used several biblical texts to do what Luther insisted had to be done with every text of the Bible, namely, to find in the text that which drives home the message of Jesus Christ (*was Christum treibt*).

Academic dean John Damm spoke to the charge that the faculty denied the third use of the law. Dressed, as I was, in a black suit and clerical collar, a receding hairline emphasizing his full face, Damm cited page and paragraph of the Formula of Concord to demonstrate that faculty members affirmed what the Lutheran confessional writings affirmed about the third use of the law. He explained how the CS curriculum was designed to help students be faithful to the proclamation of both law and gospel.

As I sat on the platform with my three CS colleagues, I was struck by the humor of what was happening. Before we left St. Louis, Andrew Weyermann, a faculty member who served as a kind of "house whip" to get things accomplished, told the four of us that for the sake of the seminary we should appear in New Orleans without beards and without clericals. I took him so seriously that I bought a red and white sports jacket to wear in New Orleans. But here we were on the convention platform, two of us in clericals, two of us with beards!

When the three hours for discussion had expired, the parliamentary wrangling resumed. Combined Committee Number 2 and 3 wanted to submit an amendment to Resolution 3-09. A delegate wanted to challenge the constitutionality of the resolution. Other delegates wanted to hear from the CS BoC. The delegates agreed that the committee that had worked out the arrangements for the orderly preceding session should propose further arrangements. So over the lunch hour I once again took part in working out a procedure to help the convention figure out what to do with a resolution that was condemning the CS faculty. I felt like an accused criminal who had been asked to help the jury determine the quickest and most orderly way to effect an execution.

After lunch Resolution 3-09 was again the order of business. Wiederaenders as chair ruled out of order the motion to declare the resolution unconstitutional. The two committees presented their amendments, and members of the BoC addressed the convention. William Buege presented the reasons why the BoC was convinced it had been given the responsibility to make the decision concerning the faculty by the previous convention. BoC chair George Loose explained that the Synod bylaws gave the BoC supervisory responsibility over doctrine at CS and that the duly constituted BoC had not found reason to judge any faculty member guilty of false doctrine. Kurt Biel pointed out that the BoC had not been given the privilege of distributing to the delegates its response to the published criticisms of some of its members. Walter Dissen and Edwin Weber explained why they felt it necessary to issue their "supplementary" reports. The delegates agreed to receive the BoC's reply, and a response to the reply from the dissident BoC members.

The committee's amendments to Resolution 3-09 made it clear that what was being condemned was a theological position rather than particular people, even though everything else in the resolution attributed the position to what was called the faculty majority, to distinguish them from the five Preus supporters among the faculty. The amendments added a resolve that turned the whole business over to the BoC. It was safe to do that at this point since the election results had made it clear that Preus now controlled the BoC.

The amendments were approved. Debate was cut off. By a vote of 574 to 451 the convention declared the CS faculty to be teaching false doctrine that "cannot be tolerated in the church of God."

A year before, I had asked myself whether Preus actually expected the people of the Synod to believe that the faculty held positions that they publicly disowned. Apparently Preus did expect them to believe that, and a majority of convention delegates did believe it—even though four representatives of the faculty in their presence told them it was not so. On the eve of the New Orleans convention I had told myself that "people in the middle" would put forth major efforts to avoid a split and to bring about a compromise. At New Orleans there was no middle. The Synod had become so polarized that delegates were either in one camp or the other.

One of what I considered Preus's chief goals for the convention remained to be accomplished. Having taken care of the faculty, it was now necessary for the convention to come to terms with me as leader and defender of the faculty. The conclusion of the syllogism had to have an additional application.

On Monday evening of the convention, before the Preus buzz saw started turning, I received a phone call from Lewis Niemoeller, chair of Committee Number 3 on Seminary Issues. It was shortly after 11:00 P.M. and I was already soundly asleep. Fully aware of the crisis in which I was involved, I was determined to get a good night's sleep each night during the convention so that I could handle whatever stress a new day would bring. Niemoeller asked if I would come to a meeting with him and Jacob Preus in the president's suite the next morning at 7:30.

When I awoke the next morning, I was not sure whether I had actually received the phone call or whether it had been a dream. My wife thought she remembered a phone call, but she had really slept through it all. I called John Damm of our faculty and told him my problem. He agreed to call Niemoeller on some pretext and find out if there really was to be a meeting. A few minutes later Damm called back to tell me that the phone call was no dream. I was expected in the president's suite at 7:30.

I was at the door at the appointed hour, and Niemoeller invited me into the spacious suite of rooms reserved for VIPs. Jacob Preus greeted me with a perfunctory handshake. Niemoeller poured me a cup of coffee and invited me to sit down on the sofa as he occupied a chair nearby. Preus stood off in the distance sipping coffee, then setting the cup down, pacing back and forth, alternately picking up the cup for a sip of coffee and inhaling on a cigarette.

Wearing a dark suit with a flashy tie, the cowlick of his dark hair invading his forehead, peering through his glasses, Niemoeller leaned toward me and spoke in a lugubrious voice that oozed pastoral concern for me. Preus and he had arranged this meeting, he told me, in the hope of avoiding major embarrassment for me at the convention. Committee 3 had produced a resolution that required that I resign my office as CS president before the close of the convention or be removed from office. The resolution specified the reasons for asking for my resignation. Preus and he did not want to present the resolution to the convention, Niemoeller told me, and would not do so if I would agree on my own to resign. In that event a very different resolution would be presented, one thanking me for my service and commending me for my churchmanship.

I asked if I could see the resolution. Niemoeller reached into his briefcase and produced it. I scanned it and saw that it was every bit as bad as Niemoeller had said it was. When did he want an answer? I asked. He needed to know by 3:00 that afternoon, he told me, in order to meet the duplicating schedule to get the material into the delegates' hands for the next day's business. If he did not hear by 3:00, the resolution he had shown me would be printed for distribution to the delegates. I told him that I would have an answer by 3:00. Rising from the sofa and setting down my almost-full coffee cup, I glared coldly first at Niemoeller and then at Preus, thanked them for the meeting, and left.

I had known instinctively what I should do, but I owed it to CS and the Synod, and to myself as well, to check it out with close colleagues and friends. I went back to my hotel room and told Ernestine what had happened. She embraced me and said simply, "You know what you have to do." I reported on the meeting to my CS faculty colleagues over sandwiches as we lunched in my room. They were almost too embarrassed to respond. Edgar Krentz spoke for them. He said that he could not tell me what to do but that I should disabuse myself of the illusion if I was thinking that my resignation would mean that Preus would go easier on the faculty. I sought the counsel of BoC chair George Loose and a few other trusted friends.

At 2:30 P.M. I made my way through the section reserved for voting delegates in search of Niemoeller. I found him in a room behind the platform, attending a committee meeting. We talked in the ramp area. I told Niemoeller that I had talked to friends and to God and had decided that I would await the action of the convention. Niemoeller urged me to reconsider for the good of the Synod and CS as well as for my own. I told him that I was not guilty of the crimes of which his committee was accusing me and therefore could not in conscience resign to spare myself the embarrassment of having them made public. I was convinced, I told him, that my call as CS president had come from God, and I therefore could not be a participant in political chicanery to remove me from the office to which God had called me.

The next day Resolution 3-12 was included among the materials distributed to the delegates for convention action.[23] It accused me of failure to fulfill my responsibility as the spiritual, academic, and administrative head of CS. With allegations numbered from one to ten, it charged me with teaching and advocating false doctrine, with irresponsible use of my office, with demeaning BoC members and faculty members, with intimidation and defiance and insubordination, and with failure to carry out my pastoral duties toward students. The resolution called on me to resign as president and professor effective August 1, 1973, and to announce my resignation before the end of the convention. In the event that I refused to do so, the resolution authorized the president of the Synod to dismiss me.

By the morning of the last day of the convention there had been action on only three of the sixteen resolutions prepared by Committee Number 3 on Seminary Issues. The convention had approved Resolution 3-01, making Preus's "A Statement" binding on the Synod. It had approved bylaw changes essential for the seminaries to continue to receive accreditation. It had condemned the CS St. Louis faculty for teaching false doctrine. Still awaiting convention action were Resolution 3-12, calling for my resignation; Resolution 3-10, which called on those BoC members who supported me to repent and to resign; and eleven other resolutions of lesser importance. On Friday morning, July 13, 1973, the orders of the day were changed "so that matters relating to Concordia Seminary, particularly those dealing with Dr. Tietjen,"[24] could be brought before the convention at 11:00 A.M.

What response should I make to a convention resolution requiring me to resign? I knew what I wanted to say. For me the question was how to say it. I wanted to speak to convention delegates as fellow Christians. I wanted to talk and act like "a called and ordained servant of the Word,"[25] proclaiming the Christian gospel, making it clear that I was a disciple of Jesus ready to follow in his steps wherever they would take me. On my ever-present yellow pad I wrote down notes of what I might say. Then I made my way through the section of voting delegates once again and approached the platform to request that I be called on for a point of privilege immediately after convention action on Resolution 3-12.

Shortly before 11:00 A.M. the ushers began distributing a document to the delegates. It was Resolution 3-12A, entitled "To Deal with Dr. John Tietjen Under the Provisions of Synod's 'Handbook.' "[26] It was a short resolution. It said that since there was not adequate time left to deal with the issues listed in Resolution 3-12 and since there were adequate procedures in the Synod's *Handbook* to deal with them, "the matter of Dr. John H. Tietjen as president and professor of Concordia Seminary, Saint Louis, shall be dealt with in such manner as is permitted under applicable substantive and procedural provisions of the *Handbook* of Synod."

When 11:00 A.M. came, a representative of Committee 3 presented Resolution 3-12A, explaining that it was taking the place of Resolution 3-12. Then under prompting from committee members, he explained that as far as the convention was concerned Resolution 3-12 did not exist since it had never been officially presented to the convention. The committee was presenting instead Resolution 3-12A. There was, of course, the problem that the first "whereas" of the resolution referred to Resolution 3-12, but a helpful amendment substituted the numbers of certain convention overtures for Resolution 3-12. But, delegates pointed out, Resolution 3-12 proposing ouster and reprimand had indeed been given to them whereas Resolution 3-12A now before them said that there were adequate procedures available to deal with the issue without following a course of action that made public accusations and did not give the accused an opportunity for defense. A motion to include within the new resolution an apology to me for the distribution of Resolution 3-12 was voted down. When all the maneuvering was over and debate had been shut off, the convention adopted Resolution 3-12A by a standing vote of 513 to 394.

I stood up and moved to microphone nine as vice-president Edwin Weber, who was chairing this session, explained that I had asked to make a statement and invited me to do so. What was I going to say? Most of what I had prepared to say in response to Resolution 3-12 was not appropriate for Resolution 3-12A. As I stood at the microphone, looking toward the voting delegates, many of whom had turned around in their seats to look at me, what I should say and how I should say it became clear.

"I should like to speak two words to the convention," I began. "Forgive me, one is a hard word. The second is a good word. The hard word is this: I believe I have been grievously wronged by the convention." I listed the reasons. First, I pointed out that the inclusion of many overtures dealing with me in the *Convention Workbook* was a violation of my constitutional rights. Then, I reported the early-morning offer of Preus and Niemoeller to me to resign to spare myself the embarrassment of the charges in Resolution 3-12 and my refusal to do so on the grounds of conscience. I pointed out that Resolution 3-12 had been circulated and, even if it had been withdrawn, the delegates all knew what it said and its accusations were being reported all over the nation. I concluded my "hard word" by saying, "Instead of reprimanding Committee 3 for presenting that material to you rather than recognizing as they now do that adequate procedures are available in the *Handbook* to deal with the matter, you declined to apologize to me."

Then I went on to speak the "good word":

> Even though I have been wronged, I forgive you. I forgive you because I think you really do not know what you are doing. I think in time you will recognize what you are doing and you will grieve over this day. But more important, I forgive you because of the suffering and death of our Lord Jesus Christ and because his blood takes away all our wrongs. . . .
>
> In conclusion I should like to say one thing more. At the beginning of this school year, at the opening service, I preached a sermon in which I asked the seminary community to fix all eyes on the cross. I reminded them of the words of St. Paul that we should know nothing except Christ and him crucified. I pointed out that if we were to undergo suffering of one kind or another in the course of this year, let it be for the sake of the gospel. The gospel is indeed something worth suffering for. I understand the implications of the action which you have just taken for my future, and I shall be prepared to meet with the Board of Control when these "matters" are referred to them. But I want to assure you that, as God gives me strength, wherever I am and whatever I do, I will do my best to see to it that I proclaim nothing except Jesus Christ and his death on the cross. And I pray that it will not be too long hence when the Lutheran Church–Missouri Synod will once again be able to forget everything except Jesus Christ and him crucified. May God bless you.[27]

Bedlam broke out on the convention floor, and the chair ended the session. Hundreds of people, many of them donning black armbands, gathered around to embrace me and to shake my hand. Ernestine, who sat in the visitor section in the rear of the hall next to Shirley Loose, wife of the BoC chair, was instantly surrounded by CS students. Dennis Laherty and Boyd Faust spoke for them in expressing their grief and offering their help. The students escorted Ernestine to the Rivergate hallway, where several hundred people were gathering for a service of Holy

Communion planned by a local pastor. I was whisked off to a press conference.

Later that day Oliver Harms called to ask Ernestine and me to go to dinner with him and his wife, Bert. I had to decline, having already agreed to be the guest of lay delegate Merrill Gille, a long-time friend from my days as an assistant pastor in Teaneck. With Gille on one side and Ernestine on the other, I walked to Antoine's for dinner wearing my red and white jacket, to let the world know that the gloom and doom of church politics could not destroy the joy of my resurrection faith.

9 ———◆

KANGAROO COURT

The debate had been going on furiously for two hours after the motion had been introduced around 11:00 A.M. on Saturday, August 18, 1973. The Board of Control of Concordia Seminary in St. Louis, Missouri, was holding its first meeting, a specially called one, following the July convention of the Lutheran Church–Missouri Synod in New Orleans. It was a sweltry summer day. In spite of the air conditioning the temperature in the CS board room felt a great deal hotter than the temperature outside.

The day before, newly elected member Ewald J. Otto had been elected chair of the BoC for the next two years. Otto now sat where I was accustomed to see George Loose, who had presided at BoC meetings since I had arrived at CS in 1969. Otto was short, thin, with hollowed cheeks and a gaunt face, staring blankly through dark-rimmed glasses. Also in attendance was newly elected member Alfred Briel, coatless but wearing a tie with his short-sleeve shirt, his full face crowned with a shock of graying hair arranged with a swirl atop his brow. Of the remaining nine board members only Kurt Biel was absent; he was in Europe when he received notice of the meeting.

The BoC had reorganized. Not only was Otto in the chair, but Edwin Weber had been elected vice-chair, Walter Dissen secretary, and Charles Burmeister treasurer. The new Preus majority was firmly in control. Dissen had called William Buege, who was then the ranking BoC officer as vice-chair, and had informed him that he had been in touch with a majority of members. They wanted a special meeting on August 17–18, 1973, for the purpose of taking up the matters that the New Orleans convention had referred to the BoC. Buege had obliged and under the date of July 31, called the meeting.

The motion that was being hotly debated had been introduced by Weber and seconded by Dissen: "That since our chairman has reported that parts (a) and (b) of 6.79 of the Synod's bylaws have been a fruitless attempt, that the Board now under 6.79(d) suspend Dr. Tietjen from the office of president and professor of the Seminary immediately because of the gravity of the situation and the serious harm that can result to the Synod and the Seminary if the problem is not faced resolutely now."[1]

What the first part of the resolution meant to say was that the attempts to resolve a problem under bylaw 6.79a. and b. had proved fruitless. Bylaw 6.79 had been adopted at the LCMS New Orleans convention, spelling out due process procedures at the Synod's schools of higher education. The new rules were part of a wider effort to meet the concerns of the CS's accrediting agency, the American Association of Theological Schools, which had suspended its accreditation a year earlier over the intrusion of the Synod's president and Board for Higher Education into the affairs of CS's governing board. Bylaw 6.79 listed thirteen steps, a. through m., describing procedures to be followed from the introduction of charges against a faculty member all the way to the person's removal from membership in the Synod.

Section a. of bylaw 6.79 specified that a board of control, in the event that it received a formal charge against a faculty member, must require the complainant to meet with the faculty member to "attempt to find a peaceful and amicable resolution of the matter." Section b. specified that if such an attempt should prove unsatisfactory, the school's president (or its board chair if the president had been accused) should "attempt to deal with [the accusation] to the satisfaction of all concerned." Section d. provided for the possibility that the board could "suspend the faculty member from his teaching duties" if the board deemed the charge "serious enough to threaten immediate harm to the accused or others by his continuance as a member of the faculty."[2]

The motion before the BoC proposed that the conditions specified under sections a. and b. of bylaw 6.79 had been fulfilled and that the BoC should avail itself of the possibility provided in section d. The board should, then and there, suspend me from being a professor and president of CS. Charges had been preferred against me, the condition envisioned in section a. of bylaw 6.79. Two clergy members of New Orleans floor Committee Number 3, Leonard P. Buelow of Green Bay, Wisconsin, and Harlan H. Harnapp of North Platte, Nebraska, had submitted the charges in a nine-page letter addressed to the BoC under the date of August 8, 1973. I received my copy on August 14, three days before the BoC meeting. The postmark indicated that the letter had been sent to me via air mail special delivery from Green Bay only the day before.

There were ten formal charges in the letter, identical in wording to the accusations that had appeared in Resolution 3–12 of the New Orleans convention, which had been circulated to delegates but never officially presented.[3] Buelow and Harnapp charged me, first of all, with "allowing and fostering false doctrine"[4] and presented four pages of material allegedly in support of the charge. In addition, they charged me with failing to mediate and settle doctrinal disagreements within the faculty; being administratively irresponsible; assuming BoC duties and prerogatives; intimidating BoC members; demeaning faculty members; defying the office of the synodical president; refusing to cooperate with the synodical president; being insubordinate to the BHE; and failing to maintain careful watch over the spiritual welfare, personal life, and conduct of the student body.

In their letter Buelow and Harnapp stated that as members of New Orleans Committee Number 3 they had discussed these matters with me as required in section a. of bylaw 6.79 and were now presenting the charges in writing as required by 6.79b. They advised the BoC that the documents issued by the Commission on Theology and Church Relations during the controversy fulfilled the bylaw requirement that the commission be asked for an opinion if the charge was doctrinal in nature. They urged the BoC to exercise the authority granted in 6.79d. to suspend me.

On August 17, the BoC first disposed of a number of preliminary matters and granted former Synod president Oliver Harms an opportunity to share his concern that the BoC should work for reconciliation in the Synod. Then the BoC turned its attention to the charges against me. Walter Dissen moved and Alfred Briel seconded that the BoC acknowledge that "the requirements of bylaw 6.79(a) have been met" and that the BoC direct that I meet once more with the accusers, and that "such parties report back to the Board of Control not later than 3 P.M. today." When I pointed out the impossibility of meeting in St. Louis with people who were in Wisconsin and Nebraska, Dissen said that Buelow and Harnapp were in St. Louis in response to an invitation from him.

William Buege challenged the legality of dealing with the charges on the grounds that the issue was not included on the stated agenda for the special meeting. Otto ruled that the charges were pertinent since they had to do with New Orleans convention resolutions, and the BoC sustained his ruling by a vote of 6 to 4. After much wrangling they recessed for lunch.

When the BoC reconvened at 2:00 P.M., it was clear that the 3:00 P.M. report time was impractical. Herman Scherer proposed a substitute motion: to receive the charges from Buelow and Harnapp and to instruct them to carry out the provisions of bylaw 6.79a. Weber amended the motion to require that I meet with Buelow and Harnapp at 7:00 that evening. When the BoC approved the amendment and the motion, Buege, Nickel, Roschke, and Scherer asked that their negative votes be recorded on the grounds that the action was not in compliance with bylaw 6.79a.

I protested the action. I argued that the BoC had no legal right to act on a convention resolution that was itself illegal because the Synod had violated its own bylaws in receiving the overtures on which the resolution was based. I joined with other members of the BoC in asserting that the BoC's action was illegal because the issue it dealt with was not on the announced agenda and because it violated the intention of bylaw 6.79a.

Furthermore, I stated that it was my considered judgment that it was not possible for me to receive a fair hearing because a majority of the BoC was on record as having prejudged my case. The chair invited me to amplify my concern. I called attention to the many editorials in *Affirm* in which Ewald J. Otto, now the BoC chair, had spoken out in judgment against me. I pointed out that Alfred Briel had been a member of Committee Number 3 in New Orleans and had participated in issuing Resolution 3–12 that had condemned me. In addition, I stated that the Evansville *Press* on July 28, 1973, had quoted Briel as saying concerning my doctrinal position, "The man is in error . . . no doubt about that." I stated further that Burmeister and Fincke had issued one "minority report" to accompany the BoC's report to the New Orleans convention; Dissen and Weber had issued another, in which they had condemned me on the same charges now being brought against me. My protest fell on deaf ears.

The BoC recessed for the day at 6:30 P.M. Shortly before 7:00 my meeting with Buelow and Harnapp began. Harnapp crossed and uncrossed his long legs as he tried to make his slender body comfortable, his face rigid and unsmiling. Buelow, of medium build, leaned back in his chair, trying to relax, a hint of a smile on his face. When I asked them why they had not come to me first with their concerns before taking them to the BoC, Buelow responded in an unctuous pulpit tone that they had no need to do that because their accusations were public knowledge. I informed them that it was untrue that, as they had said in their letter to the BoC, they had already discussed these charges with me. The fact was that I did not know who they were until I invited them into my office. Harnapp gruffly disputed my assertion, insisting that I knew very well who they were.

I asked Buelow and Harnapp if they were interested in the peaceful and amicable resolution envisioned in bylaw 6.79. When they said they were, I told them that I would be glad to respond to their charges once I had the opportunity to prepare my thoughts and to gather the material necessary to show them that they were wrong. Every time either of them asked me a question about one of the charges, I assured them that I would respond to their questions at a subsequent meeting when I was prepared to deal with their accusations. At 8:15 P.M. our meeting ended.

When Buelow and Harnapp were gone, I telephoned Richard Duesenberg. He and his twin brother Robert were attorneys in the St. Louis area and several weeks earlier had offered to give legal counsel without charge to me or to faculty members. The Duesenberg brothers were Lutherans, graduates of the Missouri Synod–related Valparaiso University, and friends of several members of the faculty. Although they were both conservative theologically, they were distressed over the New Orleans convention resolutions. Both were short of stature, with flaming red hair and freckled faces.

I had had a preliminary conversation with Richard Duesenberg late in July and talked with him in earnest after the Buelow-Harnapp charges arrived. He had assured me that nothing could happen at the August 17–18 meeting. After all, the charges were not on the stated agenda for a special meeting, and the provisions of the new bylaws were specific about the steps that had to be followed. When I reported to Duesenberg over the telephone what was happening at the BoC meeting, he was stunned and appalled. I told him that it was clear to me that I would be suspended before the meeting ended. He dictated to me words that I could use if the BoC should act against me.

When the BoC reconvened the following morning at 9:00, Ewald Otto as chair held out a sealed envelope, presented it to Walter Dissen as secretary, and asked him to read the contents. Inside was a letter from Buelow and Harnapp, written in longhand on stationery of the Hilton Inn near the St. Louis airport, and dated August 18. The letter informed the BoC that the efforts of Buelow and Harnapp to find a peaceful and amicable solution were fruitless and that they wanted to proceed to the next section of bylaw 6.79.

I reported to the BoC concerning my meeting with Buelow and Harnapp and my readiness to meet with them at a future time concerning their charges. I pointed out that the provisions of 6.79a. had not yet been fulfilled and that the BoC would be acting illegally if it proceeded to the next step.

After some discussion Alfred Briel made the motion, seconded by Eugene Fincke, "That the board direct its chairman and its executive officer, Dr. John Tietjen, to meet with Pastors Buelow and Harnapp pursuant to bylaw 6.79(b)." After considerable discussion, the motion was adopted, and Buege, Nickel, Roschke, and Scherer recorded their negative votes. Otto then declared a recess in order to conduct the envisioned meeting. The BoC upheld the chair's ruling when Buege challenged it. Once again Buege, Nickel, Roschke, and Scherer recorded their negative votes.

The meeting was recessed at 10:05 A.M. In the corridor, waiting for a meeting they knew was going to take place, were Buelow and Harnapp. We met in my office, standing the whole time. Buelow and Harnapp claimed that the charges against me had been before the church for a long time and that I had already responded to them in various writings. Therefore there was no point in further meetings with me. I said that I had been perfectly willing to discuss the charges with Buelow and Harnapp but the BoC's action in proceeding to the next step in the bylaws now made that impossible. As Buelow and Harnapp departed and Otto made his way back to the board room, I called Richard Duesenberg to tell him what had happened.

At 11:00 A.M. the BoC reconvened. After Otto reported on his fruitless efforts to solve the problem that Buelow and Harnapp had raised, Weber made the motion reported above, for my suspension. First Paul Nickel and then Herman Scherer tried a number of parliamentary moves to prevent the action. At approximately 1:00 P.M. the resolution was adopted. Once again Buege, Nickel, Roschke, and Scherer recorded their negative votes.

I reached within my coat pocket and pulled out several three-by-five-inch note papers and flipped to the appropriate one.[5] Before the meeting I had written down what I would say if the BoC required me to affirm Preus's "A Statement of Scriptural and Confessional Principles." Late the night before, after my phone call to Duesenberg, I wrote out what I would say if I were suspended and if the BoC appointed an acting president. I asked for the floor and read from the note in front of me: "I consider it my obligation to continue as president and to continue to exercise my responsibilities. To do otherwise would impose a risk of malfeasance in office and would be submission to an illegal and *ultra vires* [beyond the scope of legal authority] act of the Board."

Ewald Otto looked at me with his mouth open. Walter Dissen stared at me, his eyes blazing anger. Charles Burmeister broke the silence, suggesting that the BoC talk about what I had said. What struck them was my use of the phrase *"ultra vires."* No matter how versed I may have been in Latin, they knew that phrase came from a lawyer and that I was acting on the basis of legal counsel. With Dissen making the motion, the BoC resolved to solicit the opinion of legal counsel immediately. They recessed at 1:40 P.M.

When they reconvened at 2:25 P.M., CS legal counsel Philip Draheim was present. He informed the BoC that earlier in the day attorney Richard Duesenberg had called him to inform him of what was happening at the BoC meeting and of the advice given me that any action to suspend me at this meeting would be illegal. Further, Draheim reported that Duesenberg had announced that if the BoC enacted its suspension, a lawsuit would be filed on Monday morning, August 20. I was excused from the meeting at this point.

When I returned about an hour later, I learned that the BoC had resolved, with Buege making the motion and Roschke seconding, to "delay implementation of its suspension resolution until the Board has received a legal opinion from its counsel as to whether the Board's action is legally proper and until it has received an opinion from the Commission on Constitutional Matters that 6.79 is applicable to the president of the institution in his presidency and that the Board has followed proper procedure pursuant to 6.79."

All that was left to be done at the meeting was to work out a news release agreeable to all concerned. The BoC had suspended me, but its suspension was in a state of limbo. In spite of all the machinations I was still president of CS.

The action of the August 17–18 meeting clarified the intentions of the new BoC. From the moment the New Orleans convention ended, people had speculated about what the BoC would do. Would it take action against me first, or the faculty first and then me, or both at the same time? Would CS open in September for the fall term? How could it, with all but five members of the faculty identified with a position that had been condemned as "not to be tolerated in the Church of God"?

Jacob Preus himself contributed to the rumors. Personally and through others he spoke first to one member of the faculty, then another, about reaching an accommodation with us. Arthur Ahlschwede, executive secretary of the Synod's BHE, claimed to speak for Preus in contacting faculty member Carl Volz, professor of historical theology: "We need to work something out. Tietjen goes, and the rest of the faculty stays. Think it over. Call me back and tell me what you think." Preus himself told Volz: "Tietjen and a few others must go, but the school must open and go on. Think it over and call me back." I asked Volz to find out which deal was on. In my behalf Volz told Ahlschwede, "Tietjen is open to any reasonable offer. What do you have in mind? Why not call Tietjen yourself?"[6]

Ahlschwede did call me on July 20. "What can I do for you?" he asked. "I don't know," I responded. "What do you have in mind?" "When does the board meet?" Ahlschwede asked cryptically. "Let me know what I can do to help." To which I answered, "If you think of any way you can help, let me know."[7]

Roland Wiederaenders came to see me on July 23. He explained that Preus and Ahlschwede had discussed with him finding some procedure to avoid precipitous action on the part of the newly elected BoC in dealing with me and the faculty. Wiederaenders told me he was asked to speak for Preus in approaching me about "adjusting" my position in keeping with the Synod's decision at New Orleans and in making the same request of the faculty. Preus changed his mind, however, "because he did not want it to be said that he was making an end run on the Board of Control."[8] Wiederaenders was to approach me not as Preus's representative but as my personal friend.

Wiederaenders had two proposals to make concerning the faculty. They could accept "A Statement of Scriptural and Confessional Principles" and announce their action to the BoC. In addition they could draw up a list of the issues as they understood them. I summarized for Wiederaenders how the faculty saw the situation and what they were planning to say publicly. At no point did Wiederaenders make any proposal to me about my future, although Preus a few days later told the Council of Presidents that I had turned down an offer of reconciliation presented to me in Preus's name. In fact Wiederaenders had made it clear that there was no way out of the problem confronting CS except for us to knuckle under and accept as binding a doctrinal statement we in conscience could not approve.

On Friday, July 27, Preus arranged a meeting in his office with faculty member Duane Mehl, professor of practical theology. In a phone conversation a few days earlier, Preus had assured Mehl of a continuing position at CS. Preus stressed that it was essential that Mehl arrange for a meeting between Preus and a group of the faculty. Preus said the faculty had two aces up their collective sleeve: one, "I do not want to close the seminary," and two, "I do not want all that blood on my hands."[9] On Monday, July 30, Preus phoned Mehl, stressing the urgency of the meeting with members of the faculty because BoC members were intending to suspend operations at CS for the fall term. On August 1 Mehl put in writing what he had communicated to Preus by phone: The faculty majority would be glad to meet with Preus when they were all back in town following the summer vacation. The proposal for a meeting should be addressed to them through their president. My status as CS president would have to be the first item on the agenda.

On August 18 the BoC's aborted attempt to suspend me clarified how the Preus majority intended to handle CS. Their course would become crystal clear in the months ahead. Had there been a serious intention to suspend CS operations for a time? Perhaps. But more than likely that was a bargaining chip to get favorable action out of the faculty while at the same time encouraging the faculty to think that they needed to ally themselves with Preus to avoid what a determined BoC might do. What the BoC majority really had in mind was to take over the presidency so that they would have free reign to do anything else.

What should the CS faculty do about the New Orleans convention resolutions? Answering that question consumed faculty time and attention in the days immediately following the convention. On July 14 the faculty's representatives and I arrived back in St. Louis to a tumultuous welcome by hundreds of people from CS and the city's Lutheran community. We went straight from the airport to the CS chapel, where faculty member Arthur Carl Piepkorn presided and preached at a service of holy communion. After a Sabbath day's rest we went to work.

The Faculty Advisory Committee met on July 16 to reflect on assessments of two of its members. At this point the FAC consisted of seven members: Robert W. Bertram, the systematics theologian who gave leadership in theological articulation; Richard R. Caemmerer, senior member of the faculty, who had shaped much of the theology of his colleagues; Alfred O. Fuerbringer, who as my predecessor brought with him extensive synodical experience; Edgar M. Krentz, New Testament scholar, who had emerged as one of the faculty's leaders; Robert H. Smith, younger New Testament theologian gifted with clear expression; and Andrew M. Weyermann, ethicist who kept his colleagues focused on practical issues and was FAC chair.

Krentz proposed to the FAC that the faculty issue a statement of conscience and protest, bluntly attacking the New Orleans resolutions, inviting others to join in the protest, and announcing the faculty's decision to stand firm until removed from office. Weyermann related the seminary situation to what was happening in the Synod. He assessed that the Missouri Synod as we knew it no longer existed and that the Preus party, entrenched for a long time to come, would turn the Synod into a sect. He argued that our days at CS were numbered and that, having been condemned together, we needed to stand together in demanding that the Synod right the wrongs committed at New Orleans, thus provoking the Preus regime into further use of its power and turning CS into a paradigm of what would happen to others throughout the Synod. Weyermann proposed that the faculty lead the way in forming a coalition of congregations under a confessional banner to facilitate "free and open fellowship with other Lutherans and engage in more open ministry within the structure of the Lutheran Church–Missouri Synod as long as this is possible."[10]

On July 17 the FAC convened small group meetings of the faculty to share its thinking and to receive recommendations from what was now regularly called "the faculty majority." Many suggestions came out of the meetings, including proposals to go on strike, to set up a seminary in exile, and to excommunicate the faculty "minority." On one item everyone was agreed: A bold and public rejection of the New Orleans actions was needed. The FAC gave Edgar Krentz the task of producing a draft in consultation with Norman Habel, George Hoyer, and Robert Smith.

On July 23 the faculty majority adopted "A Declaration of Protest and Confession," and fifty-one members of the faculty and executive staff signed the document. After chapel worship the next day, Richard R. Caemmerer read the document to the seminary community assembled in front of the statue of Martin Luther at the entrance to the quadrangle. Reading with a voice full of passion that belied the frailty of his body, Caemmerer protested the wrongs of the New Orleans convention: the judgment about false doctrine, the violation of evangelical discipline, the breach of contract in judging the faculty by an imposed doctrinal norm, the elevation of tradition above Scripture, the use of coercive power to establish truth, the alteration of the Synod's confessional standard. With fervor Caemmerer read what we confessed: our longing for peace and unity, our ordination vow, an open Bible unfettered by human rules, our commitment to the teaching of law and gospel, our determination to continue in our teaching vocation.

For us all, Caemmerer intoned: "Our church confronts a crisis. The Gospel is at stake. Our church is in danger of losing its truly Lutheran character and of becoming a sect." Caemmerer appealed to fellow members within the Synod to join in a common movement of protest and confession.

During the last week in July three students came to see me in my office: Robert Preece, student body president who had graduated in June and was now serving a Missouri Synod congregation in Waterloo, Illinois; Stephen Hitchcock; and Leon Rosenthal. They presented to me a "Gift of Thanks and Support" in the amount of $1,500 that had been contributed by students and graduates of the previous academic year. Realizing that serious problems lay ahead for us, students had raised funds for the benefit of my family and the families of faculty members.

About the same time I received a number of other unsolicited gifts from pastors and laity of the Missouri Synod to be used for the defense and support of the faculty. What should I do with the gifts? How should I place them in escrow? I wanted to avoid any charge of misappropriation of funds. On the advice of attorney Richard Duesenberg, we established a not-for-profit corporation and deposited the funds in an account in its name, the Fund for Lutheran Theological Education, or FLUTE. We now had an organization and the nucleus of funding to engage in the defense and the support of the faculty.

From August 26 to 28 more than eight hundred members of the LCMS gathered in Chicago from all over the country for "A Conference on Evangelical Lutheranism." At the New Orleans convention Bertwin Frey and Dean Lueking, the leaders of the loyal opposition within the Synod, had announced that they would convene a meeting shortly after the convention in order to assess what had happened and to determine what to do next. Lueking invited a number of people to work together to plan the meeting, including me. Among the planners were Richard Jungkuntz, the executive of the Commission on Theology and Church Relations, who had been the first person to be removed from office after Preus's election and who was now serving as provost at Pacific Lutheran University in Tacoma, Washington; and C. Thomas Spitz, Missouri Synod pastor who was serving as general secretary of the Lutheran Council in the U.S.A. and who made it clear to Lueking and Frey at the New Orleans convention that he was eager to be involved in a movement of protest and confession. By the beginning of the next year Spitz had left his LCUSA post to serve as pastor of a Missouri Synod congregation in Manhasset, New York, so that he could devote himself fully to the protest movement without compromising the inter-Lutheran organization.

The people who came together for the Chicago conference could be described as trauma victims of the New Orleans convention. They had experienced the onslaught of what some called the Preus juggernaut and were concerned about what was going to happen to people in the Missouri Synod. Among many proposals there was almost unanimous agreement on the need for an organization to unite people to protest what was happening within the Synod and to stand together in a mutual defense pact. Under the guidance of Lueking as chair, those gathered in Chicago issued a statement that protested "errant actions" of the New Orleans convention and pledged "spiritual concern, financial support, and a share in the risks involved" for any who found themselves in jeopardy because of their opposition to convention actions.[11] The conference participants set in motion the legal incorporation of the movement of protest and confession into a national organization, whose name would be determined later. They elected ten members to serve as a board of directors and gave the board the responsibility of choosing five additional members to ensure proper representation of gender, race, and region.

Within a month the new board had met and chosen the additional five members, with me included among them. The organization had a name, Evangelical Lutherans in Mission, or ELIM. Samuel Roth, the articulate spokesperson for the moderate cause at the New Orleans convention, had been named president; Elwyn Ewald, a returning missionary from New

Guinea, who claimed that he had turned down an offer from Preus to serve on the Synod's staff, had been designated general manager. A mutual defense league, much larger and more inclusive than FLUTE, was ready for action.

The new board of ELIM recognized that communication was a top priority and authorized the publication of a newspaper. Larry Neeb, who had gained considerable experience in communications through his work for CS, was asked to be editor. Neeb engaged Richard Mueller and David Roschke, two students who had considerable expertise in the area of communications, to assist him. He surrounded himself with an editorial board of communications experts, among whom was Elmer Kraemer, longtime editor of newspapers within the Missouri Synod, who gave considerable assistance in the early stages of publication.

Beginning in October 1973 *Missouri in Perspective*, a biweekly newspaper, began circulating throughout the Synod, informing its readers of the latest actions of the Preus administration and presenting the opinions of the leaders of the movement of protest and confession. With prodigious energy the editors succeeded regularly in scooping other publications in reporting the fast-breaking events of the LCMS controversy. Circulation soon reached 150,000.

In the face of the Preus onslaught against CS, the faculty and the BoC had taken their case to the people of the Missouri Synod at the convention of New Orleans. In a highly politicized and completely polarized convention, Preus won and CS lost. Now, with the formation of ELIM, CS no longer stood alone. Many at CS hoped that with a grassroots organization and an effective journal of communication, it might still be possible to rouse the people of the Synod into action.

Once invited in, Richard Duesenberg, the St. Louis attorney who had offered legal counsel *pro bono*, jumped into the arena with both feet. On August 28, 1973, and again on September 11, he wrote letters to all the district presidents of the Missouri Synod, with copies to the synodical president and vice-presidents, informing them of what happened at the August 17–18 meeting of the BoC. He wrote the letters without my knowledge so that I could not be held accountable for his action. His brother sent a similar letter on August 31. In the letter of August 28 Richard Duesenberg wrote, "What took place on August 17 and 18 falls miserably short of any standards of fairness, let alone of standards required by law or expected of a Christian church body." In the letter of September 11 he recounted in detail how the BoC had moved through the steps of the bylaws in "less than 36 hours" to suspend me from office, and then frankly and bluntly appealed to the district presidents to use their influence on the Commission on Constitutional Matters to reverse the decision of the BoC.

In delaying implementation of the action to suspend me, the BoC had decided to ask the Commission on Constitutional Matters for an opinion on whether bylaw 6.79 applied to the president of a synodical school as president rather than as faculty member, and whether the BoC had followed the procedure envisioned in bylaw 6.79 in suspending me. Both the majority and the minority members of the BoC were eager to share their views with the commission, and so the commission invited "both parties" to appear at the commission's meeting on September 21, 1973.[12] When Richard Duesenberg offered his help to the "minority" faction of the BoC, they asked him to represent them before the commission.

After hearing the views of both sides of the BoC, the Commission on Constitutional Matters concluded that bylaw 6.79 did indeed apply to the CS president and that the BoC had the right to suspend me. Had the BoC correctly followed the procedures of bylaw 6.79? Instead of rebuking the BoC for its cavalier handling of the bylaw, as Duesenberg had insisted should be done, the commission found it hard to believe that I should not have been expecting to respond to the charges.

"Nevertheless," the commission concluded, "it would seem that the procedural requirements of Bylaw 6.79 may not have been adequately fulfilled . . . and that reasonable time intervals may not have been provided between the procedural steps called for in Bylaw 6.79." The commission therefore recommended that the BoC revert to the first step of the bylaw and "provide reasonable time to answer charges, so that no person . . . can say that any action against him was precipitate or that he was not treated 'in the spirit of Christian love.' (Bylaw 6.79a)."[13] Without any question about the outcome, the BoC was instructed to go through the process more slowly.

The BoC convened a special meeting on September 29, 1973, to deal with the action of the Commission on Constitutional Matters. After reviewing the commission's opinion, the BoC called on Leonard Buelow and Harlan Harnapp to communicate with me and to meet with me promptly, no later than October 15, 1973. Then, voting on a motion made by William Buege and seconded by Paul Nickel, the BoC rejected a proposal to "lift the suspension of Dr. John Tietjen."[14] When I inquired what my status was, Ewald Otto as chair responded that he assumed I was in a state of suspension. I told him that the BoC could not have it both ways—there could not be a suspension that was not implemented. I wanted a clear statement by the end of the meeting that I was not suspended or I would assume that I was suspended and would therefore take appropriate action against the BoC. Once again the majority stopped a meeting to get the advice of legal counsel. After a telephone call, Walter Dissen moved that my suspension "be vacated without prejudice" because the opinion of the Commission on Constitutional Matters had made the issue of my suspension "moot."

Both Buelow and Harnapp telephoned me, and I set up back-to-back meetings with them for October 10, 1973. I prepared thoroughly for the meetings, filling pages of yellow pad paper with notes. I concentrated on the charge of allowing and fostering false doctrine, but I also prepared material to refute the nine other charges. I was convinced that the two accusers were in collusion with the majority members of the BoC to oust me from office and that they were simply going through the motions of discussing their charges with me in order to enable the BoC to move on to the next step. Yet, believing Christian that I was, I convinced myself that with God nothing is impossible and that I should give the Spirit of God a chance to change the minds and hearts of my accusers by doing my best to show them that I did not teach false doctrine nor was I guilty of their other charges.

I met first with Harnapp and then with Buelow in my office for approximately two hours each during the morning of October 10. I taped the sessions and provided each of them with a copy of the tape. Harnapp sat rigid in his chair, looking at me with an icy stare, smoking a cigarette. Buelow was more relaxed, weighing his words carefully before responding, speaking in overly sincere tones.

I followed the same pattern in both meetings. Without much success I tried to ascertain how pastors from Wisconsin and Nebraska should have come together in filing the identical charges that had been before the New Orleans convention delegates but never officially presented to the convention, using evidence that was privileged information from convention Committee Number 3. In response to a question about how the document they submitted had been written, Harnapp said that he and Buelow had each written different sections of it; Buelow said that he had written a draft and had revised it on the basis of Harnapp's suggestions.

I spent most of the time of the two meetings refuting the charge of false doctrine by describing the interrelation of Scripture and gospel. Then I showed how the evidence they had presented in support of the other nine charges was based on misunderstandings and did not support their accusations. Neither of them said much. Harnapp said from time to time, "I'm listening, John. I'm listening." Buelow also made the point that he wanted to hear me out.[15]

At the end of both meetings I asked Harnapp and Buelow if they were satisfied. Harnapp, shifting in his chair, said he was not sure. Buelow hesitated for a moment before saying he was not satisfied. Both said they wanted to go home and listen to the tapes to reflect on what they had heard. I asked them both to meet with me again and gave them a set of materials with questions to reflect on for our next discussion. Neither would say whether we would meet again, but both said that they would call me to give me their answer.

When the BoC met on October 15, 1973, Eugene Fincke was not present, and thus one person was missing from the Preus party's one-vote majority. Perhaps that was the reason Buelow and Harnapp agreed to have another meeting with me. We set the date for October 26 and agreed that the three of us would meet together in my office.

We spent most of the time talking about the doctrinal issues in their first accusation against me, ranging all the way from Genesis to Revelation and dealing repeatedly with the issue of the relation of the Scripture and the gospel. After almost two hours I pointed out that they had not yet said anything about the material I had presented to them on the other nine charges. Had I convinced them? For example, did they agree that I did not change the BoC's minutes?

I had explained that after being unable to reach BoC secretary Walter Dissen because he was out of town, I had included within the minutes Dissen had sent me for distribution to the BoC members, a statement I had made at the BoC meeting, which the BoC wanted me to include in the minutes. I pointed out that the BoC had approved those minutes the way they were distributed to them; no one, including Dissen, had raised any question about them.

I could not believe my ears: Buelow and Harnapp remained convinced that I had changed the minutes. They alluded to a two-page letter in Dissen's possession that had convinced them that I had done so. Nothing I said could dissuade them. In exasperation, I prayed God's mercy on them in just so many words. I said that if they were incapable of understanding what I was saying to them concerning the minutes, how could I expect them to understand anything else I had presented to them?

Buelow and Harnapp had not dealt with any of the questions or the material I had given them at the previous meeting. They said they saw no reason why they should. We had dealt with only two of the ten charges, but they had to go. "I would like to continue," Harnapp said, rising from his chair, "but I have a plane to catch."[16]

I was not surprised when Buelow and Harnapp informed the BoC at its November 19, 1973, meeting that they had complied with bylaw 6.79a. and were now asking the BoC to proceed to 6.79b. What was shocking was the document that accompanied the letter, entitled "Formal Charges against Dr. John H. Tietjen, President of Concordia Seminary." The document was twice as long as the one they had submitted in August. There were now twelve charges. One new charge accused me of "rebelling against the very Synod, which he has been called to serve." The other new charge: "Dr. Tietjen has not been honest with us."[17] It cited the two letters Richard Duesenberg had sent to the district presidents as evidence that I was not functioning in a fraternal and confidential spirit. Besides the two additional charges, I had not seen or discussed with Buelow and Harnapp half of the material presented as evidence in support of the charge of false doctrine. Curiously, the reference to changing the minutes that had appeared in the August document had been removed.

Walter Dissen and Alfred Briel were ready with a motion: "that the Board of Control shall, and it does hereby, direct the chairman of the Board of Control to attempt to deal, to the satisfaction of all concerned, with the matter of the charges against Dr. John H. Tietjen. . . ."[18] In the course of the discussion the chair had to declare a fifteen-minute recess so that the five members who were not a part of the BoC majority and had not seen the material submitted by Buelow and Harnapp would have time to read it. I pointed out that the BoC could not proceed to the next point in the bylaws until Buelow and Harnapp had met with me to discuss the material I had not seen before. They proceeded anyway, adopting the motion by a 6-5 vote.

The November BoC meeting, in spite of all that had preceded it, was shocking, nonetheless. At the outset of the meeting Walter Dissen submitted a whole new agenda to take the place of the agenda I had submitted. In the course of the meeting, when preprinted resolutions were distributed, it became clear to the minority members of the BoC that the results of the meeting had been predetermined by the majority. It was clear, to me that the purpose of the meeting was simply to rubber-stamp in the presence of the minority members decisions that the majority members had already made.

As its first item of business the BoC dealt with the issue of Ralph Bohlmann's status as a member of the faculty. Bohlmann, tall, with a thin, angular face and a head of thick, wavy hair, professor of systematic theology, was one of the five dissident faculty members. According to rumor, Bohlmann like his colleague Martin Scharlemann had expected to be chosen as CS president at the time I was elected—especially since, according to unofficial reports, he had received several hundred nominations for the position, far more than anyone else. In the light of his friendly smile and quiet manner, it took me a while to conclude that he had joined with several of his colleagues to help Jacob Preus achieve his goals for CS. In fact, during the synodical controversy Bohlmann served as chief theologian and doctrinal strategist of the Preus administration.

In 1970, after Richard Jungkuntz had been removed from office as executive secretary of the Commission on Theology and Church Relations, the BoC granted Bohlmann a two-year leave to serve as the commission's acting executive secretary. When the two years were up, he asked for an extension of the leave. The BoC agreed but stipulated that his status as a faculty member would end if his contract with the commission was again renewed. Because he had been appointed to a four-year term as executive secretary of the commission, Bohlmann's status as a faculty member was about to end. But the Preus-controlled BoC reversed the decision and extended Bohlmann's faculty status. I surmised that the majority wanted to keep Bohlmann on the faculty so that he could serve as acting president when I was suspended.

Next, the BoC changed the CS retirement policy, declaring that all faculty members who had reached the age of sixty-five would be "honorably" retired or put on modified service as of February 1974. The retirement policy had been that faculty went on modified service at age seventy-two, with mandatory retirement set at age seventy-five. The BoC's action meant that seven of the most distinguished faculty members were given three months' notice of retirement. Affected by the action were Herbert J. A. Bouman, Richard R. Caemmerer, Alfred O. Fuerbringer, Arthur Carl Piepkorn, Arthur C. Repp, Alfred von Rohr Sauer, and Lorenz Wunderlich.

Then the BoC insisted on giving prior approval to contracts for each nonmember of the faculty who taught at CS, required that I submit for the BoC's review the syllabi for all courses taught at CS, and demanded that faculty members inform the BoC what they were doing about courses affected by the actions of the New Orleans convention. The BoC also directed me to answer for the July faculty protest, my activity in behalf of ELIM, the absence of faculty members from campus to speak out in the church during the last week in October, my relation to FLUTE, and a number of other matters.

As a final coup de grace, without meeting with him and without giving him a reason, the BoC decided not to renew the contract of faculty member Paul Goetting, whose trip to the Missouri Synod's sister church in India the BoC had approved a month earlier. When the report of the November BoC meeting filtered out to the seminary community, faculty and students alike were in shock at the use of raw power.

Ewald J. Otto summoned me, Buelow, and Harnapp to meet with him on November 28, 1973, at a Holiday Inn on the outskirts of St. Louis. I asked Richard R. Caemmerer to accompany me as a witness. At the last minute Richard Duesenberg said that he would be there in order to deal with the charge leveled against me because of letters he had written.

The meeting took place in a small, dark, windowless room in the hotel. Otto sat at the end of the table farthest from the door, I sat close to the foot of the table on the left side, and set out my tape machine. Caemmerer sat to my left. Buelow and Harnapp sat on the other side of the table close to Otto. Duesenberg, sitting at the foot of the table, asked for permission to explain why he was present. When Otto granted it, Duesenberg took his own tape recorder out of his briefcase, turned it on, and explained that I had no prior knowledge of his action in writing to the Missouri Synod's district presidents and was therefore not responsible for the letters he had written. Then Duesenberg took advantage of the opportunity to read into the record some of the facts about the November 19, 1973, meeting of the BoC, information that had been shared with him by minority BoC members.

After Duesenberg left, I explained that I was present for two reasons. The first was to inform Otto that it was not possible for me to recognize him as a third-party arbiter at the meeting because of his complicity in the efforts of my two accusers to oust me from office. The second reason was to inform Buelow and Harnapp that it was necessary for them to talk to me about the additional two charges and the new evidence they had submitted before I could recognize that the conditions of 6.79a. had been fulfilled.

Duesenberg's presence had rankled my two accusers, especially Harnapp. Rising from his chair and pacing back and forth on his side of the table, Harnapp took exception to Duesenberg's ethics in sending his letter to the district presidents and blamed me for the problems he had to confront in his congregation because of Duesenberg's letter. Buelow chimed in, objecting to the fact that Duesenberg had the materials they had submitted to the November meeting of the BoC. Both of them spoke to me:

> *Buelow:* After knowing the two letters that man wrote and circulated all over the Synod, and now he's got this [the latest version of the charges against Tietjen], and you talk about brotherly? Man, how do you define the word?

> *Harnapp:* Have you learned what brotherly means?

> *Tietjen:* You fellows are funny. Do you know that? You're really funny.

> *Buelow:* I don't think so.

> *Tietjen:* You are! You're engaged in the process of stringing a man up, and you talk about your reputations. You're really—you're really—(laughing) you're really laughable![19]

When Otto tried to fulfill the purpose for which he had convened the meeting, I refused to answer any questions addressed to me about the materials Buelow and Harnapp had submitted. I explained again and again the reason for my presence. Finally, I insisted that it was Otto's duty to tell Buelow and Harnapp that the terms of bylaw 6.79a. had not been fulfilled and that it was their responsibility at least to discuss with me the two additional charges and the substantial new material they had introduced as evidence. Otto said that he could not do that without instruction from the BoC and would therefore have to report the results of the meeting to the BoC.

Caemmerer had been silent through the entire meeting. Otto asked him if he would conclude the meeting with a prayer. Simply pronouncing the apostolic benediction, Caemmerer stressed the subject words: "The *grace* of the Lord Jesus Christ, the *love* of God, and the *fellowship* of the Holy Spirit be with us. Amen."

Caemmerer and I did not speak for a while as we drove back to the CS campus. Finally, expressing my own exasperation and frustration, I said, "It's ironic. I helped to frame those bylaws by which I am now being crucified." Preus had appointed a special committee to respond to the action of our accrediting agency, the American Association of Theological Schools, which had suspended CS's accreditation a year before and had insisted, among other things, that we spell out due process procedures more clearly. I had participated in the special committee's work of devising the due process procedures adopted at the New Orleans convention.

Caemmerer, who was sitting in the front passenger seat of my station wagon, sighed. Looking straight ahead, sadness etched on his face, Caemmerer said, "That's the way it is with the law, any law. In the hands of good people even the most badly formulated laws serve a good purpose. But even the best laws can't help you if people want to use them for an evil purpose. It takes good people to make sure that good laws accomplish their good purpose."

It looked as though everything was coming to a head for the meeting of the BoC scheduled for December 17, 1973. Rumors were circulating throughout the Synod that I would be suspended at this meeting and that this time the suspension would stick.

In response to the BoC's actions at the November meeting, the faculty sent a blunt letter to the BoC accusing the majority of engaging in the process of "closing the seminary" in fulfillment of its chair's call to do so in the June 1973 issue of *Affirm*. The faculty charged the BoC majority with duplicity in declining to renew Paul Goetting's contract without a reason and in "honorably" retiring those over sixty-five years of age when in fact the reason for the action in both cases was the participation of Goetting and of six of the seven "retirees" in the faculty's "Statement of Protest and Confession" and their rejection of Preus's "A Statement of Scriptural and Confessional Principles."

All seven of the faculty members affected immediately by the new retirement policy responded to the BoC's action. Lorenz Wunderlich agreed to be retired, but the others informed the BoC that they did not want to be retired. Two of them, Arthur Carl Piepkorn and Arthur C. Repp, informed the BoC that they considered the action to be a breach of their contract and would be taking steps to ensure their civil and legal rights.

The students had spent December 5 in a "Day of Theological Reflection" to deal with the problems confronting CS, a practice that had been followed from time to time since 1969. Classes were canceled to enable students to spend a day in reflection and discussion of an issue that was of major concern to them. Out of the reflection came a document, "With One Voice," in which the students appealed to the BoC to reverse its November actions concerning Goetting and the retirement policy.

Five members of the BoC—Kurt Biel, William Buege, Paul Nickel, Erwin Roschke, and Herman Scherer—now regularly called "the board minority," submitted a strongly worded protest to the BoC, to Jacob Preus, and to the BHE concerning the predetermined decisions of the majority at the November meeting, describing them as "unbrotherly and irregular activities." They recited the events of the November meeting as evidence that "reconciliation obviously is no longer the primary objective of the Board" and that the actions of the majority had made reconciliation impossible. They declared: "If Christ's love no longer constrains us in our dealings with one another, we may still be many things as an organization, but we have forfeited our right to call ourselves the Church of Jesus Christ, who, according to His own Word, has left us but one new commandment, namely, that we love one another even as He loved us."[20]

As the report of the BoC's November meeting filtered throughout the Synod, letters began coming to the BoC asking for a reversal of the actions. One letter, from Paul E. Jacobs, president of the Synod's California and Nevada District, called on the BoC to recognize that its chair, Ewald J. Otto, had demonstrated his prejudice against me in his writings and should be disqualified from sitting in judgment on my case.[21]

The week before the December BoC meeting, Larry Neeb, director of communications for CS, came to see me several times to report the results of his conversations with Victor Bryant, the Missouri Synod's director of public relations. He and Bryant were convinced that I would be suspended at the December meeting and that my suspension would be a disaster for CS and the Synod. They had agreed to see if they could find a way through the problem.

In the course of my four years as CS president, Neeb and I had opportunity to work together closely, as any president and public relations director should. In dealing with the public media, in contacts with the church press, in producing materials for our Missouri Synod constituency, in editing and publishing CS documents during the course of the controversy, Neeb had demonstrated remarkable competence. Short and stocky, a good athlete who enjoyed sports, Neeb was a likable person who was a friend to faculty and students alike. I not only admired his ability; I trusted him as a friend.

On December 8 Neeb came to see me to tell me that Bryant was distressed about what I had said to English District president John Baumgaertner. Earlier Baumgaertner had telephoned to ask if I would be open to receive a call to a congregation. I responded that in view of the disciplinary proceedings in which I was involved and the charge of false doctrine that had been raised against me, I certainly could not agree to be open to a call.

I learned from Neeb on December 8 that Baumgaertner's phone call had been initiated by Missouri District president Herman Scherer and that Bryant had urged Scherer to make the call. Two days later Neeb told me that Bryant was also in touch with Atlantic District president Rudolph Ressmeyer, urging that he find a call for me, and that Ressmeyer had been in touch with Jacob Preus about Bryant's request. It was Bryant's opinion that the way through the problem was to get me a call so that I would not have to be suspended. In fact, one of the options Preus and Ressmeyer were considering, according to Bryant, was that I should succeed C. Thomas Spitz as general secretary of LCUSA; but the presidents of the other two churches that were members of the council, Robert Marshall of the Lutheran Church in America and David Preus of the American Lutheran Church, were opposed to the idea.

At the beginning of my conversations with Neeb I said that I did not see any way through the problem but that I was willing to listen to any reasonable proposal. In our December 8 conversation I asked Neeb how it would be possible for me to accept a call elsewhere when there were charges of false doctrine leveled against me. How could a teacher of false doctrine be inflicted on a congregation? Neeb took my question to Bryant, who in turn assured Neeb that the charges against me would be dropped if I would take a call, that he had talked to Jacob Preus, Edwin Weber, and Ewald J. Otto, who were all "in sync" with the proposal.

"We'll put it in writing," Bryant told Neeb. "In writing we'll drop the charges if John takes a call." In fact, Bryant told Neeb, the BoC would undo some of its November actions if I would take a call. It would rehire

Paul Goetting. It would drop its new retirement policy. It would impose a year's moratorium on further action against the faculty.

How could I get a call in the few days left before the December BoC meeting? Neeb asked Bryant. First Bryant said that the BoC could postpone action to January. Then he said that I would not actually have to have a call in hand. I would only need to say before the BoC meeting, "I will seriously consider a call," and I could prevent the destruction of the Synod. Otherwise the BoC would continue to move against me and against the faculty. According to Bryant, my replacement would probably not be Ralph Bohlmann because the situation then would require someone who would be hard-nosed and Bohlmann might be destroyed in the process. If I did not agree to resign or to accept a call, the acting president would probably be Martin Scharlemann.[22]

I was disgusted with the hypocrisy of it all. I told Neeb in no uncertain terms that I would not be party to such a "deal." Either I was a teacher of false doctrine or I was not, but I was not about to join in a scheme to try to save my skin in pursuit of an illusion that CS could still be saved from the Preus juggernaut. I made it clear that I wanted Neeb to stop any further negotiations with Bryant. When Ressmeyer contacted me, I explained to him, as I did to Baumgaertner, why I could not be open to a call to other service.

As I sent out agenda materials for the December meeting to the members of the BoC, I took my yellow pad in hand and step by step went through a problem-solving technique I had learned at LCUSA.[23] I wrote down my assumptions about my present situation—among them, that my ouster as president was nonnegotiable to Preus and the present Synod leadership and that the disciplinary proceedings in which I was engaged would accomplish that. I listed the alternative courses that were open to me: continue the 6.79 procedures, refuse to participate further in the procedures, accept a call, resign, litigate.

Then I wrote down what were nonnegotiables for me: resign, continue in office under the present BoC, participate in a mockery of justice, settle the problem in court, attack someone else in order to defend myself. I listed what I wanted to accomplish—among them, leave my present position, serve as a paradigm for the faculty and the people of the Synod, give a Christian witness and example, deal with the charges against me, stiffen the faculty's resistance, arouse more people within the Synod. In one column running down the left side of the page I listed my objectives and assigned weights to each. In another column across the top of the page I listed my alternatives. Then at the intersection of the columns I put a number that indicated how the alternative would enable me to achieve a particular objective. When I added up the columns, the results confirmed for me what I really wanted to do at the December BoC meeting.

Early in the afternoon of Thursday, December 13, 1973, I received a phone call that was to send a shock wave through CS with reverberations throughout the Synod. An administrator at nearby St. Mary's Health Center was on the line to tell me that faculty member Arthur Carl Piepkorn had been admitted to the hospital and had been pronounced dead. She assumed that I would want to be the one to break the news to his family. I immediately asked Ernestine to go to the Piepkorn home to be with his wife, Miriam. I called John Damm, who was not only our academic dean but a close friend of the Piepkorn family, and asked him to bring Miriam and Ernestine to the hospital, where I would inform them. I contacted George Hoyer, our dean of the chapel, and asked him to contact Piepkorn's daughters living in St. Louis—Faith, wife of a St. Louis pastor, and Angela, who was a nurse at the hospital but off-duty at the time. I went to the hospital to find out what had happened.

Piepkorn had entered a barbershop a block away from the hospital, his face flushed, and had greeted the barber cheerily. He had walked the half-dozen blocks from the CS campus to the barbershop in the cold December air. As he was taking off his overcoat, he slumped into the chair closest to the door and apparently expired.

When Miriam Piepkorn arrived at the hospital, I told her what had happened, and Damm and I went with her to the room where her husband's body lay. Looking at the now-whitened face of the man who had been one of my mentors, I prayed aloud in thanksgiving for his good witness and for all he had meant to his loved ones and friends. I prayed for strength that we all might be able to give the same kind of witness. When we left the room, Hoyer arrived with the two Piepkorn daughters. Together we all drove back to the Piepkorn house adjacent to the CS campus.

Piepkorn's study was scattered with books, newspapers, and magazine articles, many of them clearly dealing with the Missouri Synod controversy and the action of the New Orleans convention. Miriam explained that laying open his working materials all around the room was her husband's method of keeping his sources close at hand as he wrote. I had already received and sent to the members of the BoC Piepkorn's letter announcing that he would not accept "honorable" retirement as long as the blot of the New Orleans convention resolution smeared his good name. Later that day in the campus mail I received a twelve-page document on which he had been working: "The constitutionality of the actions of the President of the Synod, various Boards of the Synod, the 1973 convention of the Synod, and the present Board of Control of Concordia Seminary at St. Louis, beginning with the appointment of the Fact Finding Commission by the President of the Synod."

Clearly, Piepkorn had been deeply involved with the problems of CS shortly before his death. Many people within the CS community were convinced that the decision to retire him had killed him. Piepkorn's close friend, Gerhardt W. Hyatt, Chief of Chaplains of the United States Army, expressed the thought in a letter to me following the funeral: "I sincerely hope that he did not die of a broken heart. Yet I suspect that may be the case and I am deeply wounded by that belief."[24]

Miriam Piepkorn had a different assessment. "They thought they could retire him," she said. "God took care of that." In the next day's issue of the student publication *Spectrum* I paid Piepkorn tribute with a poem that ended:

He gave his all in the service of God,
Challenging us all to strive
For the perfection we see in God.

God has crowned his striving with perfection.

Retirement? No! No!
Resurrection!
The perfection of the life of the world to come.

The funeral took place on Monday, December 17, 1973, the day the BoC was scheduled to meet. It would have been unseemly for the BoC to do what everyone expected it to do while the body of Arthur Carl Piepkorn was being laid to rest with military honors in the National Cemetery at Jefferson Barracks, Missouri. The meeting was canceled.

Piepkorn's death had a profound impact on the CS community and on the subsequent course of events. The decision on my future was put off to a time when the students would be back from the Christmas holidays, and students and faculty were given another month to decide what they wanted to do about my suspension. Even more important was the profound subliminal impact. I was clearly the pastor of a grieving spiritual community. In a coffin laid out in state in the CS chapel people could see the ultimate price that might have to be paid for confessional integrity.

◆ ◆ ◆

The BoC held a special meeting on January 7, 1974, but took no action against me. Perhaps I was being given more time to "understand the facts of life." Perhaps the arrangements for an acting president had come apart at the last minute. At the regular BoC meeting January 20–21, 1974, the big guns had been brought to bear. The Board of Directors of the Synod was insisting that the BoC take action against me because of my involvement in FLUTE. The BHE was demanding that the BoC do something about my role in the faculty's "Statement of Protest and Confession."

Walter Dissen distributed two resolutions typed in legalese. The first, fulfilling the next step in the bylaw process, requested the Commission on Theology and Church Relations to give an opinion on the theological issue in the charge of false doctrine that had been leveled against me. None among the majority members of the BoC would state what the theological issue was when minority members asked them to do so. The second resolution, alleging that the previous steps of bylaw 6.79 had been fulfilled and that great harm would come to CS if I continued in office, suspended me as president and professor.

After heated discussion in which the minority members did all the talking, the BoC voted 6-to-5 to suspend me. I gathered up my papers and left the room. Shortly before 9:00 P.M. on Sunday, January 20, 1974, the bells in the CS tower began to toll.

10 ——◆

MORATORIUM

Four hundred students were gathered in the chapel-auditorium in Wynecken Hall on the campus of Concordia Seminary. It was shortly before 10:00 A.M. on Monday, January 21, 1974. The atmosphere was highly charged, the mood sober and somber.

Students filled nearly two-thirds of the wooden, auditorium-style chairs that were connected to one another and bolted to the floor. Some of the students were in the balcony that reached out over one-third of the seats downstairs. Most had gathered in the space below on a floor that sloped down toward a darkened stage, on which stood an altar and a lectern.

Student body president Gerald A. Miller stood at a portable lectern on the auditorium floor in front of the first row of seats. He carefully wrote down the names of students who had raised their hands to speak and was calling on them in turn. Six feet tall, with a full head of sandy brown hair and a neatly trimmed mustache, wearing black-rimmed glasses, Miller was in the final year of his Master of Divinity program. Like 150 other students, he was looking forward to commencement at the end of May and to a call, to be assigned in April, that would enable him to serve as a pastor in a Lutheran Church–Missouri Synod congregation after commencement.

The meeting he was chairing had begun after student-led worship at 8:00 that morning. Miller had announced the meeting the night before, informing the students by word of mouth or by telephone through a network of student leaders. I had spoken briefly to the students after worship. They listened in stunned silence as I told them about my suspension the previous evening and about what I was planning to say at a press conference at 10:00 A.M. that day.

Functioning in strict parliamentary fashion, the students were debating a resolution that called for a "moratorium on all classes." The resolution pointed out that I had been suspended for defending faculty members who had been accused of teaching false doctrine, that the CS Board of Control had not specified who such faculty members were, and that the students needed to know who was teaching false doctrine and what the false doctrine was "before we continue our theological training." According to the resolution, the students would willingly make up for the missed classes, but the moratorium would last "until such time as the Seminary Board of Control officially and publicly declares which members of the faculty, if any, are to be considered as false teachers and what Scriptural and Confessional principles, if any, have been violated."[1] For some time the students had been discussing informally what they should do if and when I was suspended, but they were far from being of one mind on the issue. They constantly reminded one another of the consequences of the proposed action.[2]

The students had seen what the Preus party, now dominant in the Synod, had done to the faculty at the Synod convention the previous June. They had been tuned in to the process as the majority of the BoC systematically took steps to suspend me. Their proposed action could jeopardize not just their education and scheduled commencement but their future as pastors in the LCMS. Yet many of them agreed with their president Gerald Miller. Earlier in the discussion of the resolution he had said: "I personally have had all that I can take. . . . Our life in this place is being disrupted and turned into a farce. . . . I believe we need to call a halt to our theological education under this Board of Control until it has given an account of itself, until it has proved to the church that it has been dealing justly and evangelically with its responsibilities in this place."[3]

In the course of their meeting, the students learned about other actions taken by the BoC, which was continuing its meeting begun the night before. The BoC had named faculty member Martin Scharlemann as acting president. It had implemented its retirement policy in the case of Alfred Fuerbringer, Arthur Repp, and Alfred Sauer. A murmur went through the student gathering when it was reported that Sauer was informed of his retirement through a note Scharlemann had slipped under his office door. Some of the wavering students now found themselves in agreement with their student body president.

At 10:00 A.M. the students voted. The resolution for a student moratorium was adopted by more than 70 percent—274 to 92 with 15 abstentions. The next day the students decided that those in favor of the resolution should affix their signatures to it so that the BoC would know to whom to respond. At 11:00 A.M. on January 21, 1974, Gerald Miller delivered a copy of the student action to the BoC meeting and personally handed a copy of the resolution to chair Ewald J. Otto.

Moratorium was a word fraught with special meaning at CS since six years earlier when students had declared the first moratorium at the campus. While other college and university students were conducting sit-ins, going on strike, and taking over buildings, students at CS made their protest by declaring a moratorium. With class activity suspended, students participated with faculty and administrators in intense conversations over several days. For the students at that time the issues were more freedom in choosing courses and greater student participation in seminary governance.

The moratorium in the 1968–69 academic year, the year before I came to CS, resulted in immediate curricular reform and in the creation of a Theological Education Research Committee[4] to propose longer-range change of the curriculum. It also gave students numerical equality with faculty in all official CS committees; the chief ones included the Educational Policies Committee, the Community Life Committee, and the Seminary Relations Committee. Like the faculty, the students had their own organization and government. In addition to a president they elected a vice-president, a secretary, a controller, an on-campus missions director, an off-campus missions director, and a student body publications director. These officers, along with elected representatives of the three classes that were on campus, formed the Student Administrative Council.

Already holding a bachelor's degree, seminarians were graduate students engaged in a four-year program that led to a professional degree, the Master of Divinity. They were therefore older and considerably more mature than most college and university students. Approximately one-half of them married during their seminary years and lived in apartments off-campus; increasingly they were raising children prior to graduation.

The students had watched in silence as the investigation had proceeded further and further. At the beginning many students laughed at the controversy as if it were some kind of ecclesiastical game. When the temperature of the controversy rose, some of them adopted an attitude of "a plague on both your houses" in the dispute. But as more and more of them saw firsthand what was happening, they identified with the faculty and with me. From time to time student body officers and I would arrange for convocations to bring the students up-to-date on the course of events.

There was in fact little the students could do. The outcome of the investigation ostensibly lay in the hands of CS's own governing board. The students were reluctant to take any action that would give Jacob Preus opportunity to accuse me of not being able to "control" the students, an accusation Preus made several times prior to the Missouri Synod's New Orleans convention. The problem of getting consensus for student action was compounded by the fact that in any given year only one student class had been on campus the previous year. The incoming class was new to the school, and the senior class had spent the prior year scattered around the country on internships. Only the second-year class continued in residence.

In January 1973 Amandus Derr and David Miller, second-year students at CS, concluded that the time had come to organize the students politically to assist in the Bertwin Frey–Dean Lueking organization's preparations for the New Orleans convention. Derr and Miller went on their own to a strategy session Frey and Lueking convened in Chicago January 15–16, 1973. Although in Derr's appraisal[5] their reception was less than enthusiastic, they returned to St. Louis committed to lobby convention delegates on CS issues.

Derr and Miller joined with a dozen other CS students in creating Seminarians Concerned for Reconciliation Under the Gospel, an organization that publicly disavowed official connection to CS or its student body. Among the organizers was Jacquelyn Mize, who was breaking new ground as a woman student in the Master of Divinity program, even though we could not give her any hope of ordination into the ministry of the LCMS.

Derr succeeded in convincing the leadership of the Frey-Lueking coalition that his organization could be entrusted with the names and addresses of convention delegates. Contributing his earnings as CS bookstore manager, Derr was responsible for sending biweekly first-class mailings to eleven hundred New Orleans convention delegates in May and June 1973. He provided packets of material for students to use over the Easter holiday in contacting convention delegates in their home areas. He and others in Seminarians Concerned administered a program of putting CS students in direct contact with convention delegates presumed to be swing votes. Besides Derr, Boyd Faust was another student who contributed heavily to cover the organization's expenses.

After the New Orleans convention Derr left for his year of internship, or vicarage as it is called in the Missouri Synod, and assumed responsibility for informing and organizing the CS interns. Leon Rosenthal assumed leadership of Seminarians Concerned and enlisted the assistance of a select number of returning interns in behalf of the organization. By design the organization assumed a low profile and worked behind the scenes with the official leaders of the student body. The goal was to ensure that there would be responsible student action at the appropriate time.[6]

Early in September 1973 I met in my office with Gerald Miller. It was my custom at the beginning of each academic year to meet with the new student body president to talk about the year ahead and to devise a schedule for working with him. Miller had been elected to his position in the spring term of 1972 before he went on internship, long before the New Orleans convention. Now he was the chief student leader required to function in the crisis in which the faculty and I found ourselves because of the convention's actions.

His usual friendly smile gone, Miller told me that he and his wife, Lynn, were perplexed and disturbed by what had been happening in St. Louis as they watched from their vicarage church in Wisconsin. Miller wanted me to understand that theologically he was a conservative. Although he could not condone everything the Preus administration had done, he could not understand why CS had been so combative. He wanted me to know that as student body president he would do everything in his power to undo polarization and to work for reconciliation.

How could I expect Miller to understand what he had not experienced? I myself had to learn from experience what Jacob Preus and his supporters were prepared to do. Miller, too, would have to experience it, I told myself. I supported Miller in his intention to work for reconciliation. I assured him that I would help in any way I could. Let us work together, I offered, for the good of CS and the Synod. I thought to myself that Miller was now enrolled in an "elective" course that would give him a different kind of education from the one he was expecting.

Students arriving at CS in early September 1973 learned that the BoC had suspended me and then not implemented the suspension. All except the entering students knew me well. I was an active participant in CS community life and a guest at official and unofficial student social events. As a member of the faculty I served as advisor for a half dozen students each year. Students perceived me as pastor of the CS community, and nothing hurt me more deeply than the accusation made first at New Orleans and then repeated by Leonard Buelow and Harlan Harnapp that I had failed in my spiritual responsibility as pastor of the students. Nurtured as Christians on Martin Luther's Small Catechism, CS students knew well Luther's explanation to the Eighth Commandment with its injunction about defending and speaking well of one's neighbor. Under the leadership of the SAC they did that for me.

The SAC quoted Luther's words in a letter to the BoC, writing to them as "our pastors and our brothers in Christ."[7] On the basis of experience with me, the authors of the letter disowned the description of me that had been given at the New Orleans convention and urged the BoC to undo its suspension. The SAC invited students to join them in signing the letter, and approximately three hundred did.

Gerald Miller represented the students in asking for an opportunity to meet with the BoC to present the signatures and to stress the purpose of their letter. Gathered in a special meeting on September 29, 1973, the BoC decided not to take time out for lunch. In granting an audience to Miller, the BoC gave him ten minutes for his presentation if he would appear at 11:50 A.M. with "nine milkshakes."[8] Miller had to make his case while the milkshakes were being consumed.

The November meeting of the BoC shocked the students into realizing that they would soon be attending a very different seminary from the one they had entered in September. Paul Goetting, popular teacher of the church's mission in urban society, would be gone by the end of the year. Seven of the most distinguished professors could be retired by the beginning of the winter quarter. It seemed certain that I would be suspended before Christmas. The BoC's request to see all course syllabi seemed to mean that it was intent on redoing the whole curriculum.

The students asked for a "Day of Theological Reflection." There had been such a day a few years earlier during the Vietnam War and the crisis over the deaths at Kent State University. This time the students wanted to deal with a different war as they asked to discuss the synodical controversy and its implications for CS. Faculty and students concurred on December 5 as the date.

The students who were involved with Seminarians Concerned were hard at work during the Day of Theological Reflection, calling on their fellow students to take responsible action. On the basis of the discussion that day, fourth-year student David Abrahamson worked overnight to compose a document to serve as a theological foundation for united student action. Entitled "With One Voice," the document was submitted for signature to CS students, given to the BoC, and distributed to all pastors and teachers of the Missouri Synod. Ultimately, 450 students signed the document.

"With One Voice" cited the apostle Paul's description of the church as the body of Christ to affirm an identity between the faculty majority and the students of CS: "Because as members of the Body of Christ we do not suffer alone but together, we understand the condemnation of the faculty majority of Concordia Seminary to apply also to us." The document appealed to the BoC to reverse the decisions of its November meeting and affirmed: "If the Board of Control does not reconsider its decisions it will have proceeded against all the members of the student body."

The students were surprised to discover that no less a journal than the *Christian Century* took note of their action, reporting that the students "have at last spoken up" in a document that "fully supports the beleaguered faculty." "What they have done, at great risk," the *Christian Century* stated, "is to serve notice on the church . . . that they care about Concordia and will not stand idly by while the teachers they respect are vilified. Their document is one not of despair but of hope— hope for the survival of Concordia and the re-establishment of sanity in a respected denomination in danger of self-destruction."[9]

The students had found a theological base on which to stand together with the faculty, but they had no agreed-upon plan of action as to how to respond to my anticipated suspension. CS would be in recess for the Christmas holidays, and most of the students would have scattered. The sudden death of Arthur Carl Piepkorn and the subsequent cancellation of the December BoC meeting gave the students an opportunity to regroup when they returned after Christmas.

On January 19 and 20, 1974, just before the January 20–21 meeting of the BoC, the SAC and the leaders of Seminarians Concerned came together with a number of invited guests to reflect on what additional action the students should take.[10] Distinguished University of Chicago theologian and fellow Missouri Synod Lutheran Martin E. Marty communicated by videotape to encourage the students to maintain their high standards of theology and morality. Campus pastor Elmer Witt from Chicago made an impact in urging the students to follow through on their previous actions. Student body controller George Schelter and Seminarians Concerned leader Adolph Wachsmann were especially effective in facilitating communication between official student body leaders and the leaders of Seminarians Concerned.

The group explored alternative courses of action in the event of my suspension. A moratorium seemed the only sensible course, but it was difficult to come to a consensus. On the second day of the meeting, at Gerald Miller's invitation, a number of additional students joined the meeting. They compounded the problem of reaching consensus because they had not participated in all the discussions of the day before. Finally, painful as it was, James Wind, student and member of Seminarians Concerned, asked the new arrivals to leave so that the group could come to some decision.

The students had no specific plan beyond a moratorium. They expected a moratorium to have its effect: their decision to discontinue classes would so influence the people of their church body that the BoC would reverse its decisions and the leaders of the Synod would work out a settlement of the CS controversy. The student leaders did not think much about what would take place after their action. They knew only that it was not possible for them *not* to act. They reminded one another of the truism: "All that is necessary for evil to succeed is for good people to do nothing." Miller offered a draft of a motion to declare a moratorium. By late afternoon on Sunday, January 20, the student leaders had hammered out a resolution to present to the student body.

Several hours after my suspension on January 20, Gerald Miller came to see me at my home. He showed me the resolution that would be presented to the student body the next morning and asked me to be present at the meeting at 8:00 A.M. to give the students a firsthand report of my suspension. As I agreed to be there, I said to Miller, "I just hope that everyone is carefully counting the cost."

At 10:00 A.M. on Monday, January 21, 1974, I walked into the lounge of Pritzlaff Hall for the press conference that I had asked Larry Neeb, CS's director of communications, to announce. Immediately after leaving the board room following my suspension I had called John Damm, academic dean, to tell him the news and to ask him to gather the Faculty Advisory Committee. I shared with the FAC the substance of what I intended to say at the press conference the next morning. Because the tolling bell had assembled many people from the CS community in the chapel-auditorium, I spoke to them briefly about the BoC's action and told them that I would have more to say in the morning. Then I went to work on the four-page statement I intended to make, copies of which I needed to produce to go along with 156 single-space pages of typescript that I had already produced in quantity as evidence in support of the assertions in my statement.

In the lounge of Pritzlaff Hall I walked to a table that Neeb had arranged in the middle of the room, on which media people had assembled their microphones. Television lights went on as I sat down at the table. The mounds of material I was ready to release were neatly stacked on another table. I was calm, my voice in control, but there were dark rings under my eyes from the strain of the previous day's events and from lack of sleep.

In my statement I made three major points. First, I announced the terms of the "deal" that had been proposed to me that would have made it possible for me to avoid suspension: agree to accept a call in exchange for dropping the charges against me, cancellation of the retirement policy, reemployment of Paul Goetting, and a year's cessation of activity against the faculty. I pointed out that the "deal" demonstrated that the charges against me were "nothing more than tools to remove me from my position." If there were any substance to the charges, I pointed out, then it would be "immoral to arrange a call for me and to inflict me on another community of Christian people." I stated: "In the face of such evil I cannot remain silent. . . . The members of our Synod must become aware of the moral bankruptcy of the actions of the present leadership of our Synod and of the seminary's Board of Control."

Second, I stated that I had decided not to challenge the suspension action by asking for an injunction against it in civil court. "Though I would gladly go to court to ensure the rights of others," I stated, "I prefer to endure injustice than to contend for my rights against my own church body in secular court." I said that my decision was based on my commitment to be a disciple of Jesus, who in the Sermon on the Mount instructed his followers to turn the other cheek and to give away their cloak as well when people take their coat. In accord with Jesus' injunction I did not intend to use the secular courts to stop the president of the Synod and the BoC from taking "my present position from me through a process which will also force me out of the pastoral ministry of the Synod."

Third, I announced that I would take no further action in my own defense throughout the remaining provisions of the bylaws. I charged that the proceedings to remove me from office offered no possibility of a fair and impartial judgment. "They are a charade," I said, "in which my two accusers and the majority members of the Board are seeking to fulfill the letter of the bylaws for the purpose of reaching a predetermined objective, already publicly announced by the president of the Synod, to remove me from office and from the pastoral ministry of the Synod." In support of my statement I released a six-page document entitled "Evidence," in which I documented the charge of collusion between majority BoC members, the two accusers, and the president of the Synod. In addition I released the texts of the charges submitted against me in August and November and the transcripts of my meetings with my accusers and with the BoC chair, a total of 156 pages.[11]

In conclusion I stated, " . . . there is little point in participating in proceedings whose outcome has already been determined. When people refuse to hear, there is no point in speaking. When your accusers are also your judge and jury, you already know the verdict of your trial." I stated that I refused to participate further in a process that was making a mockery of bylaws whose purpose was to assure due process. Instead, I said, "I commit myself to the righteous Judge and trust his grace and mercy because of the atoning death of Jesus Christ on the cross."

After reading my statement, I answered questions for about a half hour and then concluded the press conference. St. Louis radio and television stations reported what I had said. That afternoon a banner front-page headline in the St. Louis *Post-Dispatch* reported, "Turned Down 'Deal,' Dr. Tietjen Asserts."

Ewald J. Otto was quick to deny that there had been any offer of a "deal," and before long Jacob Preus also rejected the allegation. Faculty and students wanted to know if I could back up my assertions. I assured them that I could and that it would not be long before people would know that I was telling the truth. Before the week was out Victor Bryant, the Synod's director of public relations, issued a statement acknowledging that he was one of the agents of Preus to whom I had referred in my statement; he declared that his only concern had been for my welfare and for the good of CS and the Synod. Larry Neeb also issued a statement, confirming all the details I had included in my statement. Finally, Rudolph Ressmeyer, president of the Synod's Atlantic District, issued a statement confirming that he was one of the district presidents referred to in my statement who had been contacted by Bryant and who had spoken directly to Preus about finding a call for me.[12]

Later on Monday, January 21, I met with John Damm in his office. He said that he had been in touch with his counterparts at Eden Seminary and at the Divinity School of St. Louis University, two of the local theological schools with which CS was associated in the St. Louis Theological Consortium. They were ready to begin contingency planning for a seminary in exile. Would I give the green light? Damm wanted to know. I did.

When I learned late Monday that Martin Scharlemann was expecting to function as acting president from within my office, I spent most of the next day cleaning out my files, carefully distinguishing between personal materials and those of the office. When the job was done early Wednesday, January 23, I asked Scharlemann to come to the office. I invited him in and shut the door. I told him I had just two things to say before leaving the office to him. "The first thing is this: Congratulations, Martin! You finally made it!" When he started to object, I said, "And the second thing is this: You have your reward!"[13] As he fumed and sputtered, I strode out the door.

It was the faculty's turn to act. Immediately after my suspension the FAC met to reflect on what recommendations to bring to the faculty majority. Ralph Klein and Herbert Mayer were now members of the FAC, having been elected to take the place of the deceased Arthur Carl

Piepkorn and of Leonhard Wuerffel, who was ill. They joined Robert Bertram, Richard Caemmerer, Alfred Fuerbringer, Robert Smith, and Andrew Weyermann.

For months the FAC had been reflecting on what the faculty should do "when John is suspended." They again reviewed the options. The faculty could accept the decisions of the BoC. They could give one another permission to do whatever each thought best. They could continue to function but refuse to acknowledge the authority of the acting president. They could declare that the suspension of the president meant that all faculty members had been suspended. They could resign en masse with or without an effective future date. Most committee members favored the option of declaring that the faculty had been suspended along with me. They decided not to make a decision that night.[14]

The FAC met again at 8:30 A.M. on Monday, January 21. All agreed that vacant classrooms were the most radical and most eloquent form of Christian witness that the faculty could make in response to the suspension. The FAC agreed to recommend that classrooms should remain vacant "until the moral and theological issues are squarely faced and resolved" by an action that either clears or dismisses the faculty majority.[15] The FAC decided to make its recommendation to the faculty majority that afternoon.

Gathered in the lounge of Pritzlaff Hall on the afternoon of January 21, the faculty majority reflected on the course of the day's events. They learned that the BoC had not only "honorably" retired Alfred Fuerbringer, Arthur Repp, and Alfred Sauer but also had invited Herbert Bouman, Richard Caemmerer, and Lorenz Wunderlich to continue teaching on modified service. They learned that the BoC had declined the faculty's request to grant Piepkorn's petition posthumously to clear his name of the charge of false doctrine—on the grounds that in spite of what the New Orleans convention said, Piepkorn had not been accused of false doctrine. They learned from fellow faculty member Norman Habel that in an interview with the BoC concerning a call he had received, the BoC had refused to grant him a peaceful release on the grounds that, like all CS faculty members, he *was* under indictment by the New Orleans convention.

The faculty majority reflected at length on the FAC's recommendation. Strictly speaking, they did not have to do anything. The action of the students that morning had already closed the classrooms. But they knew that the students were waiting to see what the faculty would do. They knew also that I had been suspended not so much because of my own teaching but because I had defended theirs. By late afternoon they concluded that the decision before them was of such consequence that they needed to consult with spouses and families. They asked the FAC to produce the draft of a statement they could issue and agreed to meet again at 8:30 that evening.

Spouses joined faculty members at the evening session. Ernestine and I did not attend these early meetings following my suspension. I did not want our presence to influence faculty members. Close to midnight the meeting adjourned.

At the next day's student meeting John Glamann learned what had happened the night before. As he recorded it in his chronology,[16] "The faculty majority and executive staff passed and adopted three resolutions. First, pride in the student body, support to and for the student body, expression of gratitude for the student show of solidarity, to show concern, pastoral care, and ministry to the students who oppose the student moratorium," which meant that the faculty intended to be in ministry not only to those who supported their position but to the students who were against the moratorium. "Second," Glamann's chronology continued, "since the faculty majority holds the same faith and theological convictions as President Tietjen the faculty majority considers itself suspended also. Third, to support the students in their moratorium."

At 7:30 A.M. on January 22 the FAC received from Ralph Klein and Robert Smith an edited version of a letter to Jacob Preus that had been approved in principle the night before. Later that day the faculty majority adopted it and sent it off. They decided to address Preus rather than the BoC, on the conviction that he was in actuality the puppeteer who was pulling the BoC's strings.

The letter informed Preus that the BoC had "emptied the classrooms and silenced the teaching of the Word of God on our campus." The letter declared: "By condemning President Tietjen's confessional stand and suspending him from office, the Board of Control has condemned our own confession and has suspended all of us from our duties as teachers and executive staff members." The faculty challenged Preus either to take the lead in clearing the faculty and its president of the charge of false doctrine or to identify with the BoC action and initiate the process of dismissing the faculty for cause. The letter warned Preus that the classrooms would stay empty until "the present uncertainty . . . is cleared up." Forty-six signatures, one for every member of the faculty majority and executive staff, were affixed to the letter.[17]

Far from viewing the moratorium as some sort of school holiday, faculty and students geared up for action. Under the leadership of the FAC, with Andrew Weyermann as chair, the faculty organized into a dozen committees and task forces. Duane Mehl and David Dahline initiated efforts to help faculty come to terms with questions of reemployment. Herbert Mayer and Herbert Bouman led a task force on legal issues and worked with Richard Duesenberg to engage legal counsel. John Damm and David Yagow led a group of faculty who were responsible for dealing with a variety of educational questions, including the contingency planning for a seminary in exile. Arthur Vincent and several others were given responsibility for communications and publication. Another group had responsibility for spiritual life and counseling; another for worship and events; and yet another for emergency resources. The FAC met at least daily, often for hours at a time, to coordinate the frenzy of activity in the crisis. It designated Robert Bertram as spokesperson for the faculty.

Among the items that required the faculty's immediate attention was how to respond to the appointment of Martin Scharlemann as acting president. On January 22, in addition to the letter to Jacob Preus, the faculty majority adopted a statement on Scharlemann. In rehearsing the events from the time of Scharlemann's open advocacy of the methods of historical criticism to his attack on me, the statement revealed that Scharlemann had rebuffed the private efforts of brotherly admonition from two faculty members: Alfred Fuerbringer, who had saved him from dismissal a decade earlier; and Arthur Carl Piepkorn, his good friend and fellow chaplain who had appealed to him to repent and to recognize me as his immediate spiritual superior. The statement called on Scharlemann to resign and made it clear that the faculty would not recognize him as acting president. In addition the statement called on Preus and the pastors and people of the Synod to demand that the BoC reinstate me as president.[18]

If anything, the students were even more highly organized than the faculty. Learning from the success of the consultation the weekend before, the officially elected student officers and the leaders of Seminarians Concerned joined forces to establish a moratorium coordinating committee. Recognizing Gerald Miller as president and spokesperson, the committee designated no less than seven others as co-chairs. David Abrahamson, Gerald Miller, and James Wind were given responsibility for materials development, a code word for recommending strategies, proposals, and resolutions. A telephone hotline and emergency phone network were established to provide internal communications, and John Dornheim and David Reichert were put in charge of rumor control to ensure that students received accurate information. Different groups of students were made responsible for worship, spiritual life, and publications. George Schelter, Donald Duy, and Boyd Faust joined forces to raise and administer funds. Jonathan Kosec served as press coordinator, James Nickols as chair of national publicity, Steven Dietrich as photographer.

On the first day of the the moratorium an idea was hatched that grew to reality only four days later: Operation Outreach. Students agreed to disperse across the nation, spending from a week to ten days in reporting to the people of the Missouri Synod what was happening in St. Louis and why they had declared a moratorium. Under the coordination of Leslie Weber a total of 259 students crisscrossed the country from Wisconsin to Texas, from Virginia to California, logging more than 118,000 miles.[19]

The separate organizations of faculty and students interacted primarily through their nerve centers, the FAC and the student Coordinating Committee. Because the students and faculty operated within such a well organized and thoroughly informed network, it was sheer fabrication to say, as Preus and others did, that students were unwitting dupes of faculty manipulation or that they were mesmerized by my charisma.

In the meantime, Scharlemann got nowhere in his efforts to convince faculty and students to return to class. The student body would not officially acknowledge a student meeting he had convened on Wednesday, January 23. The actions of the BoC did not help Scharlemann's efforts. The students learned that the BoC had replaced virtually the entire academic administration with the minority members of the faculty. Robert Preus was named vice-president for academic affairs and chair of the department of historical theology. Richard Klann was designated chair of the department of systematic theology. Scharlemann himself would chair the exegetical department. Without consulting Arthur Vincent, one of the faculty majority, the BoC named him chair of the practical department, an appointment Vincent rejected instantly.

A paper war broke out. Preus responded to the faculty's letter with his own letter, stating that if the faculty still considered themselves to be members of the CS faculty and staff they should resume their regular duties and "trust that the procedures your church has established for dealing with doctrinal supervision and discipline will be dealt with in all deliberate haste." In their response the faculty wanted to know how Preus could want them back in the classroom if, as the New Orleans convention proclaimed, they were teachers of false doctrine. "Are you admitting that the present struggle is largely political rather than doctrinal?" they asked. On January 25 the faculty sent all the pastors of the Synod a mailing that included my statement and the statements made by faculty and students.

Three days later Preus unleashed a missile that exploded with the force of a megaton bomb. A thirty-page document entitled "Message to the Church" was sent not only to the Synod's pastors and teachers but to all congregational officers, lay members of the Synod's boards, and lay delegates to the New Orleans convention. It incorporated as appendices Preus's correspondence with the faculty, including a blunt, hard-hitting answer to their latest letter in which Preus made it clear that there would be no give on his part. The substance of the material was a nine-page letter in which Preus repeated the charges of false doctrine and malfeasance against me as if the due process procedures had gone to the point where the charges had been proved. With a kind of gallows humor I found it funny that he would include the charge about changing the minutes of the BoC when that had been dropped from the charges against me. Preus also accused me of engineering the decision of the accrediting agency to place CS on probation. He criticized me for forgiving the New Orleans convention delegates instead of asking for their forgiveness. He responded to my accusations of his offer of a "deal" by accusing me of "trickery" because Larry Neeb had kept a taped record of his phone conversations with Victor Bryant, a fact that provided indisputable evidence of the "deal."

On the other hand, Preus's letter was conciliatory. He spoke out against talk of a split in the Synod with a division of assets, an idea that had originated with a pastor in New York City, Richard John Neuhaus. He argued against withholding funds from the Synod. He informed everyone that he had appointed an Advisory Committee on Doctrine and Conciliation composed of fourteen members representing both sides in the synodical controversy, whose task it was to delineate the issues and propose ways of dealing with them.

For the CS faculty and students a primary focus of the Preus mailing was the sixth of the seven appendices. Appendix 6 purported to be a letter from CS students who were not in favor of the moratorium and who supported Preus and the new seminary administration. The three-page letter accused the faculty of nineteen specific past and present acts of harassment and intimidation. At the end of the letter the authors stated that they had withheld their names because of the "oppressive climate and theological perversion" existing at CS, but that their names were "on file in the office of the acting president of Concordia Seminary."

Appendix 6 was too much even for the students who had voted against the moratorium. They took the lead in trying to find out what signatures were "on file." Scharlemann refused to release names, and the students reported that they could find no one at CS who had signed the document. Three students, Charles Boerger, Leon Rosenthal, and Adolph Wachsmann, decided to act on the principles of Matthew 18 and take the matter to Jacob Preus. After much difficulty they succeeded in getting an appointment with him. They confronted him with the wrong committed by the publication of Appendix 6 and asked him to help undo the wrong he had done. Preus refused, insisting that the accusations in the document were true. As a result, perhaps fifty students who would not otherwise have done so signed on to the moratorium.

John Damm reported to faculty and students from time to time in the two weeks following my suspension on his efforts to secure alternative modes of continuing CS's educational program, including a full-fledged seminary in exile—"Seminex" for short. On February 4 Damm announced that the basic elements for a seminary in exile were in place.[20]

Students began to worry about whether they would be able to complete the requirements of the winter quarter and the 1973–74 academic year. Those slated for a year of internship wondered whether they would be going on vicarage. Students hoping to be placed into ministry were concerned about how their candidacy would be approved and how calls would be assigned.

On February 6 the faculty acted to deal with the growing student unrest. It affirmed its commitment to complete the winter quarter and to follow the curriculum as closely as possible for the spring quarter. It declared its intention of certifying and placing graduates on May 1 and of providing internships on March 22. In addition, the faculty announced its intention of offering a full-fledged program of theological education in fall 1974.[21]

On February 12 the faculty wrote to the BoC to announce its intention of resuming instruction on February 19, the day following the February BoC meeting. It informed the BoC that the instruction would take place in the CS classrooms if the BoC would take "a series of simple actions: reinstate John H. Tietjen as president together with the department heads whom you removed; issue a contract to Paul Goetting so that his teaching may continue at our institution; reverse the retirement policy announced in November and the retirements effected by your January action."

The faculty letter informed the BoC that "instruction must and will resume" on February 19 even if the BoC did not take steps to reverse the decisions of the past months. Theological education conducted by the same faculty with the same students under the same curriculum and confessional commitment would begin again, "but it will not be under your auspices and not at the customary location" if there were no satisfactory resolution of the issues.

The CS crisis produced deep concern in St. Louis and throughout the LCMS. Two days after my suspension, one thousand Lutherans in the St. Louis area gathered in the CS field house to express their solidarity with the faculty and students.

On February 6, after Scharlemann had forbidden the use of CS facilities for major gatherings, Christ Church Cathedral, the Episcopal cathedral in downtown St. Louis, was filled to overflowing as the CS and the St. Louis Lutheran communities welcomed back the students who had been participating in Operation Outreach. Missouri Episcopal bishop George L. Cadigan, who three days earlier had urged the delegates at his diocesan convention to give monetary support to the beleaguered faculty and students of CS, was present to extend a welcome. Martin E. Marty, church historian at the University of Chicago, was the featured speaker. He arrived late because bad weather had delayed his flight. He told the gathering how the taxi driver who had brought him to the church identified with the students in their struggle. In an impassioned speech in which he encouraged the students to "keep Operation Outreach going," Marty concluded with a quote from William Stringfellow: "In the face of death, live humanly. In the middle of chaos, celebrate the Word. Amidst babel . . . speak the truth."[22]

During the first week of the moratorium one hundred pastors in the St. Louis area signed a letter identifying with the faculty in their theology and rejecting the BoC's suspension of me as an act of injustice done out of prejudice. Twenty-five guest or adjunct faculty members announced that they would join the CS faculty in refusing to teach. Most of the CS clerical and secretarial staff declared that they would consider themselves dismissed if the faculty and executive staff were dismissed. The faculty and I began receiving letters and copies of letters to Preus and to the BoC by the hundreds from people all across the Synod. My mail alone ultimately filled two large boxes.

On February 1 sixty of the executives serving in staff positions for the LCMS submitted to Preus and to the Synod's Board of Directors a six-page proposal calling for "Actions that Affirm Conciliation." The proposal called for the situation to be rolled back to that of August 1, 1973, and for the appointment of a Committee on Reconciliation to work with the ACDC, whose appointment Preus had announced earlier, for the purpose of "proposing procedures and structures whereby reconciliation can be effected."

The Council of Presidents met to deal with the crisis during the first week in February. It was prepared to consider a similar rollback proposal but deferred to the Synod's BoD when Preus announced that that body was in the process of trying to bring about meetings for the purpose of mediation. Instead the Council of Presidents approved a vaguely worded resolution on the placement of students into pastoral ministry, which graduating students understood to mean that they would not be penalized in the assignment of calls to congregations because of the moratorium.

On February 11, 1974, a Missouri Synod press release revealed that the Preus-appointed Commission on Constitutional Matters had provided a "clarification" of the New Orleans convention resolution (3-09) entitled "To Declare Faculty Majority Position in Violation of Article II of the Constitution." With tortuous reasoning, the Commission on Constitutional Matters stated: "Resolution 3-09 does not condemn the doctrinal position of the faculty as a whole and/or of each individual faculty member, but it does condemn the position defined as the stance of 'the faculty majority.' "

Of course, the "faculty majority" consisted of real, identifiable people. But, the Commission on Constitutional Matters ruled, " . . . the Board of Control is now obligated . . . to determine which faculty members hold positions rejected in Resolution 3-09 and to deal with them." In my judgment the ruling was designed to take the heat off the BoC by undercutting the faculty claim that they could not return to the classroom because they had been condemned for teaching false doctrine. Any reasonable individual should be able to understand that the process of determining who actually held the condemned positions would take considerable time.

After consulting with the BoC and the Synod's Board for Higher Education, the Synod's BoD announced a forum for Friday and Saturday, February 15 and 16. Invited to the forum with the BoD's executive committee were members of the BoC and BHE, three members of the faculty majority and two of the minority, and three members of the student majority and two of the minority. Preus designated Arnold Kuntz, president of the Southern California District of the Synod, as chair of the meeting.

The forum considered a number of proposals for resolving the dispute. Midway during the forum the CS business office informed academic dean John Damm that the BoC chair, Ewald J. Otto, had issued an order not to produce the next salary checks for the faculty and executive staff. Damm called Bertram, who was one of those representing the faculty majority at the forum, out of the meeting to inform him of the development. Bertram chose to continue the conversations without reporting the phone call in the hope that there could yet be an accommodation. As the meeting was drawing to a close, Bertram confronted Edwin Weber with the information. Weber did not respond. Kuntz concluded the forum with the hope that all would now reflect on the proposals in order to consider them again at a subsequent meeting.

On the evening of the next day, Sunday, February 17, the BoC met informally with a number of district presidents prior to its regularly scheduled meeting. The district presidents had originally been scheduled to meet with the BoC during its December meeting, which was canceled because of the death of Arthur Carl Piepkorn. Present for the meeting were John Baumgaertner of the English District, Herman Frincke of the Eastern District, Waldemar Meyer of the Colorado District, Herman Neunaber of the Southern Illinois District, and Rudolph

Ressmeyer of the Atlantic District. The five presidents stressed that the LCMS was on the verge of schism as a result of the BoC's decision to suspend me; they called for a rollback to the situation as it was in August 1973. Ressmeyer charged that the BoC had not acted in the interest of the Synod or CS and had to effect a dramatic turnaround. Frincke told the BoC that Evangelical Lutherans in Mission had been virtually nonexistent in the Eastern District before my suspension but now included half the members of the district. Baumgaertner insisted that as my district president he was responsible to protect me from questionable suspension procedures. Meyer wanted to know if the BoC had actually dealt with the charges against me, eliciting a vigorous negative reaction from the BoC members who had opposed my suspension. Neunaber argued that my suspension was a demonic act that had to be corrected at all costs.[23]

When the district presidents were gone and the BoC was officially in session, vice-president Edwin Weber, Preus's official representative on the BoC (who had been present at the forum the day before without saying a word, even when confronted by Robert Bertram about the instruction not to issue salary checks) proposed the action that the BoC adopted. Couched in legalese, the resolution called on faculty and staff to indicate in writing by noon of the following day, February 18, their intention of resuming on February 19 "their respective responsibilities and functions as employees under their contracts of employment." Otherwise they would be held in breach of their contracts and considered as having terminated their employment. The resolution specified that salaries and housing allowances would stop as of January 18, which would require the board to try to reclaim one salary check already paid to faculty and executive staff. In addition, faculty and staff would have to be out of their offices and CS-owned housing as of February 28, 1974, only ten days away.

"Minority BoC members" reported that Martin Scharlemann had said in support of the motion, "The only way to deal with a rebellion is to crush it." Overcome with grief, Paul Nickel reported the board's action to Robert Bertram at 11:00 that evening. On Monday morning faculty members found a copy of the resolution in their campus mailboxes with a note from Scharlemann: "You are asked herewith to respond to the resolution below, passed by the Board of Control on the evening of February 17, 1974. You will note that your affirmative reply by noon will be appreciated."[24]

At 10:30 A.M. on Monday, February 18, the faculty majority and executive staff, together with spouses, assembled in the lounge of Pritzlaff Hall. The FAC recommended that the only response should be no response; that is, the faculty as a group should not respond. Arthur Repp reminded the faculty that Alfred Fuerbringer was awaiting surgery and that Eldon Pedersen and Leonhard Wuerffel were both very ill, and so might want to comply with the resolution. I underscored the point that the decision to make no group response did not preclude any individual from expressing compliance.

Arriving during the meeting were three representatives of ELIM, the group that had been organized several months earlier to support victims of the Preus juggernaut: Bertwin Frey, who had given leadership to the resistance movement prior to the New Orleans convention; Samuel Roth, the president of ELIM; and Elwyn Ewald, ELIM's executive secretary. Ewald reported that over the weekend there had been a meeting in St. Louis of ELIM people from all over the country for the purpose of setting up a process to raise funds for just such a moment as this. ELIM's treasury contained only $10,000, Ewald said, but the ELIM people would do their best to support the faculty in their stand.

Shortly before noon Martin Scharlemann opened the door to the room and stood there without coming in. He said that vice-president Weber had asked him to thank the faculty who had participated in the forum the past weekend for their expression of commitment to the doctrinal article of the Synod's constitution. As perplexed faculty members looked at one another or stared incredulously at Scharlemann, the acting president left the room.

When the noon hour came, faculty members, executive staff, and spouses linked arms or held hands and began singing "The Church's One Foundation," the hymn that had been the protest song at the New Orleans convention. Faculty members opened the windows of the lounge in Pritzlaff Hall so that the world outside could hear: for the fired faculty of Concordia Seminary, Jesus Christ was Lord.

Following supper that night, after our family devotions, Ernestine and I made sure our children understood what had happened. We did not normally talk much about the Missouri Synod controversy in the presence of our children. Not that we avoided it. The children talked with their peers in school and on the CS campus about what was happening. When there were major developments, we made sure that our children had accurate information. At the same time, we did not bring the CS crisis into our home. Ernestine was especially concerned to provide an atmosphere of equilibrium in our family and to make sure that our four children, each in her or his own way, felt secure.

Ernestine and I often wondered what long-range consequences the Missouri Synod controversy would have for our children, for their relation to the church, and, most important, for their Christian faith. The moratorium decision of the students gave us hope. Our children admired and respected the students at CS, many of whom went out of their way to be warm and friendly toward the children of faculty. Through the moratorium the students became heroes to our children. Those students had taken a stand at considerable personal risk for their faith and for their understanding of what was good and just in the church. Our children could not have had better models for what it means to be Christian.[25]

It was more than the day's events that Ernestine and I wanted to discuss with our children in this instance, February 18, 1974. The six of us were seated around our circular table in the ample kitchen of our campus home. Ernestine and I sat opposite each other with kindergartner Sarah and high-school senior Catherine between us on one side and high-school sophomore Laurence and seventh-grader Mary on the other. Because discussions like this were unusual in our home, Catherine, Laurence, and Mary looked at us intently whenever we spoke, their faces somber, and even Sarah realized that this was a serious time.

I began by telling what had happened earlier in the day and what it meant for most of the families who were living on the campus with us. Ernestine made sure the children understood the consequences: salaries had been cut off, and our friends were going to have to move away. We explained that ELIM was raising money and would do its best to support our friends, but nobody knew if that was going to work. Then I explained that the decision to stop salaries and to force people off the campus did not apply to our family. We could continue to live in our house for the time being. CS had no choice but to continue to pay my salary since I had only been suspended instead of being fired. But, I pointed out, it wouldn't be fair for us to continue to receive a salary when all our friends did not. We were all in the same boat, Ernestine said; because we faced the same problems, we had to share the same troubles. So, I explained, we were going to give our salary checks to ELIM, and we were going to join our friends in looking to ELIM to provide for our support. "There's no other way to go," Catherine said, and the other children nodded their assent.

I asked the children if they knew the words of Jesus telling us that we should seek first the kingdom of God and what God wants done and everything else would be ours as well (Matt. 6:33). Catherine and Laurence said they did. I pointed out that Jesus said those words just after he told his disciples to look at the birds of the air and the lilies of the field and to see how God took loving care of them. I explained that we and our seminary friends were having problems because we were seeking first the kingdom of God and were trying to do what God wanted us to do. So, I said, we don't have to worry about tomorrow. Jesus will keep his promise. God will take loving care of us just like the birds of the air and the lilies of the field.

11 ——◆

EXILE

As 11:00 A.M. was approaching on Tuesday, February 19, 1974, nearly all the faculty and students of Concordia Seminary gathered in its field house and were sitting on retractable bleacher benches, pulled open on the east side of the gymnasium for this occasion. Gerald Miller, student body president, was standing in front of a microphone set on the center line of the basketball court. The CS community had gathered for a student vote on whether students would join the faculty in resuming theological education through a seminary in exile.[1]

The director of the CS athletic program, Eldon Pedersen, had full faculty status. Affectionately called "Pete" or "Coach," he was much loved by students and faculty alike. The field house was Pedersen's domain. Acting president Martin Scharlemann had insisted that the use of CS facilities by those involved in the student moratorium had to be cleared with him. But even Scharlemann would not dare make an issue of Pedersen's turf.

Each person seated in the bleachers had in hand a one-page document.[2] On one side, printed in full, was the ultimatum of the Board of Control, requiring the faculty to resume classes that day or forfeit salaries, housing, and offices. On the other side was an agenda including a proposal for action that had the unanimous support of the student Coordinating Committee.

The meeting had been in progress since 8:30. The student leadership had asked Richard R. Caemmerer to begin the day with worship. Caemmerer had chosen as a text the words of Heb. 11:8: "It was faith that made Abraham obey when God called him to go out to a country which

God had promised to give him." Caemmerer stood holding an open Bible in his left hand, gesturing with his right. He stressed the importance of faith. He pointed out that, although faith had been his throughout his long life, the events of the past months had helped him discover in new ways the dimensions of trust and obedience that were essential to faith. He thanked God that in the closing years of his life God had considered him worthy to suffer for his faith. In suffering, Caemmerer said, we discover what it really means to believe.

For almost two hours the students listened to reports and received answers to questions. Student Dale Kuhn reported on the fruitless forum that had been sponsored by the Synod's Board of Directors the previous weekend. Faculty spokesperson Robert Bertram elaborated on the decision of the faculty to make no response to the BoC's ultimatum but to resume teaching off-campus. Paul Lessmann, faculty member responsible for internship and field education programs, responded to student concerns about internships and calls to ministry.

Academic dean John Damm dealt at length with the nature of the proposed seminary in exile and the reasons for it. "Seminex is not a new seminary," Damm explained, as he stood next to Gerald Miller, "not a new institution; it is Concordia Seminary, but in exile. Seminex represents not a departure from synod but a commitment to the synod which has been rapidly departing from the best in its tradition. It is the only way we can see to complete theological education and simultaneously to call the synod back to its own evangelical fountainhead."[3]

Why was "exile" necessary to resume theological education? Damm stated that the BoC ultimatum made it impossible to return to classes and "pretend that we can have business as usual." The situation the CS community had to face was that "the synodical administration and seminary Board of Control are silencing the Word of God, stifling the biblical gospel." Damm rehearsed the events from the beginning of the CS investigation to the action of the BoC that had precipitated the student moratorium as evidence that teaching the scriptural gospel had to be done at another place.

Damm stated that in the projected seminary in exile most classes would be held at St. Louis University and Eden Seminary, although some might take place in faculty homes and church basements. Seminex would continue the educational programs in which students were enrolled and "will see to it that all qualified students receive the proper theological degree." He expressed the hope that the crisis could be resolved and the degrees granted by CS. "However," he said, his voice rising in intensity, "if the crisis continues beyond the date set for graduation, arrangements will be made to confer the appropriate degrees through an already accredited institution." In fact, he added, Seminex would continue theological programs in fall 1974 if the crisis was not resolved by then.

"Seminex is undertaken reluctantly," Damm continued, "but in the confidence that serious dialogue will result from our action, and in the hope that dialogue will achieve genuine reconciliation." Damm voiced what many people had come to believe: Moratorium had to become exile to produce the kind of confrontation that would make genuine, reconciling dialogue possible. Exile was not permanent; it promised return. "Seminex," Damm said as an afterthought, smiling and winking at the students as he strode off, "may be the only way to reconciliation."

Shortly before 11:00 A.M. student James Wind moved adoption of the statement drafted by the student Coordinating Committee, copies of which students had before them. After rehearsing the reasons for the student moratorium and the decision of the BoC to terminate the contracts of the faculty, the statement declared, "we find it impossible in good conscience to continue our education under the present seminary Board of Control. Instead, we will continue to pursue our calling as students in preparation for ministry in the Lutheran Church–Missouri Synod under the terminated faculty. . . . We therefore resolve to resume our theological education in exile, trusting in the grace of our Lord Jesus Christ." Around 11:15 the students were ready to vote. A loud and vigorous aye resounded throughout the field house. I heard only a dozen or so nays and abstentions.

After brief instructions about coming events and procedures to follow, faculty and students climbed down from their bleacher seats to participate in a public enactment of exile, whose end result had been prearranged by academic dean John Damm but whose steps along the way had been devised overnight by student leaders. I was surprised when I saw students pick up white wooden crosses about two feet in height as they left the field house on their way to the CS quadrangle. Many faculty members donned academic robes and hoods and headed in the same direction. I put on my hat and overcoat to cope with the dank and chilly winter air and hurried to catch up. I saw that the procession of faculty and students was being led by a crucifix, and I listened as the procession participants sang what had become the song of the Missouri Synod's confessing movement, "The Church's One Foundation."

As I arrived at the quadrangle at the center of the campus, surrounded on four sides by Tudor Gothic buildings, I looked on in amazement. Planted in the frozen soil were white wooden crosses, one for each member of the faculty and executive staff, bearing our individual names in black letters. The students were planting their own crosses in the ground next to ours as they moved through the quadrangle. The seminary was turned into a cemetery.

Students and faculty moved from the quadrangle through the archway to the entrance area in the parking lot in front of the statue of Martin Luther. As they did so, they intoned Luther's hymn, "A Mighty Fortress Is Our God." Standing at the top of the entrance steps, faculty member Alfred von Rohr Sauer read a Scripture lesson from the Book of Lamentations, and Gerald Miller read the students' Seminex resolution. Then students boarded up the entrance to CS with two huge frames cut to fit the dimensions of the Gothic archway. Written across the two boards in large white letters on a black surface was the single word: EXILED.

A bell in the CS tower began to toll, deeply, mournfully, the way it had tolled two months earlier at the death of Arthur Carl Piepkorn. Student Charles Muse, who was carrying the processional cross, started walking down the driveway from the CS entrance to DeMun Avenue. He was followed by a student carrying an eight-foot banner depicting the stump of a felled tree from which a new shoot was growing. The banner had been fashioned by Doris Graesser, wife of faculty member Carl Graesser, using a design created by faculty member Robert Werberig to serve as a symbol for those who were going into exile. As students and faculty joined in the procession, the tolling bell was submerged in a resounding peal from all the bells in the tower carillon, and sadness gave way to joy.

It was ironic. The procession into exile was taking place one year to the day after the previous seminary governing board had publicly announced its decision to "commend" every member of the faculty as faithful to their commitment to the Scriptures and the Lutheran Confessions.

The procession wound its way to DeMun Avenue, the eastern boundary of the campus, and to a small city park area across the street. There John Damm stood waiting with Walter Brueggemann, the academic dean of Eden Theological Seminary, who was representing both his school and the Divinity School of St. Louis University. In a brief ceremony I presented to Brueggemann our students and our faculty, who were now to be adjunct faculty of Eden and St. Louis University.

I spoke briefly to those assembled in the park, using as my text a portion of the same book from which Caemmerer had begun the day, Heb. 13:13–14: "Let us, then, go to him outside the camp and share his shame. For there is no permanent city for us here on earth; we are looking for the city which is to come." For me the seminary pilgrim procession was not really an exile with the hope of a return but an exodus like Abraham's to an unknown promised land.

More than anyone else, John Damm was responsible for the formation of Concordia Seminary in Exile. With the indispensable assistance of David Yagow, CS registrar, and Jeannette Bauermeister, Damm's administrative assistant, Damm explored the possibilities and put together the relationships with three other seminaries that produced the organizational framework that gave accredited standing to the ongoing educational efforts of our faculty and students.

Damm was, like me, an Easterner, born in Union City, New Jersey. After graduation from Concordia College in Bronxville, New York, he attended CS. He and I were roommates there for two years before his graduation in 1951. He pursued graduate study at Columbia University and Union Theological Seminary in New York, and received a Master of Arts degree in 1952 and a Doctor of Education degree in 1963. He studied as a Fulbright Scholar at Friedrich Alexander University in Erlangen, Germany. Ordained in 1951, Damm served as assistant pastor and director of Christian education at Grace Lutheran Church in Teaneck, New Jersey, and developed and built the congregation's parochial school. In addition to education Damm was keenly interested in worship; during my student days he enlisted me in the cause of the Lutheran liturgical movement. In 1966 Damm was called to the CS faculty to teach in the fields of worship and education. In 1972, three years after I began serving as CS president, I appointed him academic dean in an administrative reorganization when Arthur Repp stepped down as vice-president for academic affairs.

Of medium height, struggling to hold in a midriff bulge, Damm had a full face with thick lips and thinning black hair. He was always dressed in clerical garb. Dominant were his penetrating eyes that sparkled with joy and could glower in anger. Deeply spiritual, he helped shape the worship life at CS and fostered appreciation for the arts. A gourmet cook, he often entertained students and was among the most loved and respected of the faculty. Damm shared my conviction that theology should not exist for its own sake but had to be in the service of ministry. A professor in the department of practical theology, he was eminently practical in his approach to the problems at CS.

Having served as a faculty representative at the New Orleans convention, Damm geared up for action in the weeks following it.[4] He canceled a week of speaking engagements and his own vacation in order to prepare to be of help to students. On his instruction David Yagow made copies of all CS student records so that, should there be a new seminary administration, Damm and Yagow would be able to give counsel to students.

When the August suspension effort made clear what the BoC intended to do, Damm organized a task force of faculty and students to consider the possibility of a counter-seminary next to CS. Through September and October the task force looked at alternatives. One was to use, during evening hours, the classrooms of the Christian Brothers High School adjacent to the CS campus or of St. Luke Roman Catholic parochial school several blocks away. Office space above a florist two blocks from the campus might be used for administrative purposes.

At about that time, Robert Bertram in collaboration with Edward Schroeder came up with a theological educational program they called "Crossings." They envisioned it as their professional future when it was no longer possible to serve at CS. "Crossings" was a program of lay theological education that made use of the small-group process for intersecting the teaching of Scripture with the issues of daily life. The "Crossings" model led Damm and his task force to explore another alternative, conducting seminary education in small groups in the homes of faculty members or in church basements and classrooms.

By the end of October the task force had concluded that neither alternative was feasible. The counter-seminary had no possibility of accreditation; few students showed an interest in the idea; there was little possibility of garnering the necessary financial support. According to Damm's assessment, the students at that time were divided about what response to make to events at CS. So also was the faculty, the majority of whom were determined to stick it out and fight the battle through on the campus. Late in October, convinced that the BoC wanted other heads besides mine, Damm began contacting individual faculty members whom he considered especially vulnerable to encourage them to look for other employment.

In November, as a result of conversations with students, Damm realized that the students who were in their final year were particularly concerned over what was happening and might need special assistance to complete their programs. Would it be possible to salvage their degrees in a bona fide way? Damm asked himself. On the third Saturday of November, Damm convened a meeting of his counterparts at three institutions of the St. Louis Theological Consortium: Walter Brueggemann of Eden Theological Seminary, John Rybar of Kenrick Seminary, William Sullivan of the Divinity School of St. Louis University, along with the executive of the consortium, Sister Angelita Meyerscough.

The St. Louis Theological Consortium had come into existence some six years earlier for the purpose of fostering cooperation among St. Louis area theological schools and providing students with opportunities for cross-registration. The faculty and administration of CS had been instrumental in creating the consortium and was the catalyst for cooperative activity among the theological schools. Although cooperation was limited, the consortium provided the opportunity for school administrators, especially the deans, to get to know and work with one another. Within six years a family feeling had developed among the leaders of the consortium.

The family feeling was present at the meeting Damm convened at CS late in November. Damm described the CS situation to his colleagues and laid out the problem that could confront senior students unable to put up with what might happen following my suspension from office. Damm's guests stated their willingness to help. Rybar, expressing personal concern, made it clear that Kenrick Seminary would probably not be able to do much because it was a diocesan seminary. Brueggemann and Sullivan were sure that their schools would help if only they could be shown how.

Early in December Damm and I attended a meeting of the presidents and deans of all the Missouri Synod institutions of higher education, which the Synod's Board for Higher Education had convened in Chicago. There both of us realized that we could not count on any other Missouri Synod school for help. The school administrators were sure that what was happening to the St. Louis seminary could not happen to them. As I later described it, "The participants in that conference—the leaders of our system of schools—tried to discuss the future of our schools without any reference to what was being done to Concordia Seminary! While the house of our educational system was burning down, the leaders of that system were talking about rearranging the furniture!"[5]

Piepkorn's death increased Damm's despair, and he began to make plans for his own future, contacting friends about positions in the secular world. After the Christmas holidays it was the students who gave Damm an upsurge of hope. Together, Damm and the students reflected on what could be learned from the experience of Dietrich Bonhoeffer and his little seminary in Germany's "confessing church" during the Nazi era. Perhaps even with a remnant of forty students and ten faculty, a seminary in exile could make a witness.

The student moratorium and the action of the faculty caused Damm's hopes to soar. I encouraged him when he asked to pursue a seminary in exile, and he went to work with dispatch. Together with David Yagow and Jeannette Bauermeister, Damm canvassed the possible locations: Marillac College, a Roman Catholic school farther out in St. Louis County; a public school and a Jewish synagogue in nearby University City; Second Presbyterian Church in the west end of St. Louis; Forest Park Community College in St. Louis. None of the locations, however, was suitable.

Neighboring Fontbonne College, a Roman Catholic women's school in the city of Clayton, seemed the best location. It had an unused building that included classrooms, a chapel, and small dormitory rooms that could serve as offices. When the school's administration was open to the proposal, Damm took me to the campus to show me the possibilities. But the school's president reported that, in a canvass of the school's governing board, the board's chair, an Episcopal layman, had expressed opposition because the arrangement would involve the school in the internal dispute of another educational institution. Damm met with the man but after two hours of conversation could not dissuade him. So Damm ruled Fontbonne out of consideration.

In the meantime David Yagow had initiated conversations with the registrars at St. Louis University and Eden Seminary concerning course schedules and use of classrooms. Jeannette Bauermeister had explored with administrators at the two schools the potential use of space for offices, worship, and community life. On February 2 Damm came to the conclusion that the university's Divinity School and Eden Seminary were the only viable options for location of a seminary in exile.

On February 4 in a meeting held at the Divinity School on Lindell Boulevard in midtown St. Louis, what came to be called the Joint Project for Theological Education was born. Present for the meeting were Walter Brueggemann of Eden Seminary, William Sullivan and his assistant Joan Smith of the Divinity School, Yagow, Damm, and Bauermeister. They worked out the details of an agreement according to which the Divinity School and Eden Seminary would join together in a project in which the former "faculty majority" of CS would serve in behalf of the two schools for the purpose of completing the theological education of CS students.[6]

According to the agreement, the faculty formerly at CS would become adjunct faculty of the Divinity School and Eden Seminary. The program of instruction would be the one formerly in use at CS. Students would be registered jointly at both schools sponsoring the project. Neither school would be responsible for the salary of the faculty. Both schools would be reimbursed for use of classrooms and offices. Student fees would defray the expenses. The two schools would appoint a director to administer the project.

In the two weeks that followed, Yagow worked with Damm in the production of class schedules for 170 courses for the completion of the work of the winter quarter and for registering students for the spring quarter. As a result of small-group discussions held with students from February 11 to 13, Damm became aware that almost the entire student body would likely be enrolled in the seminary in exile. Sullivan and Brueggemann reviewed the proposal with the accrediting agency for theological schools to get that agency's informal approval.

One major problem still needed to be resolved. According to the present proposals for a seminary in exile, graduates would have to receive their degrees from either a Roman Catholic university or a seminary of the United Church of Christ. What the Joint Project for Theological Education needed was a Lutheran seminary participant so that conservative Missouri Synod students could receive their degrees from a Lutheran institution. Damm turned for help to the Lutheran School of Theology at

Chicago, a seminary of the Lutheran Church in America. Its president was Walter F. Wolbrecht, whose position as executive director of LCMS Jacob Preus had gotten the Synod to abolish in 1971. I had tried to engage Wolbrecht as an administrator for CS but could not get the BoC's approval. The Chicago seminary recognized Wolbrecht's administrative skills and appointed him as its president.

In January 1974, in the time before my suspension, the presidents and deans of Lutheran seminaries held their annual meeting in St. Louis. In the course of the meeting Damm and I met informally with Wolbrecht and Wesley Fuerst, academic dean of LSTC, about how other Lutheran seminaries might be helpful to our students. Wolbrecht and Fuerst consulted with others. One idea was to apportion our students in groups of thirty or forty to other Lutheran seminaries to complete their education. For family and financial reasons, however, the idea was not workable.

On January 28 Damm renewed contacts with Wolbrecht and Fuerst and asked whether the faculty of LSTC would be willing to grant degrees to graduating seniors who completed their degree requirements under the CS faculty but not under the CS governing board. Under date of February 14, 1974, Fuerst responded that the faculty of LSTC was ready to enter into negotiations to work out the arrangements.

On February 16 in a meeting on the campus of Eden Seminary in Webster Groves, Missouri, Sullivan submitted to Brueggemann and Damm a revised draft of the agreement that had been worked out almost two weeks earlier. Sullivan and Brueggemann agreed to present the agreement concerning a Joint Project for Theological Education to the presidents of their respective schools for approval.

On Monday, February 18, the day the CS faculty refused to submit to the BoC's ultimatum, Damm walked into William Sullivan's office at St. Louis University Divinity School at 5:00 P.M. for a meeting of the principals involved in the proposed Joint Project for Theological Education. Present in addition to Brueggemann, Damm, Sullivan, and Joan Smith were Robert T. Fauth, president of Eden Seminary, and Edward J. Drummond, executive vice-president of the university, who was serving as acting president following the retirement of Paul J. Reinert.

According to Damm, the meeting went well as the participants reviewed the details of the Joint Project. Then the direction changed as Drummond raised a number of issues that he described as negative points of view. Fauth, raising his eyebrows and creasing his forehead beneath his curly hair, picked up on what seemed to be Drummond's lead and added to the list of problems. He shook his head in resignation, sighing that he doubted he would be able to sign the agreement. Damm's heart sank. The CS faculty had already announced its intention of resuming classes in exile and was counting on the arrangements. Then

Drummond, pursing his lips and speaking with carefully articulated words, reversed himself and spoke positively for the agreement. Peering out above his glasses, he announced that he was prepared to sign the agreement. It would of course be necessary, Drummond pointed out, for Fauth and him to get the approval of the key members of their governing boards. Both agreed to do that.

Damm kept his joy in check, realizing that executives often use boards as means to make the negative decisions they themselves are unwilling to announce. At midnight Brueggemann called Damm to tell him that Eden's officials had agreed to enter into the Joint Project. Damm could not reach Sullivan until the following morning while the students met to decide whether they would agree to a seminary in exile. When Damm got through to Sullivan shortly after 9:00 A.M., he learned that Drummond had not yet received board approval.

On the phone Damm and Sullivan scrapped the students' plans to walk in procession from the CS campus to the university five miles away in midtown St. Louis. Participants in a seminary in exile had better not show up to be received at a place that had not yet officially decided whether to welcome them! Instead it was agreed that the procession would go to the DeMun park just off campus, where Brueggemann would receive them.

John Damm positioned himself midway between the telephone in Eldon Pedersen's field house office and the activities going on in the gymnasium so that he could respond in either direction when needed. At 11:15 A.M., while the students were voting their approval of a seminary in exile, Damm was on the phone with William Sullivan, receiving at what was truly the eleventh hour the good news that St. Louis University officials had approved the agreement. David Yagow went quickly to the door of the field house to hand out schedules for the classes that were to begin the next day at St. Louis University and Eden Seminary.

Damm had made it happen. A program of Lutheran theological education was going to take place under the auspices of a Jesuit university and a seminary of the United Church of Christ. In a few weeks the LSTC would also be a full-fledged member of the Joint Project for Theological Education.

◆ ◆ ◆

On Wednesday, February 20, 1974, Concordia Seminary in Exile began functioning on the campuses of St. Louis University and Eden Theological Seminary. The nerve center of Seminex was a large high-ceilinged room about fifty feet square on the first floor of the building that housed the Divinity School of St. Louis University in midtown St.

Louis. Called the Commons from the days when it served as a student dining room, the room was now the Seminex "Community and Communications Center."

The place was usually bedlam, filled with students and faculty, some engaged in animated conversation, some trying to read, the telephone ringing, information being shouted above the din. Registration for the spring quarter took place in the Commons on March 10, 1974, enrolling almost four hundred students in the Seminex programs. One hundred students chose to enroll in the programs of 801, as the seminary that had been left behind was now called. It was referred to by the numbers of its DeMun street address because faculty and students refused to acknowledge that the Clayton school was Concordia Seminary.

In the northeast corner of the room Lucille Hager set up the Seminex "library," which consisted of a table serving as a counter to serve students, a series of bookcases containing books on loan from the personal libraries of faculty members, and two or three folding chairs for the director of the library and her staff. In the southeast corner was the "Communications Center," with mailboxes, daily announcements, a table holding various handout items, chairs behind the table for those who were handling "rumor control," managing the only telephone available to the whole community, or organizing student activities.

A dozen tables, castoffs reclaimed from university storage rooms, and metal folding chairs were distributed throughout the room. Large bulletin boards, filled with news clippings, notices, want ads, and housing opportunities, dominated the wall at the south end of the room. In the northwest section of the room, not far from the room's main entrance, were two chairs set against the wall under a sign that read, "Prof. Caemmerer Enter Without Knocking." The sign had hung for decades on the door of Richard Caemmerer's CS office. He brought it with him to the Commons, and he could regularly be found underneath the sign, talking to students.

If the Commons was the nerve center of the Seminex institutional body, the chapel in DuBourg Hall was the heart. This chapel was no longer used by the university. According to a news report,[7] Cardinal John J. Carberry, who did not have jurisdiction over the Jesuit university, had nevertheless insisted that the Jesuit chapel in Fusz Hall should not be available for Seminex use. The university made its old chapel available, and daily the Lutherans of Seminex filled its pews. Surrounded by the stations of the cross and other signs of Roman Catholic piety, the people of Seminex made the chapel resound with evangelical preaching and lustily sung chorales. Here faculty and students and staff wrestled day by day with the problems of faith and the moral issues of the controversy in which they were involved.

The brains of the Seminex operation was located on the ground floor of the Divinity School in a single office where all the work of administration took place. The staff of the Divinity School had made the office available by doubling up in other offices. Damm, Bauermeister, and Yagow operated out of this room. They had to climb three flights of stairs for contact with the secretarial staff, run by Rosemary Lipka and headed by Verna Renner, who were located along with typewriters and a copy machine in a single large classroom on the top floor of the building.

The limbs of the Seminex institutional body were the classrooms scattered throughout the university's many buildings and the administration building of Eden Seminary twelve miles away in suburban Webster Groves. In addition to classroom space, Eden Seminary provided housing for a number of Seminex students, especially graduate students from overseas. At first the new administration at CS insisted that any students not registered for the spring quarter would have to leave CS housing. They relented when they realized that empty housing generated no income.

The CS administration also relented on the eviction notice given to faculty and staff when the public, churchly and secular, expressed outrage that families were given only ten days to find new quarters. The deadline was extended from February 28 to March 28. Faculty and staff, however, were determined to leave as soon as possible.

The faculty organized a task force to assist in relocation. Orville Brotherton, pastor of Second Presbyterian Church, had been aware of the search for classroom space for a seminary in exile. When Brotherton learned of the housing need, he put Seminex faculty in touch with a member of his congregation who was the head of West End Investment Co., owner of a large building with vacant apartments in the west end of St. Louis. Oxford Apartments, as the building was called, had emptied slowly over a number of years as the neighborhood changed from white to black. It was a gracious building consisting of large four- and five-bedroom apartments with foyers, sunrooms, and walk-in closets. West End Investment Co. offered the apartments to the faculty without a lease and with the understanding that they should pay whatever they could afford. A half-dozen faculty families moved in.

On March 10 the faculty families that were living on the CS campus organized what they called "the biggest garage sale in the world" and hundreds of people from the St. Louis area descended on the campus for the sale. Faculty member Holland Jones, who was licensed to drive a moving rig, teamed up with students in forming "Streaker Express" to move faculty families. Under the leadership of Wanda Weber, a St.

Louisan whose sons Leslie and Paul were seminary students, Project Concern organized teams of St. Louis Lutherans to clean apartments for the faculty, to help with the move, and to stock the new homes and apartments with food staples.

The Tietjen family helped our neighbors move. Ernestine served lunch or supper on moving days. Our older children helped with packing and carrying boxes and furniture. We all watched dolefully as one by one the houses around us became vacant and we stayed behind. With nearly all students and faculty elsewhere, the seminary had indeed become a cemetery, the vacant buildings standing as monuments to a life and time now dead and gone.

In the weeks and months following the formation of Seminex, I was out of town more than I was in St. Louis. I traveled all over the country to tell the Seminex story, speaking in four or five different locations a week. To help pass the time on the never-ending succession of airline flights, I began reading Shakespeare. A nephew in New York, Douglas Spadaro, had given me a pocket edition of Shakespeare's works as a Christmas present. On each trip I stuffed a few books from the forty-volume set into my coat pockets. Before long I had read through all forty.

Seminex asked me to teach, something I had not had time to do since my arrival at CS in 1969. Under the jurisdiction of the Joint Project for Theological Education I taught two courses in American Lutheranism during the spring quarter, one in a classroom at St. Louis University, the other at Eden Seminary. Except for my teaching responsibilities, I was officially not involved with Seminex, although I was available for counsel whenever I was in town. John Damm had been appointed director of the Joint Project; with Jeannette Bauermeister, David Yagow, and several other administrators, he managed Seminex.

Basic policy decisions were made by the two committees that had been in charge during the moratorium, the Faculty Advisory Committee for the faculty and the Coordinating Committee for the students. The name of the faculty committee was an anachronism; it had become the faculty's executive committee. Major policy decisions were made by the whole community, faculty and students consulting together in a kind of town meeting. Radical democracy was the rule during the first months of Seminex. Students and faculty spent as much time on issues of governance as on education.

My suspension and the formation of Seminex evoked an overwhelming outpouring of financial support. Evangelical Lutherans in Mission reported early in March 1974 that it had received cash gifts and pledges totaling more than $700,000. Our faculty and executive staff missed one paycheck; after that ELIM's coffers had sufficient funds to pay the salaries of faculty and staff and the other expenses of Seminex.

Financial support was needed for more than a seminary in exile. While most of the attention was focused on the dispute at CS, a long-festering problem finally broke out in the Missouri Synod's department of missions. On January 12, more than a week before I was suspended, the Synod's Board for Missions decided to dismiss James W. Mayer, the much-respected area secretary for missions in South Asia and Oceania, who had served in that position for twelve years after fourteen years as a missionary in India. The dismissal brought to a head the conflict that had been going on for more than two years between the staff and the board and between factions within the board.

The Preus party in the Synod succeeded in taking over majority control of the Synod's Board for Missions at the Milwaukee Convention in 1971 and installed one of the party's leaders, Waldo Werning, as chair. For the next two years the new majority sought to reverse the mission policies that had been constructed on the basis of a series of Mission Affirmations adopted by the Synod at its convention in Detroit in 1965. The work of the staff under the direction of executive secretary William H. Kohn became increasingly difficult as Werning and other majority board members began to exercise specific staff responsibilities and found fault with staff performance. Late in 1972 the board dismissed Martin Luther Kretzmann, the distinguished staff member who, after long service as a missionary in India, performed an analysis of the Synod's mission enterprise that led to adoption of the Mission Affirmations.

James Mayer was tall and trim, his long face accented by a high forehead and brushed back hair, his eyes ever alert and sparkling, a mustache and beard framing a mouth always ready to smile. He spoke with passion, his voice resonantly rising to a crescendo and then falling away to a whisper. He was creative and resourceful, impatient with bureaucracy, the kind of person who would stand up to critics and reciprocate in kind. The "majority members" of the Board for Missions found in him too much of an impediment to their plans for the reorganization of Missouri Synod missions. Mayer's dismissal was a clear sign of what lay ahead for the Synod's mission program.

The mission staff refused to acquiesce to the board's dismissal action. In a letter of January 17, 1974, to Jacob A. O. Preus the staff went on the offensive against the board majority. They told Preus, "the dismissal of Dr. Kretzmann and Rev. Mayer are symptoms of a much deeper problem that threatens to reverse the forward thrust of missions which our

Synod has enjoyed under the blessings of the Holy Spirit."[8] They described the problems in detail and called on Preus to help reverse the direction of the Board for Missions.

When the news of Mayer's dismissal reached the sister churches of the Missouri Synod overseas, some of the leaders of those churches joined the staff in protesting the actions of the board. President Waima Waise and missionary Erwin Spruth of the Wabag Lutheran Church in New Guinea came to the United States to express the concern of the overseas church in person.

In the meantime the crisis at CS had exploded. By the end of January there were two fronts in the LCMS controversy, one at CS in Clayton, the other in the headquarters of the Synod in downtown St. Louis. Synod staff people, district presidents, and others in the Synod were demanding a rollback of board actions to undo my suspension and the dismissal of James Mayer. The BoD, as the top governing board of the Synod, found it necessary to enter the controversy on both fronts.

On February 1 the BoD proposed an early meeting of mission board and staff to work out the problems in the mission area, offering a committee of its members to give assistance. A month went by before Werning convened a meeting. The BoD proposed a mediation process with a mediator shuttling back and forth between meetings of board and staff to work out a compromise. Staff members insisted on face-to-face meetings with a three-person panel of mediators. Another month went by without action. On March 29 the BoD unilaterally announced that the mediation process would be replaced by a study of the entire mission operation under a five-person commission.

At a special meeting of the Board for Missions on April 5–6, 1974, the board majority tabled action on reinstating Mayer and refused to respond to other proposals of the mission staff designed to effect reconciliation. The mission staff discovered what CS faculty and students learned from their participation in mediation efforts with the BoD: In the hands of the Preus administration, mediation efforts meant quieting the opposition in order to confirm the actions that had prompted the need for mediation.

On April 10, William Kohn, who for months had resisted staff pressure to take a stand, submitted his resignation as executive secretary of the Board for Missions, giving as reason the board's refusal to reinstate Mayer in spite of the appeals of sister churches. Kohn declared that his resignation protested "against the legalism of the Board for Missions in its dealing with people, against the spirit of isolationism and separatism as it has developed in the Board's outlook on missions and against its arbitrary use of power to achieve greater centralization."[9] One week later, four more mission staff resigned: Wolfgang Bulle, a physician who was secretary for medical missions; Marion Kretzschmar, administrative assistant for designated gifts; Walter H. Meyer, secretary for North America; and William F. Reinking, secretary for Africa and the Middle East. One month later Paul H. Strege, area secretary for East Asia, joined them in resigning.

On May 10–11, 1974, under the auspices of ELIM, a new agency for world missions was organized in St. Louis. Called Partners in Mission, the agency began as a division of ELIM and engaged four of the resigned staff to conduct operations: James Mayer, Walter Meyer, Marion Kretzschmar, and Paul Strege.

As I observed, the CS community learned early how little it could expect from the mediation efforts of the Missouri Synod's BoD. After the first two days of such efforts on February 15–16, 1974, the CS BoC on February 17 issued the ultimatum that resulted in the firing of the faculty. The community was wary when the Synod's BoD renewed mediation efforts with Seminex. Representatives of the Seminex faculty, Robert Bertram, Richard Caemmerer, Robert Smith, and Andrew Weyermann, met with the executive committee of the BoD on February 24 and received from them a proposal that mediation be initiated by an impartial mediator moving back and forth to separate meetings of three designated representatives of the faculty and of the BoC.

The entire Seminex community was involved in determining a response to this proposal. First the FAC, then the faculty, and finally the entire community acted on the response. The exile community submitted a counterproposal that called for free and open discussions instead of secret meetings, a panel of four distinguished persons instead of a single mediator, the inclusion of students in the negotiations, the participation of Preus in the discussions, and mutual agreement on panel members and procedures rather than unilateral arrangements and decisions. Faculty representatives presented the proposal to the BoD's executive committee on March 14.

The committee, however, would not move from its proposal of a single mediator and submitted guidelines for the mediation efforts that specified that at least "at the outset a single mediator will be used."[10] The committee's proposal was unacceptable to the Seminex community. On May 2 the committee and the faculty representatives met again. The committee proposed that the mediation effort should begin with a single mediator and the disagreements on how to proceed should be the first order of business. The faculty representatives agreed but proposed their own wording.

The faculty representatives and the executive committee were in the process of agreeing on the words to be used. Then in mid-May the BHE asked the boards of control of the Synod's two seminaries to give priority consideration to the Seminex faculty in making new faculty appointments. The BoC of the St. Louis seminary proposed to the BoD that the "mediation process be held in abeyance until the Board of Control has had sufficient opportunity to implement the recommendation of the Board for Higher Education."[11] The BoD concurred, thus unilaterally ending any possibility of a mediation process.

On May 29 faculty representatives met with three representatives of the CS BoC, including Ralph Bohlmann, who had just been named acting president of CS. Martin Scharlemann had resigned as acting president on April 15 because of "nervous exhaustion."[12] Faculty representatives reiterated the Seminex stand on the need to reverse BoC actions on suspension and retirement. Board representatives proposed a process of interviews for new positions on the faculty. Meeting early in June, the faculty declined the interview proposal and issued a counterproposal for fraternal discussions involving faculty, students, board, and synodical president, a proposal that was to be realized several months later.

Of greater significance than the negotiations involving faculty were those that affected students. Early in February the Council of Presidents had stated its intention of placing CS students in positions of internship and permanent positions of ministry, but the district presidents had not expected the problems involved in the formation of a seminary in exile.

At a meeting of the Council of Presidents March 18–22, 1974, a compromise was worked out on the internship question that made possible the placement of Seminex second-year students in Missouri Synod "vicarages." Their internship would be supervised by the BHE in consultation with the executive committee of the BoD and the placement officers of Seminex. After learning about the action of the Council of Presidents, Seminex students announced that they would accept no supervision except that of Seminex. The internship assignments had been made, however, and 124 Seminex students were able to go to authorized internships.

The placement of Seminex graduates was another matter. On March 23, 1974, the Preus-appointed Commission on Constitutional Matters declared that Seminex candidates were not eligible for ministry in the Missouri Synod and that no congregation could issue a call to a Seminex candidate without forfeiting membership in the Synod. According to the ruling, "it is clear from the bylaws that only those candidates who have been properly certified and assigned may be ordained,"[13] and because Seminex was not a seminary of the Synod, its faculty had no power to approve candidates for ministry in the Synod.

Meeting from April 29 to May 3, 1974, the Council of Presidents tried to work out a compromise within the bylaws as interpreted by the Commission on Constitutional Matters. On May 3 it adopted a series of resolutions on placement, the key one of which asked the faculty still remaining at CS to review a list of graduates recommended by the Seminex faculty and to endorse them for ministry in the Synod. The resolution further specified that if a student's candidacy was "challenged by a member of the 801 faculty, the concern of the challenge shall be investigated by a five-man interview committee," consisting of three district presidents and one faculty member from each of the schools. The committee would "determine the justice of the challenge and so advise the 801 faculty."[14]

The people of Seminex swallowed hard and accepted the compromise. On May 8, Robert Preus, who was functioning as president because of Scharlemann's resignation several weeks earlier, informed Seminex fourth-year class president Daniel Comsia that Seminex candidates would have to be interviewed on doctrinal concerns, attitudes, and the Synod's constitution and bylaws. The following day Comsia informed Robert Preus that interviews of Seminex students were not included in the Council of Presidents resolution and would have to be authorized by the Council of Presidents before Seminex students would submit to them.

On May 17 the Council of Presidents met again for the purpose of assigning calls to candidates. The district presidents were fairly evenly divided between "moderates" and "conservatives," although the presence of the synodical vice-presidents gave the balance of power to the conservatives. In my opinion the moderate district presidents never understood their own strength or the power that the Council as a group might have been able to exercise within the Missouri Synod. One moderate district president did understand it. Herman Neunaber, president of the Southern Illinois District, tried to give leadership to the moderate group within the Council, but they apparently would not let him do it. Nor did anyone else in their number emerge as leader.

Whenever the Council met on the CS campus, it was my custom to invite the district presidents to my home after an evening session to relax over refreshments. In the course of time only the moderate district presidents came. The number of guests varied. There could be as many as fifteen or as few as six. In connection with the meeting on May 17, nine or ten gathered in our living room. I decided to use the occasion to unburden my heart and soul on the need to give Seminex graduates calls to ministry.

I began by sharing with the district presidents something that Jaraslav Pelikan, the noted Yale historian and Luther scholar, had said in class when I was a student of his at CS. In describing the book-burning bonfire for which Luther shared responsibility after he received the papal bull of excommunication, Pelikan said that the really significant action was not that Luther burned the papal bull but that he threw the book of canon law into the fire. Luther wanted everyone to understand that Christians as individuals and as the church had to live by the gospel and not by the law.

Look what is happening to this church of ours that bears Luther's name, I said to the assembled district presidents. We have reinvented canon law and call it the *Synodical Handbook.* [15] We carry it around in our briefcases and rarely make a move without consulting its bylaws. The Commission on Constitutional Matters, which in times past met rarely, now meets almost every month to hand down rulings about how the bylaws have to be understood, adding bylaw on top of bylaw. We all know that it is only right and fair to assign calls to Seminex's graduating seniors. But synodical officials have invoked the letter of the law to say it cannot be done. Maybe it is time for another bonfire, I added.

Several district presidents took issue with me and stressed the importance of rules and laws. They pointed out that laws are created not only to provide recognizable, acceptable regulations for life in community but to prevent the arbitrary use of power. We have to have laws just because the church is a human institution, they said, and we have to live by the laws we have. If we do not like the laws, we have to work to change them, they added.

I replied that they were giving me the same speech I used to give when as a loyal member of the establishment I defended the institution and its rules. Through the controversy, I pointed out, I had learned something significant about law and its use: Even the best laws are no protection against abuse. Instructions about changing laws you dislike have a hollow ring when you know that the tendency of law is to favor those in power and not the dispossessed. Behind every law is a higher law that the specific law seeks to encode and that sits in judgment on it.

To support what I was saying, I quoted Scripture, pointing out that familiar texts had taken on new meaning for me as a result of the controversy. I referred to the story in which the religious authorities objected when Jesus' disciples broke the Sabbath law by plucking grain on the Sabbath. In his response Jesus said, "The Sabbath was made for the good of humanity; humanity was not made for the Sabbath" (Mark 2:27). A higher law of justice and love stood behind the Sabbath laws. If Jesus' disciples could break divine rules, we can dare to break our own in order to meet the demand of the higher law of justice and love.

In Matthew's account of this event (12:1–8), I pointed out, Jesus tells his opponents to learn what Scripture means when God says: "It is kindness that I want, not animal sacrifices."[16] The rules of the bylaws have to be ignored if they stand in the way of justice and love, I insisted. The Council of Presidents needs to do what is right even if it isn't in the bylaws, I urged my captive audience. Tell the people of the church that the situation you confronted was one that bylaw framers had not envisioned. You had to make an exception in order to do what was right.

I knew that my radical counsel had little chance of success even among my sympathetic listeners. At the meeting the Council of Presidents capitulated to CS's insistence on interviews. In addition it officially placed all candidates except those of Seminex.

The graduating students of Seminex were once again faced with a decision crucial to their future ministry in the LCMS. On May 20, 1974, they adopted two resolutions unanimously in which they refused the interviews and the process for placement approved by the Council of Presidents. They stated, "submission of our qualifications for certification to the administration of 801 DeMun would lend endorsement to that administration and thus negate our confessional witness against it." They affirmed, "we cannot in good conscience . . . participate in a program of interviews which allows Concordia Seminary, 801 DeMun, to serve as a final judge of our qualifications for the ministry in the Lutheran Church–Missouri Synod."[17]

The next day the graduating students resolved to "communicate our willingness to receive calls from congregations of The Lutheran Church–Missouri Synod which are willing to recognize our certification by the faculty of Concordia Seminary-in-Exile."[18] The placement committee of the Council of Presidents had tentatively assigned calls to most of Seminex's graduating students in the hope that the compromise for their certification would work out. On the basis of that information the placement officials of Seminex contacted congregations directly to see if they would accept the candidates who had been tentatively assigned to them. The faculty and students of Seminex wrote an open letter to the people of the Missouri Synod appealing for calls to ministry for the Seminex graduates.

"Where do we go from here?" was the topic of my address to the Seminex community assembled for commencement on Friday evening, May 24, 1974, a clear and crisp spring evening in St. Louis. Commencement was traditionally held outdoors in the CS quadrangle. Exiled from the campus, we had to find another location. Jeannette Bauermeister made arrangements for the commencement to take place in another quadrangle one mile east of CS on the campus of Washington University in St. Louis.

I spoke from a large platform arranged at the north end of the quadrangle and looked out over nearly two thousand people seated in chairs facing the platform or standing in the back and around the sides. In the assembled congregation were family and friends of the graduates and many supporters from the St. Louis area. Present were the members of the board of directors of ELIM. Also present was Erwin Roschke, member of the Board of Control of Concordia Seminary, who had come to see the graduation of his son Ronald. Behind me the entire Seminex faculty and staff were seated. With them in the front row were Walter Wolbrecht and Wesley Fuerst, president and academic dean of LSTC, present for the purpose of awarding degrees in behalf of the schools that were participating in the Joint Project for Theological Education.

The students had requested that I give the commencement address.[19] I focused on the issue of justice, calling attention to the seemingly unlimited ability of the people of the Missouri Synod to endure injustice. "We are in our present spot," I pointed out, "precisely because of our confessional and moral stand. Is there no justice? Can't the leaders and the people of our church see what is wrong? Aren't they going to do something about it?"

Warning against the twin dangers of yielding to despair or insisting on vengeance, I described the justifying grace of God, who in Christ justifies the ungodly and frees believers "for the task of securing justice for others as God has done for us." I hailed the students as "a group with a rare moral sensitivity." I told them, "I have watched you cut right through a problem to the heart and core of an issue. You have a special capacity for distinguishing right from wrong. The church and the world desperately need people like you."

"Where do we go from here?" I asked. I called on the graduates to continue their bold witness, committing themselves to the work of bringing people "the ultimate justice of God's justifying grace" and called attention to a number of issues in the city of St. Louis, in the nation, and in the world that were crying out for people to do justice. Underscoring the uncertainty of their own personal futures, I called on the graduates to put their trust in God. "Through others in the church who are concerned about justice and even through those who are not, God will be at work to open up your future."

Following my address Wolbrecht awarded degrees to the students of Seminex. The diploma said it all:

> The Lutheran School of Theology at Chicago, upon the recommendation of the faculty and on the authority of the Board of Directors, together with the

recommendation of the exiled faculty of Concordia Seminary, St. Louis, Missouri, and with the certification of the Joint Project for Theological Education Adjunct Faculty and the concurrence of the faculties of St. Louis University School of Divinity and Eden Theological Seminary that all work as set down in the program of Concordia Seminary as it was accredited by the American Association of Theological Schools has been completed, hereby confers the degree of Master of Divinity . . . .

We had reached our objective of graduating our seniors with a bona fide degree. Now we were more determined than ever to help them find places of ministry and to continue our seminary in exile.

PART 3 ◆

"For Where Two or Three Come Together"

12 ——◆

A GROWING BRANCH

Like a parade of ants lugging the means of survival to their nest, students and faculty of Concordia Seminary in Exile moved north on Grand Avenue in St. Louis carrying the seminary's worldly possessions from a building numbered 306 to one two blocks away numbered 607. August 5, 1975, was moving day for Seminex. Students found it simpler to carry smaller and lighter items, such as cartons, lamps, and folding chairs, to the seminary's new location rather than wait for them to be moved by a van and a small truck that had been volunteered for the move.

Outside 306 North Grand, a crew of students and faculty was loading the van and truck with desks, sofas, and library books. Another crew of students and faculty was carting boxes and furniture down from the second floor of the building that had housed Seminex for most of the past year above the Worth department store on the corner of Grand and Lindell Boulevard in midtown St. Louis. Still another crew of students and faculty was boxing books and other material and attaching labels with floor and room numbers to indicate their location in Seminex's new home. At 607 North Grand, yet another crew of students and faculty was setting up house on the three floors that Seminex had leased for the next academic year.

In charge of the move was Jeannette Bauermeister. Dressed in jeans and a T-shirt, Bauermeister moved back and forth between the two buildings, directing the flow of traffic and giving instructions about what should go where. She had served as a teacher in the parish schools of several Lutheran Church–Missouri Synod congregations before John Damm invited her to be his administrative assistant at Concordia

233

Seminary. Of average height, with fashionably short hair, Bauermeister seemed to be on a perpetual diet to stay thin. A good teacher, she demonstrated that she was also a first-rate administrator, willing to make difficult, even unpopular, decisions if they were for the benefit of the seminary. As Damm's assistant she gained experience in all areas of Seminex's operations and as guardian of the budget required us to live within our means. On her own time she began a course of study whose long-range goal was ordination to the pastoral ministry.

The relocation was the second one in the short history of the seminary since the move into exile in February 1974. At the beginning of the 1974–75 academic year Damm and Bauermeister acted to relieve serious overcrowding in St. Louis University's School of Divinity and leased the space on the second floor at 306 North Grand in what had previously been a dance studio. The administrative offices of Seminex were moved there, and the dance hall itself became the new Commons, the center of communication and community life. The library, which Lucille Hager had named Patmos, after the island of exile where revelation came to St. John the Divine, was moved from the Divinity School to the new location.

To greet people as they came through the door and climbed the stairs to the second-story Seminex facilities, faculty member Robert Werberig crafted out of wood a huge representation of the symbol he had created for the banner that had led faculty and students into exile: a felled tree stump from which a new branch was growing. The symbol was based on passages in the Hebrew prophets[1] that promised the emergence of a righteous branch out of the stump of the Davidic royal line to rule the people of Israel, a messianic prophecy that Christians applied to Jesus. The symbol, which Werberig had modified to include flowing lines representing the waters of baptism, had become the Seminex logo, communicating to people the meaning of the Seminex experience.

The decision made in June 1974 to continue the seminary in exile required a review of the space arrangements that had been devised with St. Louis University and Eden Seminary on a temporary, emergency basis. As Damm reminded us, "When you have to move in with your relatives, you had better know when it's time to leave so you don't wear out your welcome." Moreover, during the 1974–75 academic year St. Louis University had received a new president, Daniel O'Connell, and he was in the process of making major administrative changes. One change involved closing the School of Divinity and consolidating the teaching of theology within an undergraduate department. William Sullivan had resigned as dean of the Divinity School in protest. We at Seminex grieved over the decisions, remembering what had happened to us a year earlier and wondering how much the Divinity School's hospitality to us was responsible for the new administration's decision. In a cordial meeting, O'Connell made it clear to Damm and me that the university would need the space we were using but wanted to continue a relationship with us as good neighbors.

Following the general principle of governance in operation at Seminex, Damm convened a group of faculty and students, called the Task Force on Self-Development and Location, to deal with the location question. The task force concerned itself primarily with criteria, affirming that one of the chief criteria for location should be proximity to St. Louis University in midtown St. Louis. The people of Seminex were eager to continue the arrangements that made it possible for faculty and students to use the university library and for students to have the benefit of athletic and other student facilities. Damm and Bauermeister tried to find suitable sites.

Midtown St. Louis had been in serious decline for more than a decade. Many apartment and commercial buildings were vacant. Homeless people prowled the area, and prostitutes walked the streets. For the sake of the university as well as out of civic concern, Paul Reinert, retired St. Louis University president now named chancellor, led the way in 1974 in forming New Town/St. Louis, Inc., a community renewal agency composed of businesses and organizations in the midtown area. Jeannette Bauermeister served on its board of directors as the representative of Concordia Seminary in Exile.

Through her contacts with New Town/St. Louis, Bauermeister became aware of possible sites for Seminex. One location, known as the IBM Building because of its previous occupant, was a relatively new square structure on Lindell Boulevard, west of Vandeventer Avenue, a block from St. Louis University. The vacant building consisted of three floors of space with module-like partitions that could be rearranged. The proposal called for a lease-purchase arrangement for the second and third floors of the building; Seminex would lease the two floors for a year and could then decide whether to purchase the building and rent out the first floor to tenants.

The other site was in what was called the University Club Building at 607 North Grand Avenue, two blocks north of St. Louis University. The University Club, which owned the building and had used the top six floors for club purposes, had moved into new facilities and was considering selling the building to several tenants rather than tearing it down, if new tenants for the top floors could be found to make the old but still serviceable building commercially viable. The proposal was that Seminex would lease floors ten through twelve with the possibility of adding other floors later. The club facilities included a grillroom, several dining rooms, a library, and game rooms; they could be adapted as classrooms, chapel, and library.

The IBM Building was the riskier option for us because it included the possibility of purchasing the building after a year, even though we had no down payment and no assurances of a loan. The UC alternative was less risky and offered facilities that, while not ideal, could be made to work. On the other hand, the IBM Building would be our own building and could be shaped however we saw the need. Because it was more serviceable and more challenging, I advocated the IBM Building location.

John Damm and Jeannette Bauermeister favored the UC building: Damm because it was the less risky, more practical alternative, and Bauermeister because she liked the graciousness of its rooms and envisioned their potential. The new Seminex governing board decided in favor of the UC location at a meeting on May 15, 1975, and Bauermeister eagerly took up the task of turning club facilities into a seminary.

At first Seminex leased only three floors of the UC, continuing to house its administrative offices at 306 North Grand. But within the year we had moved our administrative offices and leased floors nine through fifteen at 607 North Grand. Floor eleven was the main center of activity, with the chapel at one end in what had been the club library, the Commons at the other end in what had been the grill, and classrooms in between. The Werberig symbol of the branch growing from the felled tree, which had greeted people at the previous Seminex location, had been carefully dismantled and reassembled near the elevators on the main floor of the new location. Student Kevin Hormann crafted the pews and the altar for the chapel; the marble slab that had been used for carving roast beef in the grill was reshaped to serve atop the altar.

The growing Seminex library was housed in the elegant two-story former dining room on the thirteenth floor. Lucille Hager and her staff were kept busy accessioning books received as gifts, especially the ten thousand volumes that comprised the libraries of deceased faculty members Paul Bretscher, Carl Meyer, and Arthur Carl Piepkorn, which their widows had donated to Seminex. These collections served as the basis of a whole new seminary library fashioned by Hager and her Seminex colleagues on the basis of a principle of cooperation with the libraries of Eden Seminary and St. Louis University, making duplication of many resources unnecessary.

Faculty offices were on the tenth floor, administrative offices a floor below. The facilities included handball courts on the fourteenth floor. The crown jewel of the new Seminex home was the fifteenth floor, a glass-enclosed room on top of the building that provided panoramic views of the city. The room was ideal for community meetings and festive celebrations. The Seminex Guild furnished the fifteenth floor facilities with stove, refrigerator, dishes, tables, chairs, and other homelike amenities.

The Seminex Guild developed out of Wanda Weber's efforts to help CS move into exile. There had been a Women's Guild at CS. The new Guild refused to limit its membership to women, and men participated regularly in its meetings. Its primary focus was to be of help to students; its charter members took exiled Seminex students into their homes. Rejecting elaborate organizational structure, the Seminex Guild entrusted its activity into the hands of a few. Neva Merzlok and Elaine Maxeiner chaired the organization in its first years. Ruth Scheurmann served as treasurer. Ethel Dierker was in charge of Seminex receptions and other events. Marcle Bremer Childs and Lucy Carter gave leadership in later years. Ernestine Tietjen was involved in the midst of it all. Whatever the need—for furniture, for library equipment, for a women's resource center—the Seminex Guild was there to help. For the move to the new Seminex facilities, the Guild furnished food to hungry movers.

The move to the UC building, more than the move the year before, signaled the serious intention of the seminary in exile to continue its mission. The message was clear: The branch growing from the stump of the felled tree was alive and well.

A great deal of thought and much hard work had to be expended to enable Seminex to get to the point where it could make such a significant decision about its location for the future. When it became clear in spring 1974 that the Preus administration had no real intention of ending the "exile" of faculty and students, the people of Seminex took steps to make Seminex an independent institution. With the help of legal counsel J. Peter Schmitz, the Faculty Advisory Committee submitted articles of incorporation and drafted corporate bylaws.[2] Concordia Seminary in Exile was officially incorporated in the state of Missouri on June 21, 1974. The seven members of the FAC were the new corporation's first, interim board of directors.

The bylaws named faculty and students as two classes of members of the corporation, who together with Evangelical Lutherans in Mission had the responsibility of electing the institution's Board of Directors. Remembering the trauma that had occurred under an autocratic board, the bylaw framers established a "Guiding Principle" for the organization as bylaw 5.1: "The corporation shall be governed by the principle of mutual respect, openness and trust . . . rather than by authoritarian or hierarchical principles. In accordance with this principle the Board of Directors, the faculty, the administrative officers and the student body shall at all times seek the counsel and advice of each other and shall report openly to the larger constituency at regular intervals." The bylaws called for separate faculty and student coordinating committees to organize the "counsel and advice" of the member classes for the governing board. Amendments to the bylaws required a two-thirds vote of faculty, students, and board, with each group voting separately. The interim Board of Directors named John Damm to serve as acting president until the regularly elected governing board could follow the bylaw procedures for choosing a president.

The entire elected board met for the first time on November 29, 1974, and elected its officers. Chosen as board chair was Richard J. Jungkuntz, provost of Pacific Lutheran University in Tacoma, Washington, who had been instrumental in founding ELIM. Jungkuntz's heritage was both German and Native American; the combination was evident in his swarthy, angular face set beneath a thick shock of stiff, graying hair. Jungkuntz combined theological depth with administrative competence. In a departure from the tradition of CS, two of the elected board members were women: Norma Everist, Missouri Synod deaconess from New Haven, Connecticut, who was elected vice-chair of the board, and Sydney Krampitz, member of the faculty and director of nursing programs at Elmhurst College in Elmhurst, Illinois.

In order to ensure adequate information and continuity with the past, the bylaws of the Seminex corporation specified that for the first two years students and faculty should each elect two board members. The student members were Leon Rosenthal, who had played a leading role in the student moratorium, and Robert Rimbo, whom the board selected to be its secretary. The faculty representatives were two of the key members of the Faculty Advisory Committee, Robert Bertram and Andrew Weyermann. Other members were Norman Brinkmann, pastor of a Missouri Synod congregation in Westwood, New Jersey, and graduate of the Synod's seminary in Springfield, Illinois; Richard Fox, distinguished black advocate of civil rights and an official of the State Department in Washington, D.C.; Carl Halter, former faculty member at Concordia Teachers College in River Forest, Illinois, who resigned in protest against the policies of the new president, Paul Zimmermann, and became director of continuing education at Valparaiso University in Valparaiso, Indiana; and Kenneth Kramer, an attorney from Wichita Falls, Texas, who had received theological training at CS before entering the legal profession and was chosen board treasurer.

The board heard with approval a report from Damm that Seminex had applied for associate membership in the Association of Theological Schools, the first step on the way to full accreditation. It requested that faculty and students be ready to submit candidates for president by the time of the board's next meeting.

Registration reports for the fall 1974 term proclaimed Seminex's strength. Registration totaled 446 students, 419 of them in the Master of Divinity program. Bishop Stephen Neill of the Church of South India was teaching as a guest professor. John Groh, ousted from a teaching position by the governing board of Concordia Teachers College under new president Zimmermann, had begun teaching in the area of church history; and Arlis Ehlen, whose contract had been terminated by the CS Board of Control, was engaged to teach Old Testament.

With no housing of its own to offer, Seminex had been resourceful in helping students find housing, primarily in St. Louis's west end and south side. Creative plans were being developed to ensure placement of students in internships and calls to ministry.

There was a symbiotic relation between Seminex and ELIM. Seminex depended on ELIM for its survival financially and for help in recruiting students and placing graduates. At the same time Seminex was a paradigm for the people of ELIM, illustrating through its experience what others could expect to happen to them.

The first assembly after ELIM's founding was held August 26–28, 1974, in the O'Hare-Kennedy Holiday Inn in the Chicago suburb of Rosemont. The direst predictions of ELIM's founders had been confirmed. Not only was there a seminary in exile and a new mission enterprise as a result of actions by the Preus administration, but the repressive spirit had also resulted in the loss of significant numbers of faculty at Concordia Teachers College in River Forest, Illinois, and at Concordia Theological Seminary in Springfield, Illinois. These resignations were causing serious problems for many members of the Synod's professional staff.

With Samuel Roth, ELIM's president, in the chair, giving patient but firm and good-humored leadership to the discussions, ELIM members reflected on what should be the shape of their confessing movement. Many of the fifteen hundred people who had come together wanted ELIM to engage in political action in preparation for the 1975 Missouri Synod convention in Anaheim, California, in order to undo the actions of the 1973 convention that produced the Synod turmoil. Others wanted ELIM to gear up for mutual support in the face of more severe repressive measures expected at the next convention. No one wanted to be accused of schism by talking about forming a new church. A few, I among them, felt we needed to take action that would enable us to be ready when the time came, as it surely would, for a new church to be formed.

Elwyn Ewald, ELIM's general manager, in his report to the assembly,[3] criticized those in the confessing movement who were "trying to say we are still part of the system of our denomination and are simply asking that system to recognize us." Ewald had become ELIM's general manager after a decade of service in New Guinea, during which he had become the chief administrator of the Missouri Synod mission there. On his return to the United States in summer 1973, Ewald had been hired by Synod president Jacob Preus to serve on his staff. After a few days of seeing what was happening at the New Orleans convention, Ewald had resigned in protest.

Short and stocky, with a full head of brown hair, speaking matter-of-factly, almost flatly, Ewald summoned the people of ELIM to rebellion. Using imagery from the black civil rights movement, Ewald charged that many people of ELIM willingly sat in the back of the Missouri Synod bus or painted themselves white "and then sat sweating in the front of the bus hoping nobody would recognize our ghettoese." He said, "I personally relate best to the few who just sit in the front of the bus, without asking permission." He outlined a nine-point program of action, concluding, "Let's sit in the front of the bus doing what we must and let the problem of what to do with us be the denomination's problem."

I laid down a similar challenge in a sermon at the assembly Eucharist. I described what we were experiencing in the controversy of the Missouri Synod as the pangs of birth. Using as my text the apocalyptic vision of a new heaven and a new earth in Rev. 21:1–5, I talked about our preference for the old order of things and our desire for the status quo as we used to know it in the Missouri Synod. Yet, I pointed out, God had put everything in the world under judgment and was in the process of making all things new.

"Shall we stand in God's way by trying to hold on to the past?" I asked. "Shall we interfere with God's work by seeking to preserve institutions and organizations already consigned to destruction?" Quoting Jesus' words in Matt. 8:22 about letting the dead bury their own dead, I said: "The Lutheran Church–Missouri Synod we have known is dead. The organization that has given us life and nurtured us is no more. Its structures are hopelessly corrupt. Its leadership is morally bankrupt. Let the dead bury their own dead."[4] I urged the people of ELIM to see God's life-renewing work going on among us in Seminex's exploration of new ground in theological education and in the creative way Partners in Mission was proposing to carry out the church's mission. "Rather than consuming ourselves in efforts to recapture organizational machinery to restore a nostalgic former status quo," I said, "we should devote ourselves to the life-creating mission to which our God has called us."

"Does that mean leaving the Missouri Synod behind?" I asked. "Why should it?" I countered. "If there are structures and functions in the old system that can still help us with our mission of bringing God's gift of life to the world, let's use them. If the institution is going to stand in our way, ignore it or bypass it. If the powers that be throw us out, what does it matter? 'The old has passed away, behold the new has come.' . . . Brothers and sisters in Christ," I concluded, "this is a time of travail. Don't be afraid of the pangs of birth."

◆ ◆ ◆

At the ELIM assembly I was still the president of CS, although I had been suspended from office six months earlier. In that half-year period the BoC had not proceeded with the next steps in the bylaws to remove me from office. The next step required that a faculty hearings committee review the charges against me, but the five faculty members left at CS had publicly called for my ouster and were clearly prejudiced against me. By the 1974 fall term the BoC had assembled a new faculty, and three of them, Louis A. Brighton, Arthur F. Graudin, and Robert G. Hoerber, were designated members of the faculty hearings committee.

The committee announced that it would conduct a hearing with me on August 30, 1974. In a letter to the BoC I explained that on the occasion of my suspension I had made it clear that I would take no further action in my own defense because the BoC's proceedings offered no possibility of a fair and impartial judgment. I stated that my position had not changed.[5]

The committee canceled the hearing but persisted in efforts to meet with me. In my response I warned the three new faculty members not to become participants in a mockery of justice that would only bring God's judgment down on them as it surely would on the BoC. They wrote back asking to talk to me about my concern. So on August 23, 1974, at 3:00 P.M. I walked into the office of Louis Brighton in Wynecken Hall, where he and the other two committee members were already present. As the meeting progressed it was clear that they thought they could turn the conversation into an informal hearings session or at least get me to talk theology. I explained that I would be glad to talk theology freely and openly with them when they were no longer participants in a judicial process whose purpose of ousting me from office had already been established. I repeated what I had told them in my letter, and when they realized that I meant what I said about not participating further in the process, they ended the meeting.[6]

Not all my friends were happy with my decision to remain silent. At the ELIM assembly some of them took me to task publicly. They argued that I should make use of every opportunity to defend my theology and my administration of CS. To refuse to do so could be misunderstood as believing that I was "above the law." The people of the Synod would become more convinced of my accusation of corruption in the Preus administration, they argued, if I were to cooperate fully at every level and still be removed from office.[7]

I had carefully thought through the consequences of my decision in January. I was heartened when I received from Martin Luther Kretzmann, the respected Missouri Synod missionary-theologian who had been removed from his staff position by the Preus administration, a quotation from a theological work published in India that commented on Jesus' silence during his trial (Matt. 26:63). "To plead one's cause before a tribunal is to acknowledge it as one which at any rate desires to do justice; it is morally to bind oneself to respect the verdict. Christ knew that the tribunal before which he stood was not a court of justice, but a conspiracy. Had there been among his judges any desire at all to do justice, it might have been worth while to state a case."[8]

I was not surprised to learn subsequently that the faculty hearings committee had found me guilty.[9] They did not find in favor of three of the ten charges: that I was administratively irresponsible, that I was insubordinate to the Synod's Board for Higher Education, and that I failed to maintain careful watch over the spiritual welfare, personal life, and conduct of the student body. On the chief accusation of "holding, defending, allowing, and fostering false doctrine," however, I was "guilty as charged."

The bylaw procedures specified that after receiving the findings of the faculty hearings committee, the BoC could hear other witnesses before making a decision. "This decision shall in no case be rendered without having given the accused a personal hearing, with right of counsel, and with adequate opportunity for the preparation of a response to the charge. . . ."[10] At its September meeting the BoC received the findings of the faculty hearings committee and set October 11–12, 1974, as the date for my opportunity to be heard.

When I was officially informed of the meeting, I wrote to explain that "parental responsibilities require that I be out of town on those dates."[11] Several weeks earlier, when Ernestine and I had taken our daughter Catherine to St. Olaf College in Northfield, Minnesota, for her first year there, we had agreed to return for Parents Weekend, October 11–13. I was not about to let the BoC charade prevent our planned reunion. When Ewald Otto wrote back to question the veracity of my reason for not being able to attend, I replied: "I regret if my response to your letter inconveniences you and the other members of the Board of Control. I am sure that you do not object that I take my parental responsibilities seriously. Does the Board of Control intend to fulfill the provisions of Bylaw 6.79j? Then it will have to choose a meeting date when I can be present."[12]

Ernestine and I had a lovely weekend with Catherine at St. Olaf College, watching a football game, listening to a band concert, attending a reception by the school's president, Sidney Rand. On Sunday, October 13, after worshiping in the college chapel, I was given an urgent message to call a telephone number in St. Louis immediately. I recognized the number as John Damm's and called him. Damm wanted me to know before I arrived back in St. Louis what the BoC had done the day before. "October 12," he said, "you know what day that is." "Sure," I answered, "Columbus Day." "No," he said, "it's the day of the Lutheran Martyrs of Florida." I groaned at the "inside" joke. I regularly made fun of Damm's insistence on commemorating on October 12 what I considered to be a spurious sixteenth-century martyrdom.

We arrived back in St. Louis early in the afternoon the next day. We were no sooner in the house when Herman Scherer, president of the Synod's Missouri District and member of the BoC, was at our door. His smile of greeting vanished as I invited him in. No, he didn't want to sit, he said. He had been designated by the BoC to tell me in person that I had been found guilty and had been removed from office. "I am so sorry, John," he said. "I'm sorry, too, Herman," I answered, "but I'm not surprised, and neither are you. Thanks for telling me personally." We shook hands, and he left. I couldn't understand why Scherer, who had not voted against me, I knew, would agree to do the dirty work of the BoC majority. Perhaps it was to spare me a much more difficult confrontation.

A letter from board chair Ewald J. Otto, dated October 12, 1974, notified me in writing of the action. Contrary to the findings of the faculty committee, the BoC had found me guilty of all ten charges that Buelow and Harnapp had submitted in August 1973. My salary would stop as of November 15, 1974, and I had until the end of December to vacate the house in which we were living.

The Seminex community acted to surround me and my family with love. In the early evening of October 16, Ernestine, our children, and I made the same walk taken by faculty and students eight months earlier from the CS campus to the park on DeMun Avenue. There in a special ceremony Richard R. Caemmerer, acting in behalf of the assembled Seminex community, embraced us and received us into exile. From there we drove to our home congregation, Mount Calvary Lutheran Church on the corner of Union Boulevard and Welles Avenue on the north side of St. Louis, where James D. Fackler was pastor. Members of the Seminex community joined with the predominantly black inner-city congregation for a eucharistic service, at which John Damm presided and Andrew Weyermann preached, to celebrate my continuing ministry in the church.

Ernestine had already gone to work to find a new home for us. Within two weeks we had purchased a serviceable and gracious old house, built at the time of the 1904 St. Louis World's Fair, on Pershing Street, close to the western end of the city. Holland "Casey" Jones's "Streaker Express" and Seminex students helped move us into our new home on December 19.

When our former house on the CS campus was empty, I stayed behind to make sure that it was properly cleaned. Ernestine had requested that the last item to be removed should be the large wooden crucifix that had graced the hallway. With the crucifix in hand, I left the house and drove down the northern lane of the campus to the exit on DeMun Avenue. I stopped as I got to the end of the lane and got out of the car. I looked back at the campus buildings with a heavy heart. In response to the words of Jesus about what to do when the people of a place do not receive your greeting of peace (Matt. 10:14), I shook the seminary dust off my feet. Then I got back into my car and drove to our new Pershing address, bringing the cross of Christ into our new home.

In the meantime, Richard Caemmerer, who had chaired the search committee when I was called as president of CS in 1969, was designated chair of the presidential search committee at Seminex. The new corporate bylaws specified that the committee must submit at least two names for faculty approval and recommendation. Working through the process, Caemmerer submitted my name and that of John Damm to the Seminex Board of Directors at its meeting January 31–February 1, 1975.

In choosing me as president, the Board of Directors stated: "The Board recognizes the divine call originally extended to Dr. Tietjen under the date of 19 May 1969 to become president of Concordia Seminary, St. Louis, Missouri, and by this election indicates that they are inviting him to continue the exercise of that call in the office of the president of Concordia Seminary in Exile."[13] I was deeply grateful for the board's interpretation of its action. I was convinced that the call God had extended in 1969 was still in effect, and I was eager to resume my responsibilities as president. I saw the mission of Seminex to be crucial and indispensable. In my letter of acceptance I described Seminex as "a major center of the confessing movement" within the Missouri Synod with responsibility for "the work of redesigning theological education for mission and ministry in the final quarter of the twentieth century."[14]

The Preus administration viewed the vigorous activity of ELIM, Seminex, and Partners in Mission as a serious threat to its control and did everything it could to stamp out the confessing movement within the

Missouri Synod. On June 3, 1974, the Board of Directors of the Synod distributed to all pastors and congregations the text of resolutions it had adopted censuring ELIM and warning Synod members against joining it. Pointing out that ELIM solicited funds for a seminary, a mission society, publications, and an organizational structure, the BoD charged that ELIM was "substantially a church within a church." Recalling a 1971 synodical resolution, the BoD said that congregations and individuals within the Synod "have no right under the constitution of the Synod" to join organizations to "achieve purposes for which the Synod itself exists or to carry on activities which rightfully belong to the duly elected or appointed officials of the Synod."

In May 1974, when Seminex students refused to submit to interviews by the few remaining faculty of CS in order to be assigned calls to ministry, the Seminex faculty appealed to Missouri Synod congregations for calls in behalf of graduates. The faculty distributed a four-page printed document challenging the ruling of the Synod's Commission on Constitutional Matters that congregations could not call Seminex graduates without forfeiting their membership in the Synod. Arguing on the basis of the provision in Article VII of the Synod's constitution dealing with the advisory nature of the Synod, the faculty stressed the congregation's autonomy and its right to call Seminex graduates.

Writing to district presidents on June 7, 1974, Preus warned the officials not to place, ordain, or install Seminex graduates without certification by the CS faculty. To do so, he wrote, "would be a clear violation on the part of the District president, and pastor of the District who may be involved, as well as the congregation receiving such candidate. . . . I can see no other alternative than that such an ordination and installation would be declared null and void." Any district president who did not abide by the regulations of the Synod "would have to be considered in violation of his oath of office."

In spite of the warnings, Seminex graduates were received into ministry in the Missouri Synod, in many cases with authorization by a district president. By August 1974, 75 percent of the graduates who had asked to be placed in ministry had received calls. Yet there were reprisals. In a bizarre development in fall 1974, CS closed the doors of the Fuerbringer Memorial Library to Seminex students and faculty. Even former CS president Alfred O. Fuerbringer, who was responsible for building the library and after whose father it was named, was denied admittance.

Jacob Preus went on the offensive at a meeting of the Council of Presidents September 16–20, 1974. He read a 28-page document[15] that detailed the history of the Council of Presidents and the relation of the district presidents to the Synod, the synodical president, and the Synod's

BoD—all designed to make it clear that the district presidents were officers of the Synod with responsibility to fulfill its constitution and bylaws. A concluding section discussed the placement of Seminex graduates, listing the names of students whose ordinations had been authorized and the names of nine district presidents who had issued authorizations. Preus charged, "this action of nine District presidents has brought The Lutheran Church–Missouri Synod to a very grave hour in her history. Not only has the corporate integrity of the Council of Presidents been virtually destroyed so that any future resolutions of that body will have little credibility, but the very life of our church body is threatened by the deliberate violation of constitutional authority." Preus announced his intention of meeting with each of the district presidents involved and warned: "If such efforts prove fruitless, I would expect these District presidents in conscience to resign their office."

Mediation proposals and "reconciliation" discussions were also used to silence the confessing movement. At the height of the turmoil over the moratorium following my suspension, Preus announced the appointment of an Advisory Commission on Doctrine and Conciliation, thereafter known as the ACDC, with seven moderate members balanced by seven conservatives. The stated purpose of the ACDC was to define the doctrinal issues at stake in the controversy. While people were being removed from office on the basis of Preus's own resolution of the issues as he had defined them, Preus offered people the hope that the ACDC might be a means to bring peace to the Synod.

Writing almost two years after the creation of the ACDC, *Missouri in Perspective*[16] editorialized that the commission was a "cruel hoax" created "not to foster reconciliation and doctrinal discussion, but to control the outrage that many Lutherans felt following the totally unwarranted and unjust Tietjen ouster." Pointing out that the conservative members of the commission "had a miserable attendance record, were perpetually late in presenting papers for discussion and publication, and finally succeeded in sandbagging the entire effort," the publication asked, "what has happened to the ACDC? What was supposed to happen? Nothing! Nothing at all."

Another effort at "reconciliation" was the convening of what was called the Committee of 20, created as an outgrowth of the Seminex faculty's call for frank and open discussion of the issues. The committee consisted of representatives of the faculty and students of Seminex, the faculty and BoC of CS, the BHE, the Commission on Constitutional Matters, the Synod's BoD, and Jacob Preus. The committee met twice, on October 2 and 23, 1974. In between the first and second meetings, the BoC completed the process of ousting me from office. The Seminex participants announced at the meeting on October 23 that they saw no reason to participate further in meetings designed for reconciliation when the other side in the controversy made reconciliation impossible.

Another effort at "reconciliation" involved a committee called the Five and Five, consisting of five representatives of the Synod's BoD and five representatives of the ELIM board. Meetings were held on December 6, 1974, and January 8, 1975. ELIM participants pointed out the problem they had in participating. They noted that discussions were repeatedly convened after oppressive actions had been taken. Then the discussions served the purpose of quieting the people of the church while the oppressive actions were not reversed and in some cases continued. The ELIM members warned that they would not be participants in such a diversionary activity.[17]

On February 14, 1975, the ELIM representatives called a halt to further meetings. In a statement to the committee of the Synod's BoD they said: "We call your attention to the fact that although you appeared to share our concern that there be no further terminations of ministry connected with the controversy while discussions were going on, a member of the synodical president's staff and a synodical vice-president aided and abetted efforts that succeeded in terminating the ministry of a parish pastor in the St. Louis area. This seems to us a vivid example of what we indicated earlier, that even while discussions are called for, the purge goes on."[18]

The biggest push for reconciliation was initiated by former synodical president Oliver R. Harms and had widespread support. It called for a theological convocation to discuss the issues in controversy in the Synod. The convocation brought together more than three hundred pastors, teachers, professors, and laity at CS April 14–18, 1975. It featured major essays presented by representatives of both sides in the controversy and provided for discussion group sessions and for peer group meetings to present findings.

I was one of Seminex's participants in the convocation, setting foot on the CS campus for the first time since the previous December. I became even more convinced, as I wrote in an article at that time in *Christianity Today*,[19] that the doctrinal issues were a smokescreen hiding grasps for ecclesiastical power. Archconservatives at the convocation insisted that we had talked about the doctrinal issues long enough and needed now to move against those who disagreed with their hard-line position. But the majority of the participants were convinced that, even though we did not all see everything the same way, we did not have the kinds of differences that would make it impossible for us to live together in one church organization. The convocation ended with calls for peace.

Jacob Preus geared up to win the war at the Anaheim convention just a few months off.

◆ ◆ ◆

An unexpected event affecting my relation to the Missouri Synod took place just before the Anaheim convention. It must have surprised Jacob Preus as much as it did me. One of the grounds for removing me from office as CS president, false doctrine, was also grounds for removing me from office as a pastor of the Synod. In such a case, the bylaws specified, "the District President of the accused shall be so notified and a transcript of the proceedings shall be forwarded to the District President," who would then have to review the case and decide whether to remove the accused from "membership in the Synod."[20]

I was a member of the English District and had been from the time of my ordination in 1953. A president of the English District had installed me into office as CS president in 1969. But a bylaw adopted at the New Orleans convention in 1973 stated that a clergy member serving an educational institution of the Synod "shall be under the ecclesiastical supervision of the President of the geographical District in which the institution is located."[21] Yet my pastoral membership was not transferred to the Missouri District, the geographical district in which CS was located. I was still a member of the English District, serving as the chair of its Board for Missions and Church Extension and, following my ouster as CS president, serving under call from the district as a theological consultant.

The CS BoC asked the Commission on Constitutional Matters to which district president it should send a transcript of the proceedings concerning my removal from office. The Commission on Constitutional Matters replied on February 21, 1975, that the appropriate district president was that of the Missouri District.

With the legal assistance of attorney J. Peter Schmitz, Harold L. Hecht, recently elected president of the English District, challenged the commission's ruling in a four-page brief.[22] He pointed out that the pertinent bylaw clearly stated that "the matter must be forwarded to the District President *of the accused.*" Hecht cited still another bylaw, 5.11: "When a member of the Synod is accused of an act or of conduct which could result in expulsion from the Synod under Article XIII of the Constitution, the accusation shall be addressed in writing to the President of the District in which said member holds membership."[23] No matter what a recently adopted bylaw might say about ecclesiastical supervision of clergy serving at educational institutions, Hecht insisted, it was clear in which district I held "membership." At a meeting April 11–12, 1975, the Commission on Constitutional Matters stood by its ruling.

On May 29, 1975, Herman Scherer, president of the Missouri District, announced that he was disqualifying himself from considering my case. His involvement as a member of the BoC that had called me as president and his participation in the proceedings of the BoC that resulted in my dismissal made him "subject to conflicts of interest," he said. He turned the case over to the first vice-president of the Missouri District, Oscar A. Gerken, pastor of a Missouri Synod congregation in Cape Girardeau, Missouri.

Gerken was known as a theological conservative. Several of his brothers were also pastors in the Missouri Synod. Two of them were supporters of ELIM; one of these had a son, Daniel, at Seminex. Oscar Gerken's position against ELIM and Seminex was well known among the members of his congregation. My only contacts with him had been at meetings of the CS BoC on the rare occasions when Scherer could not be present and Gerken had represented him.

Gerken wrote me on June 5, 1975, to inform me that he was in the process of reading through the voluminous material he had received. He asked to meet with me at my earliest convenience. "I am requesting that just you and I be present for this conference, and my basic reason for this request is to preserve a spirit of trust and confidence." I phoned him and told him about my stance of not participating in efforts to defend myself. He said he understood but wanted to be able to talk to me brother to brother. He offered to come to St. Louis, and so we set June 24 as the date.

Gerken and I met in my small Seminex office in space that had been reclaimed from a dance studio. We sat in armchairs in the cramped area between the front of my desk and the door. Gerken had a ruddy face with a long nose, the length accentuated by a receding hairline, and he had dark, flashing eyes. He reached into his briefcase for a set of papers and for a large pad. "I have come to the conclusion that you are not guilty of false doctrine," he said, "but I want to ask you some questions to be sure." I was stunned. I stared at him in silence, so deeply moved I didn't dare try to speak.

Gerken explained that he was dealing only with the question of my personal doctrinal position, not with the charge that I allowed the false doctrine of others or with any of the other charges that had to do with the conduct of my office as president. He proposed that we go through the material submitted by my accusers in connection with the charge of false doctrine so that he could be sure he understood my position. I answered his questions, and he wrote as I spoke. When he was finished, he asked that I keep our meeting in confidence until I heard from him.

When Gerken left, I closed my office door, sat down at my desk, and wept quietly.

On June 29, 1975 (which he noted was Saint Peter and Saint Paul the Apostles' Day), Gerken released his findings concerning "The Case of the Charges Against Dr. John Tietjen" in a seventeen-page document. He dealt with fifteen distinct charges in eight separate categories. His form was to present the charge made by my accusers in their own words, then my response in words as he had written them down in my office, and finally his conclusion. In a final section entitled "Summary Conclusion" Gerken wrote: "Although I do not agree with Dr. Tietjen on some matters, I do not believe that he is a false teacher who is to be excluded from the ministerium or fellowship of The Lutheran Church–Missouri Synod." In a final paragraph he issued a plea: "I call upon all members of the Synod to join me in praying that the 1975 convention of the Synod will 'keep the unity of the Spirit in the bond of peace' (Eph. 4:3) and proclaim that 'JESUS CHRIST IS LORD, to the glory of God the Father!' (Phil. 2:11)."

◆ ◆ ◆

"Jesus Christ is Lord" was the theme of the Fifty-first Regular Convention of the LCMS, meeting in the Convention Center of Anaheim, California, July 4–11, 1975. Oscar Gerken's hope that his action in my case would have a reconciling effect on the convention was not to be fulfilled. As far as the convention was concerned, *Missouri in Perspective* editorialized after the meeting, "One would never have guessed that Dr. John Tietjen, a focal point of the controversy, had been cleared on all charges of false doctrine—and by a respected 'conservative.'"[24]

Calls for reconciliation abounded at the convention. In his opening address synodical president J. A. O. Preus urged support of floor committee resolutions as a way "to build golden bridges" in the controversy troubling the Missouri Synod. But the golden bridges, one delegate observed as the eight-day convention neared its end, were "marked by one-way traffic."[25] Moderate members of the Synod were to discover that reconciliation was spelled with the letters of capitulation.

For two years tales of strife had propelled the Missouri Synod onto the front page of religion news. A confessing movement had coalesced in the formation of ELIM. A seminary in exile and an agency for world mission had come into existence outside of the structures of the Synod. Many professors at the Synod's institutions of higher education and staff officials in St. Louis had either resigned or been ousted from office. The Synod's work program was in trouble as congregations diverted funds to other causes. But the 60 percent majority that had supported Preus in

New Orleans held up at Anaheim. While calling for reconciliation, the Preus party consolidated its power and adopted courses that required capitulation.

The power of the Preus party and of Preus himself was nowhere more evident than in the elections. The convention delegates elected 130 out of the 131 candidates endorsed by the Preus party in an "election guide" distributed by the party's journal, *Affirm*. The only candidate on the list not elected was incumbent Board for Missions chair Waldo J. Werning. Here Preus's personal power was apparent. Werning had crossed Preus in dismissing James Mayer from his mission staff position in January 1974 (see chapter 11) and required Preus to do battle on both the seminary and the mission fronts. Preus did not forget.

One of the major issues for the moderates of Missouri was the action of the New Orleans convention that made Preus's "A Statement of Scriptural and Confessional Principles" binding on Synod members. The Anaheim convention reaffirmed the statement and its binding status. The convention took several actions concerning Seminex. It asked Séminex supporters to close the school "in the interest of promoting peace and harmony" in the Synod.[26] It set up procedures for the appointment of a committee to meet with Seminex professors to determine "which former faculty members adhere to the false doctrine specified by the Synod"[27] in the resolution of the New Orleans convention that had condemned the faculty's position. It warned Seminex that the continued use of the name "Concordia" would bring on legal action. It urged congregations that had received Seminex graduates to conform to the Synod's bylaws or face possible expulsion.

The convention also decided to move Concordia Theological Seminary at Springfield, Illinois, to the campus owned by the Synod in Ft. Wayne, Indiana, closing Concordia Senior College on that campus and transferring its program to the school at Ann Arbor, Michigan. Concordia Senior College had been the feeder school for the vast majority of students who enrolled at CS and had supplied most of the students who had registered at Seminex in fall 1974. The faculty and administration of the Senior College could not believe what was happening. They had tried hard to be neutral in the synodical controversy.

In a highly emotional session by a vote of 601 to 473, the delegates declared the activities of ELIM to be "schismatic" and "offensive" to the Synod and warned the supporters of ELIM that "appropriate action" would be taken against them if they continued to participate. The resolution asked the supporters either to resign from ELIM or to terminate their membership in the Synod. In the case of employees of the Synod the resolution asked for the enforcement of the Synod's constitution and bylaws when "patient and pastoral admonition has proven futile."[28]

The most far-reaching action of the convention was the resolution that censured eight district presidents for authorizing the ordination of Seminex graduates. The resolution called on the presidents to comply with the bylaws of the Synod or to resign. If they failed to comply, they were commended to the president of the Synod for pastoral care and discipline. If that failed, Preus was authorized to inform their districts "at least 60 days before the beginning of the next regularly scheduled District convention, that a vacancy exists in the office of said District President" and that the district had to elect a successor.[29]

In a statement to the convention in behalf of the eight presidents, Emil Jaech declared:

> . . . the final judgment concerning our continuing service to the church as district presidents rests with the congregations of our district which elected us to office. We intend to take our case to them. If they agree with your judgment, we will accept that decision. But they must ultimately decide this issue. Action by a synodical convention providing for the removal of district presidents is unprecedented and unheard of among us, and represents a threat to the rights guaranteed to all of our congregations by the synodical constitution.[30]

I was a visitor at the convention in Anaheim with no official responsibilities. Unsurprised by the convention actions, I spent a good bit of my time reading in the California sun beside the pool at the Quality Inn, where I shared a room with Seminex colleague Edgar Krentz. During the two years since the New Orleans convention I had learned that we were wrong in expecting that things would go differently if only the people of the Missouri Synod could be informed about what was happening. The people had had ample opportunity to find out and were perfectly willing to endure all that had happened and more.

I came to realize that "church" really went on at two levels. There was the organized church, composed of a small minority of people who were interested in structure and concerned about what happened in conventions. Then there were the people, the rank and file who constituted the vast majority of church members but who really had no interest in church structure and convention resolutions. The rank and file could not care less about what was happening to the Synod. Preus had convinced a small majority of the organized church, especially the laity in that group, to give him the support he needed to keep "Bible doubters" from subverting the Missouri Synod's doctrinal foundations.

There were people who understood and who cared. There were the students who had declared a moratorium and risked their future to go into exile. There were the faculty members who stood together for what they knew to be right at the risk of their careers. There were the countless people in all parts of the Synod who supported the activities of ELIM when it was not popular to do so. There were increasing numbers of people—officials, pastors, and laity—who were willing to stand up and be counted and to pay the price of rejection and ouster.[31]

I was personally convinced that God was at work. "Our Lord was at work through the actions of Anaheim," I reported to the Seminex community on my return. I said that I did not have a blueprint of God's plan for the future except that I was convinced Seminex was part of the plan. "God is bringing a new creation out of the old order just as new life comes from the death of the old."[32]

Samuel J. Roth, president of ELIM, presented a similar vision in his analysis of the convention. Pointing out that the Synod's leadership had made "obedience to synodical authority" the chief issue in Anaheim, Roth warned, "We can expect a policy of harassment by hard-liners throughout the Synod against anyone they suspect of 'moderate' leanings. The purge is on. . . . Where is God leading us?" Roth asked. "We must be sure as we seek the answer that God is at work in all of this. God's work is resurrection and new life. In Christ we shall find it!"[33]

Seminex professor Edgar Krentz described the Anaheim convention in terms of death and transfiguration. "It was a decisive ending and a new beginning," he wrote, "as decisive as death and transfiguration. There the LCMS died as an evangelical church and was transfigured into an ideologically directed ecclesiastical power group." But another death and transfiguration was going on, Krentz explained. "Many of those who saw the on-going synodical suicide at Anaheim also experienced the newness of the transfiguring power of God. . . . For many Anaheim showed that the future lies in God's hands. And God was sowing the seeds of that future at Anaheim."[34]

At Seminex we sought to nurture the branch of new life that was growing from the stump of the felled tree. On assuming office I began work on the articulation of a statement of purpose that would say who we were and would envision our future. Faculty, students, and governing board joined in a process that produced a two-page statement adopted by all three groups in fall 1975.

According to the statement of purpose, "Concordia Seminary in Exile (Seminex) is a school of theology in the confessing movement that has emerged from within The Lutheran Church–Missouri Synod. It has an interdependent relation with that movement. It functions as a theological center of the movement and attunes its purpose and function to the movement's developing needs." Affirming the traditional commitment to

Scriptures and Lutheran Confessions, the document said: "In its educational program Seminex prepares people for forms of ministry of Word and Sacraments that seek to meet the needs of the church's mission in the contemporary world. As the confessing movement may require, it is ready to assist in preparing people for a wide range of other ministries of proclamation and service." The concluding paragraph looked to the future: "Seminex seeks to be an instrument and object of God in God's work of refining and renewing the church. With fellow Christians of the confessing movement it seeks to follow God . . . to new institutional realities and new opportunities for mission and ministry."[35]

The obstacles that stood in the way of achieving Seminex's purpose were considerable. Preus understood that we could not survive if we could not place our graduates, and he did everything in his power to close the doors of placement to us. We knew it was crucial to get our graduates into ministry and made their placement our number one priority. With the assistance of ELIM we convened in 1975 a meeting of ELIM representatives from the Missouri Synod's districts in order to devise new procedures for gathering information on vacancies and for working directly with congregations in the placement of our graduates. By the end of 1974 virtually all of that year's graduates had been placed. By the end of the next year 75 percent of our 1975 graduates had found their way into ministry. Graduating students took the initiative to look for openings in ministry. Under the capable direction of H. Karl Reko, Seminex devised a new method for relating ministerial candidates to congregations and other agencies in the church.

If placing our graduates was crucial, so was enrolling new students. At CS the admissions program was like a funnel receiving the graduates of Missouri Synod colleges, particularly Concordia Senior College, and of independent but church-related schools such as Valparaiso University. What had been an admissions program at CS became a full-fledged recruitment program at Seminex.

The obstacles in the way of recruitment were considerable. The actions of the Anaheim convention in declaring ELIM's activities schismatic and in calling on Seminex to go out of business made it difficult for our recruitment teams to be welcomed in Missouri Synod schools. Little by little even the friendly schools succumbed to control by the Preus political party.

In September 1975 Harvey Stegemoeller, president of Concordia College in St. Paul, Minnesota, resigned rather than implement the governing board's disciplinary measures against faculty members who supported ELIM, notably world-renowned organist Paul Manz, who refused to discontinue his practice of playing benefit recitals for ELIM. Six months later Robert Schnabel resigned as president of Concordia College in Bronxville, New York, after reaching an impasse with his governing board.

By working through faculty members friendly to Seminex, first David Reichert and, later, faculty member Carl Graesser were creative in gathering lists of prospective students who were attending synodical schools. They arranged meetings with students off-campus, often in faculty homes. Seminex students accompanied them and were effective in encouraging others to follow them to the exile seminary in St. Louis.

Along with placement and recruitment, funding became a major problem. With all of its good intentions ELIM did not have enough money to fund the increasing number of causes that were in need of help. Seminex budgets were dependent on what ELIM could provide. The efforts of the Seminex board to bridge the huge gap between Seminex salaries and those of other seminaries could not be fully realized.

In December 1975 the ELIM board faced up to a serious cash flow problem that developed following the Anaheim convention. Seminex was informed that it could expect to receive only that percentage of ELIM income that the Seminex budget represented in the overall budget of ELIM. In addition ELIM asked Seminex to undertake a serious study of the future direction of Seminex that would analyze its market in relation to its purposes. In other words, ELIM was asking Seminex if it was not time to retrench, to streamline operations in an effort to reduce costs.

By April 1976 the study ELIM had requested was completed. It included a thorough analysis of recruitment and placement possibilities, faculty-student ratio, faculty salaries, cost-per-student expenditures, and future trends. The conclusion was that Seminex was operating with considerable economy but needed to pay attention to a gradual decline in enrollment.[36] Seminex never did get all the funds it requested from ELIM. At the same time it never spent more than it received.

Not all the Seminex problems came from outside. During the 1975–76 academic year Seminex experienced the beginnings of internal problems. Paul Bauermeister, who had been called at the beginning of the year to serve as dean of community life, put the problem into context in a report to the Seminex board for its May 1976 meeting: "During the early days of Seminex, the powerful galvanizing force of the exile kept almost the entire community in a highly excited and exhilaratingly united state. . . . With the passage of time, the acquisition of our own facilities, the accreditation effort and the increasing stabilization of our total situation, more usual patterns begin to emerge again among students."[37]

Bauermeister reported that the year began and ended with high spirits, but that there were low spots along the way:

In the Fall semester there were strong rumors among students of a large transfer of students to 801. The complaint seemed to be that Seminex, with its increasingly institutionalized stance, was becoming merely an '801 East.' Therefore why not go to 801 West and assure yourself of a Call? The record shows no mass return to 801. . . .

In the Spring semester, the issue was a most unfortunate one, a dissatisfaction with administrators over some temporary administrative guidelines developed regarding certification and placement, specifically the certification and placement of the homosexual student. In the minds of most people the guidelines were in no way a departure from earlier practice and principle. Nonetheless, the flap was noisy and unpleasant. The guidelines were seen variously as an improper usurping of community power by administrators or as a demonstration of Seminex's lack of faithfulness in advocating for the oppressed or as an unwarranted intrusion into the student's sense of Vocation.

The "guidelines" and "principles" became an issue because of students' assumptions about the practice of governance at Seminex. Before I had been chosen to serve as Seminex president, students and faculty were well on their way to devising a system of internal governance. They completed the work shortly after I was installed into office. At the heart of the system was a process that called for faculty and student groups to propose policy to the seminary governing board on the basis of recommendations from faculty and student committees. When I presented the proposal concerning internal governance to the Seminex Board of Directors at their May 1975 meeting, I was surprised when they did not act on my recommendation to adopt it. They chose instead to commend the faculty and students for their work and to appoint a board member to serve on the "evaluation committee studying the working of the internal governance structure."[38] The board anticipated that the proposed governance structure would cause problems and needed revision.

The notion that faculty and students had to produce clearly articulated policies on the basis of which administrators could act caused the problems in spring 1975 to which Paul Bauermeister referred. Administrators got into trouble when they acted on the basis of traditional understandings that did not allow the placement of practicing homosexuals into ministry. Some students refused to recognize "policy" in whose formulation they had not participated. Bauermeister also reported, "A long-existing tension between faculty and administration . . . is finding current expression in concern about our form of internal governance." The tension and his own vocational concerns led Bauermeister to ask to be relieved of his administrative responsibilities so that he might devote himself to teaching. The problems concerning "policy" and internal governance would not go away.

As 1975 drew to a close I addressed a Christmas message to the
Seminex community. In part I wrote:

> The day is gray and gloomy as I look out at Grand Avenue from my office
> window. . . . A chill wind nips at noses and gloveless hands and huddles
> people in doorways and against plateglass windows as they wait for buses
> to take them home.
>
> Winter is on us. A semester hurtles to an end. Another year draws to a
> close.
>
> And we are still here! By God's grace we are still here. We who are at
> Seminex are still here. . . .
>
> No chill wind of winter need dismay us. No handwriting of doom written
> large on the wall of our lives can frighten us. The End holds no threat.

> Behold, a Branch is growing
> Of loveliest form and grace,
> As prophets sung, foreknowing;
> It springs from Jesse's race,
> And bears one little Flow'r
> In midst of coldest winter,
> At deepest midnight hour.

> The Word has been made flesh! We have been born anew! . . .
>
> We live in hope! At Seminex! In ministry! As church! For the world!
>
> God has opened up our future. We have no blueprint for tomorrow, but
> we have God's promise that He is already there and will be there with us.
> So we follow where God leads.[39]

13 ——◆

A CLAY POT

It was after 10 o'clock in the evening, Saturday, June 19, 1976. The festive banquet held at the end of the third day of a convention of the English District of the Lutheran Church–Missouri Synod had come to an end. Most of the nearly five hundred delegates and friends who had attended the banquet were preparing to set out on a five-minute walk from the banquet room on the campus of Concordia Teachers College in River Forest, Illinois, to the facilities of Grace Lutheran Church, where F. Dean Lueking was pastor.

As people began walking to the nearby church in the warm night air, they were led by a crucifer carrying a processional cross flanked by two persons carrying torches. People carrying convention banners fell in behind them. Without marching band or beating drum the people formed a parade, walking unhurriedly two or three abreast, or in groups of five or six, not worrying about precision, as the long procession moved in the moonlit night from college campus to church.

How like the seminary's move into exile two years ago, I thought to myself as I walked in the parade, and yet how different. The mood was festive, not somber. Far from being silent, participants chatted happily, laughing as they walked. They were breathing great sighs of relief. The difficult decision had been made. These English District delegates were on their way to celebrate the re-formation of the English Synod of The Evangelical Lutheran Church.

At the beginning of the convention two days earlier, on the afternoon of June 17, the mood was grim. Missouri Synod president Jacob A. O. Preus had moved against English District president Harold L. Hecht.

259

Implementing a resolution of the 1975 Missouri Synod convention at Anaheim, Preus had dismissed Hecht from office along with three other district presidents. In addition, Preus had named Paul Barth, a conservative pastor of an English District congregation in Buffalo, New York, as acting president of the district. Hecht, refusing to acknowledge the validity of Preus's action, was functioning as district president by presiding at the convention. Preus himself was scheduled to be present for the convention business.

Harold Hecht had been president of the English District for only two years. When John Baumgaertner decided to retire as president at the convention in June 1974, Hecht, who had been serving as executive secretary, was elected by one vote over former district president and moderate leader Bertwin Frey. Hecht knew that his one-vote majority had come about through the backing of the convention's conservative delegates, who represented about one-fourth of the district's constituency. He nevertheless implemented the convention's resolutions that were opposed to the position of district conservatives and of Jacob Preus and his administration. Hecht made it clear that he intended to carry out the convention mandate that he support the right of congregations to call graduates of Concordia Seminary in Exile, and he authorized their ordinations.

A special convention of the English District was held in September 1975 to deal with the decisions of the Anaheim convention. In "A Position Statement" the English District reiterated its support for Evangelical Lutherans in Mission, whose activities had been condemned at Anaheim. The district reaffirmed its support for Seminex and directed Hecht to continue to ordain Seminex graduates in spite of the decision by the Anaheim convention that presidents who did so would be removed from office. In addition, the statement declared that the delegates were prepared to take action "to revert to our status as an independent Synod or to seek other institutional affiliation" if there were efforts "to discipline the District or its members because of this confessional stance." The statement authorized the district's board of directors "to initiate such action" if necessary.[1]

On April 2, 1976, Preus declared that the office of president of the English District was vacant. Former president John Baumgaertner took the lead in establishing a standby corporation, the English Synod of the ELC. There had been a time when the English District had been the English Synod, a church organization independent of the Missouri Synod although related to it. In 1911 the English Synod had become the English-speaking district in the overwhelmingly German Missouri Synod. As the Missouri Synod became an American church, there were unsuccessful efforts to amalgamate the English District into the Synod's geographical districts, including as recently as the Missouri Synod's Anaheim convention in 1975.

Some in the English District proposed that the convention should adopt changes in the district's articles of incorporation and in its bylaws that would, lock, stock, and barrel, transform the district back into an independent synod. But the Board of Directors of the Missouri Synod had warned that such an action would be illegal and that the Synod would take legal steps to block it. From the legal perspective there seemed to be no way to reconstitute the English Synod except for the congregations of the district, one by one, to decide to join it.

Others in the district were urging that the district simply ignore Preus's action and conduct business as usual. But as Hecht told the English District convention in his president's report, the synodical administration refused to recognize the validity of any of his official acts. The experience, he said, was like writing his name in water. The Synod threatened further action if Hecht continued in office beyond the time of the convention. A few in the district urged caution and compromise and wanted to maintain the status quo as much as possible. Such a course was unacceptable to most because it would mean that the district would have to agree that Hecht be replaced even though he had done what the district had asked him to do.

At a meeting of the board of directors of the English District immediately prior to the convention, Hecht made his position clear. His thin face haggard from the pressure he had been experiencing, his eyes flashing, Hecht spoke staccato-style, often in incomplete sentences. He did not know what others were going to do, he said, but he knew what he had to do. There was no way he could continue to function as president. When the convention was done, so was he. The people of the district either had to capitulate to Preus and the dictates of the Anaheim convention, or they had to form a new church.

Board members urged Hecht not to do anything until convention delegates had an opportunity to decide the future of the district. If Hecht acted too soon, board members argued, delegates would feel that Hecht was abandoning them. The consensus of the board as the meeting ended was that "the pressure for resignation and movement into an alternate structure had best come from the floor."[2] Hecht agreed not to resign immediately, but board members realized they would have to hurry to catch up to their leader.

As the convention of the English District was called into session in the college gymnasium, John Baumgaertner, suave, urbane, and articulate retired president of the district, convened the first meeting of the board of directors of the English Synod of the ELC in a room in the

Koehneke Center of the campus. Present were all the directors named in the articles of incorporation.[3]

The English Synod board approved a plan that was to be presented to interested convention delegates during a recess. The plan called for the activation of the new synod within six months or as soon as fifty congregations had agreed to join. Events moved more rapidly than anticipated. On the following day, June 18, a resolution was introduced at the English District convention calling for a process of orderly and peaceful separation from the district for the purpose of joining together in a new English Synod. The English Synod board asked its legal counsel, Seminex's attorney J. Peter Schmitz, to draft a constitution.[4]

During the evening session on June 18, with Jacob Preus present and observing, the convention adopted the proposal for a peaceful separation by a vote of 296 to 75. At the close of the evening session John Baumgaertner presented the draft of the constitution approved by the interim board a few hours earlier. In an emotional surge English District convention delegates moved to the front of the convention hall to sign the constitution as an indication of their intention of becoming part of the new synod.

In a late-night session on June 18 the interim board of the English Synod decided to accept the offer of Faith Lutheran Church in Livonia, Michigan, that its facilities should be the location of the office of the English Synod. The board asked Baumgaertner and me to serve as a committee to propose a slate of officers for the new synod. In a meeting at breakfast Baumgaertner and I discovered that overnight we had both come to the same conclusion—that Harold Hecht and the other officers and board members who had served the English District should be invited to serve the English Synod in the same capacity. The interim board approved our proposal at noon that day, June 19.

While the English Synod board was meeting, the English District board of directors met for lunch. At the meeting Harold Hecht announced his resignation as president of the district effective at the end of the convention so that he could be free to help form the English Synod. One by one board members followed Hecht's lead. Four of the five vice-presidents and all but one member of the board resigned to clear the way for the election of new members and officers of the board by those convention delegates who were intending to stay as members of the district. In the presence of Jacob Preus and LCMS legal counsel Philip Draheim, the plans were laid for an orderly and peaceful separation.

As Preus and Draheim left the room, the English Synod board members entered it and discovered that Hecht and the other members of the district board had just resigned. The resigned officers and board members readily agreed to serve as leaders of the new English Synod.

Later that night, following the banquet and the moonlight procession, the delegates and guests of the English District filled the fellowship hall of Grace Lutheran Church. John Baumgaertner introduced the first elected members of the English Synod board of directors. When Baumgaertner called out the name of Harold Hecht, the cheers were tumultuous and the applause long. Although short in stature, Hecht stood tall because of the leadership he had given.

Hecht spoke briefly, thanking everyone for their confidence in him and announcing that as soon as the convention ended he would be in contact with English District congregations about the procedures for joining the new English Synod. August Brunn was introduced, and the veteran district pastor expressed his gratitude to God that he would be able to leave Missouri Synod problems behind and end his ministry in the same English Synod in which he had begun his spiritual life.

Baumgaertner invited me to address the gathering. I said, "See what we have done." Pointing back to the Missouri Synod college campus, I said, "We have processed from over there to here. We have moved from the English District to the English Synod. We are the same people, and we have the same leaders. But the old has become new."

Others too were troubled by the decisions of the Anaheim convention. One month after the convention more than three thousand members of ELIM gathered in Rosemont, Illinois, August 13–15, 1975, for the third annual assembly of the organization, the biggest in its three-year history. Under the steady guidance of president Samuel J. Roth, they tried to determine what should be the response of the confessing movement to the Anaheim convention's condemnation of their activities and the threat of repressive action against eight of the district presidents who identified with their cause.

In sharp contrast to the deep political division evident at the Anaheim convention, the people at the ELIM assembly would not take action until they had reached consensus. They were far from united about what to do. An analogy that emerged at the assembly described them as people who were gathered at different stations along a railroad track. Some had already boarded the train; others were waiting for the train to come; still others were not sure they wanted to take the ride.

In the majority were those who wanted not to continue the political battle but to "begin to form a new association," and the assembly endorsed their intention. It recognized that for some the time had not yet come to make such a wrenching decision. It blessed those who saw the need to "carry out their mission and ministry within the institutional context of the Missouri Synod." In a unanimously adopted resolution charting the future of the confessional movement, the assembly authorized convening clusters of congregations in February 1976 to define directions for establishing a new structure.[5]

Leading the way in sounding the call to form a new structure was ELIM general manager Elwyn Ewald, who said that the Missouri Synod was no longer a "viable instrument for mission and ministry." Every board and commission of the Synod, Ewald noted, "is now in the hands of those who are against what we stand for. I am convinced that we are to be something other than what we have ever been before."[6] The newness for which Ewald called was evident at the assembly in the significant leadership exercised by women members of ELIM and in the participation of a large number of black Lutherans.

The major resolution adopted at the assembly acknowledged that Lutheran Church in Mission was a "promising alternative" for some in the movement. Lutheran Church in Mission was a standby corporation created February 7–8, 1975, at a meeting in Chicago of representatives of forty-nine congregations in twenty-two states. It was designed as a corporation that "will have the capability of functioning as an interim church body when and if its members find that to be necessary."[7]

Lutheran Church in Mission was organized under the guidance of C. Thomas Spitz, Jr., the former general manager of the Lutheran Council in the U.S.A., who resigned to become pastor of a congregation so that he could take up a leadership role in the ELIM movement. Big and tall, his long face crowned with thick and frizzy black hair, Spitz spoke with a loud and resonant voice that commanded attention. An expert at principles of organization, he was elected president of the corporation.

Spitz and the others who formed the organization were convinced that it was only a matter of time before a new church structure would be needed for the people in the Missouri Synod's confessing movement. They wanted to have an organization visibly on the scene to give hope to those who were finding it difficult to continue to function within the Missouri Synod. They viewed the structure as a life raft "to rescue the floating bodies and those on the verge of jumping overboard from the LCMS."[8] They were perfectly willing to participate in some other plan for the future, but they hoped to do some of the homework necessary in forming a new church organization, such as drawing up pension and health benefit plans.

The leaders of Lutheran Church in Mission distributed application forms for membership at the ELIM assembly in August 1975 and announced plans for a convention in January 1976 to decide whether to activate the organization. In January it was clear that no ground swell of support had developed, so the organization continued in a holding pattern.

By early 1976 a new scenario of the future had been sketched by leaders of the confessing movement, which tied the formation of a new church to Jacob Preus's actions in removing district presidents from office. Omar Stuenkel, pastor of a congregation in Maple Heights, Ohio, who joined with Spitz in calling for the formation of Lutheran Church in Mission, informed those who were eager to see the new church activated, "Most of [the leaders of ELIM and of the English District] want to be forced out so that they are the victims and not the actors in a division."[9] The ouster of district presidents was viewed as the "trip wire" that would cause pastors and congregations to rally around their district presidents, who in turn would have no choice but to lead them into new regional associations, which in turn would join together to form a new church organization.

On February 26–28, 1976, at a meeting in Chicago that issued from ELIM's efforts to cluster congregations, the leaders of the moderate movement within the Missouri Synod organized a Coordinating Council to help chart the course for the future. Invited to serve on the council were the eight district presidents whose continued ministry was in jeopardy, four ELIM members named by its board of directors, two persons designated by the board of Lutheran Church in Mission, and two persons chosen by the newly organized National Council of Afro-American Lutherans. The purpose of the Coordinating Council was to assure that its member groups engaged in a united course of action for the future. At the organizational meeting of the council in March, Elwyn Ewald, ELIM's general manager, was chosen executive secretary.

The big question was: When and how would the wire trip? For a long time after the Anaheim convention Jacob Preus took no action on the resolution requiring eight district presidents to express compliance not to authorize the ordination of Seminex graduates or be removed from office. Each of the eight district presidents convened a convocation, conference, or convention in their districts to take their case to the people. All received strong support for their stand.

The eight presidents met in Chicago with leaders of ELIM on October 28–29, 1975, and issued a joint statement, declaring: "Where there are pastoral needs and congregations call candidates loyal to the Scriptures and the Lutheran Confessions, we will continue to support their right to do so and to do what we can to encourage and protect that ministry." They also expressed support for the ELIM decision to bring about the "clustering" of congregations: "Unless there is a genuine reformation in the thinking of Synod's leadership and an honest attempt to address the problems which are tearing us apart, many of our congregations will have no other alternative but to seek new associations. We will support them in the pursuit of that interest."[10]

On October 29, 1975, Preus finally began the process required of him by the Anaheim convention. In letters written to the eight district presidents, he asked that they give their "stated compliance" with the Anaheim convention action by the time of the Council of Presidents meeting in mid-December. Preus sent an additional letter to Southern Illinois district president Herman Neunaber, initiating the pastoral process required by the Anaheim resolution for district presidents who refused to state their "compliance." Neunaber received this special attention because the convention of his district was scheduled to meet before the other seven districts, on February 20–22, 1976. Preus needed to act sixty days prior to the district convention if Neunaber was to be removed from office, according to the stipulations of the Anaheim convention resolution.

Neunaber, who had served as pastor of a prominent Missouri Synod congregation in Belleville, Illinois, was elected president of the Synod's Southern Illinois District several years before my arrival at CS. Short and stocky in nature, his eyes carefully taking in whatever was going on around him, his face set with serious concern as he dealt with problems, Neunaber had tried to keep the leadership of the Council of Presidents in the hands of the moderate district presidents after Preus was elected synodical president. His efforts failed by one vote when one of the moderate presidents left the meeting early.

Neunaber surrounded himself with bright young pastors in his district and made effective use of their theological insights and writing skills. Only by coincidence was his district's convention scheduled before the conventions of the other seven district presidents who were under fire. But Preus was probably not unhappy to have to deal first with the district president who had been a thorn in his flesh at meetings of the Council of Presidents.

Receiving strong support from the board of directors of his district, Neunaber met with Preus on December 2 and 15, 1975, and on both occasions affirmed the position that he and the other seven district presidents had expressed publicly. Preus therefore convened a meeting of the Southern Illinois District's board of directors, its circuit counselors, and its Anaheim convention delegates to discuss the issue on December 20, just before the sixty-day deadline for removing Neunaber from office. At the December 20 meeting Neunaber again received strong support from the people of his district.

Following the meeting Preus decided not to remove Neunaber from office but instead to convene a series of seven meetings throughout the Southern Illinois District to take his case to the people in advance of the district convention in February 1976. Preus himself admitted that he was taking a risk, gambling that he could convince the people of the district to require their district president to capitulate to the demands of the synodical convention. The seven meetings were attended by capacity crowds in which Preus and Neunaber squared off on the issues. Preus, speaking extemporaneously and changing his message from meeting to meeting, was all smiles and charm as he asked that the February convention adopt resolutions agreeing not to call "improperly certified candidates" as pastors and urging Neunaber "to give his stated compliance to the regulations of the Synod." Neunaber, his voice steeled with determination, spoke from a prepared text as he maintained his position that until Seminex professors received justice from the synodical administration, those who stood with them should be guaranteed the protection of the Synod's constitution.

At the Southern Illinois District convention in Belleville, Illinois, February 20–22, 1976, Preus did not succeed in getting the delegates to require their president to conform to the Anaheim decision. By an 85 to 70 vote the convention adopted a strong resolution reaffirming the district's call to Neunaber and commending him for his stance. But the results of the convention were mixed. The delegates declined other proposals that were in support of Neunaber, specifically a resolution recognizing Seminex as a legitimate seminary of preparation for ministry. The contest was a draw.

The day after the convention, February 23, the deadline for action against California and Nevada district president Paul Jacobs, Preus announced in a letter to LCMS members that he would not vacate the offices of Jacobs, Northwest district president Emil Jaech, or Colorado district president Waldemar Meyer. In what he called an "appeal for understanding," Preus expressed the hope that his action would improve the climate in the Synod. Preus said that he had acted as he did because the three district presidents had not authorized any ordinations of Seminex graduates since the Anaheim convention, which was not in fact the case. Jacobs and Jaech had each ordained a Seminex graduate in late January. Preus expressed the hope that the remaining four district presidents would state their compliance by mid-April, the sixty-day deadline prior to each of their conventions.[11]

Responding on March 21 with a statement of their own, the eight district presidents accused Preus of misstating their position. They declared, "Attempts to divide us or to disrupt our united response by approving some of us and threatening others will not succeed." They warned that there would be no genuine peace "until we deal with the real issues in the controversy instead of the symptoms." Among the issues, they listed a false understanding of authority in the church, the threat to the rights of congregations, attempts to settle doctrinal issues "by majority vote rather than by the Word of God," and injustice done to teachers of the church by "refusal to follow Matthew 18 and the Synod's own procedures for due process."[12]

On April 1 the eight district presidents met with the Synod's BoD in an effort to avert disaster. On April 2 Preus acted. Four district presidents were removed from office: Herman Frincke of the Eastern District, Harold Hecht of the English District, Rudolph Ressmeyer of the Atlantic District, and Robert Riedel of the New England District. They rejected the action as invalid. The other four district presidents did the same. The wire had been tripped.

The Coordinating Council met on April 14, 1976, and agreed to incorporate a new church structure and to organize regional groupings of congregations that would comprise the new organization. By the end of April a new church had been incorporated in the state of Illinois as The Association of Evangelical Lutheran Churches, referred to by the acronym AELC. Elwyn Ewald convened meetings of congregational representatives in nine major metropolitan centers. By the end of May ninety representatives of the regional gatherings met in St. Louis to plan for regional constitutional conventions in preparation for the constituting convention of the AELC.

The leaders of the Coordinating Council knew that much depended on what the eight district presidents would do among the pastors and people of their districts in behalf of the new church organization. Only in the English District, because of the forthright stand of Harold Hecht, was there an immediate decision to recognize that the time had come to leave the structures of the Missouri Synod behind so that the mission and ministry to which the district was committed could continue. The conventions of the Atlantic, Eastern, and New England districts gave strong support to all three district presidents and strong reaffirmation of the positions that had led to the problems. Although the people at the conventions talked about moving out into new structures, they in effect set up new trip wires to make that happen—namely, further coercive action by the Synod in the form of legal action against the districts.

But the movement to establish a new church had begun and would not be denied. In August Herman Neunaber resigned as district president in order to be able to help congregations organize the Great Rivers Synod. In September Rudolph Ressmeyer and Robert Riedel resigned to do the same for the East Coast Synod. In October Waldemar Meyer of Colorado found it impossible to continue functioning as president of his district. In November five synods of the proposed AELC held constituting conventions: East Coast, English, Great Rivers, Pacific, and Southwest. Each of the synods chose delegates to constitute the new church at a meeting in Chicago on December 3–4, 1976.

The number of congregations that helped form the synods of the AELC or that joined it later was considerably less than the leaders of the Coordinating Council had anticipated. It had been expected that twelve hundred Missouri Synod congregations would join the new church, but only 250 did so. Even the English Synod, the largest of the AELC synods, received only a little more than half the congregations that could legitimately have been expected to leave the English District, judging from the actions of its convention delegates.

A number of factors worked to keep the AELC small. Pastors who wanted to join could not bring their congregations along because they had neither properly informed them about the events in the Missouri Synod nor adequately prepared them for the formation of a new church. In many instances a majority of congregational members could not make the move into a new church because they could not get the necessary two-thirds majority required by their constitution. Vocational and security concerns caused previously outspoken pastors to be silent when the time for decision arrived. Some pastors and congregations chose rather to "stay and fight." Some did not want to risk conflict within the congregation for the sake of their mission. Others decided that institutional affiliation was not that important.

It was instructive to discover who did and who did not join the AELC. During the heat of the controversy, when I addressed gatherings of supporters, people would regularly say to me, "Hang in there, John. We're behind you." To comments like that Ernestine would say to herself, "Yes, you're behind us. But how far behind?"

Many people did back up their words with deeds. Robert Studtmann, pastor of a congregation in the conservative region of Great Bend, Kansas, took the people of his congregation into his confidence and kept them informed about events in the Synod. He and his congregation led the way in forming the Southwest Regional Synod of the AELC, and he was chosen as its bishop.

Ralph Petering, a layman who had resigned in protest from the Missouri Synod's Board of Trustees, gave leadership to members of his congregation in Ladue, Missouri. Even though they might have had the votes to prevail, they decided not to get involved in an acrimonious battle over the congregation's property. They simply left it behind, organized the Lutheran Church of the Living Word, and ultimately rented space in a Methodist church so that they could devote their financial resources to the church's mission.

The constituting convention of the AELC was quite different from a LCMS gathering. There were only 172 delegates instead of the 1,100 at Missouri Synod conventions. Seventy percent of the delegates were laity, and of these one-third were women, a marked difference from previous patterns. The worship forms used during the convention included a variety of cultural expressions to celebrate gospel, church, and mission.

In adopting a sparse constitution for the AELC, the delegates bound themselves to the doctrinal position of Scriptures and Lutheran Confessions, the same position they had championed in the Missouri Synod. As evidence of their determination not to produce another permanent church body, the delegates approved a provision in the constitution calling for a review every two years to evaluate the need for the continued separate existence of the organization. The AELC assumed the role of the "life raft" that Lutheran Church in Mission had intended for itself, seeking to haul aboard Missouri castaways for a future yet to be determined.

The delegates committed themselves wholly to Lutheran unity, offering the hand of fellowship to all Lutheran churches, expressing the desire for continued relations with the Missouri Synod, and endorsing membership in LCUSA and in the Lutheran World Federation. They adopted a resolution encouraging the regional synods to follow the lead of the Pacific Regional Synod, which at its constituting convention had approved the ordination of women.

William Kohn, former executive director of the Board for Missions of the Missouri Synod and now pastor of a congregation in Milwaukee, was elected president. Will Herzfeld, black pastor of a congregation in Oakland, California, was elected vice-president. In a meeting immediately following the convention the AELC Board of Directors elected Elwyn Ewald executive secretary, the chief staff officer of the new church.

I was asked to preach the sermon at the convention's service of Holy Communion, held at Grace Lutheran Church in River Forest, Illinois, several miles from the convention hotel. For my text I used the words of the apostle Paul in 2 Cor. 4:1–15 to describe the AELC as a clay pot containing a spiritual treasure, the gospel. Fragile and flawed as we were, small as we likely would continue to be, God was giving us "opportunity to start anew," I said, "free from the shackles and obstacles that have made mission and ministry so difficult these past several years."

Our peculiar experience confronted us with a special challenge of service, I said. I described five features of the challenge. As people who had contended for the gospel, we had a calling to make the gospel alone the center of our life together. As people who had to fight to survive, we needed to make mission rather than survival the goal of our new organization. As victims of oppression we had to identify with the oppressed and make sure that liberation from oppression was central in our mission. As those who had learned that people were more important than rules, we had to put our structures and rules in the service of our mission to people. As people who had experienced the tragedy of division, we had to foster the unity that God had given us with fellow Lutherans and with other Christians.

I pointed out that we should not be ashamed of our clay pot character. It would help us to discover with the apostle Paul that strength is made perfect in weakness. "Through the weakness of Christ's suffering on a cross," I said, "God created the power of new life. Don't be afraid to follow the Lord. Be weak as Jesus was weak. Serve as Jesus served. Love as Jesus loved. It all leads to a cross, but that is the way to resurrection and eternal life." Then, holding up a common clay pot I had brought into the pulpit with me, I said, "This is what we are." As I said, "Now this is what we are called to do," I placed the pot on the altar as an offering to God.

The formation of the AELC had major implications for Seminex. The AELC came into existence just because of actions taken against Missouri Synod leaders who had supported individuals and congregations who in turn had supported Seminex in its confessional stand against the LCMS. Seminex would obviously be related to the AELC, but how?

The formation of the AELC also had profound implications for ELIM. The AELC was formed by people of ELIM. Much of the energy, creativity, and funding that had been channeled through ELIM would now be directed to the AELC, leaving ELIM diminished. But ELIM was the funding agency for the support of Seminex. How should Seminex relate to ELIM as it looked to future relations with the AELC?

In spring and summer 1976 I worked hard to find answers to these questions. I had to try to build a consensus among groups whose ideas and interests were not identical: the people of ELIM, many of whom would not be in the AELC yet supported Seminex; the leaders of the AELC, some of whom worried that a large seminary with a big budget would be an albatross around the neck of the new church; the Board of Directors of Seminex, people who took seriously their responsibility to represent all the people of the confessing movement; the Seminex faculty, who had sacrificed a great deal and whose careers were at stake in the decisions; and the Seminex students and their families, who had risked much by choosing to be at Seminex and for whom the AELC was a sign of hope.

The fast-breaking events that led to the formation of the AELC did not allow enough time for the consensus-building process of governance

at Seminex to take effect. Nevertheless, I worked with the governance process to produce an agreement on Seminex's relation with the
AELC. I worked first with a task force of faculty and students, then
with that task force expanded to include board members, and finally
with that group along with a committee appointed by the Coordinating
Council that was forming the AELC.

Among the options available, the most desirable seemed that Seminex should be the seminary of the AELC. At the same time, because of
Seminex's size and because some of the constituency it served would not
be a part of the AELC, Seminex should not be exclusively the seminary of
the AELC. We concluded that the "AELC and Seminex should be related
to each other as partners in the church's mission."[13] As partners Seminex
would serve as the seminary of the AELC, and the AELC would participate in Seminex's governance, cooperate in the recruitment, certification, and placement of candidates for ministry, and work with Seminex
to assure adequate financial support.

We had enough consensus to send up a trial balloon at the ELIM
assembly August 18–20, 1976, in Rosemont, Illinois. In a major presentation on "Seminex and Its Future" I outlined the vision: "Seminex functions as a theological center of the confessing movement, whatever form
the movement takes, and as a partner with the AELC in carrying out the
church's mission, both of us—Seminex and the AELC—expendable in
the cause we serve." After I described the implications of the vision, the
assembly affirmed it.

The proposal of the joint task force received the endorsement of the
Seminex community and of the Coordinating Council. At its constituting
convention the AELC implemented the proposal in a resolution establishing a partnership relation with Seminex. In the agreement the AELC
authorized the Seminex Board of Directors to issue calls to Seminex
faculty and staff in behalf of the AELC and its congregations. It also
agreed to participate in the process of electing members of the Seminex
governing board.

The decision on Seminex's relation to the AELC made it clear that
Seminex would continue to relate to the people of ELIM who were not in
the AELC, but we could not afford to assume that ELIM would continue
to provide the funding we needed. We had to be responsible for our own
funding. That meant taking the risk of asking the people of ELIM to
redirect their gifts.

In dealing with the funding issue, I felt it was necessary to have the
counsel not only of people from Seminex and the confessing movement
but also of professional people knowledgeable in the funding of seminaries. Lilly Endowment, Inc., gave Seminex a $5,000 grant for consultant
purposes. When asked for ideas, Jesse Ziegler, executive director of the

Association of Theological Schools, suggested I contact Warren Deem of Wilder Deem Associates, a management consulting firm in New York City that had been helpful to theological seminaries, and Herbert Jones, vice-president for development of Garrett Evangelical Seminary in Evanston, Illinois.

Deem and Jones were intrigued by the notion of establishing a development program from nothing and agreed to help, Deem offering to give counsel on the larger issues, Jones agreeing to give basic, practical help. Both men maintained that it would be best if Seminex could receive one-half of its support from the AELC institution and the other half from individuals. Such a pattern, they said, would ensure a solid core of funds coming from an annual institution budget and at the same time would require the seminary to be responsive to the concerns and the will of the people in its constituency. The pattern they suggested was the goal toward which Seminex would strive.

First we needed to ensure ongoing support. Jones and I conferred with ELIM president Samuel Roth, ELIM general manager Elwyn Ewald, and James Mayer of Partners in Mission, which had decided to follow our lead and raise its own funds as well. We agreed to ask the people of ELIM to redirect their giving in such a way that in the future they would send to Seminex two-thirds of what they had been giving to ELIM and would divide up the remaining third between ELIM and Partners in Mission. We set October 1976 as the time to make the appeal. Ewald and I wrote separately to the people of ELIM, and the people of Seminex followed up with telephone calls to ELIM's major donors. Seminex alumni were organized to call the next level of donors.

Raising our own funds required us to make major administrative changes. Mark Roock, who had been our communications officer, became director of development within a division of seminary relations headed by Larry Neeb, who continued as editor of ELIM's newspaper but turned over day-to-day responsibility to Richard Mueller as managing editor. Processing an anticipated million dollars a year required an expanded accounting office. Jeannette Bauermeister, who had assisted John Damm in bringing Seminex into being, took on the accounting responsibility and was soon director of the division of business management.

In November 1976, like a young bird testing its wings, we were on our own, dependent for our survival on whatever we were able to raise in gifts. Some people grumbled about the need to write three checks in place of one, but year-end gifts were good. From February through May 1977 it looked as though we were going to be in serious trouble, and that situation had profound consequences for our May staffing decisions. But a surge of gifts in June and July, induced by our frank and urgent appeals, enabled us to reach our goal.

For fiscal year 1976–77 we had raised a million dollars in gifts. More important, the people of ELIM had done just what we had asked. When we at Seminex, Partners in Mission, and ELIM compared records, we discovered that donors had given to Seminex two-thirds of what they had been giving to ELIM and had divided the remainder equally between ELIM and Partners in Mission.

The new relationship of Seminex to the AELC suggested to many that we should change our name, putting an end to the rhetoric about being Concordia Seminary "in exile." The Missouri Synod's convention in summer 1975 had threatened legal action if we did not desist from using the name Concordia. Although our legal counsel assured us that we had nothing to fear from such a suit, we did not want to pay the costs of extensive litigation. We informed the administration of CS that we might decide to change our name as our circumstances changed if they did not push us to do so. They agreed to back off for the time being, but in May 1976 the BoC renewed the legal threats.

In fall 1976 the Seminary Relations Policy Committee, one of four major policy committees composed equally of faculty and students, conducted a town meeting to acquaint everyone with the issues involved in a name change. The committee adopted criteria for use in choosing a name. Its recommendation, "SEMINEX–Evangelical Lutheran School of Theology," was not approved by the faculty. By May 1977 the committee had agreed on another name, "Seminex–Christ Seminary," which received the endorsement of the faculty. Students at first did not approve but endorsed it in a second vote. At its May 11–12 meeting, however, the Board of Directors did not provide the necessary approval.

One part of the problem was the conviction of some faculty and students that there should be no change in our corporate name at all. Some made it a confessional issue, insisting that it was an essential part of our witness that we continue to be Concordia Seminary in Exile for as long as the issues that made that witness necessary had not been resolved. The inability of the community to decide what to some seemed a matter of no real consequence underscored the difficulties in the Seminex governance provision requiring consensus among board, faculty, and students.

In September 1977, in frustration, the executive committee of the Seminex Board of Directors created a board-faculty-student committee to find a way through the impasse and to submit a proposal for board action and recommendation to faculty and students. The committee proposed the name "Christ Seminary–Seminex." The board adopted the recommendation at its meeting October 28, 1977. Out of weariness, faculty and student groups agreed. The seminary now had a new name to go with its new circumstances.

In partnership with the people of AELC, Seminex did its best to rise to the challenge presented by new life in new organizational entities. Neither as seminary nor as church did we want simply to replicate the past. Although there was much in our past that was good and needed to be continued, we were eager to respond to the power of God's new creation that we were convinced was at work in our midst.

At Seminex we developed a new way of funding seminary education in partnership with individuals and congregations and with the AELC. In time we received one-third of our support through grants from congregations that included us in their budgets, the other two-thirds from gifts of individuals. Year after year we raised the million dollars necessary for our operation. The people of the AELC developed a new method of funding the mission enterprise. Adapting the model used by Partners in Mission, AELC synods served as switchboards to connect mission needs with resources. The method worked without central control, although the national structure of the AELC was habitually short of funds as a result.

The people of the AELC worked closely with Seminex in efforts to find ministry for our graduates. The AELC was small, but it received a disproportionately large number of our graduates into pastoral ministry. One reason is that the people of the AELC recognized the graduates as gifts of God and developed creative ways to put them to work. Another reason was acceptance of the notion of "worker-priest" ministry, according to which a person worked at another job to earn funds necessary to support the work of pastoral ministry. Seminex's director of placement, H. Karl Reko, became an expert within Lutheranism on the "worker-priest" concept and shared insights with the church at large. Still another reason was the readiness to recognize that pastoral ministry could be done in a wide range of contexts in addition to that of the congregation. For example, in Cleveland, Ohio, Lutheran Metropolitan Ministry Association, under the leadership of Richard Sering, received nearly a dozen Seminex graduates for a variety of ministries, such as ombudsmen for nursing homes, advocates for fair housing, and administrators of school integration.

Seminex welcomed women into its ordination programs and helped make congregations ready to receive women interns. Within a constituency that had no experience with women in pastoral ministry, it affirmed the validity of ordaining women. (On May 14, 1976, Janith Otte graduated from Seminex as the first woman candidate for pastoral ministry, and a little more than a year later was ordained to become the first woman pastor in the AELC.) The leaders of Seminex and of the AELC worked together at the task of helping the people they served live out their commitment to the equality of women and men in the life of the church.

With chapel worship continuing to serve as the center of community life, Seminex devised new ways of working to be a community. Without housing of its own, Seminex helped students find apartments in St. Louis and organized clusters of faculty and students in different parts of the city. These clusters became sharing groups within the larger seminary community and developed projects for ministry to their neighborhoods.

Seminex devised new ways of assessing progress in readiness for ministry, through use of the tools of the Association of Theological Schools and through annual conferences that provided for peer involvement in the assessment of growth. Through a grant from Lilly Endowment, Seminex professor Herbert Mayer developed models of theological education that made use of the small-group process. Although the Seminex curriculum was fairly traditional, academic dean John Damm pressed faculty to develop new methods of teaching. The faculty initiated a process of annual review for themselves that included service to the church and to the St. Louis community along with teaching and scholarship as areas for review.

Seminex received full accreditation from the Association of Theological Schools just two years after its founding. Its library, although small, was a model for how to develop a new library in cooperation with existing ones and was one of the first seminary libraries to make full use of computer technology.

Seminex also became a leader in the area of ecumenical relations in St. Louis. CS, however, opposed our entry into the St. Louis Theological Consortium, the cooperative agency for seminaries that our faculty helped establish, and the consortium soon died. We replaced it with bilateral and multilateral arrangements with Eden and Kenrick seminaries and with St. Louis University. In addition to cross-registration for students, we shared faculty among our schools and taught courses together across denominational lines. Seminex led the way in initiating and sponsoring ecumenical services in St. Louis, and I became the spokesperson for Lutheranism on a variety of public issues in the city.

Seminex's location in midtown St. Louis had a profound effect on efforts to "contextualize" education. The wailing sirens never ceased, screaming into everyone's consciousness the needs of the world around us as we engaged in the study of theology. The presence of hundreds of students and faculty in the area was one of the factors that contributed to community renewal.

In 1977 life-threatening problems emerged at Seminex. From the time of its heady beginning Seminex annually experienced a decline in enrollment. The larger classes that had moved into exile from CS were graduating, and each year the number of entering students was smaller. The shrinking of the student body posed serious questions.

Some faculty and students, while favoring Seminex's partnership with the AELC, thought that I was focusing too much attention on the AELC and had abandoned the moderates who were left behind in the Missouri Synod. Others thought I did not properly appreciate the form of governance that had been devised for Seminex and did not sufficiently utilize the consensus process of decision making. On January 3, 1977, the faculty and I spent a day together to discuss concerns. We met in a classroom in our new facilities on the eleventh floor of the University Club building. I listened for several hours and then responded. I talked to the faculty about the future of Seminex. I explained my assessment that we would not have had a future at all if Jacob Preus had not dismissed four district presidents and Elwyn Ewald and Harold Hecht and others had not taken the lead to form the AELC.

Leaning forward in a wooden chair with a tablet writing arm, looking intently at the faces of faculty and staff cramped together in chairs like mine, I spoke with passion about my conviction that Seminex and the AELC were a "revelatory-redemptive act of God," calling us to a mission whose purpose and outcome could not yet be discerned and to a faith that did not count the odds but expected to experience divine strength in the midst of human weakness.[14]

I pointed out that we confronted three critical problems: fund raising, recruitment of students, and placement of our candidates for ministry—any one of which could end Seminex. We needed to maintain a strong faculty while we trimmed down to a size that corresponded to our student body and our income. We would not be able to solve the problems apart from strong and effective leadership. By leadership I did not mean authoritarian dictation, I explained, but consensus building. Nevertheless, leaders had to be given the freedom to lead.

The meeting may have improved communication, but the problems remained. The difficulty that administrators had with the internal governance process, on which the dean of community life had reported earlier,[15] increased. I personally found that the process made it almost impossible to engage in holistic planning for the future. Those who had fashioned the internal governance process or were its supporters felt that administrators were abandoning one of the essential elements of what it meant to be Seminex. Some were unhappy that in place of decision making by faculty and students each functioning as a group, and by the two groups acting together in town meetings as in the days of moratorium and early exile, we had returned to more traditional patterns for managing the institution in which administrators functioned prominently.

The crisis came as Seminex reassessed its staffing needs. The reassessment was the direct result of the financial crunch Seminex experienced in fall and winter 1976, a crunch so serious that the board authorized the administration to borrow up to $50,000 internally from board and faculty members if necessary to continue operations. The Seminex Board of Directors initiated the assessment, asking for a staffing proposal that, on the basis of both a 250-person and a 300-person student body, would "identify by position-name and number the optimum/minimum teaching and administrative faculty, executive staff and supportive staff by which the work of the school could be carried on."[16]

A faculty-student task force proposed a procedure for producing the staffing report. All faculty and staff were involved by department and staff unit in assessing the needs and producing the data for the report. The statistics of the report made it clear that reducing between seven and twelve faculty positions was appropriate, depending on the size of the student body. As the report stated: "The net result [of the study process] is a consciousness on the part of all members of the Seminex community that there is an urgent need for the Seminex community to face facts, trim itself for the tasks ahead, and still maintain a quality confessional theological education."[17]

At its meeting January 21–22, 1977, the Seminex Board of Directors reviewed the report and resolved to ensure that staff would be adequate "to meet a 300 member student body for the next two years" and to prepare for reductions in staff in the event that "student enrollment is lower than 300 or that funds are not available for a 300 student program."[18]

Decisions on the size of staff had to be made at the May meeting of the board because policy required one year's advance notice of any intention not to renew contracts—all of which, under Seminex's non-tenure, two-year contract policy, would come due at the end of July 1978. The faculty-student task force on staffing produced guidelines for dealing with contract renewals in the light of the board's January action on staffing. The guidelines stipulated criteria to be used in deciding whether to renew contracts, required me and the academic dean to interview all faculty prior to the decision, and put the responsibility for the decision in my hands.

Aware that there would probably have to be some reduction in faculty, the task force proposed that faculty should be placed into three categories: category A for those whose contracts were to be renewed;

category B for those whose contracts would not be renewed at this time but who would be assured that every effort would be made to do so before the present contract period was up; category C for those whose contracts would not be renewed and who would be counseled and helped to find ministry elsewhere. The category proposal along with the rest of the guidelines had been proposed by faculty and had the approval of the whole faculty. John Damm and I, along with Andrew Weyermann, who had succeeded Paul Bauermeister as dean of community life, interviewed all members of the faculty and staff prior to the May meeting of the Board of Directors.

The board meeting began on Wednesday evening, May 11, 1977, in a conference room on the twelfth floor of the UC building. After taking care of a number of other matters, the board turned its attention to the staffing issue. First it ratified the guidelines submitted by the faculty and agreed to follow them. Ralph Klein and Robert Smith (advisory faculty members present at the meeting) gave assurance that the board had correctly understood that the faculty had, in this instance only, "waived advance notice of intention to recommend against contract renewal."[19]

Meeting with me in executive session, the board reviewed staffing needs on the basis of the data that had been submitted in January. We considered the names and positions of all faculty and staff in regard to contract renewal. I urged that the board should put no one into category C, thus postponing the decision of which faculty and staff would not be reengaged. Members of the board pointed out that it was clear that the total number of faculty and staff should be reduced by at least seven in view of enrollment figures and the serious financial situation, and that there should be contingency plans to reduce faculty by an additional five. The board gave me until the following morning to decide which seven I would propose should not have contracts renewed and which five should be put into the holding pattern.

At home that night I spent several hours poring over names and data. I did not sleep well for the few hours that were left and came to Seminex the next morning nervous and edgy, my stomach rolling. In the board meeting I once again urged against a final decision not to renew anyone's contract. The board insisted on my naming seven faculty as those whose contracts should not be renewed and my reasons for selecting them. When I had done the deed, they asked for an additional five names in case further reductions were necessary. The board adopted my recommendations.

Commencement was the next day. In order not to spoil the festive occasion I informed no one about the board's action until the ceremonies were over. Then I began the process of personally visiting the twelve faculty and staff members and telling them of the decision. The outcry of lament was loud and long. Whatever else the faculty and staff may have expected the board to do on the staffing question, they did not anticipate that the jobs of so many would be in jeopardy.

Faculty response varied. They had approved in principle the plan to reduce their number, but they could no longer accept it once names were attached to numbers. Some found fault with the procedure, arguing that individuals were not notified in advance that their contracts might not be renewed, that a disproportionate number of faculty in the Practical Department had been affected, that the chairs of the departments should have been consulted before the decisions were made, or that I had used a criterion not included among those the faculty had recommended. Some saw in the decision conclusive evidence that my style of administration did not allow room for the consulting process. A few could offer only shocked protest, complaining that the board's treatment of the faculty was no different from that of the CS BoC.

The faculty met on May 26, 1977, to deal with the uproar. In a letter the faculty asked the board at its August meeting to "redo . . . its arithmetic regarding staffing needs," pledging "to work more energetically than ever in the areas of financial development and recruitment" and agreeing to commit themselves to "new arrangements," such as "income-sharing, worker professorhood, and theological education by extension." The faculty also asked for a meeting as soon as possible between representatives of the board and representatives of the faculty and the students.[20] On June 17, 1977, I convened a meeting of three faculty, three students, and three board members, in which board members responded to presentations made by faculty members on the process used in the staffing decision, on the consequences of the decision, and on future options. The full board received a report of the discussions at its August 12–13, 1977, meeting.

The Seminex Board of Directors reviewed its staffing decision and adopted a statement to be given to the faculty and students. After responding to a number of the faculty's problems with the board's decision, the statement declared: "The Board reports that the result of its reconsideration of both the arithmetic supplied by the faculty staffing proposal and the financial and enrollment factors available at the time of the difficult decisions has been a conviction that its conclusions were responsible and necessary. The Board believes that the administrative members of the Seminex staff implemented the Board's action responsibly and with a concern for those involved." The statement went on to declare the board's hope that those in category B could be retained if enrollment and finances warranted.[21]

Returning students in September 1977 renewed the uproar over the staffing decision. In what at times was heated and acrimonious discussion it became clear that the disagreement was not just about who should and should not be on the Seminex staff or what procedures should have been followed, but about the nature and purpose of Seminex itself and how it should go about conducting its affairs. The malaise was so bad that I feared we might do to ourselves what all the forces marshaled against us had not been able to do to us: close Seminex.

The Board of Directors tackled the problem head-on at its meeting on October 28–29, 1977. It resolved to inform the five faculty in category B that it intended to renew their contracts. It reaffirmed its decision of the previous May not to renew seven contracts, pointing out to the faculty that the board had not received from the faculty "new mathematics and new wisdom" that would have made it possible to alter the decision. Addressing itself to the bigger problem present in the community, it called for an "early review of both bylaws and internal governance procedures" and authorized an expenditure up to $10,000 to engage an "outside, neutral, and objective consultant to facilitate the process of the review of the nature, mission and governance" of Seminex.[22]

When faculty and student groups concurred with the board's proposal concerning a consultant, the board contracted for the services of Mobley-Luciani Associates, a group that the AELC Board of Directors had engaged to do a major study of the future direction of the AELC. Louis Mobley conducted numerous meetings and hearings both within the Seminex community and with its constituency. At the meeting of the Board of Directors on January 27–28, 1978, Mobley was ready with a report and recommendations.

Mobley proposed that Seminex engage in goal setting, which he described as an open-systems network for interrelating the members of a community for the purpose of achieving agreed-upon results. He suggested a goal for Seminex to be achieved by May 1, 1978: "A goal-setting task force has processed high priority goals for Seminex." The priority goals had to do with purpose, survival, and goal-setting. The task force would consist of five persons, representing board, faculty, administration, and students, plus the Seminex president as coordinator. The board adopted Mobley's proposal.[23]

The five-person task force created three additional task forces for the purpose of dealing with the three high-priority goals. Before May the three task forces reported significant results. The purpose task force had formulated a preliminary statement of purpose and a process for refining and adopting it. The survival task force chose to substitute "minimum conditions" for "survival" and agreed on a preliminary statement of what those conditions should be and a process for coming to agreement on the statement. The goal-setting task force proposed that for the year ahead the

Seminex community should use goal setting as the way to get things done and proposed a process of review at year's end.

At the board's meeting in January 1978, when it had informed me of its intention to renew my contract the following year, I had responded that I was not sure whether I would accept. By May 1978 there was new spirit and renewed community at Seminex, and I agreed to continue to serve.

Several months later, through an extensive consulting process, the Seminex community agreed on a statement of purpose that described our understanding of who we were and what we were about:

> In response to God's call Christ Seminary–Seminex serves God and God's church in mission to the world by equipping people for and involving them in various forms of ministry. It seeks to achieve its purpose through quality programs of theological education which witness to the centrality and suffi- ciency of the Gospel of Jesus Christ and its radical implications for faith and life and which are offered in a worshiping, nurturing, and risking commu- nity. It does its work in commitment to the Scriptures and the Lutheran Confessions, in partnership with the Association of Evangelical Lutheran Churches, and in cooperation with Lutherans and other Christians.[24]

Even more important, the community was making use of the state- ment of purpose in agreeing on goals that the community would work to achieve. In a strange and unexpected way I was in charge of a process of planning I had wanted but had been unable to engender before.

If the Missouri Synod conflict was a major learning experience for me, so was the internal conflict at Seminex.[25] Among other things I came to understand clearly the paradox of institution—all institutions includ- ing ecclesiastical ones. The paradox is this: Institution is essential for the church's ministry, and at the same time institution is inimical to the church's ministry. For the sake of the church's ministry it is essential to come to terms with both elements of the paradox.

Early on in Seminex history a myth developed about its origin. The myth was that Seminex came into being spontaneously and functioned in its early days without organization, freely, through the consensus of its members. Underlying the internal conflict at Seminex, especially among many students, was the assumption that institution was an evil that had to be avoided at all cost. At issue in the argument over internal governance was the claim that Seminex was wrongly reverting to modes of institution from which the founders had set themselves free in the moratorium and exile from CS.

Anti-institutionalism was a fact of life in the AELC. Because of the experience with oppressive authority in the Missouri Synod, the founders of the AELC sought to avoid all hierarchical authority. The focus within the AELC was on the congregation and then on the synod with minimal structure and authority given to the AELC. Some set community over against institution and celebrated the freedom to function without the trappings of institution.

There was a high degree of organization among faculty and students during the time of moratorium and exile. Seminex came into being as a result of complex organizational agreements with three seminary institutions. Seminex could continue to exist only because of the prior existence of ELIM and its extensive support system. In spite of the efforts of anti-institutionalists, the AELC was an institution like any other with the pluses and minuses of all institutions.

As the Apology to the Augsburg Confession states,[26] the church is not a platonic ideal but an empirical community that exists in the world, subject to the same pressures as any other human organization. The church cannot function without an institutional form, just as God's justifying grace needs the means of Word and Sacraments to enter into human life.[27] The church's ministry requires the structure of organization. The only question is whether the structure will help or hinder the church in accomplishing its mission.

But institution that is essential for the church's ministry is also inimical to it. That was a hard lesson for an organizational person like me to learn. Institution is not neutral but is predisposed to evil. Each institution is pervaded by the principalities and powers against which Christians wrestle. Institution is a part of what it means to be human, and it participates in the fallenness of our human condition. Institution dehumanizes, perpetrates injustice, and opposes God even when it is in the best of human hands, even when it is in the hands of Christians.

Institution becomes an end in itself rather than a means. In the Missouri Synod controversy, many moderates could not think of leaving the Synod because the synodical organization had become sacrosanct to them. Pastors would not make an issue of the controversy within their congregations lest they disturb the status quo. At Seminex, preserving the institution required that we tell some of our faculty and staff that they could no longer work with us in the community they had helped create.

Institution requires the compromise of integrity. Everyone has to engage in compromise in order to accomplish anything meaningful; we are willing to sacrifice a little principle for the sake of a greater good. But institution asks us to compromise to the point of selling our soul. I am convinced that 40 percent of those in the Missouri Synod compromised their integrity rather than pay the price of following through on the principles to which they were committed. We at Seminex were continually tempted to back away from our convictions in order to ensure ongoing financial support from our friends.

Institution tempts its participants to engage in manipulation and to use power to achieve the goals of ministry. It seduces us to measure success by human standards rather than by faithfulness in walking the way of the cross. It requires the use of power to achieve results in direct opposition to the words of Jesus to his disciples, "This is not the way it shall be among you" (Matt. 20:26). At issue in Seminex's internal controversy was the conflict between faculty and students and administration and board over the locus of power.

The problem is that we have to live with the paradox of institution. We cannot escape the tension imposed by the paradox. We cannot do without institution, because it is essential for ministry. We cannot enjoy what is good about institution without experiencing and participating in its subversion. We have to work with institutions and make them work for us. We have to do our best to see to it that they remain means to good ends. We have to make the church's ministry our priority and use institution as means to ministry. Then, in spite of our best efforts, we have to acknowledge and confess our sins, knowing that our best efforts will not be good enough.

Oscar Gerken's conclusion that I did not teach false doctrine and was therefore not to be removed from the Missouri Synod's pastoral office rankled the conservatives in the Synod. Moderates kept pointing to the decision as evidence that there had been no real justification for my ouster as CS president, that the formation of Seminex was justified, and that district presidents rightly authorized the ordination of Seminex graduates. My case was proving to be a great embarrassment to the Preus administration.

Some Preus supporters argued that Gerken had acted wrongly; they said that under bylaw 5.13 he should have suspended me from the pastoral office and turned the case over to the Missouri District's Commission of Adjudication. *Affirm*, the journal of the conservatives, argued that Gerken had erred in procedure by interviewing only me and not my two accusers. Once again the ever-ready Commission on Constitutional Matters was called upon to provide a solution. In a ruling issued on September 20, 1975, the Commission on Constitutional Matters said that Gerken did have the authority to decide that I was not guilty and did not have to interview the accusers in arriving at his decision.

Then, incredibly, the commission stated that Gerken's action in finding me not guilty constituted failure to act, a condition addressed in bylaw 5.13: "If the District officers fail to act, the President of the Synod, by virtue of the power given him in the Constitution . . . may on his own initiative institute proceedings, take administrative action, and, if necessary, present charges to the appropriate District Commission of Adjudication."[28] Because Gerken had not suspended me, the commission argued, he had "failed to act." The commission ruled that my two accusers therefore had the right to appeal Gerken's decision to the president of the Synod, although the bylaw said nothing about such a right.

Leonard Buelow and Harlan Harnapp appealed. As I said when I learned of the appeal shortly after it was made on October 23, 1975, "I have been expecting the appeal. . . . The Preus administration has to have a scalp to show for all its bluster about false doctrine."[29] Jacob Preus, whose dictum "Tietjen must go," was well known throughout the Synod, clearly could not decide the issue himself. But it took him eight months to decide what to do. On July 1, 1976, he turned the appeal over to Theodore F. Nickel, third vice-president of the Synod, and asked him to decide the case.

Theodore Nickel had retired from the pastorate of a congregation in Chicago. For many years he had served as chair of the Synod's Commission on Theology and Church Relations and considered himself an expert theologian. During Oliver Harms's presidency Nickel had been the darling of the Synod's moderates. After 1969 he regularly spoke the Preus party line. Short and bald, he had a hearing problem that made him strain his head forward, squint his eyes, and cock his ear.

Nickel did not contact me until November 1976. I gave him my standard response: my door was always open but I was not participating further in the legal process. Nickel persisted in wanting to meet with me. He asked me to come to the Missouri Athletic Club in St. Louis or to his hotel room at the St. Louis airport. When he realized that I was not going to comply, he came to see me.

We met in my office on the ninth floor of the UC building on January 27, 1977, sitting in two green plastic-covered chairs that had been purchased from Goodwill. It was a strange meeting that lasted for more than four hours. Nickel did almost all the talking, a phenomenon that was a normal experience whenever you were in his company. When on rare occasions I would respond to correct a misimpression he had or to agree with an emphasis he made, he would interrupt and launch into another theological lecture. I got the impression that he was having difficulty hearing me physically, whatever his bias may have been. He would have gone on for hours longer, I was sure, but at 5:20 P.M. I pointed out that we needed to be out of the building at 5:30 or we would be locked in.

On March 28, 1977, Nickel sent me a fifteen-page, single-spaced letter in which he asked me to abjure certain positions that he said I held. I held them, he said, because I had "allowed and fostered" the false doctrine of others. He reminded me that Oscar Gerken had not dealt with that charge. "I am certain that you have noted," Nickel wrote me, "how I have dealt chiefly with charges that were not touched upon in your meeting with Pastor Gerken. . . . But this is a crucial point, for if a pastor or a responsible administrator allows or fosters the teaching of false doctrine, he is as guilty as if he had taught false doctrine himself." Gerken's "exoneration" therefore "must be regarded as incomplete."

Nickel and the Preus party were obviously trying to find a way of finding me guilty of false doctrine after all without saying that Gerken was wrong. In my response I called Nickel's attention to the immorality of what he was saying: "I am condemned as guilty of false doctrine in the name and place of unnamed others whose teaching I allegedly allowed and fostered though they have not been condemned or even been given a hearing."[30] I asked Nickel: "Doesn't simple morality require it first to be proven that the teaching by others which I have allegedly allowed and fostered is actually false before I can be condemned for allowing and fostering it? Or are you proposing a new application of the Caiaphas principle?"[31]

Letters for the record went back and forth over several months. Finally, on September 28, 1977, Nickel announced to the Synod: "Doctrinal statements, made or supported by Dr. John H. Tietjen have been found to be contrary to the Holy Scriptures and the Lutheran Confessions. Dr. Tietjen has refused to modify, correct or withdraw any of these statements. . . . Dr. John H. Tietjen is, therefore, no longer a clergy member of the Lutheran Church–Missouri Synod and not eligible for a call." I did not make much out of receiving Nickel's letter. We all knew it would come. A week later I received a letter from James Mayer in behalf of the Partners in Mission staff thanking me for the witness I had given in not participating in the process against me. Mayer wrote: "What has been finally formalized last week was as predictable as the coming Winter: The only *out* the Devil ever has is to blame the victim for the atrocity."[32]

◆ ◆ ◆

I would not be telling the truth if I said that my ouster from the Missouri Synod did not matter to me. It is true that I had become a member of the English Synod of the AELC and was under call from

Christ Seminary–Seminex. Nevertheless, what the Missouri Synod did to me wounded me deeply. But I had counted the cost in signing on as a disciple of Jesus. I told myself that I had no right to be surprised that I was expected to share in Christ's suffering as I took up my cross to follow in his steps. All around me I could see that we were experiencing the promised result of discipleship: new life was rising out of the death of the old. Seminex and the AELC were frail and flawed as common clay pots, to be sure. But in those clay pots was a spiritual treasure. As I looked to the future, I wondered: What plans did God have for such weak vessels?

14 ◆
A YEAST IN FLOUR

Around 7:30 A.M. on January 12, 1982, as I drove into the parking lot of the University Club building where Christ Seminary–Seminex was located, I could not believe my eyes. Water was flowing from the top floors down the side of the building and in the subfreezing temperature was producing a massive waterfall of ice. Sparkling icicles were dangling everywhere.

I rushed into the building to find out what was going on. In the lobby a dozen people were standing around, trying to figure out what to do. All the elevators were inoperative, so I dashed out of the building entrance to the back stairs and ran up nine flights to the floor where Seminex's administrative offices were housed. Water was cascading down the stairs as I went up.

I telephoned the manager of the building to tell him what was happening. He said I must be exaggerating and he would get there when he was ready to do so. I reported the problem to the police and called the city's water department and Union Electric to tell them to shut off the water and the electricity, hoping to prevent injury to people.

I inspected the Seminex floors to assess the damage. Water was everywhere. On some floors the ceiling had fallen down in several rooms. The library on the thirteenth floor seemed to be hardest hit. Books in parts of the room were soaking wet. Soon the water to the building was shut off and gradually the flow subsided. As Seminex staff, faculty, and students arrived we set about the big task of cleaning up the mess.

It was not difficult to figure out what had happened. At closing time on the previous Friday the building manager had turned off the heat to

289

save money. Over the weekend, after a snow and ice storm, arctic winds had brought the temperature to below zero, a rare event in St. Louis, and the water in the building's pipes had frozen solid. When the heat came back on and the ice thawed, pipes everywhere in the building burst.

The calamity was only the most recent of the crises we confronted in the building, whose eighth to the fifteenth floors we were leasing. An optometrist and two medical doctors with offices on the premises had purchased the building from the University Club just before we moved in. They did nothing for the building except receive the rent, and that, according to them, was not enough to enable the building to break even in its operations.

In May 1981 Jeannette Bauermeister as director of the division for business management alerted the Seminex Board of Directors to some of the problems we were having with the building. In June the main air conditioning unit for the administrative offices went out, and the only way to get it repaired was for Seminex to advance cash of $7,000. In July Union Electric was about to shut off electricity to the building because of unpaid bills totaling $5,000. Again Seminex paid the bill. On July 23 a severe thunderstorm blew out large panes of glass windows from the fifteenth floor onto the parking lot below, fortunately with damage only to cars and no injury to people. In pressing to get the windows replaced, we discovered that the insurance on the building had been canceled on July 3. Because the windows could not be repaired, the fifteenth floor was no longer usable. Neither we nor our attorney could get any response from the owners.

We began to look for other locations. Jeannette Bauermeister found one right across the street, on the corner of Grand and Washington. Boarded up and vacant, the Humboldt building was attached to the Fox Theater, a classic vaudeville and movie house that had closed two years before. Leon Strauss, the president of Pantheon Corporation, a redevelopment organization in St. Louis, had purchased the theater and the Humboldt building and was intending to restore and reopen the theater for musical productions and revues. Strauss was willing to accept us into the Humboldt building on the same lease terms we had in the UC building if we should find it necessary to leave.

When the pipes burst, building management did nothing. There were no prospects for pipes to be repaired or for elevators to run again. We had no option but to leave. On January 14 I signed the lease for the Humboldt building, and Bauermeister mobilized the Seminex community to move across the street. We had to pay an exorbitant fee to get the freight elevator in working condition. I commandeered the key to the elevator and personally ran it to evacuate the Seminex portion of the building.

The move was an exercise in determination and community. Faculty and students were the movers. We not only had to pack up and move out, but we also had to clean, paint, and repair in order to move in. Under Lucille Hager's watchful care, students disassembled the 30,000-volume library shelf by shelf, carefully labeling books and shelves, and reassembled it across the street. With organ builder Martin Ott telling us how, we took apart the organ that was our prized possession and put it back together again in our new chapel space. In our old building we had to work without heat in subfreezing temperatures and cart books and organ and furniture across sidewalks and streets covered with ice and snow. All the while, we continued our educational program, transferring classes to the classroom facilities of Third Baptist Church, located on another corner of Grand and Washington.

We made the move in seventeen days. On the Saturday evening when we were done, having put the finishing touches on the first-floor chapel facing out onto Grand Avenue, snow started to fall again and did not stop until more than twenty inches of it had paralyzed St. Louis. The snow delayed the dedication of our new facilities by a few days. But we were finally safe and warm in our new address at 539 N. Grand Avenue, having learned again what it means to be pilgrim people content to live in tents. Our move from one building to another was only a sign of a much bigger move that pilgrim people would be asked to make.

"I'm not about to give the ALC's approval to a unilateral arrangement in which LSTC alone cashes in on Seminex." The speaker was Walter Wietzke, director of the Division for Theological Education and Ministry of the American Lutheran Church. His wavy hair in place, his normally sleepy eyes flashing in their deep sockets, Wietzke leaned out over the restaurant table toward me, his jaw jutting pugnaciously. He was stating bluntly the reason that he was opposed to a proposal for Christ Seminary–Seminex to move to Chicago and merge with the Lutheran School of Theology at Chicago.

I shot back across the table at Wietzke: "Why should Seminex worry about what the ALC wants? What has the ALC done to show any interest in us or in our future?" The confrontation was head-on, the conversation at white-heat when two waitresses arrived with trays of soup and sandwiches for the nine of us gathered around the table. It was about 12:15 P.M. on January 29, 1982. We were gathered in a restaurant on the lower level of the Hilton Hotel at O'Hare Airport in Chicago. We had put several tables together in an out-of-the-way corner of the restaurant so that we could talk as we ate.

The other people around the table were six representatives from Christ Seminary–Seminex and Elwyn Ewald, the executive secretary of the Association of Evangelical Lutheran Churches. We were participating in a meeting that had begun earlier in the day in a conference room on a floor higher up in the hotel. Other participants in the meeting were seven representatives of the LSTC and Lloyd Sheneman, executive director of the Division for Professional Leadership of the Lutheran Church in America. The president and a faculty representative of the ALC's Wartburg Theological Seminary were supposed to be present but did not attend.

The daylong meeting was the second one involving representatives of Seminex and LSTC and staff executives responsible for theological education in the ALC, the LCA, and the AELC. The previous meeting had taken place in November 1981. The meetings were the climax of more than three years of conversations about the relation of Seminex to the seminaries of the ALC and the LCA and almost two years of conversations between representatives of Seminex and LSTC. Under discussion were two proposals about the future relations of Seminex and LSTC.

LSTC proposed that the two seminaries relate to one another according to the Union-Auburn model. Several decades earlier Auburn Seminary had united with Union Theological Seminary in New York City in such a way that the Auburn Seminary corporation continued to exist for the purpose of using its endowments to fund several Auburn chairs for the faculty of Union Seminary. LSTC proposed that Seminex move to its Chicago campus and continue to exist for the purpose of funding a number of Seminex chairs on the faculty of LSTC.

We at Seminex proposed a merger model to LSTC. We would move to Chicago in such a way that we would merge the resources of our two seminaries in a new and larger institution. We would bring not only our faculty and students into the merger but our supporting constituency as well. At the previous meeting in November 1981 the representatives of the two schools had asked subcommittees to begin work on a statement of purpose for a merged seminary and to consider the feasibility of merger.

The work of the subcommittes had been under discussion during the morning session on January 29. The participants from LSTC were convinced that merger was not feasible. The resulting seminary would be too big, argued LSTC board member and Iowa Synod bishop Paul Werger. The financial risk was too high, insisted LSTC treasurer Richard Hoefs.

For the Seminex participants the Union-Auburn model was unacceptable. It meant that we would continue to solicit support for only a limited number of professors in Seminex chairs on the faculty of LSTC and thus would have to terminate the services of most of our faculty. If we had problems over staff reductions before,[1] the problems in the Union-Auburn proposal would be nothing short of calamitous. There was no way the Seminex community would approve such a proposal.

Walter Wietzke made it clear that not only he or his board but the ALC itself would object to any decision made by Seminex and LSTC alone. He insisted that in view of the ongoing discussions to unite the ALC, the LCA, and the AELC, no decision should be made in theological education without taking into account the impact on all the seminaries in the three churches. LSTC was not the only seminary that should benefit from the resources of Seminex, he argued.

Discouraged and frustrated as the noon hour approached, I concluded that we had reached an impasse in our discussions with LSTC and that our negotiations were probably at an end. Perhaps that's how God wants it, I said to myself, thinking that Seminex would have to continue on its own into a clouded future.

In establishing the day's agenda, we had agreed that we would spend the noon hour in caucuses according to seminary and church body to reflect on the morning session and to assess our respective positions for discussion during the afternoon session. Wietzke had no one to meet with, since WTS's representatives were not present, and there was a lot I wanted to say to him. I slipped a note to Samuel Roth, one of Seminex's representatives at the meeting, who had been elected as chair of the Seminex board of directors the previous October, and suggested that we invite Wietzke to join us for lunch. Roth looked at me with raised eyebrows, shrugged his shoulders, and nodded, as if to say, "I don't know what you have in mind, but let's do it." As the meeting was about to recess, I invited Wietzke to join the Seminex-AELC caucus for lunch, and he accepted.

Among the Seminex representatives who gathered around the restaurant table were four members of the Seminex Board of Directors. Alice Hausman, director of volunteer services at a hospital in St. Paul, Minnesota, was a leader in Evangelical Lutherans in Mission and active in the AELC. She had made the motion at the Seminex board meeting that had led to the present meeting. Richard McAuliffe, a senior officer of a Chicago bank, had been active in the Frey-Lueking movement prior to the Missouri Synod's New Orleans convention, was one of the founders of the English Synod, and was serving as treasurer of the Seminex board. Tall and balding, his hands showing the signs of crippling arthritis, he had chosen a seat close to Wietzke in order to be sure to engage him in conversation.

Tecla Sund Reklau, a free-lance editor, had spent a number of years in the work of campus ministry and was familiar with inter-Lutheran issues. Tall and thin, her face expressing her care for people, she looked for opportunities to use her experience in group process to facilitate the ongoing discussion. Samuel Roth, moderate leader at the New Orleans convention, past president of ELIM, had succeeded Richard Jungkuntz as chair of the Seminex board. Roth assumed the responsibility of moderating the luncheon discussion.

Two others were among the Seminex representatives. Robert Smith was there in his capacity as academic dean, having succeeded John Damm in the position after Damm moved to a pastorate in New York City the previous fall. Of average height, with light brown hair combed to the side, Smith took notes and was ever-ready to use his skills of expression to help formulate agreements. Randall Lee had been chosen to represent the students of Seminex at the meeting. In his final year at Seminex, tall and large-framed, his eyeglasses adding to a studious appearance, Lee was ready to share expected student reactions to proposals.

I wanted a frank, nothing-held-back meeting with Wietzke and was grateful when he responded bluntly to my request that he restate for us the position he had articulated at the meeting upstairs. I responded just as bluntly. With Roth holding the reins ever so loosely as discussion moderator, Wietzke and I talked forthrightly as McAuliffe tactfully interjected from time to time to clarify what one of us had said. Occasionally Elwyn Ewald would speak in behalf of the AELC. Some of the Seminex representatives were visibly uncomfortable with the nothing-out-of-order character of the conversation, but I knew that Wietzke welcomed frank talk and would not resent what we were doing.

The ALC owes Seminex nothing, Wietzke told me. Seminex came into being by itself. What right does it have to expect ALC help? Then why are you interfering with Seminex's efforts to join forces with a seminary of the LCA? I retorted. Seminex has actually wanted the discussions to be three-way and to include Wartburg Seminary, but your board won't let Wartburg in on the discussions.

That's because no seminary should decide its future on its own, Wietzke came back. Seminex and LSTC haven't got a right to do it either—not with Lutheran union right around the corner. Any decision about the future of Seminex has to take all of Lutheran theological education into account.

Then why haven't you supported our AELC efforts to produce a plan for the future of Lutheran theological education? I wanted to know. We at Seminex are perfectly willing to relate to other seminaries besides LSTC, but we have gotten nowhere with the requests we have made to the Consultation on Theological Education[2] about a plan that would answer our questions about where we fit in the larger picture.

Any plan for the future takes time, Wietzke argued. First the Consultation had to see what the Committee on Lutheran Unity was going to do. You have all the time in the world, I responded, but we don't. You don't understand how delicate our operation is. We have to be able to place our graduates in order to survive as a seminary. The AELC has done a fantastic job of putting our graduates into ministry, but the AELC isn't big enough. The LCA has been open to our graduates. But the ALC has slammed the door in our face. If you think we have resources that can be used to strengthen theological education in a united church, then we need the ALC's help in placing our graduates so that we can continue to operate while you use your time to produce a plan for the future.

The issues were on the table. What could be done? Could we agree on anything that we could recommend to the LSTC-LCA people at the afternoon meeting upstairs? With McAuliffe nudging and Ewald assisting, Wietzke little by little produced what became the consensus of our meeting: Seminex resources should benefit not just LSTC but other seminaries as well. Needed was a more comprehensive plan for the future to help in making the decision. The theological education staff of the three churches should consult together and with seminary presidents to determine which seminaries could benefit most from Seminex resources. While the plan was being fashioned, the ALC needed to open up its placement processes to Seminex graduates.

When we returned to the meeting room upstairs, the LSTC-LCA representatives were waiting for us. Among them were four LSTC board members: Robert Hereth, a Chicago area pastor and board chair; Donald Berg, pastor of an LCA congregation in Iowa; Richard Hoefs, executive of a major Chicago accounting firm and board treasurer; Paul Werger, bishop of the LCA's Iowa Synod. Also present were LSTC president William Lesher, academic dean Franklin Sherman, and student representative Carl Sharon; and Lloyd Sheneman of the LCA's Division for Professional Leadership.

Robert Hereth reported the results of his group's noontime conversations. Speaking softly, his round face undulating with smiles under a thinning head of hair, Hereth told the rest of us it was their consensus that we should not be discouraged by the impasse we had experienced during the morning, that we needed to continue to study and work together at solving the problem, that we should ask whether other seminaries might want to share in the resources of Seminex, and that we should broaden the discussions to include other interested schools. The rest of us looked at one another and smiled as we heard a conclusion similar to our own.

Samuel Roth reported the consensus of our group. Clearly, both groups were near agreement; a consensus would not be difficult to reach. Before the afternoon was over, we had achieved a two-page statement of agreement.[3] Among other things we said: "We recognize that the future of each of our schools must be considered in relation to the need for resources in Lutheran theological education in a united church and that a more comprehensive plan for Lutheran theological education is needed to help us determine the best use of Seminex faculty resources." In addition, we said: "We look with favor on the utilization of Seminex resources in behalf of all of Lutheran theological education in a united church with a major portion of those resources to be united with LSTC and the remainder shared with other Lutheran seminaries." We asked the theological education staff of the three churches and the presidents and deans of the two schools to figure out how to make it happen, agreeing to meet again in two months.

The impasse had been transformed into breakthrough. Richard Hoefs, shrewd financial analyst ever concerned about the bottom line, spoke for us all: "The Holy Spirit has been at work among us! How else could this have happened?"

The relations of the Lutheran Church–Missouri Synod to other Lutherans had always been strained. Even the Missouri Synod action approving fellowship with the ALC took place at a convention that elected a president whose campaign had been waged on an anti-fellowship platform. Jacob Preus as president had implemented the convention's fellowship decision, but his administration immediately began to look for ways to undo it.

On the other hand, the people who formed Seminex and the AELC represented those within the Missouri Synod who were in favor of close relations with other Lutherans. As the constituting convention of the AELC made clear, the people of the AELC wanted fellowship with all Lutherans. It was therefore only natural that we at Christ Seminary–Seminex should see our future in relation to other Lutherans.

The Lutheran world outside of the Missouri Synod was appalled at the developments that caused Seminex to come into being. A week before I was suspended as president ot Concordia Seminary, the presidents and deans of the seminaries of the LCA and the ALC wrote an open letter to the CS Board of Control, supporting the theological position of the CS faculty. In the midst of the moratorium at CS David Preus, president of the ALC, publicly expressed the ALC's "deep distress" over the conflict in the Missouri Synod.[4] Although not wanting to take sides, he said, "We are fearful of any attempt to establish standards of orthodoxy that go beyond the historic Lutheran Confessions," thus endorsing the position of the CS faculty.

Six weeks after Seminex was formed, the presidents of both the ALC and the LCA, speaking separately, urged an end to the conflict in the Missouri Synod, pointing out that it was having consequences for the work of their churches, too.[5] In urging reconciliation David Preus said, "We believe there is room in the Lutheran church for the kind of differences in theological approach which have brought you to your present impasse." Robert Marshall of the LCA made it clear that, should reconciliation not be possible, the "moderates" of the Missouri Synod would be welcome in the LCA.

The presidents of the seminaries of the ALC and the LCA gave strong backing to Seminex at the biennial meeting of the Association of Theological Schools in June 1974. The association became embroiled in the Missouri Synod controversy when earlier in the month its Commission on Accrediting voted to remove the suspension of accreditation that had been imposed on CS a year earlier. They voted to impose another suspension in its place. Many association members could not understand how they could lift the first suspension in view of what had happened at CS. Lutheran seminary presidents led the way in urging the association itself to reverse the decision of its accrediting commission. When it was made clear that association rules specified that there was no appeal from the commission's decision, the Lutheran seminary presidents joined with others in securing a strong statement of support for the Joint Project for Theological Education, under whose auspices Seminex acted, and in asserting the members' unhappiness with the commission's decision.

At its biennial convention in Baltimore, Maryland, July 3–10, 1974, the LCA invited Samuel Roth, president of ELIM, to speak. After hearing him, the convention delegates adopted "A Statement of Concern," in which they gave strong support to the cause of the moderates in the Missouri Synod struggle.

When reconciliation proved futile and Seminex continued to function, and when the AELC was formed as the church to which Seminex was related, institutional concerns emerged as decisive factors in the relation of Seminex to other Lutherans. Seminex's survival depended on its ability to place its graduates. The AELC with its 250 congregations was simply not big enough to absorb Seminex's graduates even with a declining enrollment. With Missouri Synod doors officially closed to Seminex graduates, the students of Seminex looked more and more to the ALC and the LCA.

Because of my concern for the placement of Seminex graduates, I asked William Kohn, president of the AELC, to arrange a meeting with the presidents of the ALC and the LCA in order to discuss the issue of Seminex as a pan-Lutheran seminary, serving not only the AELC and a constituency in the Missouri Synod but the ALC and the LCA as well. The meeting took place in fall 1977 at the LCA offices in New York City.

Both David Preus and Robert Marshall were friendly and concerned, but Preus made it clear he was convinced that the Lutherans of America needed fewer seminaries, not an additional one. Marshall cautioned Seminex against becoming diffuse as a pan-Lutheran seminary instead of identifying closely with the AELC and serving as its theological center. Both agreed that I should raise my concern with the staff of the theological education units of their churches, namely, Walter Wietzke of the ALC's Division for Theological Education and Ministry and Lloyd Sheneman of the LCA's Division for Professional Leadership.

I did that, over supper on a cold day in February 1978 at a meeting of Lutheran seminary presidents and deans in Minneapolis. Sheneman and Wietzke were as cold as the weather. They did not say this in so many words, but upon reflection, their message was clear: Seminex cannot make it. That does not upset us because we do not need another seminary. Do not try to push your problems off on us. We do not intend to bail you out.

I was deeply introspective on the flight back to St. Louis. Could Seminex survive? The experts, not just Sheneman and Wietzke, but others as well, had been saying all along that we could not. But we had survived thus far against impossible odds. We found it necessary to use the language of miracle to describe our experience. There it was: The branch was growing from the felled tree stump. *Should* we survive? I preferred to leave that in God's hands. We had experienced the truth of the biblical promise: God's strength is made perfect in weakness. We certainly had weakness enough. I concluded that we would have to carry on by ourselves and see what God had in store for us.

Not just Seminex, but the AELC as well saw its future in relation to other Lutherans. One year after its founding, in December 1977, the Board of Directors of the AELC considered the preliminary findings of a study that showed the members of the AELC were overwhelmingly committed to developing closer relations with other Lutherans.

The study had been inaugurated several months earlier to help the AELC leadership assess what the people of the AELC understood the AELC's mission and purpose to be. The study was being done by Mobley-Luciani Associates, the same group that proved helpful to Seminex in the crisis precipitated by reduction in staff. The data produced by the study showed that, along with a desire to support Seminex and a commitment to local decision making, the grass-roots members of the AELC were united in their desire for Lutheran union.

Several days before the December 3–4, 1977, meeting at which the AELC Board of Directors was to consider the study data, Elwyn Ewald, the AELC's executive secretary, called me to get my reaction to a proposal he was thinking of presenting. Ewald had resigned his AELC position the previous July when he came to the conclusion that the AELC was going to become "just another church body" but had agreed to give part-time service while he looked for another job. Ewald told me that he and C. Thomas Spitz, Jr., who had been appointed ecumenical officer of the AELC, had been convinced by the study data that the AELC had a special reason for being, and they wanted to know what I thought.

Both of them, I felt, were wary of Seminex, convinced that it was a drain on the AELC and its mission, determined to keep it in its place. Ewald and I would soon become close friends who completely understood and respected each other and who sought each other's counsel. But at this point both Ewald and Spitz were asking for my counsel on the assumption that they could not afford to propose something to the AELC board that I would oppose.

I was delighted by what I heard. Ewald proposed that, in view of the data showing strong AELC support for Lutheran union, the AELC should take the lead in submitting a union proposal to the ALC and the LCA. For that to happen it would be necessary to move up the AELC convention to April 1978 so that the convention could act in time to submit a proposal to the conventions of the ALC and the LCA later in the year. If the AELC Board of Directors would approve the proposal, Ewald said, he would be ready to take back his resignation and continue to serve as executive secretary. I told Ewald how pleased I was with the proposal and that I would support it at the meeting.

I had been wondering for some time if one purpose God may have had in mind for Seminex and the AELC was to serve as yeast for a larger Lutheran union. Around the time of the formation of the AELC I lectured on worship at a conference held on the campus of St. Olaf College, a school of the ALC in Northfield, Minnesota. During the conference E. Clifford Nelson, professor at St. Olaf and noted historian of Lutheranism in America, invited me to his office.

Nelson, wearing a gray sports jacket, sitting behind an uncluttered desk in a neatly arranged study, said that he could not help but see parallels between the formation of the AELC and the establishment of a group in the latter part of the nineteenth century known as the Anti-Missouri Brotherhood. The Brotherhood was a group of Norwegian Lutherans who were opposed to the Missouri Synod position on the doctrine of predestination and who withdrew from the Norwegian Synod because of their desire to promote union among all the Norwegian Lutherans of America. It took several decades, but their goal was ultimately achieved. Nelson, his eyes smiling at me through his glasses, wanted to know if I didn't see some similar purpose in the formation of the AELC.

I smiled back and told him that I was well aware of the parallels between the Brotherhood and the AELC. Perhaps in the case of the AELC, too, I said, division would ultimately serve the cause of Lutheran union. We would just have to wait and see.

The AELC Board of Directors enthusiastically endorsed the Ewald-Spitz proposal. The date of the AELC convention was moved forward to April 14–16, 1978, and a task force was created to draft a proposal to be submitted to the convention. The board decided that the proposal should go not just to the ALC and LCA but to all Lutheran church bodies in the United States. Ewald was rehired as the AELC's executive secretary.[6]

The task force met in Chicago in January 1978, and I was one of its thirteen members. Spitz brought documents to help task force members understand the relations among Lutherans in the United States and the specific efforts that were under way through a joint committee to bring the ALC and the LCA closer together. William Kohn, AELC president, and Spitz both reported on informal conversations with the presidents of the ALC and the LCA concerning the projected action of the AELC. Robert Marshall said that it was the position of the LCA to respond favorably to any proposal for Lutheran union. David Preus stated that the proposal would be an embarrassment to the ALC because the ALC considered cooperation to be a sufficient expression of unity and did not want to have to turn down a merger proposal.

Task force members decided after some debate that the AELC needed to act on its own integrity and take the risk involved in issuing a proposal that might not be favorably received. After discussion of what should be included in the proposal, the task force gave me the responsibility of producing a draft overnight for consideration the next day. I worked fast and furiously and by the next morning was ready with a draft of "A Call for Lutheran Union." The task force spent the day altering and amending it, but by day's end the proposal was ready for presentation to the AELC Board of Directors and through it to the AELC convention.

"A Call for Lutheran Union"[7] laid out the reasons why union rather than cooperation was a necessity for Lutherans in America at that time in history. It proposed that Lutheran churches in North America join "in making a formal commitment to organic church union," arguing that "organizational and polity differences are most apt to be resolved in the context of a commitment to organic church union for the sake of the church's mission." It further proposed that those churches that had acted by fall 1979 meet in a consultation "to establish an implementation process in which the people of the church at the congregational and judicatory levels will have full participation." The proposal envisioned the active participation by Lutherans at every level and in every sphere of church life in shaping the united church.

The AELC met in convention at the Red Carpet Inn in Milwaukee, Wisconsin, April 14–16, 1978, and received the proposal to issue "A Call for Lutheran Union." Before acting on it, convention delegates listened to presentations by the presidents of the ALC and the LCA.

David Preus, while affirming that the ALC was not tied to the status quo, stated frankly his conviction that merger was not necessary to express unity. He pointed out that the ALC had spent much time reorganizing its structure, was happy with its church life, and was more interested in devoting itself to the church's mission than in reorganizing church structure even for the purposes of Lutheran union. Preus went on to say that the ALC welcomed closer relations with the AELC and hoped that the AELC would join with the ALC and the LCA in their Joint Committee on Church Cooperation.

Robert Marshall pointed out that in expressing support for the union proposal that was before the AELC he was articulating the position of the LCA constitution, ratified many times at LCA conventions. Affirming respect for the integrity of the ALC and its position, Marshall joined David Preus in urging the AELC to join the Committee on Church Cooperation.

"A Call for Lutheran Union," when presented to the convention delegates for action, was approved with a standing ovation by the 135 AELC voting delegates. A little more than a year after its founding the AELC was determined to act more on the basis of its vision of its mission than its recognition of practical political realities.

Only the LCA among Lutheran churches in the United States approved the AELC proposal, accepting "A Call for Lutheran Union" at its convention July 12–19, 1978, without discernible dissent. At the ALC convention in Moorehead, Minnesota, October 18–24, 1978, president David Preus proposed that the ALC invite the AELC to become a non-geographic district of the ALC. That issue was never acted on because AELC president William Kohn made it clear in his address to the convention that the AELC did not want to choose between the ALC and the LCA. Instead the ALC convention accepted the recommendation of the ALC Church Council to deal with the AELC union proposal by including the AELC in the Joint ALC-LCA Committee on Church Cooperation, which was to be reconstituted as a Committee on Lutheran Unity.

At the Moorhead convention the presidents of the ALC, the LCA, and the AELC issued a joint statement declaring that the reorganized Committee on Lutheran Unity would serve as "the recognized, common vehicle by which the three church bodies will study the ways by which the churches can be more effective in mission." The agenda of the committee, they said, would include "the study of possible structural forms for the future."[8] There was to be no advance commitment to organic union, as the AELC had proposed. Nor was there to be a 1979 consultation to devise a process for union. But the AELC had been invited to press for its commitment to Lutheran union by participating in a top-level committee of the three churches.

The committee was composed of seven members each from the LCA and the ALC and two members from the AELC. All three churches were represented by their presidents. The secretaries of the ALC and the LCA were members. Both the ALC and LCA contingents included district or synod presidents, seminary presidents, and influential laypersons. C. Thomas Spitz was the other AELC member along with William Kohn. The first meeting of the Committee on Lutheran Unity was held January 22–23, 1979, in New York City. The CLU, the acronym by which the committee became known, agreed on a process and a timetable for considering cooperation and consolidation of the three churches.

The CLU decided to draft a proposal that included a definition of options for future relations and a description of a process for discussing the options within congregations and judicatories. The proposal was to be presented to the three churches at their 1980 conventions. Then, after reflecting on the results of polling congregations and judicatories on the various options, the CLU hoped to present a recommendation for future relations to the conventions of the churches in 1982.

The CLU met five more times in 1979 and 1980, grappling with how to define the options and deciding on the best ways to find out what the people of the three churches thought. A small breakthrough took place at the meeting of the CLU in Columbia, South Carolina, October 7–9, 1979. At that meeting the ALC participants, on the one hand, received assurance that the LCA, already committed by its constitution to organic union, would seriously participate in the study process and consider the alternatives that the CLU was proposing to recommend to the church. The LCA participants, on the other hand, became convinced that the ALC members of the committee were serious about submitting a definitive recommendation to the three churches in 1982. At that meeting the CLU voted to ask the three church bodies to consider holding concurrent conventions in 1982, within the same time period if not within the same city.

To the 1980 conventions of the three churches the CLU submitted its recommendations. They called for the distribution of materials to the congregations of the three churches that described the nature of the church and its mission and listed criteria for evaluating organizational structures. The materials invited the congregations to respond concerning which of the organizational structures they preferred. In addition the

CLU recommended that delegates to the 1981 conventions of districts and synods be polled in a standardized questionnaire concerning their preferences for organizational structure.

By the time of the 1980 conventions the CLU had decided that there were four organizational options for unity:

> *Option 1.* Three churches—the ALC, the AELC, and the LCA—continuing to function separately but seeking further areas of cooperation.
>
> *Option 2.* The ALC, the AELC, and the LCA functioning as nongeographic entities in a confederation responsible for international and some national functions, with the three former separate churches retaining most of their present practice, structure, responsibility, and authority.
>
> *Option 3.* Five to eight large geographic entities, each with its own polity, structure, and autonomy for functions within its geographic area but united in a church with responsibility and authority for national and international functions.
>
> *Option 4.* One church that delegates responsibility and authority to its regional units but maintains overall responsibility for the church's mission at home and abroad.

The three churches approved the recommendations submitted by CLU. At the AELC convention in Chicago, October 17–18, 1980, Robert Hoyt, assistant to ALC president David Preus, brought greetings from the ALC. "Your leaven will make the church come alive," Hoyt said, referring to the initiative that the AELC had taken in the Lutheran unity process. "You represent a new form of integrity; that gives you a power much larger than your size," he added.[9] The unity discussion moved from the rarified level of church leadership to the pastors and people. of the churches.

The AELC's "Call for Lutheran Union" and the formation of CLU helped to change the climate for relations among the ALC, the LCA, and the AELC. Lutheran union was now a public agenda. The issue of how to live together was high on the agenda for many in the three churches, even though David Preus and others in leadership positions in the ALC spoke out against anything more than a heightening of the status quo of cooperation in inter-Lutheran relations.

As Seminex began a new academic year in fall 1979, I felt it was essential that we come to terms with the significance of the developments for our future as a seminary. The AELC's initiative, and my own role in it, had produced many of the new developments. How did we as a seminary view these developments, and what were we going to do about them?

In September 1979 I arranged for meetings of the faculty to debate two theses.[10] In a formal debate setting, the faculty considered the first thesis on September 11: "The future of Christ Seminary–Seminex is in being an extension of what it is at present, a free seminary grounded in a Lutheran church body, serving all Lutherans, and stressing new forms for mission, ministry, and theological education." On September 25 the faculty debated the second thesis: "The future of Christ Seminary–Seminex is leading the way in the AELC's union effort through union or merger with one or more seminaries of the ALC and LCA as a contribution toward a united program of theological education for the Lutherans of America." I also arranged for student discussion of the theses.

After a number of group discussions it became clear that the faculty favored the second thesis; it was eager to help the AELC succeed in its union effort. At a meeting of faculty and their spouses on November 1, 1979, I proposed that we see our future in relation to Lutheran union developments and that within the perimeter of Lutheran union we keep all our options open. I reviewed the fast-breaking developments that were of significance for our future.

During summer 1979, representatives of Seminex, WTS, and the LSTC had met in Chicago and had agreed to work together cooperatively in a Doctor of Ministry program as the first in a series of potential cooperative endeavors. The agreement was the result of a meeting held a year earlier between representatives of Seminex and WTS, initiated by the latter, to discuss how the two seminaries might draw closer together. The WTS initiative was part of its effort to explore avenues of ongoing service at its location in Dubuque, Iowa, in opposition to a decision of the ALC's Board for Theological Education and Ministry that WTS should leave Dubuque and unite with Pacific Lutheran Theological Seminary in Berkeley, California. What we at Seminex did not know, and what few others knew, was that the proposed move of WTS to the West Coast was part of an informal agreement between ALC and LCA leaders in theological education.

Several years earlier the ALC and the LCA had formed a Consultation on Theological Education to work cooperatively in seminary education. The consultation played a significant role as broker in the efforts that led two ALC and LCA seminaries in Ohio to unite in forming Trinity Lutheran Seminary in Columbus and that produced the consolidation of the ALC and LCA seminaries in Minnesota into Luther Northwestern Seminary in St. Paul. According to the informal agreement, in exchange for LCA participation in the formation of Trinity Seminary, the ALC would provide major additional strength for PLTS, and WTS was supposed to move out of Dubuque to make that happen.

Unaware of these developments, we at Seminex agreed to explore how we might work together with WTS, but, following the AELC initiative of wanting relations with both ALC and LCA, we asked that the cooperative efforts should include the LSTC. I discussed the proposal with William Lesher, newly inaugurated president of LSTC, in November 1978, and secured his agreement to consider it. When I tried to bring our three groups together, I could not understand WTS's reluctance. What I did not know until later was that the ALC's Board for Theological Education and Ministry had reined in WTS because of its refusal to move from Dubuque. Later on it would specify that WTS could participate only in discussions about cooperation, not in negotiations for institutional consolidation. In summer 1979 the best we could arrange was an agreement to work together in the Doctor of Ministry program.

In March 1979 Lloyd Sheneman, executive director of the LCA's Division for Professional Leadership, made an official visit to Seminex. A year had passed since the meeting in Minneapolis in which I had received a strong negative response from Sheneman and the ALC's Walter Wietzke concerning Seminex's serving the ALC and the LCA in addition to the AELC. But a year later it was clear that Seminex was not going to go away. Our vital signs indicated that we were alive and well. Our graduates continued to knock on doors of LCA synods. In some cases they were warmly received; in others synodical leaders objected. Either way we posed a problem that had to be dealt with.

Sheneman arranged for me to visit his office in Philadelphia and for his associate, Walter Wagner, to spend some time at Seminex. The discussions regularized Seminex's relation to the LCA, producing policy statements that dealt with Seminex on the same terms as seminaries of the ALC. Toward the end of the discussions Sheneman informed me that I could expect to hear from LSTC president William Lesher, and that the proposal Lesher would make had Sheneman's endorsement.

In September 1979 Walter Wietzke, director of the ALC's Division for Theological Education and Ministry, made an official visit to Seminex. That is when I learned about Wietzke's appreciation for frank conversation. He, too, recognized that Seminex was not going to go away. Our negotiations with WTS showed that we had to be reckoned with. Wietzke proposed that the AELC be included as an official member of the ALC-LCA Consultation on Theological Education and said that he would arrange for an invitation so that AELC president William Kohn and I could attend the next consultation meeting. Wietzke told me that he had not given up on the proposed move of WTS to the West Coast. He asked me to think seriously about moving Seminex along with WTS so that PLTS could be significantly strengthened and so that there could be a response to the request of the ALC's Southern District for a full-fledged seminary in Texas.

Wietzke delivered on his promise, after he and Sheneman had discussed it, and Kohn and I were present for the meeting of the Consultation on Theological Education in Chicago December 14–15, 1979. We expressed our desire that the AELC be included as a member "for the purpose of exploring what needs to be done to effect a united program of reciprocal theological education" for the participating churches.[11] The AELC was subsequently formally invited to be a member, and Elwyn Ewald, AELC executive secretary, and Samuel Roth, chair of the Seminex Board of Directors, were named as AELC representatives and attended their first meeting in May 1980.

On October 18–21, 1979, I was present for the convention of the AELC's Pacific Regional Synod in Portland, Oregon. At an earlier convention that synod had adopted PLTS along with Seminex as the two seminaries to which it intended to relate. In an address to the convention I affirmed the Pacific Synod's desire to relate to a seminary in its own geographic territory and talked about the desire of the people of Seminex to support a united program of theological education even in advance of the formation of a new church.

Following my presentation Walter Stuhr, president of PLTS, invited me for a cup of coffee and talked to me about the possibility of developing closer relations between Seminex and his seminary. I expressed my openness to the proposal, although there was no way that PLTS, less than half the size of Seminex, could accommodate our entire faculty. Seminex did indeed have a variety of options to consider as it committed itself with the AELC to do everything possible to bring about Lutheran union.

In June 1980, at the biennial meeting of the Association of Theological Schools in Denver, William Lesher, president of LSTC, invited me to join him for breakfast. I assumed that I was finally to receive the proposal about which Sheneman had alerted me earlier. After our entrees arrived, Lesher, smiling between mouthfuls, told me that in the name of the LSTC board he was officially asking that Seminex consider moving from St. Louis to the LSTC campus.

This was the second time LSTC had made such an offer. Four years earlier, also during a meeting of the Association of Theological Schools, Arthur Arnold, who served as interim president of LSTC between Walter Wolbrecht and William Lesher, had suggested that Seminex come to the LSTC campus. That informal invitation came at a time when the English

Synod had just been formed and when the AELC was in the process of coming into existence. The Seminex Board of Directors approved the response I gave Arnold at that time—namely, that we could not afford to confuse people about our identity by moving to the LSTC campus at so crucial a time when our supporters were uniting to form a new church.

Lesher explained that he was making the invitation because the Jesuit School of Theology, which at the time occupied space on the LSTC campus, had decided to close operations in a year. LSTC would have space available, and he was authorized to negotiate with Seminex or to invite another Roman Catholic seminary to the campus. I gave my standard response, which by that time was becoming second nature to me: Yes, we would be glad to consider the offer; we were ready to consider any viable option concerning our future. We agreed to meet again at some time during the summer to consider the matter further.

On August 19, 1980, Seminex academic dean John Damm and I went to Chicago to meet with Lesher and LSTC dean Franklin Sherman. Here Lesher first proposed that the Union-Auburn model might be a way to bring the two seminaries together. Lesher suggested that it would be wise to spend a year in bringing our faculties together in order to test compatibility.

I explained Seminex's commitment to the AELC's union effort and therefore our preference for three-way conversations that would include WTS. I pointed out that we would need to have good reasons for a move in order to convince our faculty and students to leave St. Louis and to be able to maintain the support of our constituency. We agreed to talk to Ewald, Sheneman, and Wietzke about three-way cooperation between our two schools and WTS. We also agreed on a course of action to bring together representatives of the faculties and then the faculties themselves.

I shared the results of the Chicago meeting with the leaders of the AELC, with the Seminex faculty and students, and with the Seminex Board of Directors. I was encouraged by all groups to continue. The Consultation on Theological Education, meeting in Berkeley, California, October 30–November 1, 1980, approved the "exploratory" conversations between Seminex and LSTC, authorized WTS to join in on "patterns of program cooperation," and urged Ewald, Sheneman, and Wietzke to sit in on the conversations.

A delegation of Seminex faculty visited LSTC on November 25, 1980, and met with the LSTC faculty to share information about Seminex. Seminex was represented by John Damm, Everett Kalin, Ralph Klein, Edgar Krentz, Robert Smith, and me. A delegation of LSTC faculty visited Seminex on December 16, 1980, and met with the Seminex faculty to share information about LSTC. Representing LSTC were Carl Braaten, Robert Fisher, Franklin Sherman, and William Lesher.

On April 10–11, 1981, the faculty of WTS joined with the faculties of LSTC and Seminex for two days of discussion at LSTC. Carl Braaten of LSTC, Edgar Krentz of Seminex, and William Weiblen, president of WTS, made presentations and led discussions that enabled faculty members to get to know one another and to further assess mutual compatibility. Stereotypes were broken as each faculty saw its commonality with the others. By this time Lesher and I had come to describe the faculty get-togethers as a mating dance.

"Ascertaining the Future of Seminex" had become a regular item on the agenda of meetings of the Seminex Board of Directors and of faculty and students. At board meetings in spring and fall 1981 I described action on the "four fronts" in which Seminex was engaged. The first front was Seminex's own internal study of options for its future. The study was essential because some form of Lutheran union seemed more and more likely. If we did not decide on what our future would be, others would decide for us. Among the options were staying in St. Louis, moving to LSTC, joining with WTS in a new location, moving to the Southwest, distributing Seminex faculty to other seminaries, and going out of business. Faculty workshops engaged in the study in June and August 1981, and faculty representatives discussed the implications of Lutheran union for the Seminex situation with the executive committee of the AELC Board of Directors on July 24, 1981.

The second front was three-way cooperation between LSTC, WTS, and Seminex. At the meeting of the faculties of the three seminaries in April 1981 WTS president William Weiblen urged the three seminaries to work together in a number of areas, especially in staffing satellite centers of theological education in a number of locations in the West and Southwest. His proposals were explored by presidents and deans of the three seminaries at a meeting on June 12, 1981. But in a meeting of presidents and deans with Ewald, Sheneman, and Wietzke on September 21, 1981, Wietzke made it clear that the ALC's Board for Theological Education and Ministry was on record as opposed to Weiblen's satellite proposal for a number of reasons, the chief of which was financial.

The third front was closer institutional relations with LSTC, with the outside chance that WTS might be included. More than a year had passed since Lesher had invited Seminex to move to Chicago. The faculties of the two schools had had ample opportunity to assess their compatibility. LSTC had proposed the Union-Auburn consolidation as a potential model. Presidents and deans of the two schools assessed what our next steps should be at a meeting on August 12, 1981. I proposed merger as the model we should consider.

The fourth front was an agreement I helped secure from a January 1981 meeting of Lutheran seminary presidents and deans according to which we would join together in a two-year process to produce a plan for seminary education in a united church. Seminex and the AELC had been unsuccessful in getting the Consultation on Theological Education to produce a plan for the future that would help us determine how we should respond to the many proposals that were being made to us. The action by seminary presidents and deans got the attention of the consultation. At a meeting on May 28–29, 1981, the consultation appointed a task force to deal with the issue of a plan for the future of theological education.

At a meeting October 2–3, 1981, the Seminex Board of Directors considered all the factors impinging on the future of Seminex. Alice Hausman presented the proposal of a specially appointed committee, and the board adopted it. The proposal called for uniting Seminex and LSTC "as a new theological resource for the church" and invited the LSTC board to join with the Seminex board in a four-month process beginning in November 1981 to determine the purpose for the united seminary, the program needed to accomplish the purpose, the staff required for the program, financial feasibility, and the organizational structure required.[12]

At its meeting on November 20, 1981, the LSTC board of directors agreed to participate "in a study of the feasibility of a unification of the two schools at Chicago" and affirmed a statement of the LSTC faculty concerning "the priority of financial considerations and preference for separate governance structures."[13] As I was to discover, there were people among the LSTC faculty and governing board who held the opinion that Seminex's interest in uniting with LSTC was motivated by fear that we were about to go under and by the desire for an honorable way out. They preferred to maintain separate governance structures because they did not want to saddle LSTC with what they assumed were Seminex's financial weaknesses.

A meeting of presidents and deans of WTS, LSTC, and Seminex with Ewald, Sheneman, and Wietzke had been scheduled for November 30, 1981. It was agreed to expand the meeting to include the committees appointed by the Seminex and LSTC boards. At the meeting it was decided to do the first stage of the study proposed by Seminex. The study was to include an analysis of financial and legal feasibility and proposals for purpose and program of a united school. Two subcommittees were appointed to make recommendations to a second meeting scheduled for January 29, 1982.

For one of the subcommittees I drafted a statement of purpose that was refined and amended by action of the faculties of Seminex and LSTC. The second subcommittee concluded that it could not assess financial feasibility until costs based on program needs and size of faculty had been determined. When LSTC board members reviewed Seminex financial statements, they were impressed by the fiscal soundness of the Seminex operation. Nevertheless, there was considerable uncertainty even among Seminex board members whether Seminex's strong financial support could be maintained if the two seminaries were united. The two subcommittees presented their reports at the meeting on January 29, 1982, which produced first the impasse and then the breakthrough ascribed to the Holy Spirit, described at the beginning of this chapter.

◆ ◆ ◆

Our readiness to be a people on the move was put to a critical test after the breakthrough meeting of January 29, 1982, which had called for a more comprehensive plan to determine how to make use of Seminex resources in a number of Lutheran seminaries. Events moved quickly, too quickly for some in the Seminex community.

In connection with a meeting of Lutheran seminary presidents and deans at the Yahara Retreat Center in Madison, Wisconsin, in February 1982, Lloyd Sheneman convened a meeting of the presidents and deans of Seminex, LSTC, WTS, and PLTS together with the theological education executives of the ALC, AELC, and LCA. Sheneman and Walter Wietzke had agreed that LSTC, WTS, and PLTS were the seminaries that could profit the most from the resources of Seminex.

In one evening session the group reached agreement on what was from then on regularly referred to as the "deployment" of Seminex resources: ten faculty for LSTC, four to six faculty for PLTS, two faculty and the Seminex library for the WTS Hispanic ministry program in Austin, Texas; Seminex students to decide for themselves which of the three seminaries they would attend. It was further agreed that if possible the deployment should happen in time for the beginning of the 1983–84 academic year, just one year away. Sheneman reported the agreement to the full meeting of Lutheran seminary presidents and deans. In March and April 1982 the agreement was approved in principle by the AELC Board of Directors, the ALC Board for Theological Education and Ministry, and the management committee of the LCA's Division for Professional Leadership.

In a meeting in Chicago, April 2–3, 1982, the representatives of the Seminex and LSTC governing boards drafted a report of the agreement for submission to the two boards. In addition to the deployment of Seminex faculty to LSTC, the report presented the statement of purpose on which there had been agreement and a minimal description of program, according to which LSTC would continue its existing degree programs for a 400-member student body and Seminex would continue only its Doctor of Ministry program. The report further specified that Seminex faculty would be fully integrated administratively into LSTC, but Seminex would continue as a separate institution with responsibility for faculty salaries until the union of the Lutheran churches, at which time Seminex would cease to exist as a separate seminary. The report went into detail on the financial arrangements and concluded:

> In the event that gifts from the Seminex constituency would fall short of Seminex's commitment to support its faculty and staff at LSTC, the shortfall would have to be eliminated either through a reduction in program and staffing or through increased support from LSTC's supporting synods or through assistance from the ALC, AELC, and LCA, or through a combination of these approaches. The consensus of the committee is that finding a solution would be the shared responsibility of all parties involved.[14]

On April 12, 1982, Seminex academic dean Robert Smith and I flew to Berkeley, California, for meetings with the faculty of PLTS and the executive committee of the PLTS governing board to produce a similar report for our two governing boards. In early May we met with WTS representatives to do the same. In mid-May the governing boards of LSTC, PLTS, and WTS approved the recommendations for the deployment of Seminex resources.

I did my best to keep Seminex faculty and students abreast of the fast-breaking developments. Some faculty and a larger number of students felt that events were moving too quickly to allow for sufficient faculty and student reflection and contributions to the proposals. Some were convinced that Seminex was being required to make a decision with far-reaching consequences without sufficient time and faculty-student participation. Nevertheless, in early May first the faculty and then the students endorsed the proposed plan of deployment. Robert Smith and I, along with Everett Kalin, who succeeded Andrew Weyermann as dean of community life when Weyermann accepted a call to a St. Louis suburban congregation, completed initial interviews with faculty and executive staff to learn their preferences as to where they might like to serve.

Major organized opposition to the plan developed in advance of the May 20–21, 1982, meeting of the Seminex Board of Directors. Faculty members Robert Bertram and Edward Schroeder along with a significant number of students argued that the deployment plan did not go far enough. They proposed what they called the "A-B-C Plus" plan. *A* was for Austin, *B* for Berkeley, and *C* for Chicago. They argued that there should be a *plus* factor in the plan to deploy faculty to three seminaries: St. Louis should continue as a site for Seminex faculty and students. The three-legged stool needed to be remade into a four-legged chair, they argued, as they submitted their proposal to the Seminex Board of Directors.

In my response I pointed out that the deployment plan was delivering on the commitment we had made several years earlier to lead the way in the AELC toward Lutheran union. In advance of a decision of Lutheran churches to become one, we were going to make union happen in theological education. We were acting on the counsel we had received as to how Seminex could best serve in a united church. In our characteristic way of taking risks we were going to make our contribution several years in advance of Lutheran union. To keep even a part of our resources in St. Louis would vitiate it all, I pointed out. In fact, I said, to stay in St. Louis meant that we would not be able to get many takers for the move to Austin, Berkeley, or Chicago.

To ensure that all members of the Seminex community had an opportunity to be heard, I arranged for a two-hour open forum with the Board of Directors on the evening of May 20. There was direct confrontation between faculty and students over the issue of Seminex's future. Most of the remarks came from those opposed to the deployment, who saw the "A-B-C Plus" proposal as a way out. Some students lectured board members bitterly about leading Seminex down the path to destruction.

The following morning, after a review of all the factors, the board "joyfully and enthusiastically" adopted the deployment plan. It said that the deployment would:

a. enable Christ Seminary–Seminex to play a major role in reshaping theological education for the Lutherans of America by strengthening the program of two seminaries and by joining with a third seminary in exploring the possibility of a new seminary location;
b. continue the mission of Christ Seminary–Seminex in a new and expanded way by enabling faculty to influence larger numbers of future pastors, not only for our present constituency but for the people of the American Lutheran Church and the Lutheran Church in America as well;
c. provide opportunity for Christ Seminary–Seminex to be a partner in Lutheran union already now instead of five or six years from now.[15]

Before summer 1982 was over, Smith and I had worked out with Seminex faculty and staff and with the presidents of LSTC, PLTS, and WTS who would go where.

After the 1980 conventions of the ALC, AELC, and LCA had each approved the study process proposed by CLU, congregations throughout the three churches studied the materials distributed by CLU and filled out forms to state preferences concerning relations for the future. We at Seminex also participated in the study process. To help us in our reflections, we invited the bishops of the three churches (as the presidents were now termed after 1980) to share with us their thoughts on how Lutherans should relate to one another. To our delight all three bishops accepted.

LCA bishop James Crumley, who had succeeded Robert Marshall in 1978, could not be present but was represented by LCA secretary Reuben Swanson on February 18, 1981. Swanson explained the LCA's commitment to union with all who subscribe to the Lutheran confessional writings and declared that union would be more effective than cooperation in helping Lutherans carry out their mission programs.

AELC bishop William Kohn addressed the Seminex community on February 25, 1981, and explained that the AELC's commitment to unity stemmed from the desire of its members, dating back to their days in the Missouri Synod, to relate more effectively to other Lutherans for the sake of the church's mission. Although problems stood in the way of union, Kohn insisted that the opportunity for union needed to be grasped.

On March 4, 1981, ALC bishop David Preus told the Seminex community that the Lutherans of America did not need to merge into one church in order to work together at the church's mission. He argued, "A complicated national union of church bodies should be undertaken only when such action clearly will make the church more effective in mission."[16] In an unusually candid discussion with my class on "Church Union among the Lutherans of America," Preus told the students that he was not enthusiastic about merger because the LCA was larger than the ALC and therefore had more votes and consequently more power to shape a new church.

Within the LCA and the AELC the debate was over which form of union was preferred. Within the ALC the debate was over whether there should be a union. David Preus argued winsomely that cooperation was better than union. One by one, important leaders in the ALC spoke out for union: Walter Wietzke of the Division for Theological Education and Ministry; Fred Meuser, president of Trinity Lutheran Seminary in Columbus, Ohio; E. Clifford Nelson, professor at St. Olaf College; Lloyd Svensbye, president of Luther Northwestern Seminary in St. Paul, Minnesota, to mention a few.

The decision for the future was determined in the poll of convention delegates of ALC districts and of LCA and AELC synods in spring and summer 1981. The poll enabled delegates to state their preference between cooperation and union and among three options for union. Even before the results were announced, it was clear that the delegates of all three churches preferred union.

In September 1981 the results were released, showing that 18,504 delegates at district and synod conventions had voted in favor of union by 77 percent. Greatest support for union was in the AELC, with 96 percent in favor. Second was the LCA with 87 percent support. The ALC delegates backed union by 64 percent. The union option that received strongest support was the fourth one, calling for a strong national church with regional and local subdivisions. David Preus, recognizing that the people of the ALC were strongly in favor of union, announced that he would support their preference with enthusiasm.

The ALC's relations with the LCA and the AELC were given a strong boost in July 1981, when the LCMS at a convention in St. Louis voted by 590 to 494 to end relations of fellowship with the ALC. The Missouri Synod finally took the action threatened for a decade, citing unresolved differences on the inspiration, inerrancy, and authority of the Scriptures; the meaning of subscription to the Lutheran Confessions; the nature and basis of fellowship; the ordination of women to the pastoral office; membership in ecumenical organizations; and practices concerning lodges and similar organizations. The ALC could no longer nurture its tenuous relations with the LCMS.

After the poll results were released, the CLU moved with dispatch to submit a recommendation to the 1982 conventions of the three churches, asking them to commit themselves to union. The recommendation called for the creation of a Commission for a New Lutheran Church, composed of seventy members broadly representative of the churches, which was to work toward proposals for a new church according to a timetable that would enable the new church to begin functioning by January 1, 1988. Of the seventy commission members, thirty-one each were to come from the ALC and the LCA and eight from the AELC. It was recommended that half of the members be from the laity, and half of the clergy be parish pastors; at least 40 percent of the members be women; and at least one-sixth be from ethnic and racial minorities in the church. The bishops of the ALC, LCA, and AELC named Arnold Mickelson, ALC secretary, as the chief staff person of the commission, and William Kinnison, president of LCA-related Wittenberg University in Springfield, Ohio, as the chair.

The day of decision was September 8, 1982. By prearrangement the three churches held concurrent conventions, but in separate locations. The ALC met in San Diego, California; the AELC in Cleveland, Ohio; the LCA in Louisville, Kentucky. Also by prearrangement there was to be a telephone conference hookup among the conventions to report the results of the ballots on the CLU recommendations.

At approximately 5:00 P.M. Eastern time, with AELC church historian Martin Marty serving as moderator in Cleveland, the delegates of the three conventions listened to the reports of the balloting. LCA bishop James Crumley announced that LCA delegates had voted 669 to 11 in favor of forming a new church. AELC bishop William Kohn reported that the 136 AELC delegates had voted unanimously for union.

The big concern was whether the ALC would vote for union and if so whether it would be by the necessary two-thirds majority. With a hush over all three conventions as delegates strained to hear, ALC bishop David Preus announced that the ALC had voted 897 to 90 for a new church, a preference of more than 90 percent.

After several minutes of pandemonium at all three conventions Martin Marty set the decision within its historical context and led the three gatherings in a prayer that asked the Spirit of God to call to "ever deeper levels of unity" and to enlighten with the fire of Pentecost "so that we can see our new mission."[17] Fellow Lutherans in Cleveland, Louisville, and San Diego united in singing the hymn that the 1973 LCMS New Orleans convention had seared into my heart, "The Church's one foundation is Jesus Christ, her Lord."

I was overcome with awe as I reflected on the pilgrimage that had brought me from St. Louis through New Orleans to Cleveland. The moment was too solemn for me to join in the handshaking and hugging going on among the AELC delegates. I quietly withdrew to get my sermon ready for the evening Eucharist, deeply moved that through the grace and power of God Seminex and the AELC had served as a yeast for union in the bushel of flour.

15 ——◆
ONE CHURCH
MADE NEW

"O Lord! O Lord, the smoke!"

The preacher was Walter M. Stuhr, president of Pacific Lutheran Theological Seminary of Berkeley, California. He spoke the words dramatically from the lofty pulpit of historic Saint Paulus Lutheran Church in downtown San Francisco, a Gothic structure that had survived the 1906 San Francisco earthquake and fire, whose congregation had left the Lutheran Church–Missouri Synod to help form the Association of Evangelical Lutheran Churches and its Pacific Regional Synod. The billowing smoke of incense had risen high to the wooden rafters of the church at the beginning of the service to accompany the words Stuhr was now quoting in his sermon. Everyone knew about the smoke. Not only had they seen it; the sweet fragrance of incense filled the air.

Stuhr was speaking to a pan-Lutheran congregation that had assembled on Friday, February 13, 1987, for a special service of Holy Communion written and composed by Christ Seminary–Seminex professors Walter Wangerin, Jr. and Paul Manz to help Lutherans celebrate the formation of a new Lutheran church. Entitled *"Una Sancta:* A Mass in Thanksgiving for the Unity of the Body of Christ," the service provided new words and new music for the church's historic eucharistic liturgy. Stuhr made it clear that he was talking not just about the smoke of incense but the "smoke" of Seminex and the AELC. With a smile on his lips to accompany his ever-smiling eyes, Stuhr asked the assembled congregation a series of questions:

317

What is it that makes a band of renegade professors think that they *can* or even *ought* to be supported by the voluntary contributions of individuals and congregations for even one year, let alone ten or twelve years? What is it that makes a relative handful of dissident Lutherans interject themselves into the counsels of the LCA and ALC, as equal partners, and then say, "As long as we're at it, why not form a totally new Lutheran church?" And succeed! "Just as we planned it," I can almost hear them say. What is it that gives a couple of members of that community the temerity to compose a whole liturgy, hymns and all, and then present it with the expectation that it will be used to inaugurate the new Lutheran church?[1]

Stuhr said that he raised the questions to acknowledge the "smoke" of Seminex and the AELC and "to express a word of gratitude for their courage, commitment, and creativity—for the smoke signals the presence of the purifying fire of God in their ministry."

The San Francisco service was one of fifteen such celebrations in major metropolitan centers around the United States sponsored by Seminex and the congregations of the AELC in cooperation with the synods and districts of the Lutheran Church in America and the American Lutheran Church. Jeannette Bauermeister, now Seminex's vice-president, who had fulfilled a lifelong dream by completing seminary course work and being ordained to pastoral ministry, was helping to lead the service. Paul Manz, who composed the music for the service, was the organist.

As in the other locations, we invited the local Lutheran bishops to join in the service with us. Participating were Stanley Olson, bishop of the LCA's Pacific Southwest Synod; Walter Grumm, bishop of the AELC's Pacific Regional Synod; and Bruce Lundberg, pastor of a congregation in Auburn, California, representing Nelson Trout, bishop of the ALC's South Pacific District. Creating a service to help Lutherans celebrate the formation of a new church was Wangerin's idea. I learned about it in a conversation with Paul Manz when I talked to him about a memorial for my sister, Wilma T. Weyermann, who had died in the summer of 1983, when Seminex left St. Louis. A memorial fund had been established in her name at Seminex. Andrew Weyermann, her husband, who had been a member of the Seminex faculty and was now serving a congregation of the LCA in Wilmette, Illinois, had proposed that we use the memorial funds to commission a musical work in her memory.

When in fall 1984 I raised the idea of a musical work with Paul Manz, who had become a member of the Seminex faculty a year earlier, he pulled out of his jacket pocket a letter he had received a few days earlier from Walter Wangerin, proposing that the two of them collaborate in the creation of a new eucharistic service for use at the time of the formation of the new Lutheran church and for ecumenical celebrations of unity. I arranged for a meeting with Manz and Wangerin, at which it was agreed that Seminex would commission them to create the proposed eucharistic service in memory of Wilma T. Weyermann and would use the memorial fund to help publish and distribute the work.

During the 1985–86 academic year we included the Kyrie and the Hymn of the Day from the *"Una Sancta"* service as part of the Paul Manz Hymn Festivals, which Seminex had sponsored in two dozen locations around the country since 1983. The hymn festivals became the center-piece of our efforts to keep in touch with our constituency and to encour-age financial support. The *"Una Sancta"* service was published in printed form several months before the September 1986 decision of the ALC, the AELC, and the LCA to form the Evangelical Lutheran Church in America a year later. So we decided to use the *"Una Sancta"* service in place of our regular hymn festival program for the 1986–87 academic year to gather the Lutherans of the three churches together to give thanks to God in advance of the formation of the ELCA.

In the New York metropolitan area, Saint Peter's Church, a congre-gation of the LCA whose modern church was nestled in the base of the huge Citicorp building on Lexington Avenue and 54th Street in Man-hattan, served as the location for the worship. In Austin, Texas, the site for the service was a congregation of the ALC, St. Martin's Lutheran Church. In St. Louis and Seattle the service was celebrated in the grand space of Episcopal cathedrals. Whatever the location, Lutherans of three church bodies came together to sing a new song for a new church.

In the rest of his sermon at St. Paulus Church, Walter Stuhr used the themes of *"Una Sancta"* to describe the significance of the formation of the ELCA. He said, "The ELCA is and must become our reenactment of the Covenant, now as a united group of Lutherans, to obey God's *voice, God's* voice, and claim our place as God's own people, now in the name of Jesus Christ, the new covenant." Stuhr went on to say that the ELCA is and must become the vision of *"empery,"* a word used repeatedly in the opening hymn of the service; that is, Stuhr explained, the ELCA must become the vision of the kingdom of God that is the unfinished work of the covenant. Finally, Stuhr said that the ELCA is and must become a contribution to healing the wounded Body of Christ, divided as it is by denominations and by internal struggles between women and men, laity and clergy.

The themes of covenant, kingdom, and unity all came together fol-lowing Stuhr's sermon as clergy and people gathered around the table of the Lord for the Great Thanksgiving. With the words of Wangerin and the music of Manz we raised our hearts and voices in doxology for the vision of unity present for us in our own new church:

One body and one Breathing Spirit,
One Lord, one faith, one Church made new,
One God and Father for the children:
    By One in All are all in you!
All glory to you, now and ever.
All glory. Amen.[2]

◆ ◆ ◆

The proposal to invite Paul Manz to become a member of the Seminex faculty emerged out of a planning session while Seminex was still in St. Louis and we were preparing for the deployment. A short, compact man with long, wispy, curly hair and a carefully trimmed salt-and-pepper beard, Manz had become world-famous as an organist and composer of hymn improvisations. He was in constant demand for organ recitals and hymn festivals, for musical workshops, and as a consultant in the building of organs. He had been the cantor of Mount Olive Lutheran Church in Minneapolis and member of the faculty of Concordia College in St. Paul, an institution of the LCMS.

After the Missouri Synod's convention in New Orleans Manz became an active member of Evangelical Lutherans in Mission and played benefit recitals and hymn festivals for ELIM and for Seminex in the heat of the Missouri Synod controversy. He resigned his faculty position in 1976 when the governing board of the college in St. Paul required him to discontinue his activity in behalf of ELIM and Seminex. Mount Olive Lutheran Church, whose pastor was Alton F. Wedel, a member of the ELIM board of directors, gave Manz a full-time position and called him to share his talents and gifts with the church at large. From his base in Minneapolis Manz had become an active member of the Seminex community, playing for special services, teaching in our educational programs, assisting us with counsel in the purchase of an organ.

Early in January 1983 Manz became a topic of conversation at a working luncheon for four of us who were going to share administrative responsibilities for Seminex in its deployed state. Seated in a booth with me in the Ladle restaurant on Sarah Avenue in midtown St. Louis were Jeannette Bauermeister, our director of business management; Christopher Eldredge, assistant director of recruitment; and David Krause, who had succeeded Mark Roock as director of development when Roock left to accept a development position at Washington University. We were talking about ways of supporting the Seminex faculty and considering whether we could get enough support for endowed professorships. Krause smiled through his blond beard and suggested that Manz's popularity might make it possible for us to fund a Paul Manz chair of music. Bauermeister looked wistfully at us as she toyed with the Ladle's diet plate and said, "Wouldn't it be great if we could put Paul Manz into the chair?"

We all looked at one another and realized we had come up with an idea worth pursuing. We discussed with enthusiasm how we could make it work and how Manz could be of service to Seminex in our efforts to communicate with our constituency and to raise funds during the time of our deployment. We were confident that through Seminex-sponsored recitals and hymn festivals Manz would raise more for us than the cost of his salary.

Later that day Bauermeister broached the idea to Manz. I talked it over with William Lesher, president of Lutheran School of Theology at Chicago, and with Seminex board chair Samuel Roth. Krause phoned David Abrahamson, former Seminex board member who was pastor of the Evangelical Lutheran Church of St. Luke in Chicago, about the possibility of Manz serving the congregation as cantor. Everyone expressed interest. By February the Seminex board had issued a call to Manz to join the Chicago-bound contingent of our faculty in September, and by April he had formally accepted.

It was natural, then, for Seminex to propose faculty status to Walter Wangerin, Jr., when he and Manz began collaborating on the "Una Sancta" service. Wangerin was a 1977 graduate of Seminex who was serving as pastor of an AELC congregation in Evansville, Indiana, acclaimed for his work as an author and as a preacher. Tall and thin, with sensitive blue eyes, dark brown hair, and a droopy mustache, Wangerin had decided to devote himself full-time to a ministry of writing. In 1985 we claimed him as an adjunct member of our faculty and made his services available on a part-time basis to LSTC.

During Seminex's final year in St. Louis much of our time and effort was devoted to planning and preparing for the deployment of our resources to the three other seminaries. The decisions as to which faculty would go where were made cooperatively by faculty members, the Seminex administration, and the presidents and deans of the three seminaries. Four members of the Seminex faculty committed themselves to serve at PLTS in Berkeley, California: Carl Graesser, George Hoyer, Everett Kalin, and Robert Smith. Three of the four were exegetes and were to provide PLTS needed strength in the biblical area. PLTS was in the process of revising its curriculum, and these four professors participated in meetings in Berkeley and in St. Louis to assist in the final revisions.

H. Lucille Hager agreed to be a part of the WTS program in Austin, Texas, where she would be responsible for the Seminex library. Because the Austin program was in collaboration with the Episcopal Theological Seminary of the Southwest and took place on the campus of that seminary, it agreed to house most of the Seminex library on the ground floor of the Episcopal seminary library and to store the remainder at Texas Lutheran College in Seguin, Texas, where it could be readily retrieved when needed. Several faculty to whom we proposed a move to Austin decided for personal reasons to stay in St. Louis. After the deployment was in effect, we worked out arrangements with WTS for John Constable to teach in the Austin program.

Nine of the Seminex faculty agreed to move to LSTC: Mark Bangert, Paul Bauermeister, Robert Bertram, Robert Conrad, Frederick Danker, David Deppe, Kurt Hendel, Ralph Klein, and Edgar Krentz. They complemented LSTC's strength in historical and systematic theology with major stress in biblical studies and in the practice of ministry. They were joined by Paul Manz and by two retired faculty members, William Danker and Leonhard Wuerrfel, who wanted to become part of the seminary community in Chicago. Seminex faculty agreed to adapt themselves to the LSTC curriculum until the two faculties could together produce a revised curriculum.

Out of the planning process came a decision that a core group of administrators would move to Chicago with the LSTC-bound faculty contingent to be responsible for the management of the Seminex operation in deployment and for raising the funds necessary to undergird the faculty's work. Agreeing to serve with me in administering Seminex in its deployment were Jeannette Bauermeister, Christopher Eldredge, David Krause, and Rosemary Lipka.

Early in the planning process we sought the counsel of our accrediting agency, the Association of Theological Schools. We were informed that to continue as an accredited educational institution it was necessary for us to maintain at least one degree program of our own. We decided to retain as our own the Doctor of Ministry program, a degree we had begun to offer a few years earlier for those who were engaged in the practice of ministry and wanted to work toward an advanced professional degree. We agreed that our faculty would teach in the programs of the other three seminaries for all other degrees, including the basic Master of Divinity degree. Therefore at the beginning of the 1983–84 academic year Seminex's only students were D. Min. students. Other Seminex students who were continuing their studies were counted in the programs of the schools they had chosen to attend.

The state of Illinois contributed to our decision about which degree program to offer. As a Missouri corporation Seminex had to register as a "foreign agent" to award degrees in Illinois. The Illinois Secretary of State would not approve our application without the endorsement of the Illinois Department of Higher Education. As academic dean Robert Smith and I learned in a visit to the department's offices in Springfield, Seminex had to apply for degree-granting authority and could begin to grant degrees only one year after the application had been approved.

Seminex was anything but a stranger to the Illinois Department of Higher Education. Late in 1974 Harold M. Olsen, chair of the Board of Control of Concordia Theological Seminary in Springfield, Illinois, had formally challenged the legality of the degrees awarded by LSTC to Seminex students the previous May under the arrangements of the Joint Project for Theological Education (see Chapter 11, pp. 216–18, 229). After investigation the department director, John W. Goudy, ruled that no fraud or other irregularities were involved. Later, when the administration of Missouri Synod president Jacob Preus decided to move the seminary from Springfield to Fort Wayne, Indiana, Olsen solicited the help of Seminex treasurer Richard McAuliffe to prevent the move. There was little that McAuliffe could do.

William Kelley, associate director of the higher education department, understood the Seminex situation and was helpful to Smith and me. He suggested that the best and simplest procedure would be for Seminex to limit itself to the Doctor of Ministry degree. Smith and I produced the voluminous material required to accompany the application for degree-granting authority. The request was approved on November 1, 1983. One year later we had authority to grant the D. Min. degree in Illinois.

We decided to complete our work in St. Louis with a series of special celebrations. In March we launched a special thanks-offering campaign, entitled "Founded in Courage—Continuing in Hope," and raised close to $100,000 to help us make the moves to Austin, Berkeley, and Chicago. Under the supervision of seminary relations director Larry Neeb we produced a special illustrated commemorative booklet that highlighted the ten years of Seminex in St. Louis.

We created an official alumni/ae association and invited our former students back for a three-day academic convocation prior to commencement under the theme "No Continuing City." Featured speakers included Walter Brueggemann of Eden Theological Seminary in St. Louis, who had been instrumental in the founding of Seminex; David Lotz, a fellow Lutheran teaching at Union Theological Seminary in New York City; Will Herzfeld, pastor from Oakland, California, who was vice-president of the AELC; and our own alumnus Walter Wangerin, Jr. Paul Manz teamed up with the Seminex Chorus under the direction of Mark Bangert for a presentation of Handel's "Dettingen *Te Deum*" at Christ Church

Cathedral, the Episcopal church that was the setting for so many celebrations of worship during our time in St. Louis.

Our final commencement in St. Louis was, as many described it,[3] a bittersweet occasion. There was sadness that it was the last commencement of our own, but there was also joy over the continuing and expanding mission of Seminex in three other locations in anticipation of the union of three Lutheran churches. We had, after all, decided to lay down our institutional life for the sake of the greater mission of the church. Commencement itself took place diagonally across the street from Seminex in the house of worship of Third Baptist Church. The reception was held, by special arrangement with the management, next door to Seminex in the grand refurbished lobby of the historic Fox Theater, dominated by two majestic plaster-of-paris lions that flanked the staircase leading to the balcony.

We conducted our final summer session and then held an auction to sell off our meager worldly goods. In a hot and humid St. Louis summer without air conditioning, we packed up whatever we intended to take with us to our three locations. The library was moved first, and Lucille Hager attended to its installation in Austin. We assisted faculty and families in their moves. Finally, after everyone else had moved out, Jeannette Bauermeister and I supervised the move of files and furniture to Chicago.

The temperature was over one hundred degrees when the moving van arrived at LSTC. We concluded that through the weather Chicago had found a way to make St. Louisans feel at home. We moved into what a few years earlier had been the site of the Jesuit School of Theology and took over two apartments on the first floor of the building for our administrative offices. The rooms were small, the windows looking out onto brick walls, but we transformed the place into our home. We affixed to the glass doors at the front of the building the sign Marcie Bremer Childs had presented to us at our June commencement in behalf of the Seminex Guild to give us identity in our new location. Seminex had now moved into the fifth address in its ten years: 5430 South University Avenue, Chicago.

Some of Seminex's best contributors warned us against moving out of St. Louis, predicting that the deployment would be a financial disaster. They warned us that our supporters still within the Missouri Synod, who by our estimates provided one-third of the gifts we received, would discontinue their gifts because of the move. They pointed out that many of our friends in the AELC would stop giving on the assumption that our financial needs were now being met through the ALC and the LCA. We too wondered how we were going to appeal for gifts without a seminary of our own.

After the move that prophecy seemed to be coming true. For several weeks we received almost no mail, even though we had provided all our supporters with contribution envelopes bearing our new address. When contributions did start coming in, receipts were below the usual low level of August and September.

The core group, as we called the administrators now responsible for Seminex, put heads together and worked at finding a solution. We shared the problem frankly in a mailing to all our supporters. We produced a special issue of *Together*, our Seminex newsletter, featuring what we called "The ABC Connection." There we personalized what Seminex was doing with action photos of faculty and staff in their assigned locations in Austin, Berkeley, and Chicago and with quotations from them describing their new ministry. In addition, we mobilized the faculty to telephone the pastors of all the congregations that were supporting us to urge their continuing support.

A trip to San Francisco provided an idea that was to make the difference for our financial survival. I had agreed to preach at the opening service of the new academic year for PLTS on September 14, 1983. Paul Manz needed to be on the West Coast at that time for a recital. We decided to arrange for a Seminex-sponsored Paul Manz hymn festival in San Francisco in connection with my trip and to have an alumnae gathering and a dinner for our donors in the San Francisco bay area. Jeannette Bauermeister and David Krause accompanied Manz and me to the West Coast to make arrangements.

We could not have been happier with the results. The alumni turned out in force for a luncheon at a bay restaurant, some coming from as far as two hundred miles away. The donors' dinner in the fellowship hall of St. Paulus Lutheran Church demonstrated to us that at least our supporters in the San Francisco area were pleased with the deployment. The brainstorm occurred in connection with the hymn festival. In the offering during the service about two hundred people in the congregation contributed some fifteen hundred dollars. We asked one another what would happen if we *really* tried to raise money. What if we told people that their hymn festival offerings would be matched?

On our return to Chicago I arranged to meet with Ruth Graefen, who with her husband, Rudolph, was a major Chicago area contributor to Seminex. Her husband was now in a nursing home suffering from Alzheimer's disease. After attending worship at Good Shepherd Lutheran Church in Palos Heights, Illinois, I proposed that she come to dinner with me and my wife. At dinner I explained Seminex's needs to Mrs. Graefen and told her about our experience in San Francisco and our desire to use hymn festivals to help raise funds. I asked her if she would be willing to use her next gift to match offerings received in our hymn festival program. Looking at me with her smiling eyes, she told me I could count on a gift of $10,000.

We pulled out all the stops in planning the next hymn festival for the New York City area in November. Former academic dean John Damm, now serving as pastor of Saint Peter's Church in Manhattan, agreed to make the church facilities available to us. We were astounded at the results. We had assumed that the $10,000 matching gift would be enough to cover gifts received at several hymn festivals. Instead, almost all of it was needed to match the gifts received in New York.

We scrambled to find major donors who would agree to match gifts received at a hymn festival scheduled for St. Louis in early December. Three donors pledged to match gifts up to $12,000. The St. Louis hymn festival provided us with $15,000 in offerings, several thousand more than the matching funds we had available. The pursuit for matching gifts continued as we scheduled hymn festivals in other metropolitan areas through the rest of the academic year. By the end of the year we had received more than $115,000 through the hymn festival program, making the difference between disaster and survival in deployment.

For the next three and one-half years hymn festivals were at the center of our fund-raising efforts, and in four years we sponsored eighty-nine such events and raised more than $717,000. Not only were the events rewarding financially but we also met with Lutherans and shared the Seminex spirit with them. In place after place people of the Missouri Synod told us that we provided them the opportunity to be together again with their friends in the AELC. The people of the ALC and the LCA came to the hymn festivals to celebrate unity.

Seminex did indeed foster Lutheran union in theological education. Our four faculty at PLTS strengthened the programs at that seminary and enabled PLTS to expand its contribution to the Graduate Theological Union, an ecumenical enterprise in theological education in Berkeley. The Seminex professors were in demand as essayists and lecturers throughout the western region of the church; I received many letters and phone calls expressing appreciation for their presence at PLTS. The Seminex library provided a major new theological resource for WTS's program in Austin. The arrival of John Constable made it possible for WTS to expand its Hispanic ministry program. In Chicago LSTC's president William Lesher made it clear that he viewed the unification of the Seminex and LSTC faculties as the beginning of a new school. Lesher led the way in ensuring the full integration of Seminex within the Chicago campus. The Seminex organ and altar enabled the people of Seminex to at home in chapel worship. Lesher made sure that the governing boards of the two schools consulted and met together regularly.

Seminex professors were given leadership responsibilities within the LSTC faculty. Edgar Krentz was named chair of one division. Ralph Klein was designated to lead the task force responsible for revising the curriculum. After a year of cooperative activity the Doctor of Ministry program was combined under Seminex auspices with Robert Conrad as director. Jeannette Bauermeister and I were included as members of the LSTC president's cabinet and participated in LSTC's strategic planning efforts. Ralph Klein expanded Seminex's theological journal, *Currents in Theology and Mission*, into a publication of the faculties of all four seminaries cooperating in the deployment. As I traveled around the country meeting with friends and supporters, I reported the good news: What we had planned was happening just the way we planned it. Our friends and supporters provided the financial resources that enabled us to carry out our mission.

As Seminex began the process of laying down its institutional life for the sake of Lutheran union in theological education, the Commission for a New Lutheran Church began the work of drafting proposals for the formation of a new Lutheran church. With its seventy members, the commission was unique in the history of church union efforts. The commission was broadly representative of the constituency of the uniting churches and not just of the key people in the churches' power structures. The recommendation for membership resulted in 40 percent of the commissioners being women and 16 percent being black, Hispanic, Asian, and Native Americans. Although this is not the place for a comprehensive history of the CNLC, the outcome of its work is a part of the story of Seminex and the AELC.

I was not included among those whom the AELC Board of Directors had selected for the AELC's eight slots on the CNLC. There was an uproar when the people of the AELC learned that the board, for the practical reason of meeting the variety of criteria involved in filling the eight positions, planned to name the AELC representatives without providing for an election at the AELC convention. In response the board reversed itself, submitting the eight names as recommendations but allowing for the possibility of additional nominations to specific slots whose criteria were very explicit.

Along with C. Thomas Spitz, the AELC's ecumenical officer, I was nominated to the slot designated as "clergy leader," for which the board had recommended Samuel Roth, the chair of the Seminex governing board. After several ballots I was elected. Isaac Freeman, a layman from Atlanta and former member of the AELC Board of Directors, and I were the two persons elected by the AELC convention who had not been nominated by the AELC board. I therefore felt a special responsibility to represent the people of the AELC in the deliberations of the CNLC. Also elected as AELC representatives were the bishop, William Kohn; the vice-president, Will Herzfeld; the executive secretary, Elwyn Ewald; Loretta Walker, a laywoman from Oklahoma City; Alice Meyer, a lay-woman from Washington, D.C.; and Janet Baumgartener, a member of the teaching ministry from Wausau, Wisconsin. The AELC delegation consisted of three clergy, one teacher, and four laity; three blacks and five whites; five men and three women; a slate that adequately fulfilled the goals of inclusiveness.

The AELC representatives had a particular role to play within the CNLC, not just within the commission itself but also in its committees and task forces. Commission members knew that their assignment was to produce a new Lutheran church, not just to merge the existing ones. They also tried to shape their decisions by their commitment to the future rather than by their loyalty to the past. Yet they also knew there was much that was good that needed to be preserved in the existing structures. At times it was necessary for AELC people to mediate in the struggles between contending ALC and LCA positions. That task was especially important in the meetings of the church body bishops and was carried out well, first by William Kohn, and then by Will Herzfeld after Kohn's retirement as bishop.

One standoff between ALC and LCA commissioners was over the location of the headquarters of the new church, with ALC people favoring Minneapolis and LCA people Chicago. Milwaukee emerged as a compromise choice under the forceful promotion of William Kohn. Then the battle lines were redrawn with many ALC commissioners wanting Milwaukee and many LCA representatives urging that the present headquarter sites of Philadelphia, New York, and Minneapolis be retained. Chicago was ultimately chosen only because the AELC board of directors reintroduced that location into the discussion and the AELC's Elwyn Ewald made a strong case for it. On the issue of site the AELC representatives tilted in the direction of the LCA.

On the issue of pensions the AELC representatives tilted toward the ALC. Rarely were the divisions in voting according to church body delegations, but pensions was one such occasion. Responsive to pressures from their constituency, LCA representatives spoke out and voted against the carefully crafted compromise that Ewald had helped produce. AELC people voted with ALC commissioners to preserve the compromise.

At the first meeting of the commission, in September 1982, a coalition developed that grew in numbers over the ensuing years until it comprised about two-thirds of the CNLC. The coalition included most of the women members and those whom we learned to call "persons of color and/or persons whose primary language is other than English."[4] At the first meeting the coalition debated the process that the commission was expected to follow and brought about the use of the consensus model of decision-making along with the use of the deliberative process under *Robert's Rules of Order*. The coalition stood together on a number of issues before the CNLC, particularly the inclusiveness principle and the proposals for representation in the new church. The AELC members of the CNLC were part of the coalition.

I was personally involved in the theological issues before the commission. Appointed to the Task Force on Theology, I produced the document that focused the issues for the task force and was one of those who helped draft the task force report. The CNLC adopted the task force recommendations concerning the new church's confession of faith, and I served with the LCA's John Reumann and the ALC's Gerhard Forde in writing and editing the confession of faith ultimately adopted as Article II of the constitution of the ELCA. Although the rest of the Report of the Task Force on Theology was not officially adopted by the CNLC, it was used as a foundation document. I was pleased to see how, little by little, not only the substance but the very phrasing of the report on matters of church's membership, mission, and ministry were incorporated into CNLC documents.

The issue of membership was supposed to be one on which the ALC and the LCA would be at loggerheads. According to their respective constitutions, the ALC defined the church's members as the congregations, the LCA defined them as congregations and clergy. At issue was the relation of clergy to the congregation and the church at large, and representation of the church in its assemblies. The proposal of the Task Force on Theology, which the CNLC accepted, cut through the problem by defining membership theologically as the baptized members of the congregations and by leaving the issues of representation and clergy responsibility to be decided in other contexts.

Contrary to the criticism of some outside the CNLC, a specific ecclesiology, or understanding of the nature of the church, was at the base of the commission's proposals on organization. That ecclesiology was implicit in the definition of members as the baptized people of the congregations. It was made explicit in the description of the church as the people of God in the constitutional article on the church's purpose. According to the constitutional documents, the ELCA should be understood not as one of the denominational organizations of Christendom but as an organizational expression of people of God who make a specific confession of the faith of all the people of God.

The CNLC's commitment to interdependence as an organizational principle was another evidence of the ecclesiology at work. That ecclesiology affirmed the nature of the church as both local assembly and universal fellowship and declared that the church was always both at the same time. It affirmed that any local assembly gathered around Word and Sacrament for the sake of the church's mission was "church." Not only was the congregation "church"; so also was the synod or district and the churchwide organization. Each in its own way was a local assembly that gave expression to the universal fellowship. None was more "church" than the other, and so the relationship was one of interdependence.

One of the several issues raised in spring 1986 by the bishops and the executive council of the LCA had to do with whether the CNLC sufficiently affirmed the corporate nature of the church. The LCA leaders argued that the CNLC proposals were too congregational in their emphasis and insisted that changes would have to be made if they were to support the CNLC proposals. Many people began to wonder aloud whether the problem would not derail the efforts to form a new church.

I could not understand the uproar. I was sure that the CNLC members agreed with the principles the LCA leaders were enunciating. I was therefore not surprised at how the CNLC dealt with the issue at its final meeting in June 1986. ALC member David Hardy proposed including in the ELCA constitution a new article on the nature of the church that was taken word for word from the LCA constitution. Hardy's proposal was adopted unanimously.

The ecclesiological understanding together with an assessment of what was necessary for ELCA Christians to be faithful in mission lay at the root of the CNLC's decisions on representation and inclusiveness. If the church is the people of God and if there are many more laity than clergy, then laity ought to have significant representation in church assemblies. The figure of 60 percent laity and 40 percent clergy was a compromise that the commission reached in response to the negative reaction of clergy to its original proposals of an even higher percentage of laity. If the church is the people of God and if there are at least as many women as men in the church, then women ought to be represented equally with men in church assemblies—another of the principles of representation in the ELCA. If we wanted the ELCA to be an organizational expression of the people of God and not an ethnic denomination with a Northern European tradition, then it would be necessary to reach out in mission to the people of an increasingly multicultural America. To be able to do so, the ELCA needed to exhibit its own multicultural diversity. The CNLC adopted provisions for the inclusion of people of color and of primary language other than English in assemblies and among the church's staff.

The understanding of the church as the people of God required the CNLC to propose a strong ecumenical posture. The people of the ELCA were not alone the people of God. So the documents produced by the CNLC affirmed unity with all Christians and committed the ELCA to act in behalf of the church's unity.

There was no question within the CNLC that the new church should be ecumenical, the only question was *how*. The issue came to a head over membership in ecumenical organizations, especially the National Council of the Churches of Christ in the United States of America. Most of the commissioners from the LCA, which was a member of the NCC, favored membership; most of those from the ALC, which was not a member, opposed it. Leaders of the two churches worked out a compromise, according to which the ELCA would continue membership in any ecumenical organizations in which one or more of the uniting churches were members and would review the question of membership in all ecumenical organizations at the first regular assembly of the church body. Instead of making the issue a battleground between two churches and requiring a resolution before union, the CNLC postponed the decision until after union.

Ministry was one of the most controversial issues before the CNLC, yet the areas of agreement were much more extensive than the few areas on which there was disagreement. The article on ministry in the ELCA constitution affirms that the call or appointment to specific ministries in the church takes place within the context of the ministry of the baptized people of God. "Within the people of God and for the sake of the Gospel ministry entrusted to all believers, God has instituted the office of ministry of Word and Sacrament. To carry out this ministry, this church calls and ordains qualified persons."[5]

The issue on which there was disagreement was whether there could or should be more than one form of the "office of ministry of Word and Sacrament." I represented the AELC position on the subject and served on most of the groups created to deal with the question. The final CNLC committee to deal with the ministry issue, chaired by the LCA's William Lazareth, used much of the material on ministry in the theology task force report to propose the compromise that succeeded: to bring the existing forms of ministry of the three churches into the new church, to add only to the ranks of pastors and lay professionals for a six-year period, and during the six years to engage in a study of the nature and forms of ministry that would result in a decision on what form(s) the new church's ministry should take for the future.

The CNLC advocated freedom and flexibility in dealing with organization and structure. On the assumption that people should be involved in decisions that affect them, the CNLC provided most guidance for structure at the churchwide level, much less at the regional and synod level, and least of all at the congregational level. It specifically proposed that "congregations and synods shall be free to organize in such manner as each deems appropriate for its jurisdiction."[6] It provided for an ongoing process to review the churchwide organization's function and structure and to develop recommendations for change.

I was personally happy with the results of the CNLC's work. Did it really succeed in producing a new church? In many ways the ELCA is a fascinating blend of outlooks and structures that were present in the ALC and the LCA. Nowhere is the blending of ALC and LCA more evident than in theological education. The ALC operated a system of national seminaries with churchwide participation in their governance and funding. The LCA seminaries were regional, relating to specific numbers of synods and receiving governance and financial support from those synods. In the ELCA the nine former seminaries of the ALC and LCA are seminaries of the whole church, but each seminary has a relation and responsibility to two regions of the ELCA and to the synods within them. So, for example, the LSTC and WTS, two seminaries cooperating with Seminex, were paired for cooperative relations with the synods of regions four and five. The ELCA churchwide organization and the synods of particular regions participate in the governance and the financial support of the seminaries.

Yet there is something new about the way theological education is handled in the ELCA. In the ALC, seminaries were the responsibility of the Division for Theological Education and Ministry, where "theological education" meant seminaries and "ministry" referred to what pastors do. In the LCA, seminaries were the responsibility of the Division for Professional Leadership, which included not just pastors and clergy candidates but deaconesses and lay professionals. In the ELCA, seminaries are the responsibility of the Division for Ministry, where ministry is understood broadly as including the baptized people of God as well as pastors and those in other forms of ministry, now brought together under the umbrella term *associates in ministry*. The Division for Ministry must deal with the concern for the theological and continuing education of pastors and associates in ministry as part of the concern for the ministry of the baptized people of God. The Division for Ministry is specifically charged with the responsibility of supporting the "ministry of the laity in daily life."[7]

In my judgment what is really new about the ELCA is the potentially new understanding of Lutheran identity implicit in the ecclesiology undergirding the organization. In the course of their history the Lutherans of America have given a number of different answers to the question of what it means to be Lutheran. Some have seen Lutheran identity in historical terms. Some have viewed it in terms of a system of doctrine. Although few wanted to admit it, most Lutherans at least for a time identified themselves in cultural or ethnic terms—for example, as German, Norwegian, or Swedish—and the cultural answer to Lutheran identity continues to be pervasive. Most recently the Lutherans who formed the ELCA have understood themselves confessionally and denominationally. In answering what it means to be Lutheran, Lutherans in the uniting churches have affirmed that Lutherans are that denomination in Christendom that witnesses to the faith of the Lutheran Confessions.

In my opinion the documents of the ELCA are proposing another answer to the question of Lutheran identity: Lutherans are baptized people of God who through their confession affirm the faith of all the baptized people of God and make a particular witness to the gospel within the people of God. Lutherans are Christians first of all, members of the one holy catholic and apostolic church. The ELCA is first of all an organization of the baptized people of God. Much more than one denomination among others, it is an organizational expression of the one church of Jesus Christ. Together with other Christians it gives witness through its confession to the one faith of the church of Jesus Christ. What makes it Lutheran is the particular witness it gives to other Christians through its confession that the teaching of justification by faith is essential to the Christian gospel.

The understanding of Lutheran identity present in the documents of the ELCA could have profound consequences for the new church's life and mission. Instead of being bound to a particular historical tradition or to a specific cultural heritage, the ELCA could be free to become the church for all the people of America. It could become inclusive of all the cultural traditions of America and reach out, not to expand the Lutheran denomination, but to incorporate people into the family of God. As it recognizes the unity it shares with all Christians within the people of God, the ELCA could play a significant role in the ecumenical movement. As people with feet planted in both the Catholic and the Protestant traditions, the ELCA could bring its confessional witness to bear toward Catholic churches on the one hand and Protestant churches on the other.

Do the people of the ELCA understand Lutheran identity as it is presented in the ELCA documents? In my opinion most people of the ELCA think that to be Lutheran means to belong to a particular denomination that has a specific doctrine and a peculiar culture. Such an understanding could prevail in spite of what the ELCA documents say. The struggle for the soul of Lutheranism, which has been going on from the beginning, will continue. At the heart of the struggle is how to answer the question of what it means to be Lutheran. The answer of the ELCA documents offers much hope for the future. The unanswered question is whether the people of the ELCA will make good on the promise embodied in its creation.

The CNLC completed its work in June 1986 and submitted its recommendations for action by conventions of the ALC, the AELC, and the LCA. It had been decided to hold the conventions of the three churches during the same period at the end of August 1986 so that the conventions could communicate with one another concerning proposed revisions in the CNLC recommendations and could vote simultaneously on the proposal to form the ELCA. The ALC held its convention in Minneapolis, the AELC in Chicago, and the LCA (ironically, in view of the LCA stance on the site of the new church offices) in Milwaukee.

The AELC met in convention August 26–29, 1986, at the O'Hare-Kennedy Holiday Inn in Rosemont, Illinois, the site of several ELIM assemblies and previous AELC conventions. Several hundred delegates and guests met to do the convention's primary business of voting on the CNLC recommendations, eagerly expectant of a positive decision on the formation of a new church. The convention Eucharist premiered *"Una Sancta: A Mass in Thanksgiving for the Unity of the Body of Christ,"* created by AELC members Paul Manz and Walter Wangerin, Jr., to celebrate the formation of the new church.

Presiding at the convention was Will L. Herzfeld, bishop of the AELC. Herzfeld had succeeded to the office at the AELC convention two years earlier, when William Kohn retired for reasons of health. The action made Herzfeld the first black bishop of a Lutheran church in America. Short of stature with curly black hair, his keen mind analyzing the issue under discussion, Herzfeld spoke from the podium with a voice that rang with authority and passion. Herzfeld and I had become good friends during the time of the civil rights movement in the United States, when as a pastor in Alabama Herzfeld had become a lieutenant of Martin Luther King, Jr., in the Southern Christian Leadership Conference. Herzfeld stood up for the faculty of Concordia Seminary during the controversy in the LCMS. At the constituting convention of the AELC he was elected vice-president, a position to which I followed him when he became bishop.

I learned much from Herzfeld about the church's need to identify with the poor and the oppressed in order to be faithful to its mission. He helped those of us in Seminex and in ELIM understand the connection between what was happening to us and the oppression others were experiencing in different parts of the world. As a result, our perspective on Christian responsibility and mission changed, and we enlisted in the cause of justice in many forms.

Herzfeld shared the major responsibilities of the final AELC convention with others. I was given the task of presenting and interpreting the CNLC recommendations to the delegates. Elwyn Ewald had the job of communicating with designated representatives of the conventions of the ALC and the LCA concerning revisions of the CNLC recommendations. Jeannette Bauermeister of Seminex served as chair of the convention committee.

According to the rules of procedure, any amendment to a CNLC proposal adopted by a two-thirds vote at one convention automatically became an item for action at the conventions of the other two churches. A negative vote on an amendment by the conventions of either the ALC or the LCA meant that the amendment failed and the original CNLC proposal was in effect. Thus, the conventions of the ALC and the LCA had to agree on any proposal to change a CNLC recommendation. Negative action by the AELC convention had no effect on the outcome of a decision. We accepted our ineffectual status, proposed by the CNLC, without complaint.

The major issues of confession, purpose, and organization received an overwhelming consensus among the people of the three conventions. The problem areas were practical: pensions, headquarters location, and size of the church council. The LCA convention tried to overturn the compromise on pensions recommended by the CNLC, but the ALC would not let it happen. The ALC convention tried to get the headquarters location moved back to Milwaukee and to increase the size of the church council, but the LCA disagreed. The result was that the recommendations of the CNLC were approved with only minor changes.

On the final vote to form the ELCA the three conventions had agreed not to announce the tallies until all the voting results could be announced at the same time through a telecommunications hookup. The interconnection among the three conventions took place shortly after noon on Friday, August 29, 1986. LCA bishop James Crumley was about to announce the results of the LCA vote when a disruption prevented the common sharing of information by the three conventions. The joy over the results of the voting could not be dimmed, however. At our AELC convention Herzfeld announced the tallies. The AELC delegates had voted unanimously, all 137 casting ballots for the formation of the ELCA. The ALC votes were 900 in favor, 37 opposed, and 5 abstentions.

The LCA votes were 644 in favor, 31 opposed. At the AELC convention the emotion of gratitude to God ran deep.

In the eucharistic service at the close of the AELC convention, Martin Marty was the preacher, just back after several months in South Africa. With his high-pitched voice Marty spoke to us profoundly yet simply about the reality of the resurrection, for Jesus and for us, in the face of our death and in the here and now. We hung on his every word. We believed in the resurrection. We had experienced its power in our lives. Out of oppression and exile and division had emerged unity and union in a new church.

The three churches had already begun the process by which to make the move into the new church organization. A team had been established to make sure the transition was smooth. The staffs of the churches were asked to figure out the details of procedures for living together in a new church and to propose budget figures for the first year of operation.

I served in behalf of the AELC in helping to flesh out the procedures and to come up with a budget for the Division for Ministry of the new church. I worked with Lloyd Sheneman of the LCA's Division for Professional Leadership and Walter Wietzke of the ALC's Division for Theological Education and Ministry and their staffs in devising procedures by which to approve and place candidates for ministry. In composing the budget Sheneman, Wietzke, and I made sure that the income and expenditure figures were adjusted for the LSTC, PLTS, and WTS to include the faculty salary figures for which we at Seminex had been responsible. The plans we had made five years earlier were to become a reality. Seminex faculty deployed to LSTC, PLTS, and WTS were to remain permanently at the seminaries they were serving.

The ELCA was scheduled to begin life on January 1, 1988. For that to happen the body needed to be officially constituted. The constituting convention of the ELCA was held at the Ohio Center in Columbus, Ohio, April 30–May 3, 1987. At Columbus more than one thousand delegates officially adopted the constitution and other documents that would serve as the basis for life together in a new church. They approved a $112 million budget and selected more than two hundred persons to serve on boards and committees of the ELCA.

As evidence of the spirit of unity the delegates selected one member from each of the three uniting churches to serve as three chief leaders of the new church. Elected as the first bishop of the ELCA was Herbert

Chilstrom, tall and fair-complexioned bishop of the LCA's Minnesota Synod, who had been a member of the CNLC. Elected as secretary was Lowell Almen, bespectacled pastor of the ALC and editor of its journal, the *Lutheran Standard*. Christine Grumm, a young and vivacious lay member of the AELC Board of Directors and of the transition team, was elected vice-president. In a moving ceremony at the Festival Eucharist, for which Chilstrom was presiding minister, the three bishops of the uniting churches, each using a separate cruet, poured wine together into a single chalice. As I looked on from my seat in the worshiping congregation, I reflected that Christ was taking the offering of our separate church lives to transform them by his own life's blood into a single and common new life.

The constituting convention opened the way to complete the rest of the transition process. Over the next few months synods were organized, boards and commissions held their first meetings, and the process for choosing staff began. In a frenzy of activity the work of three churches was brought to a conclusion, and the work of the new church was set to begin with the new calendar year.

As the uniting churches prepared for the advent of the ELCA, so also we at Seminex worked with the seminaries with which we were cooperating to make the transition. We produced covenants with LSTC, PLTS, and WTS that spelled out what would happen when Seminex went out of existence as a separate educational institution. All three schools agreed that they would become responsible for our professors' salaries as of December 31,1987, and that our faculty serving at their seminaries would continue to be known as Christ Seminary–Seminex professors. We officially turned over the Seminex library to WTS. We shared our donor and mailing lists for the western region of the country with PLTS. We assigned our organ and computer to LSTC along with whatever financial assets we might have at the end of 1987.

Just as the three churches had decided to unite through a corporate merger, we proposed that Seminex should merge with LSTC. But we had to find another way. We learned that the Illinois Board of Higher Education construed a merger to mean that a new school had been produced by the uniting schools. As a new school LSTC would have to apply, as Seminex had done earlier, for degree-granting authority from the state of Illinois and would then come under the jurisdiction of the Illinois board. It was not under that jurisdiction because LSTC had already been in existence when the Illinois board was created.

For several reasons—to insure the proper use of any future bequests to Seminex was one—we did not simply want to dissolve the Seminex corporation. Under the guidance of legal counsel we amended the Seminex articles of incorporation and the bylaws to make it a corporation that as of December 31, 1987, existed for the purpose of serving the interests of LSTC and was governed by the LSTC board of directors.

The numbers of the Seminex core group had been reduced over the years. David Krause left in fall 1984 to head a special fund-raising effort of the AELC. Christopher Eldredge moved over to LSTC at the end of 1985 to become associate vice-president of administration and finance. Jeannette Bauermeister, Rosemary Lipka, and I remained to complete the arrangements that brought the work of Seminex to a conclusion. As 1987 came to an end and a new year began, I gave thanks to God. The branch growing out of the root of the felled tree was in full bloom. The Evangelical Lutheran Church in America was a reality.

◆
EPILOGUE

A funny thing happened to me on the way to a new church. I write about the incident because of what I learned from it and because the learning experience is an important conclusion to the story I have been telling. I was elected bishop of the Chicago Metropolitan Synod of the Evangelical Lutheran Church in America, and a few weeks after my installation into office I resigned.

My election as bishop took place at the constituting convention of the synod June 5–6, 1987. I fully expected that in view of my background and experience there would be a position in the new church for me where I could continue the ministry to which God had called me. If, as I am convinced, the ELCA is the gift of transfigured life that God raised up out of institutional death, then as one who was deeply involved in the dying and rising, I would find new ways of serving in the ELCA. I did not expect to be elected bishop of a synod, but that is what happened.

I prefer not to go into detail about the reasons for my resignation, lest in a vain effort to justify myself I find fault with others. Suffice it to say that I realized that it would not be possible for me to serve without major conflict. As *The Lutheran,* journal of the ELCA, reported one year later, "Tietjen . . . resigned a month before the ELCA's start-up in a dispute with his synod council over staffing."[1] What surprised me was the reaction of many of my friends from the Association of Evangelical Lutheran Churches. Some were deeply concerned for me even without knowing the details of what had happened. But many were angry with me, downright angry, even without asking what had happened. At first I could not understand the anger. In time I did. Vicariously I represented my AELC friends.

339

As Christ Seminary–Seminex had served as a paradigm for those in the confessing movement that produced the AELC, so I as leader of Seminex was a personal paradigm for the people involved. My experiences were not mine alone. I served as exemplar for others.

My election as a synod bishop was more than a personal experience: It signaled the affirmation of those for whom I was paradigm. Others would be able to continue to speak and act through me as I represented them vicariously in my position of influence. For those to whom I was paradigm, my decision to resign meant that their place in the ELCA was diminished.

More important, to my friends in the AELC my election as synod bishop was proof of the promise that those who give their lives away for the sake of Christ and the gospel do indeed find them. Everything else does indeed come to those who seek first the kingdom of God. The tragic story of Seminex and the AELC had a happy ending. By resigning my office I had ruined the happy ending and called the truth of the promise into question.

My resignation must have wreaked havoc in the publication of a *Festschrift* edition of *Currents* that the Seminex faculty dedicated to me as Seminex ceased operations.[2] It did not take a historical critic to recognize that whole sections had been expunged from the journal to take account of the fact that I was no longer a synod bishop. It was clear to me that my colleague Jeannette Bauermeister, in presenting an overview of my ministry and citing words about faith that I had written over the years, had intended to point to me as evidence that God's promise comes true for those who believe. In expressing thanks for her good words, I wrote to my former colleague: "I think I know what had to be edited out of the article and how that applied to the words of mine which you quoted. So faith will have to continue to be faith. Its proof is still in the future. We will have to continue to trust that 'God will have new surprises in store for us' and that 'we are forever in the embrace of the tender mercy of our God.'"

Through the trauma that accompanied resignation I learned again the truth that I had confronted many times before. We may indeed experience what God promises here and now, but the fulfillment of the promise is guaranteed only ultimately when the kingdoms of this world become the kingdom of our God and of God's Christ. The substance of what we hope for, the evidence of what we do not see, is ours only by faith.

Perhaps at the end of the Evangelical Lutherans in Mission–Seminex–AELC story I was still a paradigm. On the first Sunday in Advent in 1987, as I looked ahead to Christmas, deeply wounded by my experience with the Metropolitan Chicago Synod, I wrote:

There was no room in the inn.
Outside they stayed, not in.
Among beasts the child was born
Like Adam for an Eden-like end.

Outside the walls he died.
There was no room within.
Embrace of Love reached out
And a garden bloomed from a tomb.

Outside and alien we are.
There is no room in the in.
In exile is our home.
The desert is the place to bloom.

There were many others, talented and experienced, whose expectations of serving in the structure of the ELCA were not fulfilled. As the ELCA began functioning and experienced the tensions and conflicts that would be present in the start-up of any organization, people began to wonder whether the ELCA would in fact deliver on its promise. People of color or whose primary language is other than English were disappointed with the selection of leadership. Limited financial resources called into question the ELCA's ability to reach out in mission to become the church for all of multicultural America. Perhaps the ELCA would not fulfill the expectations that it should provide new impetus for the ministry of all the people of God and for the equality of women and men in the church's life.

Even with the formation of the ELCA, exile is still our condition. The ELCA did not bring in the kingdom of God. It is an organization like any other, with all the problems inherent in human institutions. We continue to be exodus pilgrims, all of us in the ELCA, and are still on the way to the promised land. We need to remember that we live by faith and must keep our institutions in their place.

Yet I am convinced that God, who raised Jesus from the dead, worked through institutional death and transfiguration to produce the ELCA. If God was involved in bringing the ELCA into being, then God must have a special purpose and mission in mind for it. Those of us who believe that need to invest ourselves in discovering the ELCA's mission and purpose and bring it to reality. After all, faith is the substance of things hoped for, the evidence of things not seen. By faith we do indeed participate here and now in what we hope for and what we cannot yet see. By faith the ELCA can be God's instrument of new life in the world. In fact it is only as the people of the ELCA believe, that the ELCA will be able to fulfill the special purpose and mission God has in mind for it.

◆ ◆ ◆

There is much more to be learned from the story I have told. I have tried to fulfill a debt to posterity by describing events unknown to others, presenting information only I have, and sharing my perspective on what happened. But much more than that, I have tried to bear witness to the mighty acts of God in my life. Instead of simply rehearsing facts I have tried to tell what the facts mean.

At Christ Seminary–Seminex we regularly reflected on the meaning of our experiences. Every year on the anniversary of the procession into exile the people of Seminex gathered in chapel to commemorate the mighty acts of God among us. It took only two years before the majority of students who were with us had no experience with the events that had formed the seminary in exile. We found it necessary to tell the story to those who did not know it, to hand on the tradition, so that those who had not experienced it could participate in its meaning and celebrate it with those of us who did experience it. Every year in our anniversary commemoration we used a form of the Haggadah, the ritual order used by Jewish families in celebrating the Passover. In the Passover ritual children ask their parents, "What does this ritual mean?" (Exod. 12:26). The question provides the occasion for parents to relate the story of the mighty acts of God in delivering the Israelites from bondage in Egypt. At Seminex we asked the question in our anniversary commemoration and invited members of the seminary community to tell the story from their own experience.

The people of Seminex gave many answers to the question through the years. In all the welter of witness several passages of Scripture loom large. One was Heb. 11:8–16 with its message about Abraham and Sarah responding with faith to God's call "to go out to a country which God had promised" to give them. We discovered that Christians are a pilgrim people, aliens and exiles whose citizenship is in heaven. Richard R. Caemmerer, Sr., used a phrase from Hebrews 13 for the title of his autobiography, "No Continuing City."[3] As people on the way we live in trailers and tents, not in permanent houses. We need to be ready to pick up stakes and move on, and so we must travel light, always ready to change forms and structures to meet new needs. As those who await a "better country," a "heavenly country," we shape our lives more by the future than by the present or the past. For God "has prepared a city" for us and comes to us from that city to take care of our tomorrow.

Another Scripture at the heart of Seminex witness was 1 Cor. 2:1–5, the determined expression of the apostle Paul "to forget everything except Jesus Christ and especially his death on the cross." For emulating the apostle we were labeled "gospel reductionists." We did indeed gladly affirm that for Christians the gospel is central and sufficient. With the apostle we learned not to be ashamed of the gospel of Jesus Christ, trusting as he did that it is God's power to save all who believe (Rom. 1:16). To forget everything except Jesus Christ means not relying on people for success in the church, not expecting programs to ensure the church's future, not trusting laws and rules to bring about results, and not counting on the institution for survival. We have to be willing to be weak and vulnerable to be strong with the strength that comes from the Christ who died on the cross.

Seminex witness arose also out of Matt. 6:25–34, Jesus' words from the Sermon on the Mount that call us to give the kingdom of God top priority in our lives and in doing so to live one day at a time. Not everything is relative. God expects us to stand up for the truth and to do what is right no matter what the consequences. It may not be easy or pleasant to do what God wants, but we do not have to fear for our security or our survival if we commit ourselves to the rule of God in our lives.

To do what is right, it is essential to do what is just, and so Matt. 12:1–8 was central to the Seminex witness. There the one who calls himself "Lord of the Sabbath" makes it clear that because God is more interested in deeds of kindness than in ritual observance, our obedience to law has to serve the Law of Love. As people who were victimized by the use of the letter of the law, we identified with fellow oppressed in our world. We learned to look askance at the popular wisdom concerning school busing, an intransigent Israel, or divestment in South Africa. The Lord of the Sabbath requires deeds of justice and kindness that supersede our laws and rules. How hard it was to learn! To do the will of God you might have to break the law.

Among many other Scripture passages Eph. 4:1–6 stands out as central to the Seminex witness. Those of us who were involved in the fracturing and splintering of the church came to understand at the deepest levels the call "to preserve the unity which the Spirit gives by means of the peace that binds you together." The unity which the Spirit gives is vastly more than organizational togetherness. It begins in baptism and is exemplified in the Holy Communion. It involves all those who by the Spirit call Jesus Lord. We discovered the unity that the Spirit gives in the embrace of love of Christians who belonged to such disparate organizations as the Roman Catholic Church and the United Church of Christ. We had no choice but to recognize our unity with other Lutherans and to give up our organizational life to foster that unity. The Seminex witness is that we have no choice now but to recognize our unity with other Christians and, if necessary, to give up our separate existence as a Lutheran denomination to foster that unity.

◆ ◆ ◆

In the weeks following the closing of Seminex I had time to reflect on my ministry and my struggles to be faithful to the will of God. Often I would walk along the rocks that line the shore of Lake Michigan, looking out across the silvery blue water, drinking in the grandeur of the Chicago skyline, thinking, pondering, reflecting. During one of those walks I remembered the time in my youth when I heard the good news of justification by faith, and terror over future judgment gave way to peace. During another walk I heard a cacophony of voices, like the roaring waves of the lake, criticizing me, complaining. Anxiety churned my viscera, and dread deepened my depression. I remembered my teenage encounter with the gospel and heard the good news again: "In spite of your sins and failures you don't have to justify yourself. God has already justified you and through forgiveness will redeem the past and open up the future." Again peace returned.

The two events are like bridge pilings that support the span of my life. From frightened teenager to pastoral veteran of church controversy, the span of God's grace on which I have walked all my life has held firm. Justified by faith, we are free to serve and to go wherever God leads. That is the confessional principle. We can face the future with hope. God brings life out of death.

―――――◆

NOTES

PREFACE

1. *Currents in Theology and Mission* 5 (October 1978): 325–29.

1 CONTEXT FOR CONFLICT

1. A fraternal benefit insurance company with close ties to the people of the LCMS.

2. Transcribed from Sounds of Denver Convention '69, audiotape produced by the Division of Communication of the LCMS, 1969.

3. John H. Tietjen, *Which Way to Lutheran Unity?* (St. Louis: Concordia Publishing House, 1966).

4. The last named was a small church, Slovak in origin, that later became part of the LCMS. The only large Lutheran church not in the LCUSA was the 350,000-member Wisconsin Evangelical Lutheran Church.

2 AGENDA OVERHEARD

1. Frederick Danker's notes are in the author's files and are used with Danker's permission.

2. *CTM* 40 (June, July–August 1969): 434–43.

3. *American Lutheran* 43 (December 1960).

4. *CTM* 41 (January 1970): 3–9.

5. Frank Block Associates, "A Survey of Missouri Synod Pastor Attitudes toward Concordia Seminary, St. Louis, Mo.," distributed in typescript form at the April 1970 meeting of the BoC.

6. Account based on author's memo to himself written following the meeting.

7. Account based on author's memos to himself written following the November and December BoC meetings.

8. Author's personal recollection has been reinforced by letters from Martin Scharlemann to Everett Kalin and Ralph Klein, copies of which are in the author's files.

9. Quotations from copy of Martin Scharlemann's letter to Jacob Preus, April 9, 1970.

10. *Faculty Journal,* April 16, 1970, CS.

11. Minutes, April 20, 1970, BoC.

12. Letter from Jacob Preus to BoC, April 20, 1970, and two-page document entitled "Fact Finding Committee."

13. Minutes, April 20, 1970, BoC.

14. Letter from author to Jacob Preus, April 22, 1970, summarizing and restating conversation of April 21, 1970.

15. Copy of notes in author's files.

16. Minutes, September 21, 1970, BoC.

3 FISHING EXPEDITION

1. Report of the interview and quotations that follow are from the typed transcript of the tape recording of the interview, used with Robert W. Bertram's permission.

2. The terms formal principle and material principle are philosophical categories inherited from the seventeenth-century Lutheran dogmaticians. Formal principle refers to the Scriptures as rule and norm of faith. Material principle refers to the teaching of justification by faith as the essential content of Scriptures. Cf. Bertram's explanation later in the interview.

3. *Faculty Journal,* October 13, 1970, CS.

4. *Faculty Journal,* October 16, 1970, CS.

5. Extensive debate occurred at two successive monthly meetings of the BoC as to whether the substance of George Loose's remarks should appear in the Minutes. Loose finally agreed that they should be removed, but the record of what he said remains in the Minutes as circulated before they were approved.

6. Minutes, October 19, 1970, BoC.

7. Agendas and Reports, November 16, 1970, BoC.

8. Minutes, November 16, 1970, BoC.

9. *Faculty Journal,* November 3, 1970, CS.

10. Their statement appears as Exhibit G in Agendas and Reports, November 16, 1970, BoC.

11. Bylaw 6.75, *Handbook of the Lutheran Church–Missouri Synod,* 1969 edition, 132–33.

12. Quotation is from the typescript of the tape recording of the FFC's interview with Martin Scharlemann.

13. Ibid. Author never received a copy of Preus's letter of November 30, 1970.

14. Minutes, December 14–15, 1970, BoC.

15. The letter is included in BoC Agendas and Reports, January 18, 1971.

16. Minutes, January 27, 1971, BoC.

17. Agendas and Reports, February 15, 1971, BoC.

18. Agendas and Reports, March 15, 1971, BoC.

19. *Faculty Journal*, February 25, 1971, CS.

20. Quotation is from the typed transcript of the tape recording of the FFC's interview with Andrew M. Weyermann, March 27, 1971, and is used with his permission.

21. The document this group produced, categorizing and analyzing responses during the FFC interviews, totals approximately 170 typewritten pages. It is in the author's files.

22. Quotation is from the typed transcript of the tape recording of the FFC's interview with the author, March 27, 1971.

23. Author recreated the conversation from his recollection and received Weyermann's approval for its publication.

4 CONVENTION STALEMATE

1. Quotation is from the typed transcript of the tape recording of the convention; the transcript is in the author's files.

2. "President's Report," *Convention Proceedings, Forty-ninth Regular Convention, LCMS, Milwaukee, Wisc., July 9–16, 1971*, 54.

3. The full text of Resolution 2–21 appears ibid., 117–19.

4. The full text of Resolution 5–24 appears ibid., 163–65.

5. Resolution 5–24, when it was presented later, after action on Resolution 2–21, was adopted by an overwhelming vote without discernible dissent.

6. The text appears in Milwaukee *Convention Proceedings*, 119.

7. Quotation of Preus's statement to the convention is from the typed transcript of the official convention tape recording.

8. Standard parliamentary procedure allows for reconsideration of an action taken by an assembly if the motion to reconsider is made by someone who voted on the prevailing side and if a simple majority of those voting favor reconsideration. Cf. *Robert's Rules of Order* (New York: Berkley Books, 1989), 58–60.

9. The full text of Resolution Number 9 is in *Proceedings, Forty-fourth Regular Convention, LCMS, San Francisco, Calif., June 17–26, 1959*, 191.

10. *American Lutheran* 44 (August 1961): 6–10.

11. The full text of the resolution is in *Proceedings, Forty-fifth Regular Convention, LCMS, Cleveland, Ohio, June 20–29, 1960*, 112–23.

12. Ibid., 105–6

13. The report appears as Appendix E, Report of the Commission on Theology and Church Relations, *Convention Workbook (Reports and Overtures), Forty-seventh Regular Convention, LCMS, New York, N.Y., July 7–14, 1967*, 51–52.

14. Quotations are from the Solid Declaration, Formula of Concord, *The Book of Concord*, ed. Theodore G. Tappert (Philadelphia: Fortress Press, 1959), 505–6.

15. *Convention Proceedings, Forty-eighth Regular Convention, LCMS, Denver, Colo., July 11–18, 1969*, 90.

16. A typescript of the unpublished essay is in the author's file.

17. Epitome, Rule and Norm 1, *The Book of Concord*, 464–65.

18. Solid Declaration, Rule and Norm, ibid., 505–6.

19. Herman Sasse was a German theologian teaching in Australia with influence within the Missouri Synod; the quotation is from an unpublished 1962 essay.

20. Cf. chap. 2, pp. 32–33.

21. Quoted from an extensive memorandum of the meeting made by Walter Wegner, one of the CS participants.

22. Cf. chap. 3, p. 52.

23. *Spectrum* (January 11, 1971): 12.

24. Milwaukee *Convention Proceedings*, 52.

25. Ibid., 54.

26. Ibid., 55.

27. Cf. chap. 3, pp. 48–49.

28. Report based on the author's memo to himself written immediately following the meeting.

29. Resolution 2–28 appears in Milwaukee *Convention Proceedings*, 122.

30. The reported conversation was recreated on the basis of the author's recollection.

5 NO RETURN

1. Conversation recreated on the basis of the author's memo to himself, written immediately following the meeting.

2. Preus heard the address I gave at my inauguration as president of CS, in which I described my view that all of theological education must be in service of the church's ministry; cf. chap. 2, pp. 22–23.

3. Report of the Theological Education Research Committee, established by the Board of Higher Education in cooperation with Concordia Seminary the year before I arrived as president. The TERC, headed by CS professor John Damm, had completed its work, and we were eager to consider the implications of the report for our curriculum and the life of CS.

4. Author's memo to himself notes that Preus made no objection to this assessment of his aims.

5. Preus seemed not to be cognizant of it, but that parable from Luke 14:25–33 was the text for my sermon at my installation as CS president (chap. 2, p. 22), a text I deliberately chose to remind myself and others about the need to count the cost of Christian ministry before entering upon it.

6. Cf. below, pp. 80–82.

7. Arlis J. Ehlen, professor at CS; cf. below p. 80ff.

8. Quoted from author's memo to himself written September 22, 1971, to record what happened at the BoC meeting.

9. A copy of the original report is in author's files.

10. Minutes, September 20, 1971, and October 17–18, 1971, BoC.

11. Preus's letters to the BoC, copies of which are in author's files, are dated October 4, October 14, November 3, November 11, and December 7, 1971.

12. Letter from Jacob Preus to BoC, October 4, 1971.

13. Letter from Jacob Preus to BoC, October 14, 1971.

14. Preus subsequently supplied the BoC with the text of the statement he read at the BoC meeting, in a letter dated December 20, 1971.

15. *Faculty Journal*, Minutes, Faculty Meeting, January 4, 1972, CS.

16. The report was preserved on tape; a copy is in author's files.

17. Letter from Jacob Preus to Ralph Klein, December 20, 1971.

18. Letter from Robert H. Smith to Jacob Preus, January 6, 1972.

19. Letter from Ralph W. Klein to Jacob Preus, January 6, 1972.

20. Letter from Jacob Preus to the author, January 7, 1972.

21. Cf. chap. 2, p. 32.

22. Author's assessment appears in a three-page document, handwritten by the author, for his own purposes in thinking through the problem; document is in author's files.

23. Letter from author to Jacob Preus, January 13, 1972.

24. The notes describing these plans are in author's files.

25. Report based on author's memo to himself written immediately following the meeting with Preus.

26. Recollections of the phone conversation with Preus are based on author's memo to himself written January 20, 1972.

27. In author's files are his notes of his original proposal, responses from individual members of the Faculty Advisory Committee, and the proposal presented to Preus.

28. The list of objectives is as they were presented to the BoC meeting, February 18, 1972.

29. Quoted from the list of procedures as presented to the BoC meeting, February 18, 1972.

30. Ibid.

31. Minutes, February 18–21, 1972, BoC.

32. Ibid.

33. Letter from Jacob Preus to author, February 22, 1972.

34. Letter from author to Jacob Preus, March 5, 1972.

35. Minutes, March 20, 1972, BoC.

6 PREJUDGED

1. *Report of the Synodical President to the Lutheran Church–Missouri Synod, In Compliance with Resolution 2–28 of the Forty-ninth Regular Convention of the Synod, held at Milwaukee, Wisconsin, July 9–16, 1971.*

2. *Fact Finding or Fault Finding? An Analysis of President J. A. O. Preus' Investigation of Concordia Seminary.*

3. Only thirty-eight of the district presidents usually attended; distances kept the presidents of the Synod's two districts in South America from being present.

4. This and the following quotations about the action of the Council of Presidents and the Preus-Tietjen joint statement are from a letter from Wilbert Griesse to all pastors of the LCMS, September 21, 1972.

5. Letter from Jacob Preus to the BoC, March 3, 1972, which accompanied a revised form of the document he had submitted in February.

6. Minutes, March 20, 1972, BoC.

7. At the BoC meeting, March 20, 1972; cf. Minutes, BoC, 5.

8. Response of the Faculty of Concordia Seminary, St. Louis, April 4, 1972.

9. Quotations from Preus's address to the faculty are from a typescript of the address distributed to the faculty.

10. Quoted from the typescript of Bertram's presentation, a copy of which was given to Preus.

11. *Faculty Journal,* May 30, 1972, CS.

12. Quotations are from the BoC report as transmitted to Preus, which he published in *Report of the Synodical President,* 133–38.

13. *Report of the Synodical President,* 25.

14. Ibid., 22.

15. Ibid., 145–47.

16. *The Book of Concord* (Philadelphia: Fortress Press, 1959), 168.

17. Cf. chap. 5, pp. 75–77.

18. Letters from Jacob Preus to author, April 10 and May 4, 1972.

19. *Fact Finding or Fault Finding?* 2.

20. *Faculty Journal,* October 5, 1972, CS.

21. Copies of the letters, dated October 10 and 16, are in author's possession.

22. Preus sent author a copy of this letter.

23. A copy of the letter is in the author's files.

24. Recollection of the three meetings is reinforced by author's memos to himself written immediately following each of the meetings.

7 VERDICT

1. Quotations of the BoC actions in this account are from Minutes, January 15, 1973, BoC.

2. Minutes, August 21, 1972, BoC.

3. "What Does 'Inerrancy' Mean?" *CTM* 36 (September 1965): 577–93.

4. The Piepkorn interview is reported in detail as an illustration of the BoC's interview process because the BoC itself chose this same method and case when it submitted to a floor committee of the 1973 LCMS convention a four-page document entitled, *A Case in Point, or How the Board of Control of Concordia Seminary, St. Louis, Mo., Reviewed the Case of Professor Arthur Carl Piepkorn, and Why the Board Did Not Find Him Guilty of False Doctrine but Commended Him for Being Faithful to the Holy Scriptures and the Confessions of the Lutheran Church.*

5. Quotations and report of what Piepkorn said are from a written summary of the interview, which author drafted with Piepkorn's approval and which the BoC adopted and attached to the protocol copy of the minutes of its meeting, October 15–16, 1972.

6. *A Brief Statement of the Doctrinal Position of the Evangelical Lutheran Synod of Missouri, Ohio, and Other States* (the official name of the Missouri Synod at the time) was adopted by the Missouri Synod in convention in 1932 for use in

fellowship discussions with the American Lutheran Church and was subsequently reaffirmed several times as a doctrinal statement of the Synod.

7. Minutes, September 18, 1972, BoC.

8. Ibid.

9. Minutes, October 15–16, 1972, BoC.

10. Cf. chap. 6.

11. Report of what Mayer and other faculty members said in their interviews is taken from summaries of the interviews, which author prepared in consultation with the individual faculty members and which the BoC adopted and attached to the protocol copies of the BoC Minutes of the meetings.

12. Cf. chap. 6, p. 117.

13. Those two pages are in author's files.

14. Minutes, January 15, 1973, BoC.

15. Dissen's minutes indicated that in the case of Schroeder and Smith, in addition to the seven votes to commend and three to correct, there was one vote to abstain. Author's notes did not include votes to abstain in the case of Schroeder and Smith, nor could there have been such votes because the ballots on Schroeder and Smith were taken after Eugene Fincke had excused himself from the meeting.

8 RIVERGATE

1. "Reports and Overtures," *Convention Workbook, Fiftieth Regular Convention, LCMS, New Orleans, La., July 6–13, 1973,* iii. The term "sons of Missouri" was apt because the delegates with few exceptions were male.

2. Resolution appears in New Orleans *Convention Proceedings,* 133–39.

3. Reference in parentheses is to the location of the quotation in the Preface of the Solid Declaration of the Formula of Concord, *The Book of Concord* (Philadelphia: Fortress Press, 1959).

4. Portions of presentation in quotation marks are taken verbatim from the tape of broadcasts of the convention aired by KFUO, radio station of LCMS, St. Louis.

5. New Orleans *Convention Proceedings,* 37.

6. Emmet C. Rogness, pastor from Enid, Okla., reported on the secret meeting and on the delegate assessment in a confidential letter to Doctrinal Concerns People, as the Preus supporters were known; a copy of the letter is in author's files.

7. Derr reported the assessment at a student convocation at CS, May 21, 1973; a tape of the convocation is in author's files.

8. *Faculty Journal,* Minutes, March 6, 1973, CS.

9. Minutes, March 19, 1973, BoC.

10. *Info,* July 1973, analyzed the makeup of the two committees.

11. Adopted May 22, 1973, it was published as *Response of the Faculty of Concordia Seminary, St. Louis, to the "Report of the Synodical President."*

12. *Reply of the Board of Control of Concordia Seminary, St. Louis, to Statements of Some of Its Members Appearing as Section 3-01B and 3-01C in the Convention Workbook.*

13. This report is based on those notes.
14. *Info,* July 1973.
15. Cf. chap. 4, pp. 69–71.
16. A tape of the radio interview is in author's files.
17. Resolution appears in New Orleans *Convention Proceedings,* 111–15.
18. Summary of Preus's remarks is based on the Minutes of the convention, as recorded in New Orleans *Convention Proceedings,* 26.
19. Quoted in *Info,* September 1973.
20. Resolution appears in New Orleans *Convention Proceedings,* 127–28.
21. In a six-page letter to Preus following the convention, Donaho not only presented clear evidence for the illegality of the convention but also questioned many other rulings of the Synod's parliamentarian.
22. Quoted from typed transcript of the tape made from the KFUO radio broadcast of the session.
23. Resolution is included in New Orleans *Convention Proceedings,* 140–42.
24. Ibid., 43.
25. The phrase is from the Missouri Synod's formula for absolution to be pronounced on penitent sinners by its ordained clergymen.
26. Resolution appears in New Orleans *Convention Proceedings,* 140.
27. Quoted from the tape of the KFUO radio broadcast.

9 KANGAROO COURT

1. Quotations in the report of this meeting are taken from Minutes, August 17–18, 1973, BoC.
2. *Handbook of the Lutheran Church–Missouri Synod,* 1973 edition, 145–46.
3. For a report of the New Orleans convention, see chap. 8.
4. Quoted from copy of letter in author's files.
5. The slips of paper are in author's files.
6. Quoted from Minutes, July 31, 1973, FAC.
7. Quoted from a memo to himself written by the author after the phone call.
8. Quoted from letter from Roland Wiederaenders to author, August 16, 1973. Wiederaenders wrote in response to author's request that he put in writing what he had said in the meeting.
9. Minutes, July 31, 1973, FAC.
10. Quoted from Weyermann's "First Ruminations Post New Orleans," presented to the FAC on July 16, 1973, and appended to its minutes of that date.
11. Quoted from the resolutions adopted at the Chicago conference.
12. Letter of invitation is dated September 19, 1973.
13. Opinion of the commission was submitted to the BoC in a letter, September 25, 1973.
14. Minutes, September 29, 1973, BoC.
15. Cf. typed transcript of tape of the meeting, October 10, 1973.
16. Cf. typed transcript of tape of the meeting, October 26, 1973.
17. Quoted from copy of the document in author's files.

18. This quotation and others below are from Minutes, November 19, 1973, BoC.

19. Conversation is taken verbatim from the typed transcript of the tape recording of the meeting, November 28, 1973.

20. Their document as submitted among agenda materials for the December 17, 1973, meeting was entitled, "To the Members of the Board of Control and All Others Who Are Involved in a Supervisory Role at the Seminary."

21. The letter was among the agenda materials submitted for the December 17, 1973, meeting.

22. This detailed report, including quotations, is from author's extensive notes of Neeb's explicit report of his telephone conversations with Bryant. Neeb taped the conversations and quoted them in his press release.

23. Following material reports what author wrote on those pages, which are in author's files.

24. Letter from Gerhardt W. Hyatt to author, December 21, 1973.

10 MORATORIUM

1. Resolution appears in *Seminar* (special edition, 1974): 10. This magazine was published by the students of CS. This edition's purpose was to analyze issues in the controversy and to make some of the documents available to the church at large.

2. Quoted from a chronology of the events written by senior student John V. Glamann, p. 3, a copy of which is in author's files. Glamann described at the time what he saw as the potential cost to himself: "First, my further theological education and preparation for the ministry in the Lutheran Church-Missouri Synod at Concordia Seminary. Second, my graduation this May [1974]. Third, my call into the ministry of the Lutheran Church-Missouri Synod. . . . Mindful of these possible repercussions to myself and my wife I stand ready to pay whatever price I am called upon to pay as a result of my action."

3. The statement, which Miller verified personally to the author, is recorded by Frederick W. Danker, *No Room in the Brotherhood: The Preus-Otten Purge of Missouri* (St. Louis: Clayton Publishing House, 1977), 195.

4. Cf. above, chap. 4, note 3.

5. Amandus Derr, interview with author, August 29, 1988.

6. Leon Rosenthal, interview with author, August 29, 1988.

7. Letter is included in BoC Reports and Agendas, September 29, 1973.

8. Minutes, September 29, 1973, BoC.

9. *Christian Century* (January 2–9, 1974): 7.

10. Report of this meeting is based on author's interviews with David Abrahamson, Leon Rosenthal, and James Wind, August 29, 1988, and with Gerald Miller, September 5, 1988; all were participants in the meeting.

11. "Evidence" document and transcripts were published by Evangelical Lutherans in Mission (ELIM), February 1974.

12. Copies of statements by Victor Bryant, Larry Neeb, and Rudolph Ressmeyer are in author's files.

13. Reference is to Jesus' words in Matt. 6:2 about people who seek human rather than divine approval for what they do and who can therefore expect nothing more than a human reward.

14. Minutes, January 20, 1974, FAC.

15. Minutes, January 21, 1974, FAC.

16. Glamann's chronology, 4.

17. Letter was mailed January 25, 1974, to all pastors of the LCMS.

18. Copy of the letter is in author's files.

19. Information given by Leslie Weber in an interview about the moratorium experience recorded on videotape, a copy of which is in ELCA Archives.

20. Minutes, February 4, 1974, FAC.

21. Minutes, February 6, 1974, FAC.

22. Copy of Martin E. Marty's presentation is in author's files.

23. Report based on notes of the meeting made by Waldemar Meyer, a copy of which is in author's files.

24. Note and resolution were published in *Seminar* (special edition, 1974): 36–37.

25. Nevertheless, our children experienced the effects of the controversy in more ways than we realized. Sarah, the youngest, was in kindergarten at Bethel Lutheran School. Her teacher, Dorothy Hoyer, had to help the class understand what was happening at CS when one of Sarah's classmates became upset at learning that Sarah's father had been "fired." The child thought that to be fired meant to be set on fire.

Our son, Laurence, was in his second year at Lutheran High School North. One day, as he was getting things out of his locker, he overheard two first-year students talking about someone named Tietjen. They were saying that Tietjen was getting what he deserved because he was nothing but a "heretic." Laurence walked over to the two young men and asked them why they thought that Tietjen was a heretic. One responded that his father had told him that Tietjen did not believe what was in the Bible. "Well," Laurence told them, "I know he's not a heretic. I know he believes what's in the Bible." "Oh, yeah," the young man responded, "how do you know?" At that point Laurence extended his hand in greeting to both of them and said, "My name is Larry Tietjen. What's yours?"

11 EXILE

1. CS was unique among American seminaries in having a full-fledged athletic program complete with intramural and varsity sports. The program dated back to the late 1940s and 1950s when CS was responsible for providing the last two years of college and awarded the Bachelor of Arts degree. Even after the Missouri Synod abandoned the German gymnasium system for the American higher education pattern, CS continued its athletic program, quoting the Latin proverb about the need for a sound body to house a sound mind.

2. Copy of the document is in author's files.

3. Damm read from a statement he had drafted that the faculty had approved; a copy is in author's files.

4. Report based primarily on John Damm's record of what happened, which he recorded on tape January 11, 1977, a copy of which is in author's files.

5. Commencement address delivered at Concordia Seminary in Exile, May 24, 1974, and later published by Seminex.

6. Terms of the agreement for a Joint Project for Theological Education were later published in *Seminar—In Exile* (1974):3–5, a publication of the students of Seminex.

7. "Background for Seminary in Exile," *St. Louis Post-Dispatch*, February 22, 1974, 8.

8. The mission staff released the letter to all engaged in mission within the LCMS.

9. Copy of Kohn's letter of resignation is in author's files.

10. Copy of the Executive Committee's proposal is in author's files.

11. Letter from LCMS Board of Directors to Synod members, June 3, 1974.

12. As reported by CS in ELIM's newspaper *Missouri in Perspective* 1 (April 8, 1974): 1.

13. *Missouri in Perspective* 1 (April 12, 1974): 1.

14. Quoted from a copy of the resolutions in author's files.

15. *Handbook of the Lutheran Church–Missouri Synod*, 1973 edition.

16. The quotation in Matt. 12:7 is from Hos. 6:6.

17. Quoted from copies of the resolutions in author's files.

18. Ibid.

19. Later published and distributed by Seminex.

12   A GROWING BRANCH

1. Isa. 11:1; Jer. 23:5; Zech. 3:8; 6:12.

2. Articles of Incorporation and Bylaws were published in *Seminar—In Exile* (1974): 5–12.

3. Excerpts published in *Missouri in Perspective* 1 (October 7, 1974): 7.

4. The sermon and actions of the ELIM assembly were reported in *Time* (September 9, 1974): 66–67.

5. Letter, a copy of which is in author's files, was dated August 14, 1974.

6. Account based on report of the meeting tape recorded by the author immediately following the meeting. A copy of the tape is in author's files.

7. The public debate over author's stance was reported in *Missouri in Perspective* 1 (September 9, 1974): 3.

8. According to Kretzmann, the quotation is from J. R. Macphail, *Introduction and Commentary to St. Matthew* (Madras, India: CLS, 1956), 224.

9. Author received from them a signed five-page report to the BoC, dated September 10, 1974.

10. Bylaw 6.79j., *Handbook of the Lutheran Church–Missouri Synod*, 1973 edition, 147.

11. Letter to board chair Ewald J. Otto, October 3, 1974.

12. Otto's letter was dated October 7, 1974, and author's reply, October 9, 1974; copies of both in author's files.

13. Minutes, January 31–February 1, 1975, Board of Directors, Seminex.

14. Statement was the subject of a Seminex news release dated February 5, 1975.

15. Copy of the document is in author's files.

16. *Missouri in Perspective* 3 (December 8, 1975): 8.

17. Account based on author's notes taken as participant of the meeting.

18. Copy of statement is in author's files. The ousted pastor was Paul R. Heckmann, whose position was abolished by a slim majority of his congregation in Black Jack, Mo.

19. "Piercing the Smokescreen," *Christianity Today* 19 (April 11, 1975): 8–10.

20. Bylaw 6.79L., *Handbook of the Lutheran Church–Missouri Synod,* 1973 ed., 147.

21. Bylaw 1.09d., ibid., 28.

22. Copy of brief, dated March 11, 1975, is in author's files.

23. *Handbook of the Lutheran Church–Missouri Synod,* 1973 ed., 118.

24. *Missouri in Perspective* 2 (July 21, 1975): 6.

25. Quoted from News Release 75-47 of the News Bureau of LCUSA, July 15, 1975.

26. Resolution 6-02, *Convention Proceedings, Fifty-first Regular Convention, LCMS, Anaheim, Calif., July 4–11, 1975,* 141.

27. Resolution 3-03A, ibid., 94.

28. Resolution 3-06, ibid., 96–99.

29. Resolution 5-02A, ibid., 122–24. The district presidents involved were Herman R. Fincke of the Eastern District, Harold L. Hecht of the English District, Paul E. Jacobs of the California and Nevada District, Emil G. Jaech of the Northwest District, Waldemar E. Meyer of the Colorado District, Herman Neunaber of the Southern Illinois District, Rudolph P. F. Ressmeyer of the Atlantic District, and Robert J. Riedel of the New England District.

30. Ibid., 77–78.

31. I remember Ernestine's report of her conversation with the Jewish woman who worked in the tailor shop not far from home. I had dropped off a suit to be mended. When Ernestine went to pick it up, the Tietjen name made a connection with the woman. "If only I had known who your husband was," she said, "I would have said something to him. Tell him: God will take care of him; the truth will come out." As Ernestine looked at the woman's wrist, she saw the tattooed numbers from one of Hitler's death camps.

32. Statement appears in *Together,* July 18, 1975, a newsletter of the Seminex community.

33. From a column by Roth in *Missouri in Perspective* 2 (July 21, 1975): 6.

34. From a report by Krentz on the Anaheim convention in *Together,* July 18, 1975.

35. Minutes, October 31–November 1, 1975, Board of Directors, Seminex.

36. "A Study of the Future of Seminex," agenda materials, May 12–13, 1976, Board of Directors, Seminex.

37. Ibid.

38. Minutes, May 14–15, 1975, Board of Directors, Seminex.

39. *Together,* December 8, 1975.

13   A CLAY POT

1. *Proceedings, Special Convention of the English District of the LCMS, North-lake, Ill., September 19–21, 1975,* 26–27.

2. Minutes, June 17, 1976, Board of Directors, English District, LCMS, Concordia Teachers College, River Forest, Ill.

3. Original document is in author's files. In addition to Baumgaertner the directors included two district pastors, Bernard Hemmeter of Fort Wayne, Ind., and Waldemar Kissling of Detroit; and three laypersons, Wentworth Marshall of Cleveland, Richard McAuliffe of Chicago, and Marie Prange of St. Louis. At a subsequent session, retired pastor August Brunn, who as a boy had been a member of an English Synod congregation, was named to the interim board.

4. Account of the actions of the interim Board of Directors of the English Synod is based on Minutes of First Meetings, Board of Directors, English Synod of the Evangelical Lutheran Church, a copy of which was given to author by J. Peter Schmitz.

5. Quotations are from the resolution as it was published in "Special Report on the Third Annual Assembly, Evangelical Lutherans in Mission, August 13–15, 1975," *Together in Mission* 2 (1975): 3–4.

6. *Together in Mission* 2 (1975): 12–13.

7. *Catechism on LCM,* pamphlet published in April 1975 by the Board of Directors of Lutheran Church in Mission.

8. *Lutheran Church in Mission Newsletter,* 2 (February 10, 1976): 1.

9. Ibid., 2.

10. *Missouri in Perspective* 3 (November 10, 1975): 3.

11. Preus made his announcement in a twelve-page letter addressed to the members of the LCMS.

12. The district presidents sent their letter to all those to whom Preus had sent his.

13. Quoted from the partnership agreement as adopted at the AELC constituting convention, December 3–4, 1976.

14. In author's files are notes he made of what the faculty said and his response.

15. Cf. chapter 12, pp. 255–56.

16. Minutes, October 22–23, 1976, Board of Directors, Seminex.

17. Report was Exhibit C in Agenda, January 21–22, 1977, Board of Directors, Seminex.

18. Minutes, January 21–22, 1977, Board of Directors, Seminex.

19. Minutes, May 11–12, 1977, Board of Directors, Seminex.

20. *Faculty Journal,* May 26, 1977, Seminex.

21. Minutes, August 12–13, 1977, Board of Directors, Seminex.

22. Minutes, October 28–29, 1977, Board of Directors, Seminex.

23. Minutes, January 27–28, 1978, Board of Directors, Christ Seminary-Seminex.

24. Minutes, January 19–20, 1979, Board of Directors, Christ Seminary-Seminex.

25. Author shared his insights at the time with a number of groups. What follows is abstracted from a presentation made to the graduating students of Luther Northwestern Theological Seminary at a banquet sponsored by AAL, February 1979.

26. *The Book of Concord* (Philadelphia: Fortress Press, 1959), 171.

27. Cf. Article V, Augsburg Confession, ibid., 31.

28. *Handbook of the Lutheran Church–Missouri Synod*, 1973 ed., 119.

29. *Missouri in Perspective* 3 (November 24, 1975): 1.

30. Letter dated May 11, 1977, a copy of which is in author's files.

31. John 18:14 reports Caiaphas, the high priest, as saying that it was better that one man die for all the people.

32. The letter, dated October 3, 1977, is in author's files.

14   A YEAST IN FLOUR

1. Cf. chapter 13, pp. 279–82.

2. Cf. below, pp. 306, 309.

3. Statement was among materials in Agenda, February 12–13, 1982, Board of Directors of Christ Seminary-Seminex.

4. *Missouri in Perspective* 1 (February 25, 1974): 2.

5. Statements of both presidents were reported in *Missouri in Perspective* 1 (April 22, 1974): 2.

6. What the author is describing is the AELC's contribution to the Lutheran union effort as witnessed by the author. The AELC was not the only actor. For example, the Committee on Church Cooperation of the ALC and LCA recommended in January 1978 that the AELC be invited to join the committee.

7. *Missouri in Perspective* 5 (April 24, 1978): 5.

8. *Missouri in Perspective* 6 (November 6, 1978): 1.

9. *Missouri in Perspective* 8 (November 3, 1980): 1.

10. Text of the theses taken from author's memo to the Seminex faculty, September 5, 1979.

11. Quotation is from author's report in Agenda, January 25–26, 1980, Board of Directors, Christ Seminary-Seminex.

12. Minutes, October 2–3, 1981, Board of Directors, Christ Seminary-Seminex.

13. Response of the LSTC board is included in Agenda, February 12–13, 1982, Board of Directors, Christ Seminary-Seminex.

14. Report appears in Agenda, May 20–21, 1982, Board of Directors, Christ Seminary-Seminex.

15. Minutes, May 20–21, 1982, Board of Directors, Christ Seminary-Seminex.

16. *Missouri in Perspective* 8 (April 6, 1981): 5.

17. *Proceedings, Fourth Delegate Assembly, AELC, Cleveland, Ohio,* September 7–9, 1982, 13.

15   ONE CHURCH MADE NEW

1. Quoted from typescript of notes for the sermon, used with Walter Stuhr's permission.

2. *Una Sancta: A Mass in Thanksgiving for the Unity of the Body of Christ* (Madison, Wisc.: A-R Editions, 1986), 20–21.

3. Cf. report of the festival week and commencement in *Lutheran Perspective* 10 (June 6, 1983): 5.

4. The phrase, as it appears in the ELCA Constitution, 5.01.f., was devised by those in the CNLC whom it is intended to describe.

5. ELCA Constitution, 10.21; Chapter 10 is on ministry.

6. Ibid., 5.01.d.

7. Ibid., 16.31.D87.b.

EPILOGUE

1. *The Lutheran* 2 (January 4, 1989): 23.

2. *Currents in Theology and Mission* 15 (February 1988).

3. Caemmerer's autobiography was published in *Currents in Theology and Mission* 5 (October 1978): 268–315.

INDEX